Architectures, Protocols and Algorithms of Sensor Networks—Second Edition

Architectures, Protocols and Algorithms of Sensor Networks—Second Edition

Guest Editors

Bartłomiej Płaczek
Marcin Bernaś

MDPI

Basel • Beijing • Wuhan • Barcelona • Belgrade • Novi Sad • Cluj • Manchester

Guest Editors

Bartłomiej Płaczek
Institute of Computer Science
University of Silesia
Sosnowiec
Poland

Marcin Bernaś
Department of Computer
Science and Automatics
University of Bielsko-Biala
Bielsko-Biala
Poland

Editorial Office

MDPI AG
Grosspeteranlage 5
4052 Basel, Switzerland

This is a reprint of the Special Issue, published open access by the journal *Sensors* (ISSN 1424-8220), freely accessible at: https://www.mdpi.com/journal/sensors/special_issues/483B2JD347.

For citation purposes, cite each article independently as indicated on the article page online and as indicated below:

Lastname, A.A.; Lastname, B.B. Article Title. *Journal Name* **Year**, *Volume Number*, Page Range.

ISBN 978-3-7258-7909-0 (Hbk)
ISBN 978-3-7258-7910-6 (PDF)
https://doi.org/10.3390/books978-3-7258-7910-6

Contents

About the Editors

Bartłomiej Płaczek

Bartłomiej Płaczek, M.Sc. (2002), Ph.D. (2005), Habilitation (2016), is a professor at the University of Silesia, Institute of Computer Science, Poland, and an expert from the National Centre for Research and Development (NCBR). His research interests include sensor networks, smart sensors, intelligent systems, and the Internet of Things. He is the author or co-author of more than seventy papers in peer-reviewed journals and conferences and several books. He serves as a reviewer for many scientific journals, international conferences, and research foundations. Since 2010, Dr. Placzek has been a reviewer of grants and projects (including EU projects) in the field of information technologies.

Marcin Bernaś

Marcin Bernaś is an assistant professor at the University of Bielsko-Biala. His research interests concentrate on advanced artificial intelligence methods, cyber-physical system reliability, and the Internet of Things. Specifically, his work encompasses the development and implementation of machine learning models, such as recurrent neural networks, for real-time data processing, activity recognition, and cybersecurity in smart cities. He has served as a Principal Investigator for the prestigious NCBiR LIDER project, which focused on wireless hybrid sensor networks for traffic monitoring. Additionally, he actively participates in international initiatives, including the Horizon MSCA FORCE project and Erasmus+ educational projects like FAAI JOB HUB and iBIG World. His scientific achievements include over 53 publications indexed in the Scopus database with more than 440 citations. Since 2020, he has also contributed his expertise as an expert for the National Centre for Research and Development. His work has been recognized with multiple accolades, such as the Best Paper Award at the Computer Networks 2019 conference and several Rector's awards for outstanding professional and scientific activities. Furthermore, he serves as an active reviewer for numerous prestigious scientific journals.

sensors

MDPI

Editorial

Architectures, Protocols and Algorithms of Sensor Networks—Second Edition

Bartłomiej Płaczek

Institute of Computer Science, University of Silesia, Będzińska 39, 41-200 Sosnowiec, Poland; bartlomiej.placzek@us.edu.pl

1. Introduction

Sensor networks have become a background technology for a wide range of applications in industrial automation, smart cities, intelligent transportation systems, healthcare monitoring, environmental sensing, precision agriculture, and supervision of critical infrastructure [1–4]. By enabling continuous data acquisition, processing, and transmission across distributed environments, sensor networks effectively support advanced intelligent services. However, the increasing scale, heterogeneity, and performance demands of these systems impose significant constraints on network architectures, communication protocols, and the design of specialized algorithms tailored to them. We are witnessing the evolution of sensor networks from relatively simple data-collection solutions to complex, distributed cyber-physical systems. For real-world implementations, such systems must support long-term autonomous operation while ensuring reliability, scalability, and low energy consumption [5–7]. These requirements have motivated active research across many areas, including the proliferation of tiny, resource-constrained devices, heterogeneous communication technologies, application-specific quality-of-service techniques, low-latency transmission in industrial control, and high reliability, e.g., in healthcare monitoring [8,9]. Addressing the above-mentioned challenges requires innovative solutions related to different layers of the system, including hardware, network architectures, medium access protocols, intelligent data processing, and adaptive resource management algorithms.

One should also note that sensor networks play a central role in the Internet of Things (IoT), serving as the indispensable interface between the physical and digital worlds [10–12]. IoT systems rely on sensor networks and embedded devices to capture real-time information about various processes, human activities, and environmental conditions. The effectiveness of IoT applications in smart manufacturing, logistics, telemedicine, ecological sustainability, and other domains directly depends on the robustness, efficiency, and security of the sensor networks that provide input data. Therefore, advancements in sensor network design are essential for developing scalable IoT systems that can support the connectivity of numerous devices, distributed intelligence at the edge, and seamless integration with cloud and multi-access edge computing platforms. Simultaneously, the implementation of IoT systems in new scenarios introduces novel challenges for sensor networks. These challenges include the need for deterministic communication in industrial environments, energy-aware operation in large-scale deployments, support for embedded machine learning, and resilience against evolving security threats. Consequently, the convergence of sensor networks with edge computing, artificial intelligence, and next-generation communication technologies has become a central focus of research [13–15]. This convergence necessitates the development of innovative architectures that accommodate heterogeneous devices, protocols that adapt to dynamic network conditions, and algorithms

 https://doi.org/10.3390/s26072197

that optimize key performance metrics such as energy consumption, latency, throughput, and network lifetime.

This Special Issue, titled "Architectures, Protocols and Algorithms of Sensor Networks—Second Edition", builds upon the foundations established in the first edition and reflects the current state of the art in sensor network research. The eleven contributions included in this Special Issue address complementary aspects of sensor network design and operation, encompassing industrial communication architectures, real-world deployment studies, analytical performance modeling, learning-driven optimization techniques, energy-efficient algorithms, secure embedded platforms, and post-quantum cryptographic solutions. By combining theoretical analysis with experimental validation and practical implementation, these contributions collectively provide valuable insights into the challenges and opportunities shaping new solutions in sensor networks and their role within the broader IoT landscape.

2. Overview of Contributions

The contributions in this Special Issue span multiple layers of the system stack, encompassing Internet-scale measurement and distributed coordination, communication protocols and network architectures, analytical performance modeling, learning-driven optimization techniques, and hardware–software platforms that address energy efficiency, reliability, and security. Taken together, these works illustrate how advances in theory, algorithms, system design, and experimental validation support the development of scalable, intelligent, and resilient sensor network solutions for diverse application domains. The individual contributions are briefly described in the following subsections.

2.1. Architectures and Protocols for Industrial Sensor Networks

In the paper "Two-Phase Distributed Genetic-Based Algorithm for Time-Aware Shaper Scheduling in Industrial Sensor Networks" (Contribution 2), the authors address a challenge in Time-Sensitive Networking (TSN) for industrial sensor networks, namely the scalability and deployability limitations of centralized Time-Aware Shaper (TAS) scheduling under the IEEE 802.1Qbv standard. The authors observe that existing global schedulers often produce fragmented Gate Control Lists (GCLs) that exceed the per-port entry limits of commercial switches, thus hindering practical deployment in large-scale networks.

To overcome these limitations, the authors propose a two-phase distributed genetic-based algorithm (2PDGA). The first phase performs a network-wide genetic optimization to determine routing paths and transmission offsets, producing a conflict-free baseline schedule. The second phase refines the schedule locally at each switch, merging time windows and enforcing hardware-specific GCL constraints through lightweight coordination. Extensive evaluations across multiple topologies, network sizes, and guard-band configurations demonstrate that the proposed approach achieves high compliance rates under strict hardware constraints, maintains low latency, and improves the feasibility of deploying large-scale TSN-enabled industrial sensor networks.

In Contribution 7, Lacasa et al. focus on architectural challenges associated with deploying Industrial Internet of Things solutions in operational factory environments. Within the Industrializable Industrial Internet of Things (I3oT) paradigm, the authors emphasize the importance of reusing existing industrial infrastructures, such as programmable logic controllers (PLCs) and IT/OT networks, to minimize deployment costs and operational disruptions.

The proposed Cross-PLC platform enables passive and vendor-agnostic data extraction from heterogeneous PLCs by acting as a virtual PLC that aggregates and standardizes information for I3oT applications. Supporting both native PLC communication and

https://doi.org/10.3390/s26072197

HTTP/JSON-based interfaces, Cross-PLC achieves interoperability, scalability, and safety without interfering with control logic. Its implementation and validation in a real automotive factory demonstrate how architectural design choices aligned with industrial constraints can facilitate the large-scale adoption of data-driven sensor network applications in Industry 4.0.

2.2. Communication Performance, Coverage, and Analytical Modeling

In the paper "VistaScan: Optimizing Internet-Wide Scanning Through Visibility-Aware Distributed Task Allocation" (Contribution 1), Hu et al. address efficient Internet-scale network measurement for security and monitoring. The authors highlight visibility heterogeneity across networks as a key limitation of both centralized and naive distributed scanning, leading to redundant probing and incomplete coverage.

To address this issue, VistaScan leverages the principle of visibility consistency, assuming that IP addresses within the same CIDR block share similar visibility patterns. Using anchor-based probing, the system constructs a lightweight visibility matrix and applies a load-aware task allocation strategy that assigns scanning tasks to suitable nodes while filtering unreachable targets. Experimental results show that VistaScan achieves high coverage with significantly reduced probing overhead and scan time, while generalizing across services. This work demonstrates how visibility-aware modeling and coordinated task allocation enable scalable and efficient Internet-wide scanning.

Silva et al., in the paper "Radio Coverage Assessment and Indoor Communication Enhancement in Hospitals: A Case Study at CHUCB" (Contribution 3), investigate the performance of cellular communication technologies in a complex indoor healthcare environment. Through a measurement campaign conducted at the Cova da Beira University Hospital Center, the authors evaluate signal strength and quality for multiple technologies, including 5G NR, LTE, NB-IoT, and UMTS, using professional-grade spectrum analysis equipment.

The study identifies specific indoor locations with insufficient coverage and analyzes the performance differences among mobile network operators. Based on these findings, the authors propose the targeted deployment of femtocells as a scalable and replicable solution to enhance indoor connectivity. Beyond coverage improvement, the work highlights the broader implications for healthcare sensor networks, including reliable telemonitoring, real-time tracking of equipment and patients, and secure data transmission, particularly in clinical areas and resource-constrained settings.

In Contribution 10, Rodriguez-Gomez et al. revisit the classical CSMA non-persistent medium access protocol from a perspective relevant to modern sensor networks. While most analytical models assume an infinite node population, the authors demonstrate that this assumption leads to significant inaccuracies in scenarios with a limited number of active nodes and low traffic intensity.

The authors derive a closed-form expression for system throughput that explicitly accounts for a finite number of nodes, complemented by a computationally efficient approximation. Through numerical evaluation and simulation-based validation, the study reveals how throughput, delay, and energy consumption characteristics vary with node population size. These results provide important insights for the design and analysis of contention-based MAC protocols in practical sensor network deployments where the infinite-population assumption no longer holds.

2.3. Intelligent Processing and Learning-Driven Optimization in Sensor Networks

In the paper "EdgeVidCap: A Channel-Spatial Dual-Branch Lightweight Video Captioning Model for IoT Edge Cameras" (Contribution 4), Guo et al. address the challenge of deploying advanced video understanding algorithms on resource-constrained IoT edge devices. The authors note that conventional video captioning models are computationally intensive and unsuitable for real-time processing on embedded platforms.

To address this issue, the paper introduces a lightweight architecture that integrates channel attention mechanisms with state-space models through a novel Synergetic Attention State Mamba module. An adaptive attention-guided LSTM decoder further enhances caption generation by dynamically weighting visual features. Experimental evaluations on benchmark datasets demonstrate that EdgeVidCap achieves competitive captioning accuracy while significantly reducing model complexity and computational requirements, enabling practical deployment on intelligent edge cameras.

The paper "DRL-Driven Intelligent SFC Deployment in MEC Workload for Dynamic IoT Networks" (Contribution 5), by Ros, Ryoo, and Kim, proposes a learning-based framework for resource orchestration in IoT systems integrated with multi-access edge computing. The authors address the challenges posed by fluctuating workloads, limited edge resources, and stringent quality-of-service requirements in dynamic IoT environments.

The proposed framework leverages deep reinforcement learning (DRL), specifically a Deep Q-Network, to jointly optimize task offloading decisions, service function chaining, virtual network function placement, and routing. Simulation results demonstrate improvements in latency, energy consumption, packet delivery ratio, and throughput compared to baseline approaches. This contribution highlights the effectiveness of DRL in managing complex, multi-dimensional optimization problems in large-scale sensor network ecosystems.

In Contribution 9, Eriş, Gül, and Bölük focus on sustainable communication in underwater acoustic sensor networks, where battery replacement is often impractical. The authors consider a realistic stochastic model for piezoelectric energy harvesting and the spatio-temporal variability of underwater ambient resources.

They propose a distributed multi-agent reinforcement learning–based TDMA scheduling scheme that allows sensor nodes to adapt their transmission slots based on available harvested energy autonomously. Simulation results demonstrate improvements in throughput and network lifetime metrics, including the first-, half-, and last-node death times. The work illustrates how learning-enabled MAC protocols can effectively exploit ambient energy sources and enhance the long-term sustainability of underwater sensor networks.

2.4. Energy Efficiency, Embedded Platforms, and Security in Sensor Networks

The paper "A Cluster Head Selection Algorithm for Extending Last Node Lifetime in Wireless Sensor Networks" (Contribution 6) revisits the problem of energy-efficient clustering in wireless sensor networks. Unlike traditional approaches that aim to balance energy consumption across nodes, the authors formulate network lifetime as a function of node energy depletion and analytically derive a cluster head selection rule that maximizes the time until the last node dies.

The proposed algorithm prioritizes nodes with high transmission probabilities and low initial energy levels for cluster head selection and operates using distributed per-cluster computation. Its effectiveness is validated through experiments on a real LoRaWAN-based sensor network prototype, demonstrating significant lifetime improvements over state-of-the-art methods. This contribution emphasizes the importance of analytically grounded, application-aware algorithms validated in real-world deployments.

In Contribution 8, Vandervelden et al. provide a comprehensive survey and comparative analysis of Rust-based operating systems and frameworks for sensor nodes. Motivated by Rust's memory safety guarantees, the authors examine platforms such as Tock, Hubris, RTIC, and Embassy, focusing on scheduling, inter-process communication, application isolation, and networking support.

https://doi.org/10.3390/s26072197

The paper also presents a performance evaluation of scheduling latency and memory footprint, highlighting trade-offs between functionality and resource usage. By contrasting different design philosophies, this contribution offers valuable guidance for developers seeking secure and efficient software platforms for embedded sensor network devices.

Lee et al., in the paper "A Programmable Crypto-Processor for National Institute of Standards and Technology Post-Quantum Cryptography Standardization Based on the RISC-V Architecture" (Contribution 11), address emerging security challenges posed by quantum computing. The authors propose a programmable crypto-processor that extends the RISC-V instruction set to accelerate post-quantum cryptographic algorithms currently under NIST standardization.

The proposed architecture reduces code size, instruction count, and execution cycles for key cryptographic operations while maintaining flexibility to support multiple algorithms. Implemented as a coprocessor, the design enables efficient and secure cryptographic processing in embedded systems. This contribution demonstrates how hardware–software co-design can play a critical role in ensuring long-term security for future sensor network deployments.

Conflicts of Interest: The author declares no conflicts of interest.

List of Contributions:

1. Hu, L.; Shi, F.; Shen, Y.; Xu, C.; Xue, P.; Guo, B. VistaScan: Optimizing Internet-Wide Scanning Through Visibility-Aware Distributed Task Allocation. *Sensors* **2026**, *26*, 1458. https://doi.org/10.3390/s26051458.
2. Chang, R.-I.; Hsu, T.-W.; Chen, Y.-T. Two-Phase Distributed Genetic-Based Algorithm for Time-Aware Shaper Scheduling in Industrial Sensor Networks. *Sensors* **2026**, *26*, 377. https://doi.org/10.3390/s26020377.
3. Silva, Ó.; Teixeira, E.B.; Corceiro, A.; Reis, A.D.; Velez, F.J. Radio Coverage Assessment and Indoor Communication Enhancement in Hospitals: A Case Study at CHUCB. *Sensors* **2025**, *25*, 4933. https://doi.org/10.3390/s25164933.
4. Guo, L.; Li, X.; Wang, J.; Xiao, J.; Hou, Y.; Zhi, P.; Yong, B.; Li, L.; Zhou, Q.; Li, K. EdgeVidCap: A Channel-Spatial Dual-Branch Lightweight Video Captioning Model for IoT Edge Cameras. *Sensors* **2025**, *25*, 4897. https://doi.org/10.3390/s25164897.
5. Ros, S.; Ryoo, I.; Kim, S. DRL-Driven Intelligent SFC Deployment in MEC Workload for Dynamic IoT Networks. *Sensors* **2025**, *25*, 4257. https://doi.org/10.3390/s25144257.
6. Lewandowski, M.; Płaczek, B. A Cluster Head Selection Algorithm for Extending Last Node Lifetime in Wireless Sensor Networks. *Sensors* **2025**, *25*, 3466. https://doi.org/10.3390/s25113466.
7. Lacasa, A.; Llopis, J.; Montés, N.; Peinado-Asensi, I.; Garcia, E. Cross-PLC: An I3oT Cross Platform to Manage Communications for Applications in Real Factories. *Sensors* **2025**, *25*, 2973. https://doi.org/10.3390/s25102973.
8. Vandervelden, T.; De Smet, R.; Deac, D.; Steenhaut, K.; Braeken, A. Overview of Embedded Rust Operating Systems and Frameworks. *Sensors* **2024**, *24*, 5818. https://doi.org/10.3390/s24175818.
9. Eriş, Ç.; Gül, Ö.M.; Bölük, P.S. A Novel Medium Access Policy Based on Reinforcement Learning in Energy-Harvesting Underwater Sensor Networks. *Sensors* **2024**, *24*, 5791. https://doi.org/10.3390/s24175791.
10. Rodriguez-Gomez, A.I.; Rivero-Angeles, M.E.; Orea-Flores, I.Y.; Gallegos-García, G.; Chimal-Eguia, J.C. Performance Analysis of CSMA/NP under Finite Population Environments. *Sensors* **2024**, *24*, 3290. https://doi.org/10.3390/s24113290.
11. Lee, J.; Kim, W.; Kim, J.-H. A Programmable Crypto-Processor for National Institute of Standards and Technology Post-Quantum Cryptography Standardization Based on the RISC-V Architecture. *Sensors* **2023**, *23*, 9408. https://doi.org/10.3390/s23239408.

https://doi.org/10.3390/s26072197

References

1. Majid, M.; Habib, S.; Javed, A.R.; Rizwan, M.; Srivastava, G.; Gadekallu, T.R.; Lin, J.C.W. Applications of Wireless Sensor Networks and Internet of Things Frameworks in the Industry Revolution 4.0: A Systematic Literature Review. *Sensors* **2022**, *22*, 2087. [CrossRef]
2. Dahmane, W.M.; Ouchani, S.; Bouarfa, H. Smart cities services and solutions: A systematic review. *Data Inf. Manag.* **2025**, *9*, 100087. [CrossRef]
3. Kumar, H. Wireless Sensor Networks in Healthcare System: A Systematic Review. *Wirel. Pers. Commun.* **2024**, *134*, 1013–1034. [CrossRef]
4. Soussi, A.; Zero, E.; Sacile, R.; Trinchero, D.; Fossa, M. Smart Sensors and Smart Data for Precision Agriculture: A Review. *Sensors* **2024**, *24*, 2647. [CrossRef] [PubMed]
5. Ojha, A.; Gupta, B. Evolving Landscape of Wireless Sensor Networks: A Survey of Trends, Timelines, and Future Perspectives. *Discov. Appl. Sci.* **2025**, *7*, 825. [CrossRef]
6. Zhang, D.; Cui, Y.; Cao, X.; Su, N.; Gong, Y.; Liu, F.; Yuan, W.; Jing, X.; Andrew Zhang, J.; Xu, J.; et al. Integrated Sensing and Communications Over the Years: An Evolution Perspective. *IEEE Commun. Surv. Tutor.* **2026**, *28*, 5014–5048. [CrossRef]
7. Płaczek, B. Prediction-based data reduction with dynamic target node selection in IoT sensor networks. *Future Gener. Comput. Syst.* **2024**, *152*, 225–238. [CrossRef]
8. Khan, S.; Mazhar, T.; Shahzad, T.; Ghadi, Y.Y.; Hamam, H. Integrating IoT and WSN: Enhancing Quality of Service through Energy Efficiency, Scalability, and Secure Communication in Smart Systems. *Peer-to-Peer Netw. Appl.* **2025**, *18*, 249. [CrossRef]
9. Trigka, M.; Dritsas, E. Wireless Sensor Networks: From Fundamentals and Applications to Innovations and Future Trends. *IEEE Access* **2025**, *13*, 96365–96399. [CrossRef]
10. Abdulhussain, S.H.; Mahmmod, B.M.; Alwhelat, A.; Shehada, D.; Shihab, Z.I.; Mohammed, H.J.; Abdulameer, T.H.; Alsabah, M.; Fadel, M.H.; Ali, S.K.; et al. A Comprehensive Review of Sensor Technologies in IoT: Technical Aspects, Challenges, and Future Directions. *Computers* **2025**, *14*, 342. [CrossRef]
11. Pandey, S.; Chaudhary, M.; Tóth, Z. An Investigation on Real-Time Insights: Enhancing Process Control with IoT-Enabled Sensor Networks. *Discov. Internet Things* **2025**, *5*, 29. [CrossRef]
12. Jamshed, M.A.; Ali, K.; Abbasi, Q.H.; Imran, M.A.; Ur-Rehman, M. Challenges, Applications, and Future of Wireless Sensors in Internet of Things: A Review. *IEEE Sens. J.* **2022**, *22*, 5482–5494. [CrossRef]
13. Xu, W.; Yang, Z.; Ng, D.W.K.; Levorato, M.; Eldar, Y.C.; Debbah, M. Edge Learning for B5G Networks with Distributed Signal Processing: Semantic Communication, Edge Computing, and Wireless Sensing. *IEEE J. Sel. Top. Signal Process.* **2023**, *17*, 9–39. [CrossRef]
14. Seng, K.P.; Ang, L.M.; Ngharamike, E. Artificial intelligence Internet of Things: A new paradigm of distributed sensor networks. *Int. J. Distrib. Sens. Netw.* **2022**, *18*, 15501477211062835 [CrossRef]
15. Liu, F.; Cui, Y.; Masouros, C.; Xu, J.; Han, T.X.; Eldar, Y.C.; Buzzi, S. Integrated Sensing and Communications: Toward Dual-Functional Wireless Networks for 6G and Beyond. *IEEE J. Sel. Areas Commun.* **2022**, *40*, 1728–1767. [CrossRef]

https://doi.org/10.3390/s26072197

sensors

MDPI

Article

VistaScan: Optimizing Internet-Wide Scanning Through Visibility-Aware Distributed Task Allocation

Luolin Hu , Fan Shi *, Yi Shen , Chengxi Xu, Pengfei Xue and Bingyang Guo

College of Electronic Engineering, National University of Defense Technology, Hefei 230031, China; huluolin14@nudt.edu.cn (L.H.); shenyi@nudt.edu.cn (Y.S.); xuchengxi@nudt.edu.cn (C.X.); xuepengfei@nudt.edu.cn (P.X.); guobingyang@nudt.edu.cn (B.G.)

* Correspondence: shifan17@nudt.edu.cn

Abstract

Internet-wide scanning is indispensable for security research and network measurement, yet its efficacy remains limited by significant visibility heterogeneity across global networks. Traditional centralized scanners suffer from single-point failures and offer a constrained perspective, while naive distributed approaches fail to intelligently leverage visibility variations, leading to redundant effort and incomplete coverage. This paper presents VistaScan, a novel distributed scanning system based on node visibility awareness, demonstrating that the visibility pattern among IP addresses is highly consistent within CIDR blocks, enabling a lightweight method for efficient and scalable quantification of per-node visibility. It first constructs a Visibility Matrix through efficient anchor probing, then employs a load-aware task allocation mechanism that assigns each block to the most capable node while filtering out entirely invisible blocks. Evaluation across global, regional, and challenging Special-Block tasks demonstrates that VistaScan consistently outperforms five baseline methods. It achieves near-optimal coverage (97.95%, 99.05%, and 97.58%, respectively), reduces probe volume by 64–93%, and shortens completion time by 13–19× compared to conventional centralized and distributed scanners. Furthermore, the visibility matrix derived from one port (TCP/80) effectively generalizes to other TCP ports (TCP/22, TCP/53), achieving coverages of 91.09% and 87.95%—preliminarily validating the practical generalizability of our approach. VistaScan provides both a highly efficient solution for Internet-scale distributed measurement and a new theoretical foundation based on visibility consistency, advancing the field from brute-force probing toward intelligent, low-overhead, and sustainable scanning practices.

Keywords: internet measurement; distributed scanning; node visibility; visibility matrix; visibility consistency; task allocation; network architecture

1. Introduction

With the continuous proliferation of devices connected to the Internet, ensuring robust cybersecurity has become an imperative [1]. Internet-wide scanning plays an important role in cybersecurity analysis and network asset detection. This measurement technique has been used to study security vulnerabilities [2–5], host liveness [6–9], service deployment [10–16], network topology [17,18], uncover protocol weaknesses [19–21], and more. Internet-wide scanning works by initiating network connections with services on a set of given ports. So open port scanning is universally recognized as the critical first step in various types of network research. However, the scale of modern IPv4 and IPv6 networks makes exhaustive scanning a monumental task. Although modern scanning tools like ZMap [22], Masscan [23] and Nmap [24] employ centralized high-speed scanning from a single vantage point, this approach faces inherent limitations: the limited efficiency of a single node [12], network access restrictions [3,25] and IP blacklisting [9]. The research community has also recognized the fundamental constraint that no single node can see everything, and different geographical and network locations offer different views of the Internet [3,25–28].

To reduce the time overhead of large-scale scanning and detection, distributed technology was introduced in scanning and detecting network assets [29–32]. They improve probing efficiency by breaking down large-scale scanning tasks and distributing them across multiple nodes for execution. However, their task allocation strategies are often simplistic, treating different subtasks and probing nodes as interchangeable, and fail to account for the critical issue of nodal visibility divergence. Blindly assigning a CIDR block to any random node often results in insufficient coverage. If we missed certain ports from the very beginning, this omission can have significant negative implications for subsequent research, potentially resulting in the neglect of security vulnerabilities, the omission of critical assets, and a misjudgment of the overall security posture. Therefore, a more intelligent task allocation strategy is required to maximize coverage and minimize completion time.

In this paper, we present VistaScan, an intelligent visibility-aware distributed scanner for Internet-wide scanning. VistaScan is the first system that quantifies probing node visibility and, accordingly, performs task allocation and probing, the core idea of which is to assign probing tasks of different network blocks to the best-suited probing nodes. Our solution stems from a key empirical observation: Although nodes differ vastly in their global visibility (heterogeneity across nodes), a single node's visibility of IPs within a specific CIDR block is highly consistent (consistency within blocks), which we formally define as the Visibility Consistency. Based on this, the visibility of representative anchor IPs by a node can characterize its visibility of the entire block. This allows for the assessment of a node's capability without the need for a full-block exhaustive probe. Prior to executing the distributed probing, each node first performs a pre-scan of the representative IPs. The visibility scores of each node for each block are then calculated to construct a visibility matrix. Subsequently, the probing tasks are allocated in a targeted manner based on this matrix. This approach improves coverage effectiveness, reduces the total number of probe packets, shortens the overall scanning duration, and improves load balance in a distributed scanning scenario. Our core contributions are as follows.

- The first formalization and large-scale validation of Visibility Consistency. We discover and formally characterize the phenomenon that visibility remains consistent within blocks, enabling the use of a few representative IPs to infer whole-block visibility. We formulate this concept using Jaccard similarity and empirically establish /23 blocks as the optimal task allocation unit.
- A lightweight method for efficient and scalable quantification of per-node visibility. We show that using three anchor IPs from different probing sources is a practical and effective heuristic for characterizing block-level visibility. We also propose two anchor selection methods and construct a node–CIDR visibility matrix, where each value in the continuous range [0,1] reflects a node's proficiency in probing a block.
- The design and implementation of the VistaScan system. VistaScan comprises four modules: CIDR Partitioning, Anchor Selection, Visibility Matrix Construction, and Load-Aware Task Allocation, significantly improving the performance of distributed Internet measurement by streamlining evaluation, quantifying capability, optimizing assignment, and pruning infeasible work.

https://doi.org/10.3390/s26051458

We evaluated VistaScan with five baseline methods (Centralized, Union-of-All Nodes, Naive-Distributed-Random, Partitioned-Distributed-Random, Geo-Heuristic) in four metrics (Global Coverage, Total Completion Time, Total Packets Sent, Node Load Balance) across three scanning scenarios (global, regional, and challenging special block tasks). The results show that it achieves near-optimal coverage (97.95%, 99.05%, and 97.58% respectively) while reducing the total number of probes by 64–95% and overall completion time by 13-19x compared to centralized and naive distributed baselines. Crucially, we demonstrate that the visibility matrix derived from one port (TCP/80) is highly effective for scanning other TCP ports (TCP/22, TCP/53), achieving 91.09% and 87.95% coverage, which preliminarily underscores the generalizability of our approach.

The remainder of the paper is organized as follows. Section 2 details the background and motivation for this project. Section 3 describes the architecture of VistaScan. Section 4 reports the experimental setup and evaluation results, followed by a discussion of the results and limitations in Section 5. Section 6 presents the related work. Finally, Section 7 concludes this paper.

2. Background and Motivation

Distributed scanning leverages multiple geographically or topologically distinct vantage points to conduct large-scale network measurements in a parallel and coordinated manner. It offers increased scanning throughput, improved resistance to blocking, and, most importantly, diverse network perspectives. Compared to single-source methods, this approach significantly reduces scan time while enhancing fault tolerance and scalability. However, the transition to a distributed model replaces the technical challenge of high-speed packet generation with new algorithmic challenges, such as intelligent task allocation and coordination overhead. We begin by briefly summarizing current Internet-wide scanning systems and the key challenges they face.

2.1. Heterogeneity in Node Visibility

Prior studies have identified discrepancies in scanning results arising from different probing sources [3,25–27]. The paper [28] further showed that scanning from a single vantage point achieve limited coverage (miss an average 1.6–8.4% of HTTP, 1.5–4.6% of HTTPS, and 8.3–18.2% of SSH hosts) and that aggressive scanners experience significant blocking. Due to permanent and temporary blocking, probing nodes from different geographical and network locations would obtain different views of the Internet. They advise scanning from 2 to 3 sufficiently diverse vantage points to improve coverage, but this comes at the cost of a two-to-threefold increase in probing overhead.

To better understand the impact of nodal visibility on distributed probing, we designed a global-scale scanning experiment based on the MaxMind GeoLite2 database. We constructed a task list comprising 100 randomly selected CIDR blocks from each of 18 countries on six continents (excluding Antarctica) and performed scans from five geographically distributed nodes using ZMap. Each node operated at a calibrated rate of 1500 packets per second (pps), which is established in Appendix B to balance packet loss and resource usage. To reduce temporal bias, all nodes shared the same ZMap seed, ensuring target probing at approximately the same time. The experiment was repeated three times to mitigate the effects of the transient network, and the results were aggregated through a union between repetitions. This controlled setup allows us to isolate and quantify the effect of node location on visibility, independent of hardware or configuration artifacts, and provides a foundation for developing customized task allocation strategies.

The results are presented in Figures 1 and 2. Figure 1 reveals significant and systematic disparities in the results of the investigation of the same targets between nodes located in

https://doi.org/10.3390/s26051458

different regions, indicating that each node has a unique and partial view of the Internet. On average, a single node can only detect about 95% of the total assets, with the node JP having the lowest coverage at 92%. Only 87% of the target IPs were visible to all nodes. The remaining 13% exhibited distinct node-specific visibility patterns, with approximately 2% of the assets accessible only from a single probing source. This implies that these IPs can only be discovered if assigned to that specific node. Although this proportion may appear small, in absolute terms, it translates to 36,875 IPs that could be missed due to inappropriate node selection - and this is only within the 1800 CIDR blocks sampled. Given that the full MaxMind database contains 629,757 CIDR blocks, the number of potentially overlooked assets in an Internet-wide scan cannot be overlooked. If such visibility heterogeneity is ignored during distributed scanning and tasks are assigned indiscriminately, the impact on coverage could be substantial.

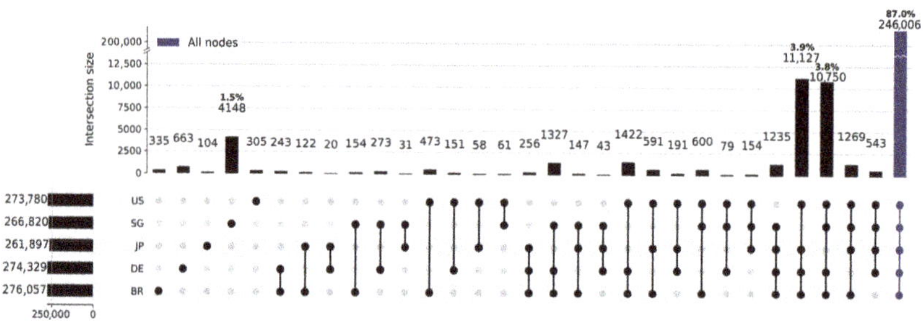

Figure 1. Heterogeneity of network visibility across nodes: IP address detection results. The significant non-overlapping areas visually confirm the systematic differences in node visibility. Only 87% of the target IPs were visible to all nodes; the remaining IPs exhibited node-specific visibility patterns. Intelligent systems must treat nodes as heterogeneous, not interchangeable.

Moreover, the remarkably low average hit rate of only 1.94% shown in Figure 2 indicates that a significant portion of the blocks and IPs in the IPv4 address space remain inactive, and the active IPs are highly sparse. If we can take advantage of this sparsity and detect these inactive blocks in advance, the probing overhead could be significantly reduced.

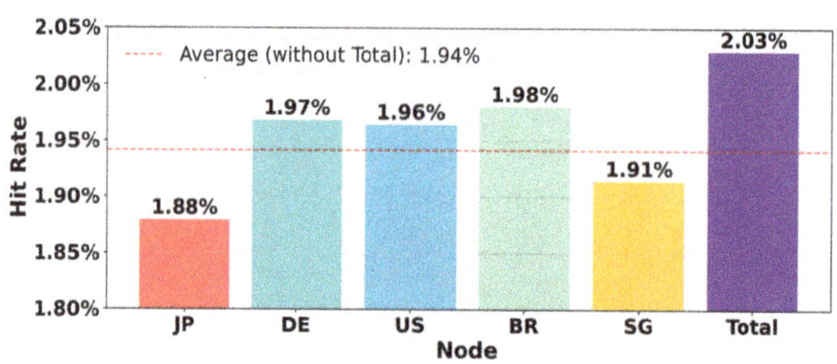

Figure 2. Hit rates by node and total. The average hit rate across all nodes is only 1.94%, indicating that active IPs in cyberspace are highly sparse. Leveraging this sparsity effectively could eliminate a substantial number of unnecessary probes.

2.2. Limitations of Existing Allocation Strategies

Despite the critical importance of accounting for visibility heterogeneity in distributed probing, existing task allocation strategies often fail to adequately leverage these differences, which may cause insufficient coverage, redundant probing, and ineffective measurements.

Random allocation: The most common baseline; it treats all nodes as equal and distributes targets randomly. This approach does not attempt to match targets with nodes

https://doi.org/10.3390/s26051458

that can see them, leading to suboptimal coverage and inefficient use of resources, as demonstrated in our evaluation (Section 4). Previous studies have proposed various distributed scanning frameworks [29–31]. These systems focus primarily on achieving load balance, improving overall efficiency, and improving the flexibility and scalability of the system. However, they share a common limitation: treating both nodes and subtasks as homogeneous and interchangeable. Their task allocation strategies are typically randomized, involving either a central controller assigning tasks uniformly or nodes automatically claiming subtasks based on their current load.

Geographic heuristics: The paper [32] showed that the regional characteristics of scanners greatly affect the scan rate and the port connection latency within the same country or region is lower than between countries and regions. Therefore, they cluster scanners based on geographical location and further assign tasks regionally using historical average latency tables, thereby reducing average detection delay and improving task completion efficiency. However, the resources of the probing node are limited; we cannot always rely on nodes located within the target region. Assigning subtasks based solely on geographic clusters also overlooks the heterogeneity of IP responsiveness within regions. Additionally, constructing an average latency table requires historical full-coverage probing data, which incurs significant computational and management overhead. However, the resources of probing nodes are limited, and we cannot always guarantee the availability of nodes within the target region. Assigning sub-tasks based solely on geographical distribution also overlooks the heterogeneity of IP responsiveness within the same region. Furthermore, constructing an average latency table relies on historical full-coverage probing data, which entails significant computational and management overhead.

Therefore, it is imperative to develop a lighter method for evaluating distributed node capabilities and an intelligent task allocation strategy that effectively leverages limited probing resources to maximize coverage and accuracy.

2.3. Problem Formalization and Key Insight

The Distributed Scanning Task Allocation Problem can thus be formalized as follows. Given a set of targets C (e.g., a list of IP addresses or CIDR blocks) and a set of distributed nodes N, find an assignment $A : C \rightarrow N$ that maximizes the number of responsive targets found, minimizes the total completion time, and balances the workload across N, subject to the constraint that a node can only probe the targets it can reach. Therefore, a pivotal and urgent task is to define the theoretical foundation for intelligent task allocation.

The key principle is to assign tasks based on node specialties to ensure workload equilibrium, and the primary challenge is to quickly and efficiently quantify and evaluate the coverage capacity of each node. Our proposed system, VistaScan, solves this problem by the key insight that while nodes exhibit vastly different visibility globally, the visibility pattern within a specific CIDR block remains highly consistent from any single node's perspective. We formalize this property as Visibility Consistency and formally validate it in Appendix C.

Definition 1 (Visibility Consistency). *For a given CIDR block $B = \{ip_1, ip_2, ..., ip_m\}$ and a set of distributed probing nodes $N = \{n_1, n_2, ..., n_k\}$, we define* visibility vector *for an IP address ip_i as a binary vector $\vec{v}_i = (V(ip_i, n_1), V(ip_i, n_2), ..., V(ip_i, n_k))$, where $V(ip_i, n_j)$ indicates the visibility of ip_i from node n_j. The degree of* Visibility Consistency *within block B is then quantified as the average pairwise Jaccard similarity between the visibility vectors of all IP pairs in B:*

$$Consistency(B) = \frac{2}{m(m-1)} \sum_{i=1}^{m-1} \sum_{j=i+1}^{m} J(\vec{v}_i, \vec{v}_j)$$

https://doi.org/10.3390/s26051458

where $J(\vec{v}_i, \vec{v}_j)$ *is the Jaccard similarity coefficient:*

$$J(\vec{v}_i, \vec{v}_j) = \frac{|\vec{v}_i \cap \vec{v}_j|}{|\vec{v}_i \cup \vec{v}_j|} = \frac{\sum_{k=1}^{k} \min(v_{i,k}, v_{j,k})}{\sum_{k=1}^{k} \max(v_{i,k}, v_{j,k})}$$

A higher consistency score indicates that the visibility patterns of IPs within the block are more homogeneous, justifying the use of representative anchor IPs for the entire block. We also quantify the Visibility Consistency of various sizes of CIDR blocks and one of the figures is shown as Figure 3, indicating that /23 is the optimal block size for overall consistency (see Appendix C.3 for details).

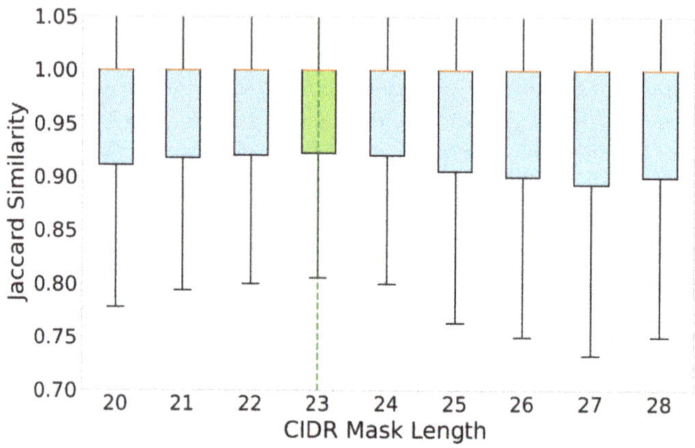

Figure 3. Distribution of Jaccard similarity across different CIDR sizes. The /23 block size exhibits a higher lower bound.

3. VistaScan System Design

The core idea of the *VistaScan* system is to assign the probing tasks of different network blocks to the best-suited probing nodes. Based on the principle of *Visibility Consistency*, the visibility of representative *anchor IPs* by a node can characterize its visibility of the entire block. This allows for the assessment of a node's capability without the need for a full-block exhaustive probe.

The architecture of VistaScan, shown in Figure 4, is structured as a modular orchestration designed to transform a raw set of scanning targets into an optimally distributed task assignment. The system begins with *CIDR Partitioning Module*, which ingests user-defined targets and leverages the MaxMind GeoLite2 database to group them by autonomous system or geography before systematically splitting them into consistent /23 CIDR blocks. These standardized blocks then pass to the *Anchor Selection Module*, which identifies a small set of representative IP addresses (anchors) for each block in two optional ways. Subsequently, the *Visibility Matrix Construction Module* coordinates a lightweight validation probe where all distributed nodes probe these anchors, resulting in a visibility matrix that quantifies the coverage effectiveness of each node for each block. Finally, the *Load-Aware Task Allocation Module* consumes this matrix to intelligently assign each CIDR block to the most capable node while maintaining global load balance across the entire system. If a network-wide visibility matrix is already available, the two modules within the dashed box can be skipped, and the partitioned user tasks can be directly allocated based on this pre-built matrix, thereby further reducing system overhead. This orchestrated workflow ensures that the expansive scanning task is decomposed and allocated in a manner

https://doi.org/10.3390/s26051458

that maximizes coverage and efficiency by explicitly accounting for the inherent network visibility constraints of each probing node in a distributed probing scenario.

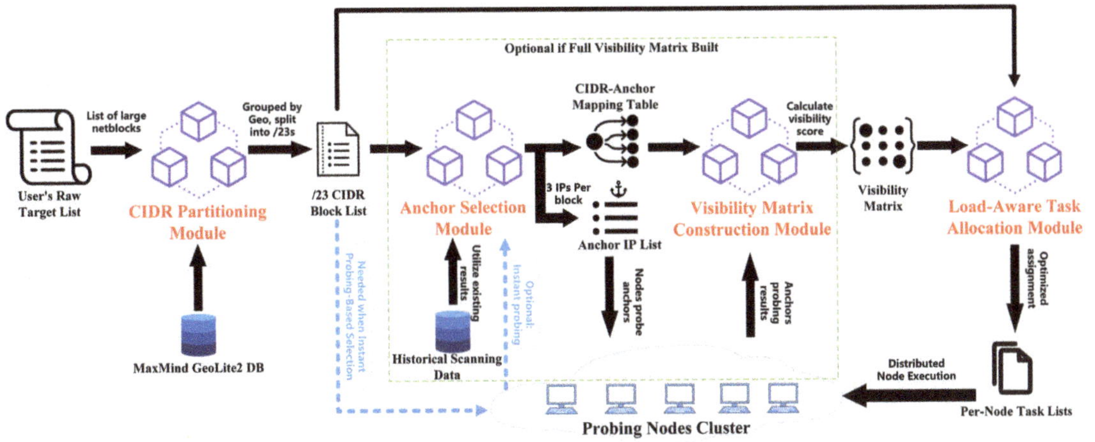

Figure 4. VistaScan system architecture overview. The system consists of four main modules: CIDR partitioning, anchor selection, visibility matrix construction, and load-aware task allocation.

3.1. CIDR Partitioning

The CIDR Partitioning Module preprocesses the user's raw input targets, which may be a list of individual IP addresses or large netblocks (e.g., a /12), and transforms them into a canonical set of mainly /23 CIDR blocks optimized for high Visibility Consistency, forming the foundational unit for subsequent processing of anchor selection and task allocation. This module optimizes load balance by refining subtasks into finer-grained units and operates in two stages.

1. **IP-to-Country Mapping:** Each IP address is mapped to its corresponding country or region using the MaxMind GeoLite2 database. This initial grouping takes advantage of the premise that IPs within the same geographic region are more likely to share network infrastructure and visibility characteristics.
2. **Canonical Splitting:** Address blocks larger than a /23 prefix are split into /23 CIDR blocks. This specific size was selected based on the analysis in Appendix C.3, which found it to be the optimal trade-off between Visibility Consistency and management overhead.

3.2. Anchor Selection

The target IP space is divided into no more than /23 blocks. For each block, we select a small set of anchor IPs to characterize its visibility. In our experiments, using three anchor IPs from different probing sources per block proved to be a practical and effective heuristic, balancing representativeness, robustness, and probing overhead. The theoretical criteria for anchor selection are detailed in Appendix D, and are supported by prior work that leverages limited sampling to infer broader network characteristics [7,12,28,33–38]. The optimal number of anchors may vary depending on network conditions and consistency levels, and is a subject for future parameter tuning. The selection of representative anchor IPs can be accomplished through two primary methods:

1. **Historical Data-Based Selection:** This approach utilizes existing probing results, requiring no additional probing overhead beyond the main task. Although compu-

https://doi.org/10.3390/s26051458

tationally efficient, its main limitation is the potential lack of timeliness in anchor IP availability, as the historical data may not reflect the current network state.

2. **Instant Probing-Based Selection:** This method involves initiating a targeted, rapid random probe for a single IP within each target CIDR block by pre-configured nodes. The results of these probes are then aggregated to generate the final anchor list. The principal advantage of this method is the strong timeliness and freshness of the anchors obtained. However, it introduces additional probing overhead and latency before the main scan can begin.

For probing tasks with stringent timeliness requirements—such as post-incident assessments or scans in highly dynamic network environments—users can perform instant anchor scanning and visibility matrix construction on a per-task basis, accepting a modest increase in probing overhead in exchange for maximum freshness. This flexibility ensures that VistaScan can be tailored to a wide range of operational contexts.

Algorithm 1 demonstrates the efficient retrieval and anchor generation process based on historical data. Its core operation involves, for each block, performing an efficient lookup to find belonging IPs from each node's perspective, randomly selecting one candidate IP per node, and finally deduplicating and sampling up to three unique IPs to serve as the final anchors for that block. The process outputs a comprehensive list of all representative IPs and a mapping of each CIDR block to its anchors. The instant probing method differs only in its data source, consuming a live stream of probe results from each node instead of querying static historical files.

Algorithm 1 Historical Data-Based Anchor IP Selection

Require: Set of distributed nodes: $N = \{n_1, n_2, ..., n_k\}$
Require: Sorted IP lists from each node's scan results: $L_{n_1}, L_{n_2}, ..., L_{n_k}$
Require: List of target CIDR blocks: C
Ensure: Representative IP list R
Ensure: Mapping M from CIDR blocks to representative IPs

$R \leftarrow \{\}$ ▷ Initialize representative IP list
$M \leftarrow \{\}$ ▷ Initialize CIDR-to-IP mapping
for each CIDR block c_i **in** C **do**
    $S \leftarrow \{\}$ ▷ Initialize set for candidate IPs per block
    for each node n_j **in** N **do**
        $I_{\text{candidate}} \leftarrow \text{FindIPsInCIDR}(L_{n_j}, c_i)$ ▷ Binary search for IPs in CIDR
        if $I_{\text{candidate}} \neq \emptyset$ **then**
            $ip_{\text{selected}} \leftarrow \text{RandomChoice}(I_{\text{candidate}})$ ▷ Random selection per node
            $S \leftarrow S \cup \{ip_{\text{selected}}\}$ ▷ Add to candidate set
        end if
    end for
    $S_{\text{unique}} \leftarrow \text{RemoveDuplicates}(S)$ ▷ Preserve order while removing duplicates
    if $S_{\text{unique}} \neq \emptyset$ **then**
        $F \leftarrow \text{RandomSample}(S_{\text{unique}}, \min(3, |S_{\text{unique}}|))$ ▷ Select up to 3 unique IPs
        $R \leftarrow R \cup F$ ▷ Add to final representative list
        for each IP ip_k **in** F **do**
            $M \leftarrow M \cup \{(c_i, ip_k)\}$ ▷ Add to CIDR-to-IP mapping
        end for
    end if
end for
return R, M

This algorithm takes sorted IP lists from historical scanning data from different nodes and a list of target CIDR blocks as input. Its design directly addresses the core requirements of representativeness and diversity by leveraging a key insight: the collective historical

https://doi.org/10.3390/s26051458

data from all nodes provide the most unbiased view of a block's visibility landscape. By performing an efficient lookup into each node's sorted IP list, it ensures computational scalability. The strategy of randomly selecting one candidate IP from each node's perspective inherently incorporates the necessary discriminative power and mitigates single-point visibility bias, as the final anchor set is distilled from a pool that reflects the heterogeneous nature of the network. Finally, the deduplication and sampling step robustly handles real-world data imperfections, enforcing a multi-anchor strategy to balance robustness with low overhead. This synergy of efficiency, built-in diversity, and practical robustness makes the algorithm a critical component for building the foundational data structures of our distributed scanning system.

3.3. *Visibility Matrix Construction*

The Visibility Matrix M is a core data structure that encodes the visibility score $M[n, c]$ for each node–block pair (n, c), where $n \in \mathcal{N}$ is a node and $c \in \mathcal{C}$ is a CIDR block. The score $M[n, c]$ is defined as the fraction of anchor IPs in block c that node n can successfully probe, formalized as:

$$M[n,c] = \frac{|\{a \in Anchors(c) \mid Probe(n,a) = \text{success}\}|}{|Anchors(c)|}$$

where $Anchors(c)$ is the set of anchor IPs for block c and $Probe(n, a)$ denotes the result of node n probing anchor a.

Algorithm 2 outlines the construction process. It first precomputes a reverse lookup table *IP2Block* to efficiently map any anchor IP back to its parent CIDR block (lines 1–3). The reverse mapping IP-to-Block ensures that determining the parent block of any visible IP is an O(1) operation, which is crucial given the scale of Internet-wide scanning. For each node n, it processes the set of anchor IPs visible to n (V_n). For each visible IP, it uses the *IP2Block* map to increment a counter for the corresponding block (lines 5–9). Finally, the visibility score for each block is computed by normalizing the count of visible anchors by the total number of anchors in that block (lines 10–13).

Algorithm 2 Build Visibility Matrix M

Require: $Anchors : \mathcal{C} \to \mathbb{A}^*$ ▷ Map: Block c to its anchor lists
1: $V : \mathcal{N} \to 2^{\mathbb{A}}$ ▷ Map: Node n to its set of visible anchors
2: $\mathcal{N}, \mathcal{C}$ ▷ Lists of all nodes and CIDR blocks
Ensure: Visibility Matrix $M[\mathcal{N}, \mathcal{C}]$
3: $IP2Block \leftarrow \{\}$ ▷ Initialize IP-to-Block mapping
4: **for** $c \in \mathcal{C}$ **do**
5:     **for** $a \in Anchors(c)$ **do**
6:         $IP2Block[a] \leftarrow c$
7:     **end for**
8: **end for**
9: **for** $n \in \mathcal{N}$ **do** ▷ For each node
10:     $Count \leftarrow \text{DefaultDict(int)}$ ▷ Initialize per-block counter
11:     **for** $a \in V(n)$ **do** ▷ For each anchor visible to node n
12:         **if** $a \in IP2Block$ **then**
13:             $c \leftarrow IP2Block[a]$
14:             $Count[c] \leftarrow Count[c] + 1$
15:         **end if**
16:     **end for**
17:     **for** $c \in \mathcal{C}$ **do** ▷ Compute final scores
18:         $M[n,c] \leftarrow Count[c] \ / \ |Anchors(c)|$
19:     **end for**
20: **end for**

https://doi.org/10.3390/s26051458

This process efficiently transforms raw probe results into a quantitative suitability matrix, which is the final, critical input for the subsequent task allocation stage.

3.4. Load-Aware Task Allocation

The central component of VistaScan before probing is its intelligent task allocation algorithm, which optimally assigns CIDR blocks to distributed nodes based on pre-computed visibility scores while maintaining load balance. The algorithm maximizes coverage probability by leveraging the Visibility Consistency property and ensures efficient resource utilization through dynamic load-aware scheduling.

Algorithm 3 encapsulates the main allocation logic. Process each CIDR block $c \in \mathcal{C}$ by first checking if any node has positive visibility ($\mathcal{M}[n,c] > 0$). For such blocks, it identifies the node(s) with the highest visibility score $\mathcal{M}[n,c]$. If multiple nodes achieve the maximum score, the algorithm selects the currently least-loaded node n^* to maintain the load balance. The selected node is assigned to the block c and its load count increases.

The algorithm separates blocks into two queues based on the availability of visibility information. The priority queue ($\mathcal{C}_{\text{priority}}$) contains blocks with established visibility patterns, which are assigned to nodes that have demonstrated the highest historical visibility scores. Tie-breaking based on current load ensures balanced distribution, which prevents node overload and ensures efficient resource utilization. Additionally, the algorithm maintains the linear time complexity $O(|\mathcal{C}| \times |\mathcal{N}|)$, guaranteeing scalability for large-scale Internet-wide scanning tasks. Our system and algorithm are fully scalable to a larger number of nodes.

Algorithm 3 Load-Aware Task Allocation

Require: $\mathcal{C}$: List of CIDR blocks
$\mathcal{M}$: Visibility matrix ($\mathcal{N}$ nodes $\times$ $\mathcal{C}$ blocks)
$\mathcal{N}$: List of distributed nodes
Ensure: $\mathcal{A}$: Block-to-node assignment
$\mathcal{L}$: Node load counts
$\mathcal{A} \leftarrow \{\}$, $\mathcal{L}_n \leftarrow 0$ for all $n \in \mathcal{N}$
$\mathcal{C}_{\text{priority}} \leftarrow []$ ▷ Blocks with $\max(\mathcal{M}[:,c]) > 0$
$\mathcal{C}_{\text{fallback}} \leftarrow []$ ▷ Blocks not in or with $\max(\mathcal{M}[:,c]) = 0$
for each block $c \in \mathcal{C}$ **do**
    if $\max(\mathcal{M}[:,c]) > 0$ **then**
        $\mathcal{C}_{\text{priority}}.\text{append}(c)$
    else
        $\mathcal{C}_{\text{fallback}}.\text{append}(c)$ ▷ For future implementation
    end if
end for
for each block $c \in \mathcal{C}_{\text{priority}}$ **do**
    $s_{\max} \leftarrow \max(\mathcal{M}[:,c])$
    $\mathcal{N}_{\text{candidate}} \leftarrow \{n \in \mathcal{N} \mid \mathcal{M}[n,c] = s_{\max}\}$
    if $|\mathcal{N}_{\text{candidate}}| = 1$ **then**
        $n^* \leftarrow$ the single node in $\mathcal{N}_{\text{candidate}}$
    else
        $n^* \leftarrow \underset{n \in \mathcal{N}_{\text{candidate}}}{\text{argmin}} \ \mathcal{L}_n$
    end if
    $\mathcal{A}[c] \leftarrow n^*$, $\mathcal{L}_{n^*} \leftarrow \mathcal{L}_{n^*} + 1$
end for
return $\mathcal{A}$, $\mathcal{L}$

Currently, we only perform the priority allocation for CIDR blocks that are present in the visibility matrix. Those blocks not included in the matrix indicate that no node currently has visibility in them and are therefore discarded directly, a decision grounded in our nodes' capability and the sparsity of active IPs (as shown in Figure 2). The fallback queue ($\mathcal{C}_{\text{fallback}}$) is reserved for blocks lacking visibility data, providing a framework for future work on complete coverage strategies.

4. Evaluation

We present a comprehensive quantitative evaluation of VistaScan against multiple baselines in Global, Regional, and Special-Block tasks. Section 4.1 covers the experimental environment. Sections 4.2–4.4 demonstrate the performance of VistaScan.

4.1. Experimental Setup

To thoroughly evaluate the performance of VistaScan, we conducted extensive experiments in a variety of scenarios. Our testbed, target selection, and evaluation methodology were designed to ensure a fair and comprehensive comparison against established baselines.

Testbed. Our distributed probing infrastructure consisted of five nodes strategically deployed throughout the world using commercial cloud services. The details of each node are summarized in Table 1. All nodes were equipped with identical hardware specifications and a 100 Mbps network interface to eliminate performance disparity caused by resource differences. This homogeneous configuration allows us to isolate and attribute any performance variations solely to our task allocation strategy and network visibility, rather than to raw computational or network power.

Table 1. Configuration of distributed probing nodes.

Node	Location	OS	Hardware
JP	Tokyo, Japan	Ubuntu 20.04 LTS	2 vCPU/4 GB RAM/100 Mbps
BR	São Paulo, Brazil	Ubuntu 20.04 LTS	2 vCPU/4 GB RAM/100 Mbps
DE	Frankfurt, Germany	Ubuntu 20.04 LTS	2 vCPU/4 GB RAM/100 Mbps
US	San Jose, CA, USA	Ubuntu 20.04 LTS	2 vCPU/4 GB RAM/100 Mbps
SG	Singapore	Ubuntu 20.04 LTS	2 vCPU/4 GB RAM/100 Mbps

Scanning Rate. To ensure fairness and prevent measurement artifacts caused by local congestion or packet loss, all experiments used a fixed scanning rate of **1500 pps** per node. This value was determined to be the optimal global rate by the calibration process described in Appendix B.

Scanning Tasks and Targets. Table 2 summarizes the three scanning tasks designed to thoroughly evaluate VistaScan under different conditions. The Global task consisting of 3 countries from each of 6 continents was designed to assess worldwide coverage. The Regional task focused on the regions where our nodes are located. The targets of these two tasks were randomly selected from the MaxMind GeoLite2 database to ensure unbiased and generalizable results. The Special-Block task was designed to stress-test the system's ability to handle challenging blocks where node visibility is highly heterogeneous, in which the targets were manually selected based on our scanning experience.

Table 2. Scanning tasks and targets.

Task Type	Countries	CIDR Blocks	Total IPs	Target Port(s)
Global	18	1800	13,936,863	TCP/80
Regional	5	500	2,689,122	TCP/80
Special-Block	15	53	3,915,152	TCP/80, 22, 53

https://doi.org/10.3390/s26051458

Baseline Comparisons. We implemented five baseline methods for a comprehensive and rigorous comparison. This design allows us to dissect and isolate the contribution of each individual component within VistaScan.

- **Centralized:** A single node (e.g., US) scans the entire target list. This baseline highlights the advantages of a distributed architecture over a traditional centralized approach.
- **Union-of-All:** All five nodes independently and simultaneously scan the *entire* target set. The final result is the Union-of-All their outputs. This provides the **absolute upper bound** for the coverage achievable by any distributed system with these five vantage points, serving as a key reference for evaluating the coverage *efficiency* of VistaScan and other methods.
- **Naive-Distributed-Random:** The original, unsplit target list of IPs is randomly and uniformly assigned to the five nodes. This evaluates a simple distributed strategy without intelligent partitioning or allocation.
- **Partitioned-Distributed-Random:** The target IP space is first partitioned into /23 CIDR blocks using the VistaScan CIDR partitioning module. Then, this list of blocks is randomly and uniformly assigned to the five nodes. This baseline isolates the performance gain that is only attributable to the CIDR partitioning step.
- **Geo-Heuristic:** Targets are assigned to the geographically closest node to them (for example, Brazilian IPs to the BR node). This baseline is only used for the *Regional task* and represents a common geographic-driven heuristic.

Evaluation Metrics. We evaluated the performance of each method based on the following metrics:

- **Global Coverage:** The total number of unique IP addresses that respond. To contextualize this absolute value and measure the efficiency of a method's coverage, we also report it as a percentage of the total unique IPs found by the *Union-of-All* baseline. This relative measure indicates how close a method gets to the theoretical maximum coverage achievable with the given set of vantage points.
- **Total Packets Sent:** The aggregate number of probe packets sent by all nodes, indicating the overall network overhead and efficiency of the method.
- **Total Completion Time:** The wall-clock time from the start of the first probe to the completion of the last probe across all nodes.
- **Node Load Balance:** The standard deviation of the number of scanning IP addresses assigned to each node, quantifying the fairness workload distribution.

4.2. Coverage Analysis

The paramount goal of a distributed scanning system is to maximize coverage. Our evaluation demonstrates that VistaScan consistently achieves near-optimal coverage across all scenarios, a direct result of its core design principle: Intelligently assigning each CIDR block to the node with the highest probability of seeing it.

As synthesized in Table 3, VistaScan's coverage remains exceptionally high and stable, reaching 97.95%, 99.05%, and 97.58% in the Global, Regional, and Special-Block tasks, respectively. This performance places it within 2-3% of the theoretical maximum (Union-of-All) and significantly outperforms all centralized and naive distributed baselines. Notably, in the Regional task, VistaScan matches the performance of Geo-Heuristic (99.05% vs. 99.35%) with significantly lower scanning overhead time consumption and without relying on external geographical databases, demonstrating the sufficiency of its empirically measured visibility matrix.

https://doi.org/10.3390/s26051458

Table 3. Synthesis of coverage results across all tasks.

Task	VistaScan	Union-of-All	Centralized					Naive-Random	Partitioned-Random	Geo-Heuristic
			JP	BR	DE	US	SG			
Global	97.95%	100.0%	92.35%	96.60%	96.08%	96.28%	96.08%	95.31%	96.08%	-
Regional	99.05%	100.0%	96.30%	96.52%	96.38%	98.94%	96.09%	96.36%	96.76%	99.35%
Special-Block	97.58%	100.0%	61.88%	93.52%	91.00%	90.03%	92.73%	66.23%	83.27%	-

The Special-Block task serves as a stress test. These blocks exhibit poor Visibility Consistency, comprising targets with pronounced visibility heterogeneity. VistaScan's robust performance here (97.58%) underscores its effectiveness even in the most challenging network environments. Crucially, this high coverage is not achieved by brute force, but through precision: the system allocates tasks based on the visibility matrix, ensuring each block is probed by its most capable node. Our method can also effectively avoid assigning tasks to nodes with poor coverage capabilities for specific blocks, such as the JP node.

VistaScan also features Cross-Port Applicability. As shown in Figure 5, we found that the visibility matrix constructed from one TCP port (TCP/80) is applicable to other TCP ports. When applied to scanning TCP/22 and TCP/53 ports, VistaScan maintained a high coverage of 91.09% and 87.95%, respectively. Within the scope of the TCP protocol that we probed, this cross-port applicability indicates that visibility patterns exhibit cross-port generalization capabilities. It enhances the practicality of VistaScan, as a single profiling phase can optimize subsequent scans for multiple TCP services, dramatically reducing operational overhead.

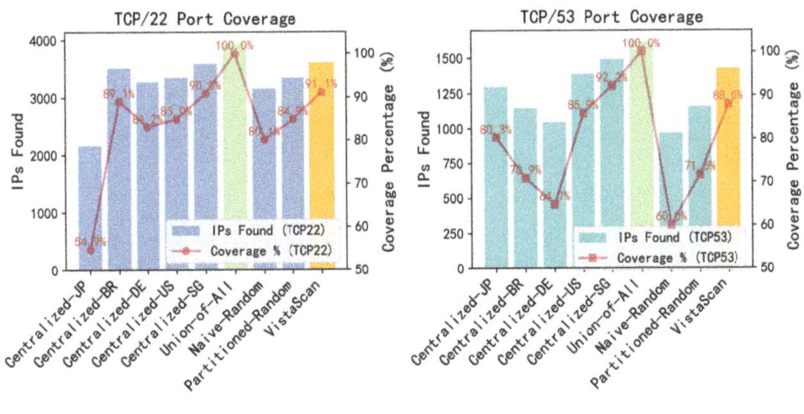

Figure 5. Cross-port coverage performance: Applying TCP/80 Visibility Matrix to TCP/22 and TCP/53 Scanning. VistaScan maintained high coverage of 91.09% and 87.95%.

4.3. *Efficiency Analysis: Overhead and Completion Time*

Beyond coverage, VistaScan's paramount advantage is its revolutionary efficiency, simultaneously minimizing two critical resources: network overhead and completion time. As shown in Figures 6 and 7, VistaScan consistently demonstrates orders-of-magnitude improvements in efficiency.

https://doi.org/10.3390/s26051458

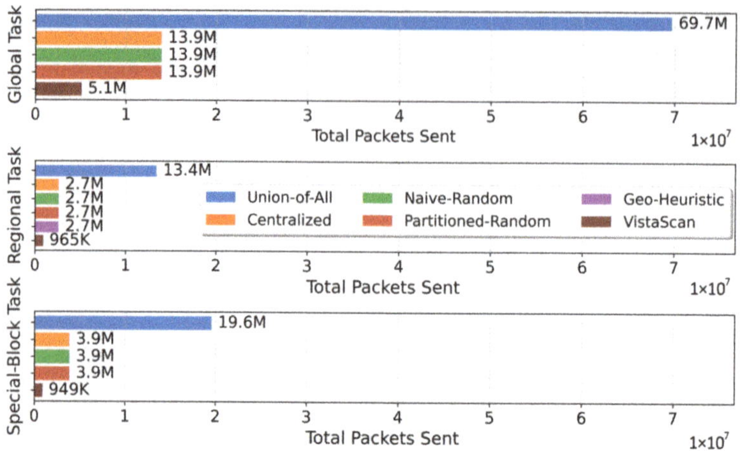

Figure 6. Total packets sent.

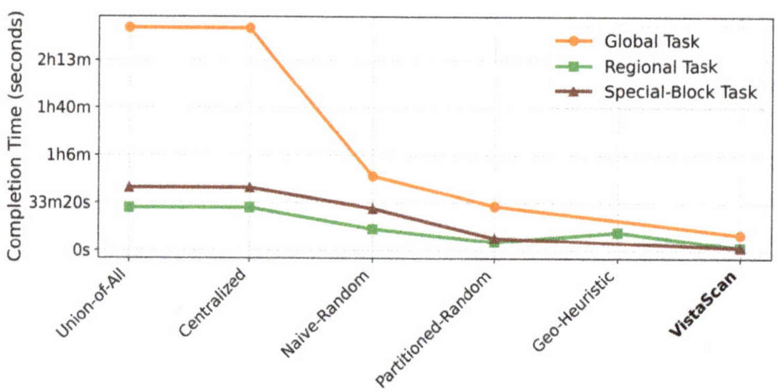

Figure 7. Total completion time.

Network Overhead: As illustrated in Figure 6, VistaScan drastically reduces the total number of packets sent. Compared to the baseline methods that scan all targets (approx. 2.7 M–39.2 M packets, depending on the task), VistaScan reduces the network overhead by 64% to 93%. This reduction is the direct consequence of its decisive filtering strategy: any CIDR block with no visible anchor IPs in the visibility matrix is pruned from the task list entirely. This avoids futile probing of network blind spots, constituting a fundamental shift from exhaustive scanning to targeted, intelligent probing.

Completion Time: Figure 7 shows the total completion time. VistaScan completes scans 13 to 19 times faster than centralized baselines. This speedup is a compound effect of (1) reduced total workload (fewer packets to send) and (2) highly efficient parallelization due to excellent load balance (analyzed in Section 4.4). For example, in the Global task, VistaScan was completed in 11 min and 34 s, compared to over 2.5 h for the centralized approaches. This efficiency enables near-real-time Internet-scale scanning, opening new possibilities for frequent monitoring and rapid incident response.

Cost of Pruning: While pruning blocks with no visible anchors drastically reduces probe volume, it inevitably forgoes scanning some IPs. To assess the potential loss of coverage, we examined the pruned blocks in our Global task. Among these blocks, the proportion of responsive IPs was extremely low—less than 0.005% of the IPs in these blocks responded to the probes, and the vast majority of pruned blocks contained no active hosts at all. In practice, VistaScan incurs only about a 2.0% coverage loss compared to the Union-of-All baseline (which represents the theoretical maximum achievable with our five vantage points). Importantly, this loss already includes the inherent coverage deficit of any single node scan (as seen in the Centralized baselines). Therefore, the additional coverage loss attributed to pruning is negligible while yielding substantial savings in probing overhead.

4.4. Load Balance Analysis

The efficiency of a distributed system depends on how well it balances workload across its nodes. Poor load balance leads to resource idle time and becomes the bottleneck for completion time.

Our analysis reveals that VistaScan's allocation algorithm achieves near-perfect load balance. As depicted in Figure 8, task completion times between all five nodes are virtually identical in all VistaScan scenarios. This is because its allocation algorithm is not only visibility-aware, but also load-aware; when multiple nodes have similarly high visibility scores for a block, the algorithm assigns it to the currently least-loaded node.

In stark contrast, other distributed strategies show a severe imbalance. The Naive-Random method leads to a highly skewed distribution of work, with the slowest node taking up to 3.8 times longer than the fastest to finish its assigned segment. The Geo-Heuristic method also exhibits a significant imbalance in the Regional task, as geographical proximity does not perfectly correlate with scan workload or link quality, nor does it guaranty balanced task allocation across regions. Compared to *Naive-Distributed-Random*, the *Partitioned-Distributed-Random* method equipped with the CIDR Partitioning Module achieves a more uniform distribution of tasks, significantly reduces the overall completion time, and exhibits superior load balance.

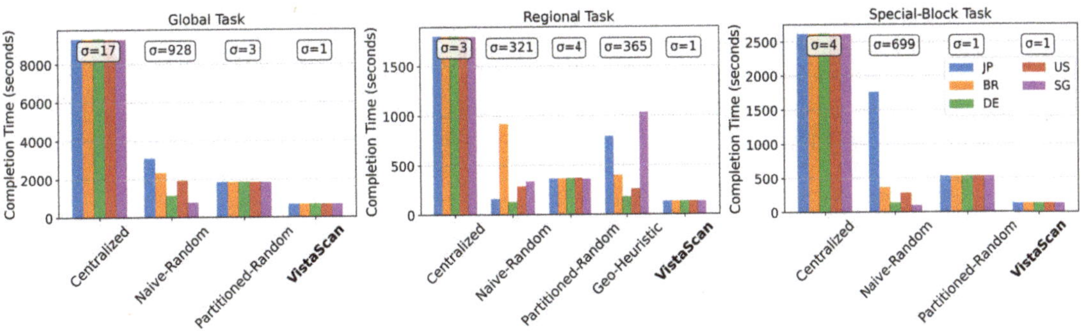

Figure 8. Load balancing performance across three probing scenarios. VistaScan demonstrates consistently excellent load balance across all nodes and tasks, while other distributed methods (Naive-Random, Geo-Heuristic) suffer from significant imbalance, leading to longer overall completion times.

5. Discussion and Limitations

Our experimental results demonstrate that VistaScan achieves significant performance improvements in various scanning scenarios. In the global scenario, VistaScan achieves higher coverage than all other methods while requiring only 36.7% of packets and 7.4% of the time compared to single-point centralized robing. In regional scanning, VistaScan achieves a nearly identical hit rate to Geo-Heuristic while using only 37% of its probe packets and 17.4% of its time, along with a more balanced node load. In addition, our method excels particularly at Special-Block tasks, outperforming all other approaches across all metrics and approaching the theoretical maximum coverage. The success of our system hinges on two validated core principles: the Visibility Consistency phenomenon within CIDR blocks and the systematic heterogeneity of visibility across geographically distributed nodes. By quantifying the latter into a Visibility Matrix and leveraging the former to make this matrix efficient to construct, VistaScan enables an intelligent task allocation strategy that is both precise and practical, moving the field from ad hoc and static allocation strategies to a data-driven and adaptive framework, fundamentally improving the efficiency and effectiveness of distributed Internet measurement. VistaScan's advantages can be summarized as follows:

- **Streamlining Evaluation:** The Visibility Consistency principle enables the inference of full-block visibility from a few anchor IPs, dramatically lowering the assessment overhead through targeted probing rather than full-block scanning.
- **Quantifying Capability:** We design two anchor selection methods and then build the Visibility Matrix through lightweight probing of anchor IPs, in which are the per-node visibility scores for each block.
- **Optimizing Assignment:** Using the Visibility Matrix to assign each block to the node with the highest probability of seeing it (the "most capable" node), while simultaneously balancing the load.
- **Pruning Infeasible Work:** Intelligently discarding blocks for which no node has significant visibility, thus eliminating ineffective probing.

However, we acknowledge several limitations of our current work that point to future research directions.

Anchor Freshness and Matrix Validity: A fundamental assumption of VistaScan is that the visibility matrix provides a reasonably stable representation of the network state. Although network paths are generally stable, events such as routing changes, outages, or filtering updates could stale the matrix over time, leading to task misassignment or erroneous block pruning. To address this, a production system requires lightweight mechanisms for periodic or triggered re-validation—dynamically adjusting probing frequency based on observed network dynamics (e.g., failure rates). Our future work will systematically address temporal robustness along two directions: we plan to evaluate the effective duration of a single constructed visibility matrix over longer time scales, and explore two lightweight update mechanisms—periodic active probing of anchor IPs (e.g., weekly), and online learning that refines visibility scores using incidental observations from main scans. Together, these approaches will enable VistaScan to adapt to gradual network changes while preserving efficiency, ensuring its viability for sustained real-world deployment.

Coverage–Completeness Trade-off: The strategy of pruning blocks with no visible anchors is the primary driver of efficiency gains. However, it inherently sacrifices absolute completeness (as achieved by the Union-of-All baseline) for efficiency. This is a deliberate and beneficial engineering trade-off for most scanning use cases. Nevertheless, for applications where finding every single responsive host is critical, our method could be extended to include a fallback mechanism where pruned blocks are periodically scanned by a random node or all nodes at a very low rate to check for changes. This is why we maintain the fallback queue ($\mathcal{C}_{\text{fallback}}$) mentioned in Section 3.4. Subsequently, a low-frequency scanning and update mechanism will be established for it.

Anchor Count Selection and Extension to UDP Scanning: While our empirical results demonstrate the effectiveness of using three anchors per block (each from a diverse source), the optimal number warrants further investigation, as it may depend on factors such as block size, network stability, and the trade-off between accuracy and overhead. Future work could explore adaptive anchor selection mechanisms that dynamically adjust the anchor count based on intra-block consistency estimates or historical data. In addition, UDP's connectionless nature, reliance on ICMP, and distinct firewall handling may produce visibility patterns that differ from TCP. While VistaScan currently focuses on TCP, future

https://doi.org/10.3390/s26051458

work should explore its extension to UDP. This requires addressing challenges in probing strategy, response ambiguity, and timeout handling, as well as validating whether Visibility Consistency holds for UDP services. Such research would broaden the applicability of visibility-aware distributed scanning.

Handling of Ultra-Low Consistency Blocks: No real-world system can rely on perfect statistical regularity, and our design pragmatically exploits the strong statistical trend of Visibility Consistency while handling outliers gracefully. We acknowledge that a small subset of blocks exhibit very low intra-block consistency, typically due to complex network configurations such as multihoming or fine-grained, IP-specific filtering policies. For such blocks, a single optimal node may not provide adequate coverage, as visibility can vary significantly even within a /23 prefix. Two promising directions for future work can address this limitation: (1) further subdividing these blocks into smaller granularities (e.g., /24 or /25) to restore high consistency with minimal overhead; and (2) employing multi-node coordinated probing, where tasks are distributed among a set of complementary nodes to maximize coverage. We plan to explore these optimizations in future work.

6. Related Works

Our work is based on and intersects with several key areas of Internet measurement and distributed systems research.

Centralized High-Speed Scanning. Modern scanning tools such as Nmap [24], ZMap [39], Masscan [23], Zippier ZMap [40], ZGrab2 [41], and LZR [42] revolutionized Internet-wide scanning by demonstrating that the entire IPv4 address space can be scanned in minutes from a single machine. With the support of high-performance I/O frameworks such as PF-RING [43], Packetshader [44] and netmap [45], port scanning time can be significantly reduced. VistaScan does not seek to replace these tools, but rather to extend their centralized paradigm. We address their inherent limitations: single-point visibility blind spots, susceptibility to IP blocking, and the physical bottleneck of a single source. VistaScan adopts their high-performance probing engines, but distributes the effort intelligently across nodes.

Distributed Measurement Systems. Distributed scanning technology reduces the time required for large-scale scanning and detection by decomposing scanning tasks and distributing them across multiple nodes. The research community has developed several distributed scanning systems [29–32]. However, their native task allocation mechanisms are often simplistic, relying on random assignment or geographic heuristics. VistaScan contributes a novel, automated, and intelligent allocation layer that could be deployed on such platforms to dramatically increase the efficiency and coverage of experiments run on them.

Efficient Predictive Scanning Systems. Predictive scanning offers a novel approach to improving the efficiency of large-scale scanning operations. In contrast to distributed scanning systems that minimize scanning duration through probing resource expansion and task partitioning, predictive scanning operates by narrowing the target space via a pregenerated prediction list. Previous works such as Smart Internet Probing [46] by training a unique XGBoost classifier [47], GPS [12], PMap [48], and IPREDS [10] have attempted to develop efficient predictive scanning systems capable of forecasting port activity on target hosts, thereby reducing the time required to discover a sufficient number of valid targets. However, after generating the prediction list, they still face the problem of determining which specific node(s) should execute the actual scanning tasks. VistaScan can act as the core distributed probing engine of these predictive systems, increasing the accuracy of their predictions effectively. Our system integrates the strengths of both distributed and

https://doi.org/10.3390/s26051458

predictive scanning, which not only increases available probing resources but also reduces the probing space, while intelligently assigning tasks to the most suitable nodes.

Studies of Network Visibility. Previous work has documented and analyzed the heterogeneity of views from different organizations [26,27], different scanning origins [28], different probing tools [40] and different probes [3], and the paper [25] further showed that web-based geoblocking is increasingly common. We have taken a step further by systematically investigating the extent to which the location of probing nodes influences the results of distributed measurements. In addition, VistaScan goes beyond observation to application. We are the first to formalize the "Visibility Consistency" hypothesis and use it as the foundational principle for building a practical, optimized distributed scanning system. Our work shows that these observed biases are not just noise to be accounted for, but a signal that can be exploited for significant performance gains.

In summary, VistaScan distinguishes itself by introducing a formal model of Visibility Consistency, which enables a lightweight node's capabilities evaluation methods and a novel task allocation algorithm that are both more efficient and provide higher coverage than existing distributed approaches, while overcoming the visibility and efficiency limitations of centralized scanners.

7. Conclusions

In this paper, we introduced VistaScan, a novel system for optimizing distributed Internet-wide scanning based on the key insight of Visibility Consistency, that the visibility pattern among IP addresses is highly consistent within CIDR blocks. This principle enabled the construction of a lightweight Visibility Matrix via anchor-based probing and informed the design of a load-aware task allocation algorithm. Our comprehensive evaluation across Global, Regional, and challenging Special-Block tasks demonstrates that VistaScan consistently outperforms existing methods, achieving superior coverage by matching blocks to the most capable nodes while significantly improving efficiency through the pruning of unreachable targets and intelligent load balancing. In particular, the visibility matrix derived from one TCP port (TCP/80) proved highly effective for scanning other TCP ports (TCP/22, TCP/53), preliminarily underscoring the generalizability of our approach. VistaScan shows how a deeper understanding of network structure can lead to substantial practical gains, opening new avenues for building efficient, large-scale distributed measurement systems that are fine-grained, low-impact, and resource-efficient.

Author Contributions: Conceptualization, L.H. and F.S.; methodology, L.H. and Y.S.; software, L.H.; validation, L.H., C.X. and P.X.; formal analysis, L.H.; investigation, B.G.; resources, F.S.; data curation, L.H.; writing—original draft preparation, L.H.; writing—review and editing, F.S., Y.S., C.X., P.X. and B.G.; visualization, L.H.; supervision, P.X.; project administration, C.X. All authors have read and agreed to the published version of the manuscript.

Funding: This research received no external funding.

Data Availability Statement: The data presented in this study are available upon request from the corresponding authors.

Conflicts of Interest: The authors declare no conflicts of interest.

Appendix A. Ethical Considerations

We strictly adhered to responsible ethical and disclosure scanning practices. All probing was rate-limited to 1500 pps per node to avoid causing network congestion, performed without attempting exploitation, and targeted only at networks where such measurement is considered acceptable practice within the security research community. The goal of VistaScan is to improve the efficiency and accuracy of security and network research and to eliminate redundant scanning with the purpose of reducing the overall burden on Internet resources, not to facilitate malicious reconnaissance.

Appendix B. Scanning Rate Calibration

In distributed measurement, the hardware performance of each node (e.g., CPU, network stack) can become a bottleneck for scanning rates. Excessively high packet sending rates may cause local packet loss, thereby distorting measurement results, while overly low rates under-utilize available resources. To ensure the reliability of all probing data, avoid distortion caused by a mismatch between hardware capability and scanning rate, and demonstrate that observed visibility differences are not due to misconfigured environments or suboptimal parameter settings, while also ensuring that all subsequent experiments operate at a sustainable and optimized rate, we first conducted a scanning rate calibration experiment for each node on 8 August 2025.

Each node was tasked with scanning a set of test targets at rates ranging from 500 to 8000 packets per second (pps), while the effective hit quantity (the number of successful responses) was measured. The test targets consisted of the top 500 CIDR blocks from the MaxMind GeoLite2 database. The scanning was performed using ZMap with TCP SYN scans targeting TCP/80. As shown in Figure A1, for our node configuration, the hit quantity of almost all nodes peaked and remained stable at 1500 pps. Beyond this rate, the hit rate declined significantly. Therefore, in all subsequent experiments, the scanning rate for each node was set uniformly to this calibrated and reliable optimal rate.

This calibration step ensures the rigor of our subsequent work in characterizing network visibility, confirming that the phenomena we observe are not mere noise. It also guarantees fairness in the comparative evaluation of method performance during experimentation, eliminating performance bias caused by improper node-specific configuration. All baseline methods are compared under optimal and consistent conditions.

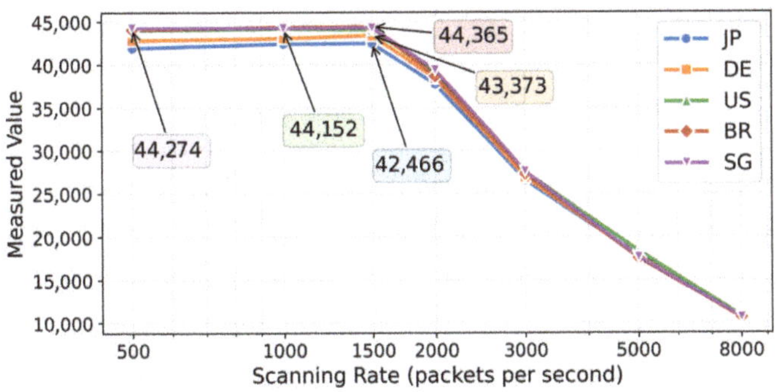

Figure A1. Rate vs. hit quantity for different nodes. Nodes BR, DE and JP peaked at 1500 pps. US and SG peaked at 1000 and 500 pps. All nodes' performance sharply degrades beyond 1500 pps. Here, 1500 pps represents the optimal trade-off between efficiency and hit rate.

Appendix C. The Key Insight: Visibility Consistency Within CIDR Blocks

The heterogeneity in node-visibility shown in Section 2.1 reveals that the Internet is not a single uniformly visible space. The set of targets that a node can successfully probe is not random but is systematically influenced by its network location (Autonomous System), geographic region, and upstream providers. This leads to a fundamental question underpinning our work, which is that within a logically contiguous portion of the address space (a CIDR block), is the visibility of each IP consistent from the perspective of distributed vantage points? To answer this, we define Visibility Consistency.

Appendix C.1. Problem Formulation and Definition

Let $B = \{ip_1, ip_2, \ldots, ip_m\}$ be a CIDR block containing m IP addresses, and let $N = \{n_1, n_2, \ldots, n_k\}$ be a set of k distributed probing nodes. The *visibility* of an IP address ip_i from a node n_j is defined as a binary function:

$$V(ip_i, n_j) = \begin{cases} 1 & \text{if } ip_i \text{ is reachable from (visible to) } n_j. \\ 0 & \text{otherwise.} \end{cases} \quad \text{(A1)}$$

For each IP address $ip_i \in B$, we define its *visibility vector* $\vec{v}_i$ as a k-dimensional binary vector that captures its global visibility pattern across all probing nodes:

$$\vec{v}_i = (V(ip_i, n_1), V(ip_i, n_2), \ldots, V(ip_i, n_k)) \quad \text{(A2)}$$

The Visibility Consistency of block B is then quantified as the average pairwise Jaccard similarity between the visibility vectors of all IP pairs in B:

$$\text{Consistency}(B) = \frac{2}{m(m-1)} \sum_{i=1}^{m-1} \sum_{j=i+1}^{m} J(\vec{v}_i, \vec{v}_j) \quad \text{(A3)}$$

where $J(\vec{v}_i, \vec{v}_j)$ is the Jaccard similarity coefficient between the vectors $\vec{v}_i$ and $\vec{v}_j$:

$$J(\vec{v}_i, \vec{v}_j) = \frac{|\vec{v}_i \cap \vec{v}_j|}{|\vec{v}_i \cup \vec{v}_j|} = \frac{\sum_{l=1}^{k} \min(v_{i,l}, v_{j,l})}{\sum_{l=1}^{k} \max(v_{i,l}, v_{j,l})} \quad \text{(A4)}$$

The value of $\text{Consistency}(B)$ ranges from 0 to 1, where:

- $\text{Consistency}(B) = 1$ indicates perfect consistency (all IPs in B have identical visibility patterns);
- $\text{Consistency}(B) = 0$ indicates no consistency (all IP pairs have completely dissimilar visibility patterns);
- Higher values indicate stronger Visibility Consistency within the block.

In summary, Visibility Consistency refers to the phenomenon that within the same CIDR address block, the visibility patterns of different IP addresses, as observed by distributed probing nodes, are highly similar or consistent. In other words, if a node in a distributed network can successfully probe one IP within a block, it is highly likely that it can also probe other IPs in the same block. Conversely, if it cannot see a certain IP, it is probably unable to see the entire block. This formalization provides a quantitative measure to validate our key insight: that IP visibility patterns exhibit strong spatial correlation within CIDR blocks, enabling efficient representative-based probing strategies. Specifically, a higher consistency score indicates greater homogeneity in intra-block visibility, robustly justifying the use of a small number of anchor IPs to accurately represent the entire block.

Appendix C.2. Verification and Analysis

To verify the rationality of our proposed Visibility Consistency, we performed a consistency analysis on the complete data set of the probe scan from five nodes in Section 2.1. We calculated the pairwise Jaccard similarity between the visibility vectors of all IP pairs within CIDR blocks of various sizes using Equation (A3), from large /20 prefixes to small

https://doi.org/10.3390/s26051458

/28 prefixes, in addition to the original, highly irregular blocks from the MaxMind dataset (/Orig). The results, summarized in Figure A2, reveal a powerful and robust phenomenon:

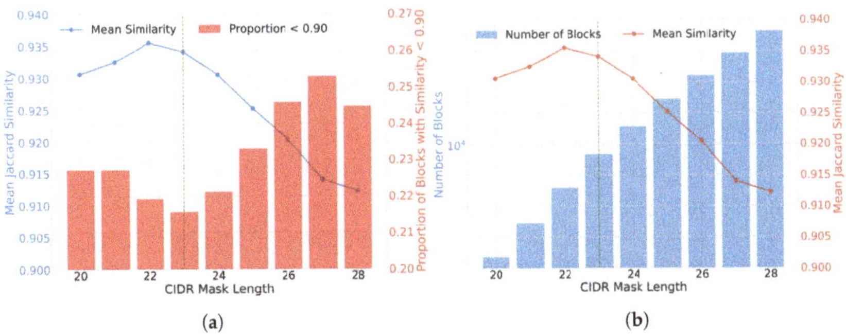

Figure A2. Characterization of Visibility Consistency across CIDR block sizes. (**a**) Trends of overall Consistency and low-Consistency proportions. (**b**) Trade-off: Number of blocks vs. Consistency.

- **High Intra-Block Consistency:** The **median** consistency score is consistently **1.00** across all block sizes. This indicates that for most blocks, knowing the visibility of one IP perfectly predicts the visibility of all others within the same block. The visibility vector of any IP is essentially interchangeable with that of its neighbors.
- **Stability Across Scales:** The **mean** consistency remains notably high (above 0.91) across all regularly-sized blocks. This demonstrates that Visibility Consistency is an inherent property driven by network routing and filtering policies, not an artifact of observation scale.
- **Existence of Outliers:** The standard deviation and the lower quartile values confirm the existence of blocks with lower internal consistency. These typically represent complex network environments such as multi-homed prefixes or blocks employing fine-grained, IP-specific filtering policies.

Appendix C.3. Selecting the Optimal Block Size

The choice of block size is a trade-off between consistency and granularity. Table A1 shows the summary statistics table of Visibility Consistency across CIDR Block Sizes. While /Orig blocks exhibit the highest mean consistency, their irregular and often large sizes render them unsuitable for fine-grained, load-balanced task allocation. Our analysis identifies the /23 prefix as the optimal operational unit for VistaScan:

- **High Absolute Consistency:** It maintains a high mean consistency score of **0.934**, ensuring the core premise of our method holds.
- **Favorable Proportion of Difficult Blocks:** The proportion of blocks with consistency below 0.90 (**21.6%**) is among the lowest for regularly-sized splits, minimizing the potential for misrepresentation by anchors.
- **Superior Manageability:** With 8798 blocks, it provides an ample number of tasks to enable efficient load balancing across our distributed nodes, without incurring the excessive overhead of managing tens of thousands of smaller blocks.

This consistency means that probing a few anchor IPs can accurately predict a node's visibility of the entire block. This high degree of intra-block consistency is the foundational insight that makes VistaScan efficient and practical. It allows us to accurately characterize the visibility of an entire /23 CIDR block by probing just a few representative anchor IPs within it, reducing the overhead of building the visibility matrix by orders of magnitude. For the optimal /23 block size, the median consistency score reaches 1.00 (indicating perfect consistency for most blocks), with a mean consistency score of 0.934. The 21.57% of blocks with a consistency score below 0.90 do not "completely fail to follow the consistency rule"—a Jaccard similarity of 0.90 still represents extremely high homogeneity in visibility patterns and does not invalidate the core premise of our method.

Table A1. Summary statistics table of Visibility Consistency across CIDR Block Sizes.

Mask	Count	Mean	Median	Std	Q1	Q3	Prop. < 0.95	Prop. < 0.90
Original	595	0.9511	1.0000	0.1211	0.9623	1.0000	0.2151	0.1361
20	2161	0.9306	1.0000	0.1248	0.9111	1.0000	0.3318	0.2272
21	3455	0.9325	1.0000	0.1268	0.9176	1.0000	0.3146	0.2272
22	5595	0.9355	1.0000	0.1231	0.9200	1.0000	0.3001	0.2193
23	8798	0.9341	1.0000	0.1281	0.9222	1.0000	0.2851	0.2157
24	12,994	0.9305	1.0000	0.1352	0.9200	1.0000	0.2872	0.2212
25	18,909	0.9252	1.0000	0.1457	0.9053	1.0000	0.2928	0.2330
26	26,194	0.9204	1.0000	0.1530	0.9000	1.0000	0.2964	0.2458
27	35,710	0.9140	1.0000	0.1632	0.8930	1.0000	0.3066	0.2529
28	48,232	0.9122	1.0000	0.1765	0.9000	1.0000	0.3001	0.2447

Appendix D. Criteria for Anchor IP Selection

Given that a few representative anchor IPs are used to characterize an entire block, the selection of these anchors is of paramount importance. We have given this careful consideration and identified the following key factors.

- **Representativeness:** The selected IPs should be representative of their block; that is, if a node can see a given anchor IP, it should be able to see the vast majority of IPs within that block. The principle of Visibility Consistency explicitly validates the representativeness of anchor IPs. In theory, the chosen IPs should exhibit the *most prevalent visibility pattern* within the block.
- **Discriminative Power:** IPs with significant variation in visibility between different nodes should be selected. Divergent probing results for an IP from different nodes help highlight the differences in their coverage capabilities.
- **Quantity:** Due to the existence of Visibility Consistency, a single IP could, in theory, represent an entire block, offering the lowest probing and maintenance overhead. However, we opt against using just one IP for two reasons. First, a considerable proportion of blocks exhibit poor Visibility Consistency, where a single IP cannot guarantee representativeness for the whole block. Second, a single IP introduces a point of failure; if that specific IP goes offline, it could lead to the erroneous conclusion that the entire block is unreachable, thereby compromising the accuracy of all subsequent processes and the entire methodology. Hence, a *multi-anchor strategy* is necessary. The multi-anchor strategy also enables the visibility of a node to a block to be represented as a score value rather than a simple binary value. This scoring provides fine-grained differentiation, directly reflecting the node's proficiency with the block, and tasks can be assigned based on these scores. Conversely, the number of anchors should not be excessively large, as too many would increase the probing and management overhead.

In summary, we should select IPs that demonstrate **high consensus but non-universal** visibility, those with the **most prevalent visibility pattern** of the block. Such anchors possess the most typical visibility pattern for the block, meaning that they are visible to most scanning nodes, but not all, ensuring both representativeness and discriminative power. Simultaneously, a multi-anchor strategy is adopted to enhance robustness.

https://doi.org/10.3390/s26051458

Since it is impractical to pre-statistically determine the visibility pattern for every block (as it would require exhaustive probing of all blocks by all nodes), achieving optimal representativeness and discriminative power in anchor selection is challenging. As a compromise, we decided to select anchors from diverse sources to maximize the variety of their origins. Relying on a single probing source to select anchors would allow the local perspective of one node to dictate the global view of a block, introducing single-point visibility bias (preference) and consequently leading to biased selection of the best probing node. To balance representativeness, discriminative power, robustness, and system overhead, we ultimately decided to select 3 anchor IPs for each block from different probing sources. This approach significantly enhances the system's robustness and accuracy while maintaining low overhead, laying a solid data foundation for an efficient and reliable distributed probing system.

This multi-anchor strategy from diverse probing sources aligns with established practices in network measurement, where a limited set of probes is used to infer larger-scale properties [7,12,28,33–38]. Although three anchors proved effective in our experiments, we acknowledge that the optimal number may vary with network conditions and consistency metrics. Investigating adaptive anchor selection strategies is a promising direction for future work.

References

1. Kaur, J.; Ramkumar, K. The recent trends in cyber security: A review. *J. King Saud-Univ.-Comput. Inf. Sci.* **2022**, *34*, 5766–5781. [CrossRef]
2. Durumeric, Z.; Clark, H.; Cody, J.; Cubit, E.; Ellison, M.; Izhikevich, L.; Mirian, A. Censys: A Map of Internet Hosts and Services. In Proceedings of the ACM SIGCOMM 2025 Conference, Coimbra, Portugal, 8–11 September 2025; pp. 147–163.
3. Durumeric, Z.; Adrian, D.; Stephens, P.; Wustrow, E.; Halderman, J.A. Ten years of zmap. In Proceedings of the 2024 ACM on Internet Measurement Conference, Madrid, Spain, 4–6 November 2024; pp. 139–148.
4. Beurdouche, B.; Bhargavan, K.; Delignat-Lavaud, A.; Fournet, C.; Kohlweiss, M.; Pironti, A.; Strub, P.Y.; Zinzindohoue, J.K. A messy state of the union: Taming the composite state machines of TLS. *Commun. ACM* **2017**, *60*, 99–107. [CrossRef]
5. Checkoway, S.; Niederhagen, R.; Everspaugh, A.; Green, M.; Lange, T.; Ristenpart, T.; Bernstein, D.J.; Maskiewicz, J.; Shacham, H.; Fredrikson, M. On the practical exploitability of dual {EC} in {TLS} implementations. In Proceedings of the 23rd USENIX Security Symposium (USENIX Security 14), San Diego, CA, USA, 20–22 August 2014; pp. 319–335.
6. Bano, S.; Richter, P.; Javed, M.; Sundaresan, S.; Durumeric, Z.; Murdoch, S.J.; Mortier, R.; Paxson, V. Scanning the internet for liveness. *ACM SIGCOMM Comput. Commun. Rev.* **2018**, *48*, 2–9. [CrossRef]
7. Cai, X.; Heidemann, J. Understanding block-level address usage in the visible internet. In Proceedings of the ACM SIGCOMM 2010 Conference, New Delhi, India, 30 August–3 September 2010; pp. 99–110.
8. Padmanabhan, R.; Dhamdhere, A.; Aben, E.; Claffy, K.; Spring, N. Reasons dynamic addresses change. In Proceedings of the 2016 Internet Measurement Conference, Santa Monica, CA, USA, 14–16 November 2016; pp. 183–198.
9. Quan, L.; Heidemann, J.; Pradkin, Y. When the Internet sleeps: Correlating diurnal networks with external factors. In Proceedings of the 2014 Conference on Internet Measurement Conference, Vancouver, BC, Canada, 5–7 November 2014; pp. 87–100.
10. Luo, Y.; Li, C.; Wang, Z.; Yang, J. IPREDS: Efficient prediction system for Internet-wide port and service scanning. *Proc. ACM Netw.* **2024**, *2*, 1–24. [CrossRef]
11. Song, G.; He, L.; Zhao, T.; Luo, Y.; Wu, Y.; Fan, L.; Li, C.; Wang, Z.; Yang, J. Which doors are open: Reinforcement learning-based internet-wide port scanning. In *Proceedings of the 2023 IEEE/ACM 31st International Symposium on Quality of Service (IWQoS), Orlando, FL, USA, 19–21 June 2023*; IEEE: New York, NY, USA, 2023; pp. 1–10.
12. Izhikevich, L.; Teixeira, R.; Durumeric, Z. Predicting IPv4 services across all ports. In Proceedings of the ACM SIGCOMM 2022 Conference, Amsterdam, The Netherlands, 22–26 August 2022; pp. 503–515.
13. Richter, P.; Smaragdakis, G.; Plonka, D.; Berger, A. Beyond counting: New perspectives on the active IPv4 address space. In Proceedings of the 2016 Internet Measurement Conference, Santa Monica, CA, USA, 14–16 November 2016; pp. 135–149.
14. Holz, R.; Amann, J.; Mehani, O.; Wachs, M.; Kaafar, M.A. TLS in the wild: An Internet-wide analysis of TLS-based protocols for electronic communication. *arXiv* **2015**, arXiv:1511.00341.
15. Pujol, E.; Richter, P.; Chandrasekaran, B.; Smaragdakis, G.; Feldmann, A.; Maggs, B.M.; Ng, K.C. Back-office web traffic on the internet. In Proceedings of the 2014 Conference on Internet Measurement Conference, Vancouver, BC, Canada, 5–7 November 2014; pp. 257–270.

https://doi.org/10.3390/s26051458

16. Durumeric, Z.; Adrian, D.; Mirian, A.; Kasten, J.; Bursztein, E.; Lidzborski, N.; Thomas, K.; Eranti, V.; Bailey, M.; Halderman, J.A. Neither snow nor rain nor MITM...: An empirical analysis of email delivery security. In Proceedings of the 2015 Internet Measurement Conference, Tokyo, Japan, 28–30 October 2015; pp. 27–39.
17. Beverly, R. Yarrp'ing the Internet: Randomized high-speed active topology discovery. In Proceedings of the 2016 Internet Measurement Conference, Santa Monica, CA, USA, 14–16 November 2016; pp. 413–420.
18. Vermeulen, K.; Rohrer, J.P.; Beverly, R.; Fourmaux, O.; Friedman, T. {Diamond-Miner}: Comprehensive Discovery of the Internet's Topology Diamonds. In Proceedings of the 17th USENIX Symposium on Networked Systems Design and Implementation (NSDI 20), Santa Clara, CA, USA, 25–27 February 2020; pp. 479–493.
19. Aviram, N.; Schinzel, S.; Somorovsky, J.; Heninger, N.; Dankel, M.; Steube, J.; Valenta, L.; Adrian, D.; Halderman, J.A.; Dukhovni, V.; et al. {DROWN}: Breaking {TLS} using {SSLv2}. In Proceedings of the 25th USENIX Security Symposium (USENIX Security 16), Austin, TX, USA, 10–12 August 2016; pp. 689–706.
20. Adrian, D.; Bhargavan, K.; Durumeric, Z.; Gaudry, P.; Green, M.; Halderman, J.A.; Heninger, N.; Springall, D.; Thomé, E.; Valenta, L.; et al. Imperfect forward secrecy: How Diffie-Hellman fails in practice. In Proceedings of the 22nd ACM SIGSAC Conference on Computer and Communications Security, Denver, CO, USA, 12–16 October 2015; pp. 5–17.
21. Amann, J.; Gasser, O.; Scheitle, Q.; Brent, L.; Carle, G.; Holz, R. Mission accomplished? HTTPS security after DigiNotar. In Proceedings of the 2017 Internet Measurement Conference, London, UK, 1–3 November 2017; pp. 325–340.
22. Durumeric, Z.; Wustrow, E.; Halderman, J.A. {ZMap}: Fast internet-wide scanning and its security applications. In Proceedings of the 22nd USENIX Security Symposium (USENIX Security 13), Washington, DC, USA, 14–16 August 2013; pp. 605–620.
23. GitHub—Robertdavidgraham/Masscan: TCP Port Scanner, Spews SYN Packets Asynchronously, Scanning Entire Internet in Under 5 Minutes—github.com. Available online: https://github.com/robertdavidgraham/masscan (accessed on 8 September 2025).
24. Lyon, G.F. *Nmap Network Scanning: The Official Nmap Project Guide to Network Discovery and Security Scanning*; Insecure: Sunnyvale, CA, USA, 2009.
25. McDonald, A.; Bernhard, M.; Valenta, L.; VanderSloot, B.; Scott, W.; Sullivan, N.; Halderman, J.A.; Ensafi, R. 403 forbidden: A global view of CDN geoblocking. In Proceedings of the Internet Measurement Conference 2018, Boston, MA, USA, 31 October–2 November 2018; pp. 218–230.
26. Chung, T.; Liu, Y.; Choffnes, D.; Levin, D.; Maggs, B.M.; Mislove, A.; Wilson, C. Measuring and applying invalid SSL certificates: The silent majority. In Proceedings of the 2016 Internet Measurement Conference, Santa Monica, CA, USA, 14–16 November 2016; pp. 527–541.
27. Hastings, M.; Fried, J.; Heninger, N. Weak keys remain widespread in network devices. In Proceedings of the 2016 Internet Measurement conference, Santa Monica, CA, USA, 14–16 November 2016; pp. 49–63.
28. Wan, G.; Izhikevich, L.; Adrian, D.; Yoshioka, K.; Holz, R.; Rossow, C.; Durumeric, Z. On the origin of scanning: The impact of location on internet-wide scans. In Proceedings of the ACM Internet Measurement Conference, Virtual, 27–29 October 2020; pp. 662–679.
29. Cao, Y.; Chen, F.; Quan, X.; Zhou, K. DLCAS: Distributed Large-scale Cyberspace Asynchronous Scanning Framework. In *Proceedings of the 2024 IEEE 24th International Conference on Communication Technology (ICCT), Chengdu, China, 18–20 October 2024*; IEEE: New York, NY, USA, 2024; pp. 1117–1124.
30. Li, L.; Wang, Y.; Zhu, D.; Li, X.; Du, H.; Lu, Y.; Qu, R.; Higgs, R. Dis-NDVW: Distributed Network Asset Detection and Vulnerability Warning Platform. *Comput. Mater. Contin.* **2023**, *76*, 771. [CrossRef]
31. Xiaopeng, T.; Di, T. A distributed vulnerability scanning on machine learning. In *Proceedings of the 2019 6th International Conference on Information Science and Control Engineering (ICISCE), Shanghai, China, 20–22 December 2019*; IEEE Computer Society: New York, NY, USA, 2019; pp. 32–35.
32. Xue, P.; Shen, Y.; Ma, H.; Hu, M. An Area-Aware Efficient Internet-Wide Port Scan Approach for IoT. *Electronics* **2025**, *14*, 1267. [CrossRef]
33. Heidemann, J.; Quan, L.; Pradkin, Y. *A preliminary Analysis of Network Outages During Hurricane Sandy*; University of Southern California, Information Sciences Institute: Marina del Rey, CA, USA, 2012.
34. Schulman, A.; Spring, N. Pingin'in the rain. In Proceedings of the 2011 ACM SIGCOMM Conference on Internet Measurement Conference, Berlin, Germany, 2–4 November 2011; pp. 19–28.
35. Tozal, M.E.; Sarac, K. Estimating network layer subnet characteristics via statistical sampling. In *International Conference on Research in Networking*; Springer: Berlin/Heidelberg, Germany, 2012; pp. 274–288.
36. Lee, Y. Improving Accuracy and Efficiency of Network Measurement by Identifying Homogeneous IPV4 Addresses. Ph.D. Thesis, University of Maryland, College Park, MD, USA, 2017.
37. Bush, R.; Hiebert, J.; Maennel, O.; Roughan, M.; Uhlig, S. Testing the reachability of (new) address space. In Proceedings of the 2007 SIGCOMM Workshop on Internet Network Management, Kyoto, Japan, 27–31 August 2007; pp. 236–241.

https://doi.org/10.3390/s26051458

38. Kardes, H.; Gunes, M.; Oz, T. Cheleby: A subnet-level internet topology mapping system. In *Proceedings of the 2012 Fourth International Conference on Communication Systems and Networks (COMSNETS 2012), Bangalore, India 3–7 January 2012*; IEEE: New York, NY, USA, 2012; pp. 1–10.
39. GitHub—zmap/zmap: ZMap Is a Fast Single Packet Network Scanner Designed for Internet-Wide Network Surveys—github.com. Available online: https://github.com/zmap/zmap (accessed on 1 September 2025).
40. Adrian, D.; Durumeric, Z.; Singh, G.; Halderman, J.A. Zippier {ZMap}:{internet-wide} scanning at 10 GBPS. In Proceedings of the 8th USENIX Workshop on Offensive Technologies (WOOT 14), San Diego, CA, USA, 19 August 2014.
41. GitHub—zmap/zgrab2: Fast Application Layer Scanner—github.com. Available online: https://github.com/zmap/zgrab2 (accessed on 1 September 2025).
42. Izhikevich, L.; Teixeira, R.; Durumeric, Z. {LZR}: Identifying unexpected internet services. In Proceedings of the 30th USENIX Security Symposium (USENIX Security 21), Virtual Event, 11–13 August 2021; pp. 3111–3128.
43. Deri, L. Improving passive packet capture: Beyond device polling. In Proceedings of the SANE, Amsterdam, The Netherlands, 30 September 2004; Volume 2004, pp. 85–93.
44. Han, S.; Jang, K.; Park, K.; Moon, S. PacketShader: A GPU-accelerated software router. *ACM SIGCOMM Comput. Commun. Rev.* **2010**, *40*, 195–206.
45. Rizzo, L. netmap: A novel framework for fast packet I/O. In Proceedings of the 21st USENIX Security Symposium (USENIX Security 12), Bellevue, WA, USA, 8–10 August 2012; pp. 101–112.
46. Sarabi, A.; Jin, K.; Liu, M. Smart internet probing: Scanning using adaptive machine learning. In *Game Theory and Machine Learning for Cyber Security*; John Wiley & Sons: Hoboken, NJ, USA, 2021; pp. 411–437.
47. Chen, T.; Guestrin, C. Xgboost: A scalable tree boosting system. In Proceedings of the 22nd ACM Sigkdd International Conference on Knowledge Discovery and Data Mining, San Francisco, CA, USA, 13–17 August 2016; pp. 785–794.
48. Song, G.; He, L.; Chen, T.; Lin, J.; Fan, L.; Wen, K.; Wang, Z.; Yang, J. PMap: Reinforcement Learning-Based Internet-Wide Port Scanning. *IEEE/ACM Trans. Netw.* **2024**, *32*, 5524–5538.

https://doi.org/10.3390/s26051458

sensors

MDPI

Article

Two-Phase Distributed Genetic-Based Algorithm for Time-Aware Shaper Scheduling in Industrial Sensor Networks

Ray-I Chang *, Ting-Wei Hsu and Yen-Ting Chen *

Department of Engineering Science and Ocean Engineering, National Taiwan University, Taipei 10617, Taiwan; f11525125@ntu.edu.tw

* Correspondence: rayichang@ntu.edu.tw (R.-I.C.); ytingchen@ntu.edu.tw (Y.-T.C.)

Abstract

Time-Sensitive Networking (TSN), particularly the Time-Aware Shaper (TAS) specified by IEEE 802.1Qbv, is critical for real-time communication in Industrial Sensor Networks (ISNs). However, many TAS scheduling approaches rely on centralized computation and can face scalability bottlenecks in large networks. In addition, global-only schedulers often generate fragmented Gate Control Lists (GCLs) that exceed per-port entry limits on resource-constrained switches, reducing deployability. This paper proposes a two-phase distributed genetic-based algorithm, 2PDGA, for TAS scheduling. Phase I runs a network-level genetic algorithm (GA) to select routing paths and release offsets and construct a conflict-free baseline schedule. Phase II performs per-switch local refinement to merge windows and enforce device-specific GCL caps with lightweight coordination. We evaluate 2PDGA on 1512 configurations (three topologies, 8–20 switches, and guard bands $\delta_{gb} \in \{0, 100, 200\}$ ns). At $\delta_{gb} = 0$ ns, 2PDGA achieves 92.9% and 99.8% CAP@8/CAP@16, respectively, compliance while maintaining a median latency of 42.1 μs. Phase II reduces the average max-per-port GCL entries by 7.7%. These results indicate improved hardware deployability under strict GCL caps, supporting practical deployment in real-world Industry 4.0 applications.

Keywords: Time-Sensitive Networking (TSN); IEEE 802.1Qbv; Time-Aware Shaper (TAS); genetic algorithm (GA); Industry 4.0; edge computing

1. Introduction

Time-Sensitive Networking (TSN) has emerged as a critical enabler for deterministic communication within Industrial Sensor Networks (ISNs), bridging traditional Information Technology (IT) and real-time Operational Technology (OT) environments [1]. By incorporating precise time synchronization and scheduled transmission mechanisms, TSN guarantees bounded latency and minimal jitter—essential properties for applications in ISNs, including factory automation, robotics, and process control systems.

Among various TSN standards, IEEE 802.1Qbv, which defines the Time-Aware Shaper (TAS), has received significant attention due to its capability to enforce precise time-triggered schedules. TAS achieves deterministic latency by scheduling the opening and closing of gates at network switches according to pre-defined time schedules, thereby controlling traffic flows strictly and predictably [2]. Deterministic end-to-end latency is particularly crucial in distributed sensor and control networks, where even minor timing violations can negatively impact system safety and performance [3].

A core challenge in the practical deployment of TSN using TAS is the generation of Gate Control Lists (GCLs) for network switches. Each GCL specifies the precise timing of traffic gate operations for all time-triggered traffic flows. Formulating a globally feasible schedule that meets strict timing constraints for all flows is inherently complex, representing a combinatorial optimization problem proven to be NP-hard [4]. Consequently, computational complexity escalates rapidly with network size and the number of scheduled flows, making exhaustive searches impractical for large-scale networks.

Currently, most TSN deployments rely on a Centralized Network Configuration (CNC) entity for schedule computation. The CNC aggregates flow requirements and calculates a synchronized GCL for each network node. Although centralized approaches can achieve optimal schedules for smaller networks, they exhibit substantial scalability limitations. Specifically, the computational burden of a centralized scheduler significantly increases as the network expands, creating a bottleneck that limits the feasible network size [5]. Moreover, the centralized architecture concentrates the computational load on a single node, which may become inefficient for the large-scale topology management.

The limitations of centralized scheduling methods become increasingly prominent in large-scale ISNs. While centralized solvers can optimize globally, they often struggle to address local device constraints efficiently. ISNs often comprise heterogeneous devices, each with distinct hardware limitations—for example, some economical TSN-capable devices support limited GCL entries due to memory and hardware constraints [6]. Centralized methods struggle to accommodate such diversity, potentially resulting in conservative schedules that under-utilize network resources. Additionally, the geographical dispersion of sensor nodes further exacerbates the inefficiency and latency associated with centralized control schemes, motivating the exploration of distributed solutions that share scheduling responsibilities across the network nodes.

In response to these challenges, this paper introduces 2PDGA, a Two-Phase Distributed Genetic-Based Algorithm specifically designed to address TAS scheduling within IEEE 802.1Qbv networks in a decentralized manner. Figure 1 contrasts a centralized CNC architecture with the proposed two-phase distributed design: (a) the CNC concentrates global scheduling, GCL computation, and resource management, whereas (b) 2PDGA performs Phase I globally (route selection, offset assignment, conflict resolution) and Phase II locally at each switch via a heuristic-based local optimizer to synthesize per-port GCLs and refine schedules, thereby improving computational efficiency and GCL compactness. The proposed 2PDGA approach divides scheduling into two complementary phases: a global genetic algorithm (GA) phase, which provides a coarse-grained optimization of end-to-end latency and preliminary scheduling across the entire network, and a distributed heuristic refinement phase, where individual network nodes independently adjust their local GCLs based on device-specific constraints and fine-tune their schedules. This hierarchical, distributed structure distributes the scheduling workload across network nodes, thereby enhancing scalability and facilitating parallel processing.

To assess practicality under hardware constraints, we evaluate 2PDGA in TSNKit on 1512 configurations spanning three topologies (Chain/Star/Grid), seven network sizes (8–20 switches), and guard bands ($\delta_{gb} \in \{0, 100, 200\}$ ns). Using CAP@N to represent strict per-port GCL entry limits, 2PDGA achieves 92.9% CAP@8 and 99.8% CAP@16 at $\delta_{gb} = 0$ ns, and maintains 97.6–98.0% CAP@16 at $\delta_{gb} = 100$–200 ns. At $\delta_{gb} = 0$ ns, the measured median/P99 end-to-end latency is 42.1/1409.8 µs. We further quantify the impact of Phase II, which reduces the average max-per-port entry count from 6.02 to 5.55 (−7.7%) over all guard-band settings ($n = 1512$). For $\delta_{gb} = 0$ ns, inter-switch coordination is required in 32/504 cases (6.3%), with 545 bytes of control traffic per case on average.

https://doi.org/10.3390/s26020377

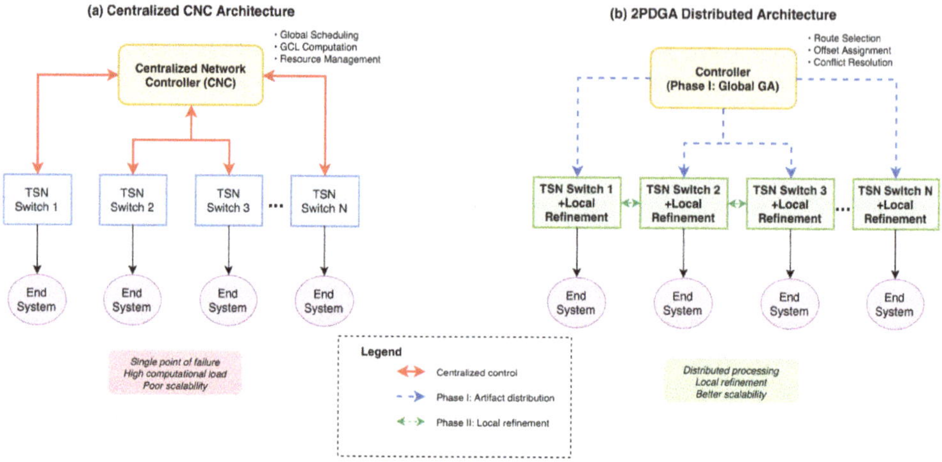

Figure 1. Centralized CNC vs. 2PDGA Distributed Architecture for IEEE 802.1Qbv TSN.

The main contributions of this paper are summarized as follows. (1) We present 2PDGA, a two-phase distributed TAS scheduling framework for IEEE 802.1Qbv, which combines a network-level GA (Phase I) with per-switch local refinement (Phase II) to effectively decouple global feasibility search from local hardware adaptation. (2) We design a cap-aware per-switch refinement procedure that specifically targets GCL fragmentation and enforces per-port entry caps; in our evaluation, Phase II is shown to reduce average max-per-port entries from 6.02 to 5.55 (−7.7%) with an average communication overhead of 545 bytes. (3) We conduct a comprehensive evaluation across 1512 configurations and varying guard bands ($\delta_{gb} \in \{0, 100, 200\}$ ns), demonstrating that 2PDGA achieves 92.9% CAP@8 and 99.8% CAP@16 at $\delta_{gb} = 0$ ns, maintains 97.6–98.0% CAP@16 at $\delta_{gb} = 100$–200 ns, and reports detailed end-to-end latency statistics (e.g., 42.1/1409.8 μs median/P99 at $\delta_{gb} = 0$ ns).

The remainder of this paper is organized as follows: Section 2 reviews related work on TAS/TSN scheduling, GA-based methods, and distributed scheduling approaches. Section 3 introduces the system model and formalizes the TAS scheduling problem and constraints. Section 4 describes 2PDGA, including Phase I global GA design and Phase II per-switch refinement. Section 5 details the experimental setup, baselines, and evaluation metrics. Section 6 presents experimental results, including CAP@N compliance, guard-band sensitivity, topology effects, scalability, and communication overhead. Section 7 concludes the paper and outlines future work.

2. Related Works

2.1. Overview of TSN Scheduling Algorithms

Precise scheduling algorithms are essential for deterministic communication in TSN, particularly when employing the IEEE 802.1Qbv TAS. The scheduling techniques for TAS generally fall into two categories: exact optimization methods and heuristic approaches.

Exact methods include Integer Linear Programming (ILP), Constraint Programming (CP), and Satisfiability Modulo Theory (SMT). These approaches theoretically guarantee optimal solutions under defined constraints [4]. However, TAS scheduling has been shown to be NP-hard, implying that the complexity exponentially grows with network scale and flow numbers [4,5]. Consequently, exact methods become computationally infeasible for large networks. For instance, Falk et al. [7] demonstrated the practical limitations of ILP-based scheduling methods, highlighting significant scalability issues when network size

https://doi.org/10.3390/s26020377

increases. Similarly, CP-based methods improve efficiency by using higher-level constraints (e.g., "all-different" constraints), yet still face scalability challenges [8].

To overcome scalability issues, heuristic methods have been widely adopted. Such algorithms, while not guaranteeing optimality, rapidly provide high-quality feasible schedules suitable for practical use. Common approaches include List Scheduling (LS) and Conflict Graph (CG) algorithms. LS employs a greedy mechanism, sequentially allocating feasible transmission slots along the routing path for each flow [9]. CG abstracts transmissions into graph nodes, where conflicts (e.g., simultaneous transmissions on the same link) are represented as edges. Feasible schedules correspond to independent sets in this graph [10]. In practice, conflict-graph-based solvers combine heuristic search with ILP calls, significantly reducing computational complexity compared to solving full ILP formulations directly.

2.2. TSNKit Tool and Benchmark Algorithms

To facilitate evaluation and comparison, the community has developed benchmark tools such as TSNKit, an open-source Python toolkit designed for configuring and scheduling in TSN environments [11]. TSNKit incorporates various well-established algorithms, providing researchers with standardized baselines. In this study, all TSNKit-based baselines were executed using TSNKit v0.2.0 with Python 3.10.18.

TSNKit supports exact methods, including ILP-based joint routing and scheduling (JRS), which simultaneously computes optimal paths and transmission schedules under strict end-to-end latency constraints. Such ILP formulations, while optimal, are practical only for smaller networks due to their computational complexity [7]. TSNKit also implements a no-wait scheduling baseline (SMT-NW), which models TAS synthesis under a no-wait constraint. Following Dürr and Nayak [12], this baseline can be solved via an ILP formulation and is commonly enhanced with a Tabu-search heuristic to improve scalability.

Additionally, TSNKit provides both LS and CG. LS assigns transmission slots incrementally along each route to minimize computational overhead [9]. In contrast, CG constructs a configuration–conflict graph in which vertices represent candidate transmission configurations and edges represent mutual exclusions; feasible schedules correspond to independent vertex sets in this graph, which TSNKit computes following the conflict-graph method of Falk et al. [10]. These diverse algorithms serve as essential benchmarks to validate the proposed 2PDGA.

2.3. Genetic Algorithms in Scheduling Applications

Genetic algorithms (GAs), a subset of evolutionary computing, are widely recognized for their robustness in solving complex optimization and scheduling problems. In the context of TSN, GA-based methods have demonstrated considerable promise in scheduling efficiency and constraint satisfaction. Several works have employed GA for JRS optimization. Pahlevan and Obermaisser [13] proposed a GA-based scheduler for TSN, encoding routing paths and transmission slots into chromosomes and evaluating solutions through customized fitness functions. This approach demonstrated enhanced schedulability compared to traditional heuristics. Similarly, Kim et al. [14] applied GA to automotive Ethernet TSN scheduling, optimizing for multiple performance metrics such as end-to-end latency, jitter, and bandwidth usage. Their results indicated that GA substantially reduced latency and timing deviations while satisfying critical real-time constraints.

Researchers have further enhanced GAs by combining them with other optimization strategies, notably Particle Swarm Optimization (PSO). Zheng et al. [15] developed a hybrid GA-PSO algorithm that periodically integrates PSO operators to enhance population diversity and convergence rates. Their results showed that hybrid approaches could signif-

https://doi.org/10.3390/s26020377

icantly outperform traditional GAs, reducing total transmission delays by approximately 8%. Despite these advances, existing GA-based approaches primarily optimize for latency or schedulability without explicitly considering hardware deployment constraints. This gap between algorithmic output and hardware capability motivates the design of 2PDGA, which indirectly promotes GCL compaction through offset clustering and path selection in Phase I, and explicitly enforces hardware caps in Phase II.

2.4. Distributed Scheduling Approaches

Distributed scheduling has proven effective in various network domains for enhancing scalability, fault tolerance, and responsiveness. In ISNs, distributed slot allocation protocols enable local coordination among nodes, minimizing the computational burden and the risk associated with single-point failures inherent in centralized systems [16]. Similarly, vehicular networks and Multi-access Edge Computing (MEC) scenarios commonly adopt distributed or hierarchical control frameworks, where multiple local controllers coordinate autonomously to manage network resources efficiently [17].

In contrast, standard TSN scheduling currently relies predominantly on CNC entities that compute and disseminate global schedules. This centralized approach introduces latency during network reconfigurations and represents a significant vulnerability due to potential single-point failures [5]. Despite the recognized need for distributed methods, few distributed scheduling solutions for TAS currently exist.

Recent exploratory research has introduced distributed scheduling methods, including reinforcement learning (RL)-based local schedulers embedded in network switches. For example, Zhong et al. [18] proposed a RL scheduler for TSN, allowing switches to autonomously adapt scheduling decisions based on local state information, demonstrating the viability of decentralized scheduling concepts. However, such solutions remain preliminary, and comprehensive distributed algorithms for IEEE 802.1Qbv TAS scheduling are still lacking. 2PDGA directly addresses this gap by integrating the global optimization capabilities of GA with localized, distributed refinements, significantly enhancing scalability and hardware efficiency in large-scale TSN deployments.

2.5. Comparison with GA-Based TSN Scheduling Algorithms

To deepen the related work discussion, Table 1 compares our proposed 2PDGA against representative genetic-algorithm-based TSN scheduling approaches in the literature. We focus on key dimensions including the scheduling architecture (centralized vs. distributed), primary optimization objectives, consideration of hardware constraints (e.g., GCL entry limits), and the intended application scenarios. This comparison highlights how 2PDGA's unique design ("global coarse optimization + local hard constraint adaptation") differs from prior GA-based solutions and clarifies its novel contributions.

As summarized in Table 1, existing GA-based schedulers [13–15] predominantly employ a centralized architecture. While these methods successfully optimize for timing metrics and search convergence, they assume idealized hardware capabilities and neglect practical device constraints such as GCL entry limits. Consequently, schedules generated by these global-only approaches may be theoretically feasible but fail deployment on commercial switches with limited memory.

In contrast, 2PDGA bridges this gap through a novel "global coarse optimization + local hard constraint adaptation" strategy. By decoupling global routing decisions (Phase I) from local hardware compliance enforcement (Phase II), 2PDGA explicitly addresses GCL entry caps and reduces schedule fragmentation at the device level. This distributed refinement ensures that the resulting schedules are not only optimized for latency but are also practically deployable on resource-constrained hardware, addressing a critical limitation in prior centralized GA methods.

Table 1. Comparison between 2PDGA and existing GA-based TSN scheduling algorithms.

Algorithm	Architecture	Objectives	Hardware Constraints	Scenario
Pahlevan et al. (2018) [13]	Centralized GA	Minimize makespan & idle gaps; Meet deadlines.	No (Focuses only on theoretical feasibility)	Automotive/Industrial TSN with hard real-time flows.
Kim et al. (2022) [14]	Centralized GA	Optimize latency, jitter, & bandwidth utilization.	No (Assumes ideal hardware; ignores GCL limits)	Automotive Ethernet (In-vehicle networks).
Zheng et al. (2023) [15]	Centralized Hybrid GA + PSO	Enhance search convergence & reduce transmission time.	No (Idealized model; ignores device limitations)	General industrial networks (Mesh/Star topologies).
2PDGA (This Work)	Distributed Two-Phase	Global latency optimization + Local hardware adaptation.	Yes. Explicitly enforces GCL entry caps&reduces fragmentation.	ISNs with resource-constrained switches.

3. System Model and Problem Statement

This section formalizes the scheduling problem solved by our 2PDGA. We first introduce the network model used by our simulator, then describe TAS, state the optimization objective and feasibility constraints, and finally recall the computational hardness of timetable synthesis. Throughout this section, we assume that all devices in the TSN are synchronized to a global clock using IEEE 802.1AS. To facilitate the description of the network model and the proposed scheduling algorithm, we summarize the key mathematical notations and parameters used in this paper in Table 2.

Table 2. Summary of Notations.

Symbol	Meaning
$G = (V, E)$	Directed TSN graph
V	Set of vertices (switches and end systems)
E	Set of directed edges (link directions)
F	Set of time-triggered (TT) flows
f_i	Flow i: $(s_i, d_i, L_i, T_i, D_i)$
s_i, d_i	Source/destination of f_i
L_i	Payload length of f_i (bytes)
T_i	Release period of f_i
D_i	End-to-end deadline of f_i

https://doi.org/10.3390/s26020377

Table 2. *Cont.*

Symbol	Meaning
π_i	Ordered list of edges in the route of f_i
$e = (u, v)$	Directed link from node u to v
t_{proc}	Per-frame processing delay at a switch
t_{prop}	Propagation delay of a link
T_{cycle}	Cycle length of the gate-control list
q_j	Queue opened by the j-th GCL entry
t_j^{start}	Start time of GCL entry j
t_j^{end}	End time of GCL entry j
$R(e)$	Line-rate of edge e (bit $\cdot$ s^{-1})
δ_{gb}	Guard band absorbing clock error and switchover
ϕ_i	Release offset of f_i in the cycle
C_v	Maximum number of GCL entries on port v
$Latency(f_i)$	Worst-case end-to-end latency of f_i
$t_{queue}(f_i, e)$	Queuing time of f_i on edge e
$t_{trans}(f_i, e)$	Transmission time of f_i on edge e

3.1. Network Model

A TSN installation is represented by a directed graph $G = (V, E)$ whose vertices V comprise both end systems and switches. Each directed edge $e = (u, v) \in E$ corresponds to one direction of a full-duplex Ethernet link between nodes u and v. Every edge is annotated with a constant line-rate, a fixed propagation delay and a per-frame processing delay incurred at the transmitting switch. Because all devices share the same global clock and operate with sub-microsecond synchronization [1], the entire network follows a common cycle length T_{cycle} without drift.

Traffic to be scheduled consists exclusively of time-triggered (TT) flows. A flow f_i is defined by the tuple $(s_i, d_i, L_i, T_i, D_i)$, where s_i and d_i denote the source and destination vertices, L_i is the payload length in bytes, T_i is the release period and D_i is the end-to-end deadline. The hop sequence $\pi_i = \{e_1, \ldots, e_k\}$ that carries the flow from s_i to d_i is assumed loop-free and is drawn from a pre-computed set of candidate routes between s_i and d_i. These candidate paths are generated by enumerating loop-free routes and filtering those that satisfy the flow's end-to-end deadline constraint D_i.

Figure 2 illustrates the graph structure and annotations $(R(e), t_{prop}, t_{proc})$ and highlights a representative TT path π_1. Directed TSN topology $G = (V, E)$ with switches and end systems. Directed edges denote link directions; edges are annotated with line rate $R(e)$, propagation delay t_{prop}, and per-frame processing delay t_{proc}. The red dashed path shows a representative TT flow along π_1.

https://doi.org/10.3390/s26020377

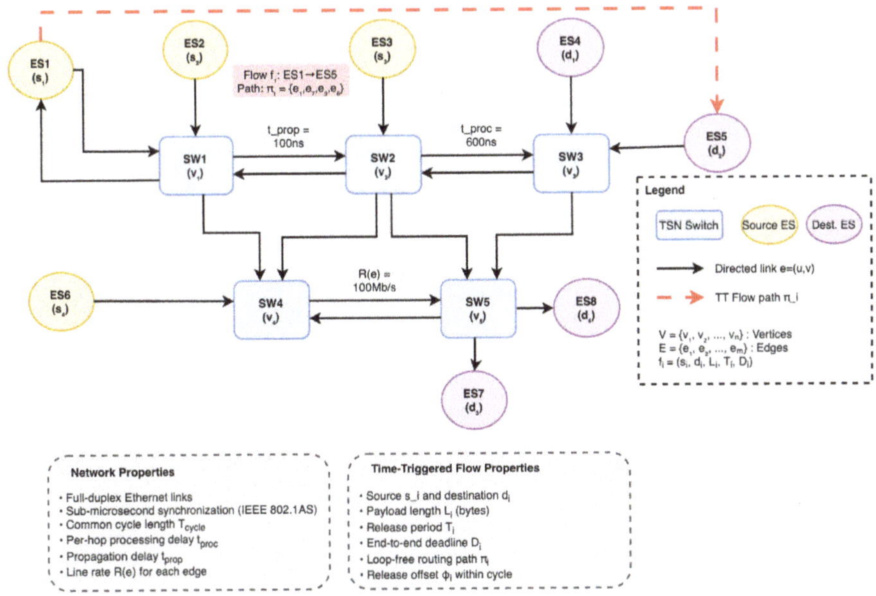

Figure 2. TSN-Network-Model (values shown are for illustration).

3.2. IEEE 802.1Qbv Gate-Control Lists

Deterministic forwarding in TSN relies on TAS introduced in IEEE 802.1Qbv. Every egress port of a TSN bridge holds a GCL that repeatedly opens or closes its priority queues at precisely defined instants. Each entry in the GCL specifies a gate state (open or closed) for each queue and the time interval for which that state is active [2]. During an "open" interval packets from the associated queue may be transmitted according to the queue's priority, whereas during a "closed" interval they are held in the queue [2]. Gate operations are driven by a global clock and repeated every cycle of length T_{cycle}; typical cycle times range from a few tens of microseconds to several milliseconds [3].

Figure 3 visualizes one T_{cycle} and the corresponding six GCL entries of equal duration. Queue 7 (TT) opens in the first, third, and sixth entries; Queue 6 (Audio-Video Bridging (AVB) Stream Reservation Class A (SR-A)) opens in the second entry and in the fourth and fifth entries. The colored arrows indicate that frames are transmitted exclusively within open windows; a small guard band is appended to TT windows to absorb clock error and switchover time. Dashed vertical markers align with GCL entry boundaries, and the table at the right lists the gate states per entry.

A list entry can be written as $\left(t^{start}, t^{end}, q\right)$, meaning that the queue q alone may transmit in the half-open interval $\left[t^{start}, t^{end}\right)$. For a TT frame of size L_i to fit entirely into a window, the window length must exceed the serialization time plus a guard band:

$$t^{end} - t^{start} \geq \frac{8L_i}{R(e)} + \delta_{gb} \tag{1}$$

Because the pattern is periodic, each flow leaves its source at a fixed offset $\phi_i \in [0, T_i)$. We define the transmission time on edge e as $t_{trans}(f_i, e) = 8L_i/R(e)$. The end-to-end

https://doi.org/10.3390/s26020377

latency is calculated as the sum of queuing, transmission, propagation, and processing delays along the path:

$$Latency(f_i) = \sum_{e \in \pi_i} \left(t_{queue}(f_i, e) + t_{trans}(f_i, e) + t_{prop}(e) + t_{proc}(e) \right) \quad (2)$$

Two families of constraints must hold simultaneously for a timetable to be feasible. First, each flow must satisfy the deadline constraint:

$$Latency(f_i) \leq D_i \quad (3)$$

Second, transmissions must be conflict-free: if two flows share an edge, their windows on that edge may not overlap, and on every intermediate switch the downstream window must open strictly after the upstream transmission and processing finish, thereby preserving causality.

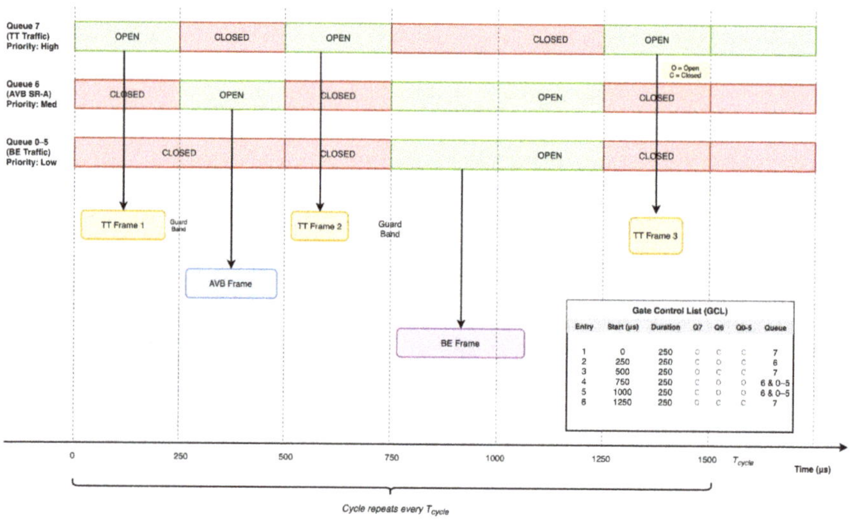

Figure 3. IEEE 802.1Qbv TAS GCL Operation.

3.3. Computational Complexity

Timetable synthesis for TAS is computationally intractable. A classical reduction maps the no-wait job-shop scheduling problem to TAS scheduling: jobs correspond to flows, machines to directed links, and the no-wait constraint mirrors the causality condition. Since the job-shop scheduling problem is a well-known NP-hard optimization problem [4], deciding TAS feasibility is also NP-complete, and minimizing the worst-case latency as posed in (2) is NP-hard. Consequently the search space grows exponentially with the number of flows and hops, and exhaustive enumeration becomes infeasible even for moderate instance sizes. These complexity barriers motivate the meta-heuristic design of 2PDGA.

4. Two-Phase Distributed Genetic-Based Algorithm (2PDGA)

This section introduces 2PDGA for synthesizing GCLs under IEEE 802.1Qbv. The algorithm separates the search into a network-wide global phase and a device-local refinement phase. In Phase I, a lightweight genetic search jointly selects a candidate route from a bounded set and a release offset within the common cycle. The outcome is a feasible, interference-free baseline that already respects link mutual exclusion and hop-to-hop

https://doi.org/10.3390/s26020377

causality. In Phase II, each switch independently improves its local windows in parallel to remove fragmentation, reduce the number of GCL entries, and accommodate hardware entry caps while preserving feasibility. The two phases exchange information only through compact artifacts (GCL, ROUTE, OFFSET, QUEUE, and DELAY). Time is discretized into slots of length t_{slot}, periods T_i are measured in slots, and the cycle length equals the least common multiple (LCM) of all periods. For causality, a conservative per-hop processing delay t_{proc}^{max} is applied uniformly across devices in the global phase. We discretize time into slots of length $t_{slot} = 100$ ns to convert the continuous-time search space into a finite domain manageable by the GA. The maximum alignment overhead is one slot ($\leq$100 ns), which is <10% of the serialization time of a 128-byte frame at 1 Gb/s.

Figure 4 summarizes the control/data flow, the artifacts exchanged between phases, and annotates the dominant costs near each loop (global $O(|F| \times G \times P)$, local $O(W \log W)$).

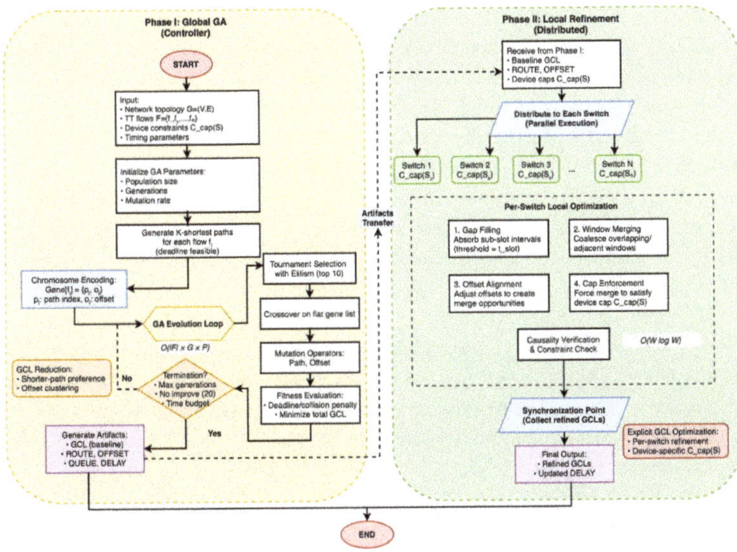

Figure 4. 2PDGA flowchart where G denotes the number of GA generations and P denotes the population size.

Phase I (left) runs a global GA to produce a feasible baseline schedule and emits artifacts {GCL, ROUTE, OFFSET, QUEUE, DELAY}. Phase II (right) performs per-switch local refinement—gap filling, window merging, entry-cap enforcement, and causality verification—in parallel, followed by a synchronization step. Complexity annotations indicate the total cost of the GA loop $O(|F| \times G \times P)$ and the dominant per-switch workload $O(W \log W)$.

4.1. Phase I—Global GA

Phase I (Figure 4, left) aims to generate a network-wide baseline timetable that eliminates conflicts on each directed link and minimizes the end-to-end latency over one cycle. The chromosome for a flow f_i contains two genes: a path index p_i and a release offset o_i.

The path index refers to a small, pre-computed candidate set of loop-free routes built by K-shortest enumeration under a hop bound. The release offset o_i is defined in $[0, T_i)$ and, in implementation, is handled modulo the cycle length for efficient vectorized reduction. Given a chromosome, the evaluator constructs, for each link, a Boolean timeline representing occupancy within the cycle. Each hop advances by the sum of serialization time and the conservative processing delay, yet only the serialization portion occupies the link timeline; the trailing processing segment enforces the no-wait causality between consecutive hops. If any occupied slice overlaps with existing occupancy on the same link, the individual is deemed infeasible and receives a large penalty. The fitness function penalizes deadline violations and minimizes average end-to-end latency. Beyond explicit optimization, Phase I incorporates two design choices that implicitly reduce GCL fragmentation: (1) path selection strongly favors shorter routes, reducing the number of hops per flow; and (2) release offsets are constrained to a small fraction of the period, causing transmissions to cluster temporally rather than scatter across the cycle. This clustering naturally produces adjacent windows on shared links, enabling consolidation without requiring an explicit entry-count term in the fitness function—which would significantly increase per-candidate evaluation cost.

The genetic configuration follows a standard yet tuned setting for TSN instances. In our experiments, we set the population size to 120 with 180 generations per restart. The algorithm performs up to 10 independent restarts within an 8 s time budget. Selection uses tournament sampling (k = 3) with elitism preserving the top 10 individuals. Crossover with per-gene exchange probability of 0.5 promotes structural mixing. Mutation operators include path mutation (20% probability) and offset perturbation (35% probability) with modular reduction to respect the bounds of both the path index and the release offset. The crossover rate is set to 0.8 and mutation rate to 0.2. The evaluator is implemented with vectorized operations to keep the per-generation cost low even for hundreds of flows. An early-stopping rule terminates evolution when the best fitness has stalled for 20 consecutive generations, which preserves quality while keeping runtime modest on larger instances.

Figure 5 illustrates the chromosome encoding structure and genetic operators designed for the Phase I global search. (a) An individual chromosome is organized as an ordered sequence of gene pairs (p_i, o_i) for n flows, resulting in a total length of $2n$ genes. (b) The path-index encoding (p_i) selects a routing path from a set of up to K pre-computed loop-free candidates subject to a hop bound. (c) The release-offset encoding (o_i) determines the transmission start time as a discrete multiple of the time slot t_{slot} within the range $[0, T_i)$, aligned to the common network cycle $T_{cycle} = \mathrm{LCM}(T_1, \ldots, T_n)$. (d) Genetic operators include crossover, which uses even-index cut points to preserve the integrity of (p_i, o_i) pairs, and shuffle mutation with modular reduction applied at a low probability (0.2) to maintain constraint validity.

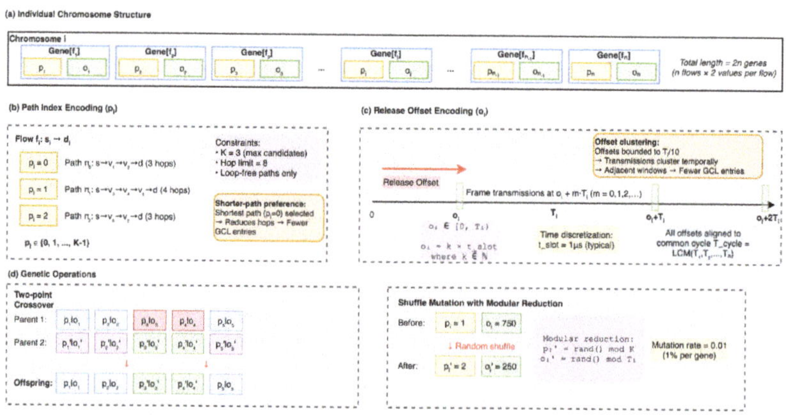

Figure 5. Chromosome Encoding Structure for 2PDGA Phase I.

https://doi.org/10.3390/s26020377

Upon completion, Phase I emits five artifacts that fully describe the baseline schedule. The GCL file lists the queue state, start time, end time, and cycle length for each directed link in nanoseconds; by construction, the marked duration equals the serialization time. The ROUTE file records the set of hops used by each flow, while the OFFSET file stores the per-flow hold time from which the original release offset can be recovered. The QUEUE file records queue assignments for each hop; in our experiments, a single time-triggered queue per port is used. Finally, the DELAY file reports the end-to-end latency achieved by the baseline timetable. Using a uniform processing delay t_{proc}^{max} strikes a safe balance: it may slightly over-approximate some hops on heterogeneous hardware, but it greatly simplifies causality checks in the global search.

4.2. Phase II—Local Refinement

While Phase I produces schedules with reduced fragmentation through implicit design choices, the resulting GCLs may still exceed hardware entry limits on resource-constrained switches. Phase II explicitly enforces hardware compliance by refining the baseline timetable using only local information, running concurrently across all switches. It employs an iterative local search procedure with domain-specific heuristics, operating on each switch independently. From the global GCL, the algorithm constructs, for each switch, a dictionary that groups windows by incident directed link; windows are converted to slot indices and sorted.

A dedicated thread invokes a local optimizer on this per-switch structure to reduce fragmentation and enforce the per-port hardware entry cap. In our evaluation, each egress port uses a single TT queue; therefore, Phase II compaction operates on TT gate-open intervals only and does not require changing queue-state vectors. The optimizer applies monotone transformations on each port timeline. The overall Phase II per-switch refinement workflow is summarized in Algorithm 1.

First, a gap-filling pass (GAP_FILL) absorbs sub-slot (or very small) idle intervals by extending/aligning neighboring TT intervals within a bounded tolerance (t_slot), effectively turning near-adjacent fragments into overlapping or contiguous intervals. Second, a merging pass (GREEDY_MERGE) coalesces overlapping/contiguous TT intervals on the same port into a single longer interval, thereby reducing the number of GCL entries. Any timing changes introduced by local alignment/merging are validated by the end-to-end delay replay and causality verification described later in this section. Third, when the number of entries on a port exceeds the device cap, the optimizer greedily coalesces the nearest compatible windows or the smallest-gap pairs until the cap is met; if a merge would invert causality, the optimizer defers that merge and prefers alternatives with minimal slack loss.

Because Phase II may shift or merge windows, end-to-end delays are recomputed over the refined lists. The ROUTE artifact is used to reconstruct the unique ordered path of each flow by inferring the successor and predecessor relationships within the set of unordered hops. The OFFSET artifact recovers the original release offset from the stored hold time and the known period. Forward propagation then proceeds hop by hop: for each directed link, the algorithm selects the first window whose start is not earlier than the current time modulo the cycle, wrapping to the next cycle only when necessary, and advances the clock to the end of that window plus the conservative processing gap. The resulting end-to-end latency equals the final time minus the recovered offset and the trailing processing delay. This recomputation is purely local to the GCLs and does not require re-invoking the global genetic search. To ensure end-to-end causality is maintained across the network, communication among devices is limited to compact summaries for the flows whose windows changed, so the message volume grows only with the number

https://doi.org/10.3390/s26020377

of affected flows and their hop counts. With sorted lists, the dominant work per switch is the initial ordering of windows, which runs in $O(W\log W)$ where W is the number of local windows; linear passes suffice for the three transformations. Since each switch optimizes independently, wall-time is governed by the largest local workload rather than the sum over the entire network.

Algorithm 1: Phase II—Per-Switch Local Refinement

Input: Baseline GCL from Phase I, device-specific caps C_cap(S)
Output: Refined GCLs satisfying hardware entry limits per switch

```
function PHASE_II_REFINE(GCL, {C_cap(S)})
    // Distribute to switches and refine in parallel
    parallel for each switch S do
      windows ← PARTITION_BY_PORT(GCL, S)
      for iter = 1 to I do                                  // I = 8
        for each port P in S.egress_ports do
          if COUNT_ENTRIES(windows[P]) ≤ C_cap(S) then continue

          // Step 1: Gap filling-absorb sub-slot intervals
          windows[P] ← GAP_FILL(windows[P], t_slot)

          // Step 2: Greedy merge-coalesce compatible windows
          windows[P] ← GREEDY_MERGE(windows[P])

          // Step 3: Offset alignment-adjust timing for merging
          if COUNT_ENTRIES(windows[P]) > C_cap(S) then
            windows[P] ← ALIGN_OFFSETS(windows[P], C_cap(S))

          // Step 4: Cap enforcement-force merge if needed
          if COUNT_ENTRIES(windows[P]) > C_cap(S) then
                windows[P] ← FORCE_MERGE_TO_CAP(windows[P], C_cap(S))

      GCL_refined[S] ← RECONSTRUCT(windows)

    // Synchronization and delay recomputation
    return MERGE_ALL(GCL_refined), RECOMPUTE_DELAYS()
function GREEDY_MERGE(windows)
          // Sweep-line merge of overlapping/contiguous TT intervals after GAP_FILL/ALIGN_OFFSETS
    windows ← SORT_BY_START(windows)
    merged ← []
    for each (st, en) in windows do
      if merged is not empty and st ≤ merged[-1].end then
        merged[-1].end ← max(merged[-1].end, en)
      else
        merged.append((st, en))
    return merged
```

https://doi.org/10.3390/s26020377

4.3. Rescue Search (Fallback Repair)

Rescue Search is a time-bounded fallback invoked only when the max-per-port GCL count still exceeds the hardware cap after Phase II refinement. It performs a small, conservative local repair (candidate offset alignment and limited path alternatives) and accepts only conflict-free schedules that meet all deadline constraints. This step is not a core contribution; it is a safety net used sparingly when cap violations remain.

5. Experimental Setup

This section details the simulation environment, network topologies, traffic workloads, baseline algorithms, and evaluation metrics used to assess the performance of the proposed 2PDGA. The experimental design is structured to rigorously evaluate the algorithm's scalability, GCL efficiency, and hardware compliance against both heuristic and solver-based scheduling methods.

5.1. Software and Hardware Environment

Experiments were conducted on a Linux workstation running Ubuntu 24.04 LTS, equipped with a 13th Gen Intel® Core™ i7-13700K CPU (24 threads, up to 5.4 GHz) and 64 GB of RAM. All algorithms were implemented and evaluated using TSNKit, an open-source TSN scheduling toolkit. To ensure reproducibility and determinism, fixed random seeds were used across all trials, ensuring that all algorithms were evaluated on identical problem instances.

5.2. Network Models and Traffic Workloads

The simulator adopted the standard TSN abstraction of a directed graph $G = (V, E)$ assuming IEEE 802.1AS global synchronization. All links operated at 1 Gb/s. To reflect the realistic forwarding latency of store-and-forward switches used in our model, we applied a per-frame processing delay $t_{proc} = 2000$ ns and assumed a negligible propagation delay ($t_{prop} \approx 0$ ns) typical of short-range industrial cabling.

To evaluate robustness against clock synchronization errors, experiments were conducted with three guard band values: $\delta_{gb} \in \{0,\ 100,\ 200\}$ ns. The guard band represents additional idle time inserted between consecutive GCL windows to prevent timing violations due to clock drift.

To comprehensively evaluate topological adaptability, we investigated three distinct network structures as illustrated in Figure 6. The Chain topology (Figure 6a) represents linear constraints common in automotive daisy-chains, challenging schedulers with accumulated hop delays and a lack of routing diversity. The Star topology (Figure 6b) models centralized industrial cells; while routing is simpler, it creates significant congestion at the central switch bottleneck. Finally, the Grid (Mesh) topology (Figure 6c) represents complex industrial mesh networks (e.g., factory floors). This topology offers high path diversity but presents an exponentially larger search space, serving as the primary stress test for scalability.

To assess scalability, we conducted a parameter sweep of the network size N ranging from 8 to 20 switches. For each size, the number of time-triggered (TT) flows (F) is scaled based on the network size to maintain a consistent traffic density of approximately 0.6 to 0.8 flows per switch. Specifically, the workload follows the relation $F = N - 4$ for $N \geq 12$, with baseline flow counts of 5 and 6 for $N = 8$ and $N = 10$, respectively. Traffic attributes are synthesized to mimic realistic industrial workloads. To prevent cycle length (hypercycle) explosion, flow periods are selected from a discrete set (e.g., 0.5, 1, 2, 4 ms) rather than a continuous distribution. To ensure algorithm robustness, we generated diverse

https://doi.org/10.3390/s26020377

traffic configurations by varying flow densities and payload sizes across experiments. The detailed simulation parameters are summarized in Table 3.

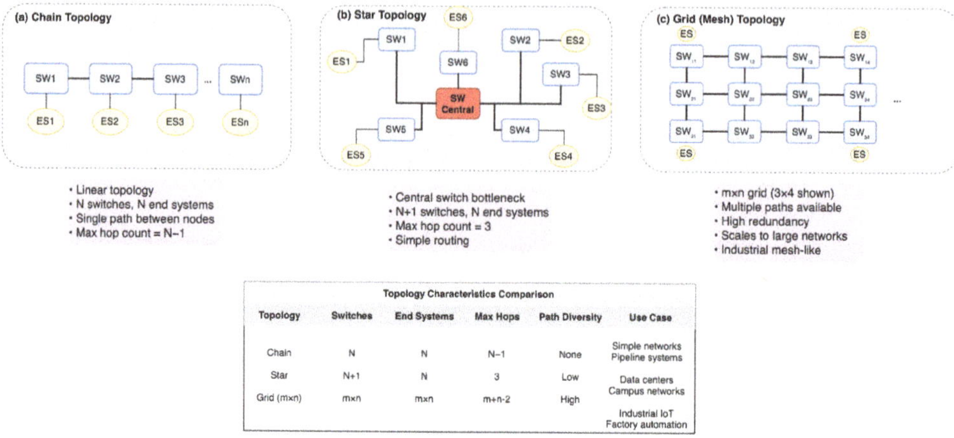

Topology	Switches	End Systems	Max Hops	Path Diversity	Use Case
Chain	N	N	N−1	None	Simple networks Pipeline systems
Star	N+1	N	3	Low	Data centers Campus networks
Grid (m×n)	m×n	m×n	m+n-2	High	Industrial IoT Factory automation

Figure 6. Test network topologies. (**a**) Chain: Linear topology with single-path routing. (**b**) Star: Centralized topology with $N + 1$ switches and low diversity. (**c**) Grid: $m \times n$ lattice structure (3×4 shown) offering high redundancy for scalability testing.

Table 3. Simulation Parameters and Traffic Configurations.

Parameter	Value/Description
Network Settings	
Link Rate	1 Gb/s
Processing Delay (t_{proc})	2000 ns
Propagation Delay (t_{prop})	0 ns
Network Size (N)	{8, 10, 12, 14, 16, 18, 20} switches
Topologies	Chain, Star, Grid (Mesh)
Traffic Workload	
Flow Count (F)	$N - 4$ (for $N \geq 12$); $\{5, 6\}$ (for $N = \{8, 10\}$)
Flow Period (T_i)	Discrete: $\{0.5, 1, 2, 4\}$ ms (scenario-dependent)
Payload Size (L_i)	256–1024 bytes
Priority	8 queues (0–7)
Algorithm Settings	
2PDGA Population Size	120 (Phase I)
Generations	180
Phase II Iterations	8

In this study, the traffic model consists exclusively of Time-Triggered (TT) flows. While industrial networks typically carry mixed-criticality traffic, we focus on TT traffic based on two key rationales widely adopted in TSN scheduling research. First, ensuring deterministic latency for safety-critical flows is the primary objective of TSN and represents an NP-hard scheduling problem in itself. Focusing on TT flows allows for a rigorous evaluation of the algorithm's scalability and hardware efficiency without the confounding variables of stochastic traffic, a strategy consistent with established studies such as Geppert et al. [19] and Dürr & Nayak [12]. Second, our model assumes the standard TSN protection mechanisms—Gate Control Lists (GCLs) that close non-TT queues during TT windows, together with guard bands at window boundaries—to protect critical transmission windows [2]. Under this strict isolation configuration, lower-priority AVB/BE frames

https://doi.org/10.3390/s26020377

are prevented from being transmitted (or being in flight) during TT windows; therefore, they do not affect the worst-case timing or feasibility of the TT schedule, allowing the TT synthesis problem to be decoupled and solved independently [4].

5.3. Algorithms and Baseline

To validate the effectiveness of 2PDGA, we benchmark it against four representative algorithms spanning heuristic, ILP-based, and solver-assisted approaches. LS [9] is used as a baseline for widely used greedy heuristics; it sequentially assigns the earliest feasible transmission slots, offering low computational cost but no guarantee of optimality. In TSNKit, CG follows Falk et al. and combines a fast heuristic with an ILP-based solver for this independent-set subproblem [10,11], providing a strong (often near-exact) feasibility baseline. We include CG to highlight that constructing a feasible schedule is fundamentally different from producing a hardware-efficient schedule, especially under strict GCL length constraints. ST/BE-Ratio applies traffic-class-aware bandwidth allocation to balance scheduled traffic (ST) and best-effort (BE) flows, representing ratio-based optimization strategies. FlexTAS-Tabu [12,20] is a Tabu-search baseline implementation provided in the FlexTAS artifact [20], following the no-wait packet scheduling (NW-PSP) formulation and Tabu metaheuristic of Dürr and Nayak [12]. For clarity, "FlexTAS-Tabu" in this paper refers to this Tabu baseline (implementation source: FlexTAS), not the FlexTAS scheduling method itself. Note that the released implementation uses a coarse time granularity, which precludes evaluation under non-zero guard band configurations; therefore, we report FlexTAS-Tabu only for $\delta_{gb} = 0$.

Regarding the configuration of our proposed 2PDGA, Phase I is initialized with a population size of 120 to ensure sufficient genetic diversity for exploring the solution space, while Phase II executes distributedly to apply local refinements such as gap absorption and window merging. This two-phase configuration ensures that hardware constraints are enforced efficiently without the excessive computational overhead typical of exact methods.

5.4. Metrics

We assess performance using the following five metrics. Schedulability Rate (SR) measures the percentage of test cases in which all flows satisfy their end-to-end deadlines.

For GCL Efficiency, consider a network with P egress ports, where g_p denotes the number of GCL entries on port p. We report: (i) Total GCL Entries ($\sum_{p=1}^{P} g_p$) and Avg GCL, defined as the mean of Total GCL Entries over all test cases; and (ii) the per-test-case maximum entries on any port, $g^{max} = \max_p g_p$ together with Avg Max/Port, defined as the mean of g^{max} over all test cases (reported as "Max/Port" in Section 6 for brevity).

Hardware Compliance Rate (CAP@N) evaluates the percentage of valid schedules that satisfy a strict per-port GCL cap N, i.e., $\max_p g_p \leq N$. Prior work indicates that practical per-port GCL capacities can range from 8 to 1024 entries depending on device class and implementation constraints [6]. To match the hardware-cap analysis in Section 6, we report CAP@8, CAP@16, and CAP@32. These thresholds reflect representative commercial limits: entry-level platforms such as the TI AM64x ICSSG provide 16 schedule entries [21], mid-range TSN switch solutions such as the Analog Devices ADIN6310 evaluation stack support 32-entry GCLs [22], and industrial switches such as the Moxa TSN-G5008 are commonly evaluated under 64-entry per-port caps [23]. End-to-End Latency is computed for each TT flow from the resulting schedule/GCLs using the end-to-end delay definition in Section 3. We report Median (P50) and P99 latency (in μs) over the distribution of per-flow end-to-end latencies for each algorithm under each guard-band setting δ_{gb}.

https://doi.org/10.3390/s26020377

Finally, Phase II Contribution quantifies the incremental improvement brought by the distributed refinement stage. Specifically, we measure the change from Phase I to Phase II in terms of Avg Max/Port (and the corresponding CAP@N feasibility), and we additionally report the coordination overhead of Phase II using communication volume statistics (bytes/messages/frames) in Section 6.7.

5.5. Evaluation Protocol

For every algorithm-configuration pair, we recorded the generated GCLs, latency statistics, and runtime. Each configuration was tested across all three guard band values (0, 100, 200 ns), yielding 1512 total test cases (504 base configurations × 3 guard bands). We performed paired statistical tests to validate that the observed differences are significant at the 95% confidence level ($p < 0.05$). This rigorous protocol ensures that reported improvements are statistically robust and not artifacts of random variation. For the 2PDGA-specific analysis, we additionally recorded Phase I/II execution times, GA convergence metrics (including generations and the converged generation), and communication overhead measured in bytes, messages, and frames.

6. Experiments and Results

This section reports the empirical evaluation of the proposed 2PDGA against four representative baselines: LS, CG, ST/BE-Ratio, and FlexTAS-Tabu. We present a comprehensive analysis spanning 1512 experimental configurations—incorporating varying guard band settings—to assess GCL efficiency, hardware compliance, robustness, and scalability. All reported results are derived from actual experiments with statistical validation.

6.1. Overall Performance and GCL Efficiency

We first examine the aggregate performance across all network configurations. Table 4 summarizes the performance for all evaluated algorithms across three guard band values. A total of 1512 experimental configurations (504 per guard band value × 3 guard bands) were evaluated. Figure 7 below provides a visual comparison of key metrics across algorithms. Table 4 reports SR, Avg GCL, Max/Port, CAP@8, CAP@16, and median/P99 latency for each guard band. The figure below (Figure 7) further breaks down these metrics at $\delta_{gb} = 0$ ns into CAP@8 compliance (Figure 7a), CAP@16 compliance (Figure 7b), and median latency (Figure 7c).

Figure 7. Overall Algorithm Comparison.

https://doi.org/10.3390/s26020377

Table 4. Overall Algorithm Performance Comparison.

Algorithm	δ_{gb} (ns)	SR (%)	Avg GCL	AvgMax/Port	CAP@8 (%)	CAP@16 (%)	Median (µs)	P99 (µs)
LS	0	100	63.65	6.401	82.1	97.4	35.4	1694.9
CG	0	100	114.52	8.788	56.5	92.7	74.5	1603.1
ST/BE-Ratio	0	100	60.01	5.875	85.1	99.2	29.5	1683.7
FlexTAS-Tabu	0	100	49.41	5.998	78.6	97.8	32.6	1241.7
2PDGA	0	100	45.54	4.998	92.9	99.8	42.1	1409.8
LS	100	100	69.2	7.393	70.8	96.8	26.8	1084.7
CG	100	100	113.54	8.752	56.7	91.5	77.9	1699.5
ST/BE-Ratio	100	100	69.2	7.393	70.8	96.8	44	863.9
2PDGA	100	100	50.1	5.871	80.6	97.6	28.3	984.1
LS	200	100	69.2	7.393	70.8	96.8	28.9	1085.2
CG	200	100	111.47	8.589	57.5	94	67.2	1685.1
ST/BE-Ratio	200	100	69.2	7.393	70.8	96.8	61.7	877.4
2PDGA	200	100	50.03	5.788	80.8	98	28.1	944.1

The proposed 2PDGA demonstrates superior GCL compactness and hardware compliance. At $\delta_{gb} = 0$ ns, 2PDGA achieves an average of 45.54 total GCL entries with an avg max-per-port value of 4.998, compared to 63.65/6.401 for LS, 114.52/8.788 for CG, and 49.41/5.998 for FlexTAS-Tabu.

More importantly, 2PDGA achieves the highest CAP@8 compliance rate (92.9%), significantly outperforming all baselines. In comparison, LS achieves 82.1% (a + 10.8% gap), ST/BE-Ratio 85.1% (+7.8%), FlexTAS-Tabu 78.6% (+14.3%), and CG 56.5% (+36.4%).

This high CAP@8 compliance enables deployment on cost-sensitive entry-level TSN hardware where other algorithms fail to achieve adequate compliance rates. Regarding latency, 2PDGA achieves a median latency of 42.1 µs ($\delta_{gb} = 0$), which is slightly higher than LS (35.4 µs) and ST/BE-Ratio (29.5 µs). However, the P99 latency of 2PDGA (1409.8 µs) is lower than LS (1694.9 µs), indicating better tail behavior and more predictable worst-case performance. This modest median latency increase is justified by the significant improvement in hardware compliance.

6.2. Hardware Compliance and Topology Analysis

Under the strict CAP@8 constraint (8 entries per port), 2PDGA achieves a compliance rate of 92.9% at $\delta_{gb} = 0$, significantly outperforming all baselines. Figure 8 below illustrates the compliance rates across different GCL entry limits. In particular, Figure 8 below compares CAP@8, CAP@16, and CAP@32 at $\delta_{gb} = 0$, highlighting 2PDGA's consistently highest compliance across thresholds.

As shown in Table 5, 2PDGA maintains the highest CAP@8 compliance across all guard band values. Most algorithms exhibit 10–15% degradation as the guard band increases from 0 to 200 ns, while CG shows minimal sensitivity since its conflict graph structure is unaffected by timing margins. Notably, 2PDGA's advantage over baselines is preserved even under conservative timing margins, demonstrating its robustness for practical deployment scenarios.

These results demonstrate that 2PDGA enables deployment in hardware-constrained scenarios where other algorithms fail to achieve compliance, providing significant practical value for Industry 4.0 applications with heterogeneous device constraints. Topology-specific behavior is summarized in Table 6 and Figures 9 and 10 below. Table 6 reports the average total GCL entries by topology, while Figure 10 below contrasts CAP@8, CAP@16, and CAP@32 compliance across topologies.

https://doi.org/10.3390/s26020377

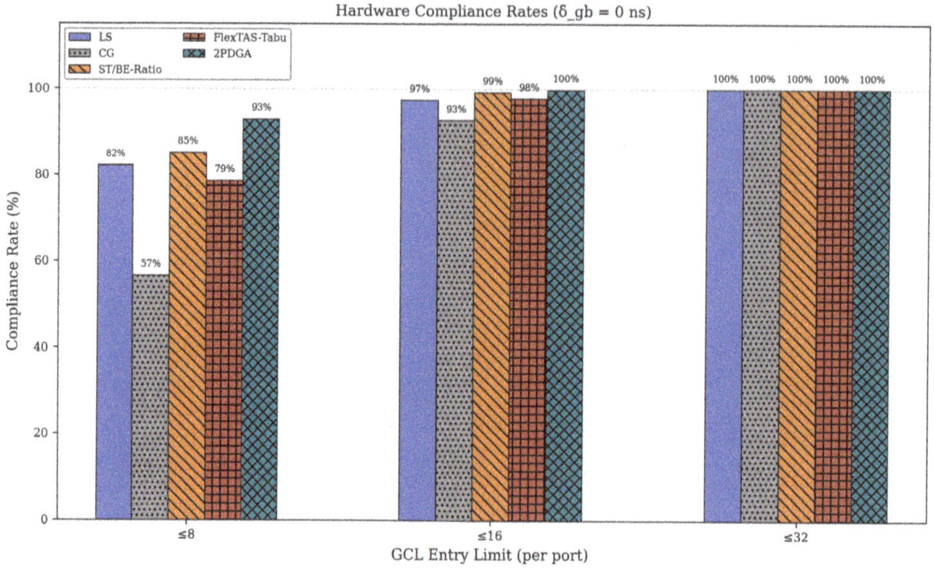

Figure 8. Hardware Compliance Rates.

Table 5. CAP@8 Compliance Across Guard Band Values.

Algorithm	CAP@8 (δ_{gb} = 0)	CAP@8 (δ_{gb} = 100)	CAP@8 (δ_{gb} = 200)	Degradation
2PDGA	92.90%	80.60%	80.80%	−12.10%
ST/BE-Ratio	85.10%	70.80%	70.80%	−14.30%
LS	82.10%	70.80%	70.80%	−11.30%
FlexTAS-Tabu	78.60%	N/A	N/A	-
CG	56.50%	56.70%	57.50%	+1.0%

As shown in Figures 9 and 10 below, 2PDGA demonstrates consistent advantages across all topologies. In Chain topology, 2PDGA achieves 78.6% CAP@8 compliance compared to only 48.8% for CG. In Star topology, the simpler network structure allows both 2PDGA and ST/BE-Ratio to achieve 100% CAP@8 compliance. The most dramatic difference appears in Grid topology, where 2PDGA achieves 100% CAP@8 compliance while CG achieves only 38.1%, highlighting 2PDGA's effectiveness in complex networks with high path diversity. The extreme gap in Grid topology (100% vs. 38.1% CAP@8) demonstrates 2PDGA's robustness in complex, high-redundancy networks typical of smart factory deployments.

Table 6. Topology Performance.

Algorithm	AvgGCL(Chain)	AvgGCL(Star)	AvgGCL(Grid)	CAP@8(Chain)	CAP@8(Star)	CAP@8(Grid)
2PDGA	70.5	19.4	30	78.60%	100.00%	100.00%
LS	106.3	33.2	51.5	57.10%	99.40%	89.90%
CG	113.5	38.9	191.2	48.80%	82.70%	38.10%
ST/BE-Ratio	97.8	32	50.2	63.10%	100.00%	92.30%
FlexTAS-Tabu	91.8	22	34.4	53.60%	94.60%	87.50%

https://doi.org/10.3390/s26020377

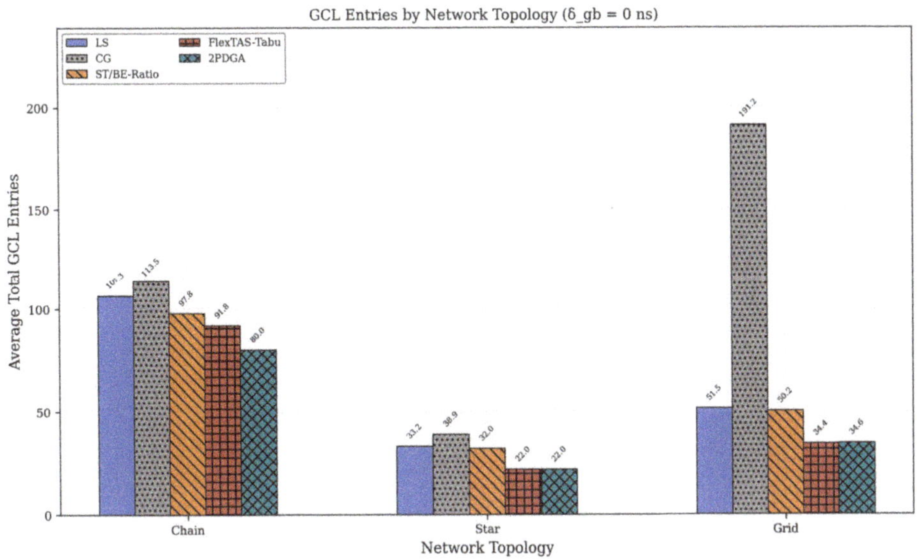

Figure 9. Topology GCL Analysis.

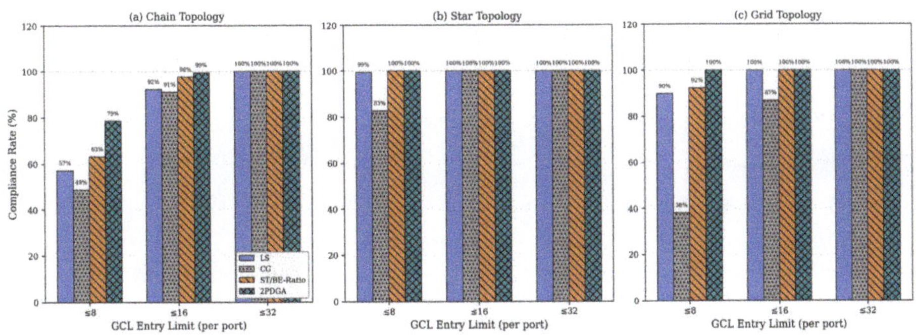

Figure 10. Topology Compliance Rates.

6.3. Guard Band Sensitivity Analysis

To evaluate robustness against clock synchronization variations, we tested all algorithms with guard band values of 0, 100, and 200 ns. Figure 11 presents the CAP@8 compliance trend across guard band configurations, with Figure 11 below explicitly comparing $\delta_{gb} = 0$, 100, 200 ns to show how each algorithm's CAP@8 rate degrades under increasing timing margins.

As shown in Figure 11, all algorithms except CG show degradation with increased guard bands, as larger guard bands reduce the effective window space for scheduling. Despite this trend, 2PDGA maintains over 80% CAP@8 compliance even at $\delta_{gb} = 200$ ns. The distributed baseline ST/BE-Ratio exhibits higher sensitivity (14.3% degradation) compared to 2PDGA (12.1% degradation), demonstrating the robustness of 2PDGA's optimization approach. Note that FlexTAS-Tabu cannot be evaluated at non-zero guard bands due to its microsecond precision limitation.

https://doi.org/10.3390/s26020377

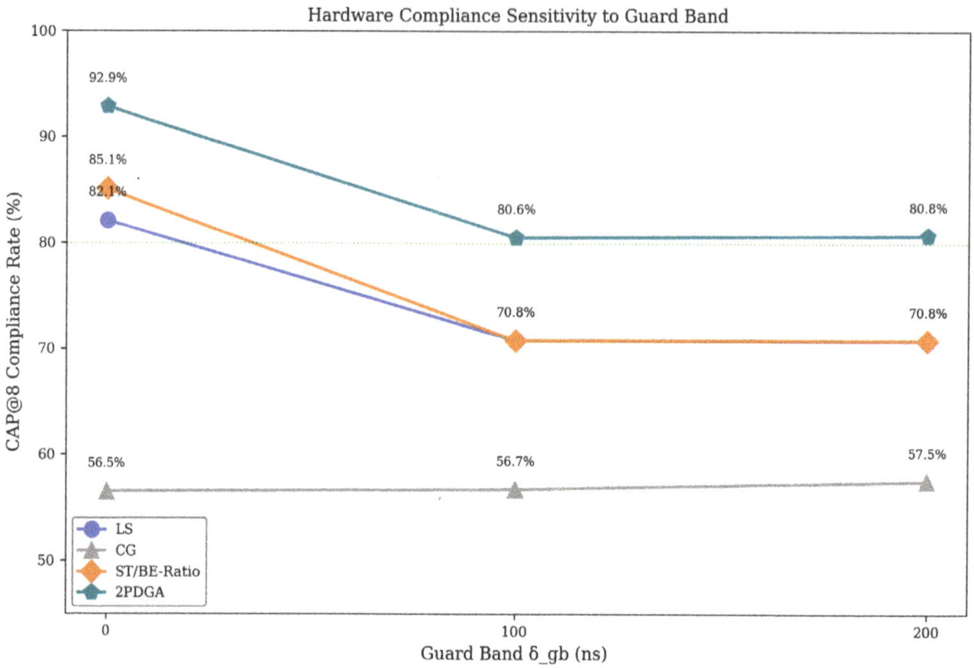

Figure 11. Hardware Compliance Sensitivity to Guard Band.

These results confirm that 2PDGA's advantage is not limited to ideal synchronization scenarios but extends to realistic industrial deployments with timing margins.

6.4. Ablation: Contribution of Phase II (Hardware Feasibility)

To isolate the impact of Phase II refinement, we conducted an ablation study comparing Phase I output (before window merging and local refinement) against the final optimized results.

Phase II includes two components: window merging, which coalesces adjacent GCL windows serving the TT queue, and per-switch local refinement, which performs gap filling/offset alignment and cap enforcement. Table 7 summarizes how Phase II changes max-per-port GCL entries across all 1512 cases (all guard bands), focusing on hardware feasibility rather than average GCL.

Table 7. Phase II Feasibility Impact (Max-Per-Port). Table 7 reports event (i) local refinement executed aggregated over all guard-band settings ($\delta_{gb} \in$ 0, 100, 200 ns), i.e., 1512 cases = 504 base configurations × 3 guard bands.

Metric	Value
Avg Max/Port (Phase I -> Phase II)	6.02 -> 5.55 (−0.46, −7.7%)
Cases with improved max-per-port after Phase II (all guard bands)	15.3% (231/1512)
Avg reduction when improved	3.08 entries

Phase II local refinement is intentionally conservative and activates only when per-port caps are at risk. Across 1512 cases, it reduces max-per-port entries by 0.46 on average, with improvements in 15.3% of cases (3.08 entries when improved). These results indicate that Phase II is intentionally conservative: its average GCL reduction is modest, but its

https://doi.org/10.3390/s26020377

primary contribution is enforcing the per-port max-per-port cap, which directly determines deployability and is reflected by CAP@N improvements in Section 6.2.

6.5. Scalability Analysis

We evaluate how algorithm performance scales with network size (8–20 switches). Figure 12 below illustrates the scaling trends for all evaluated algorithms. Table 8 lists the average total GCL entries at each network size, while Figure 12 below visualizes the same trends to highlight relative growth rates across algorithms.

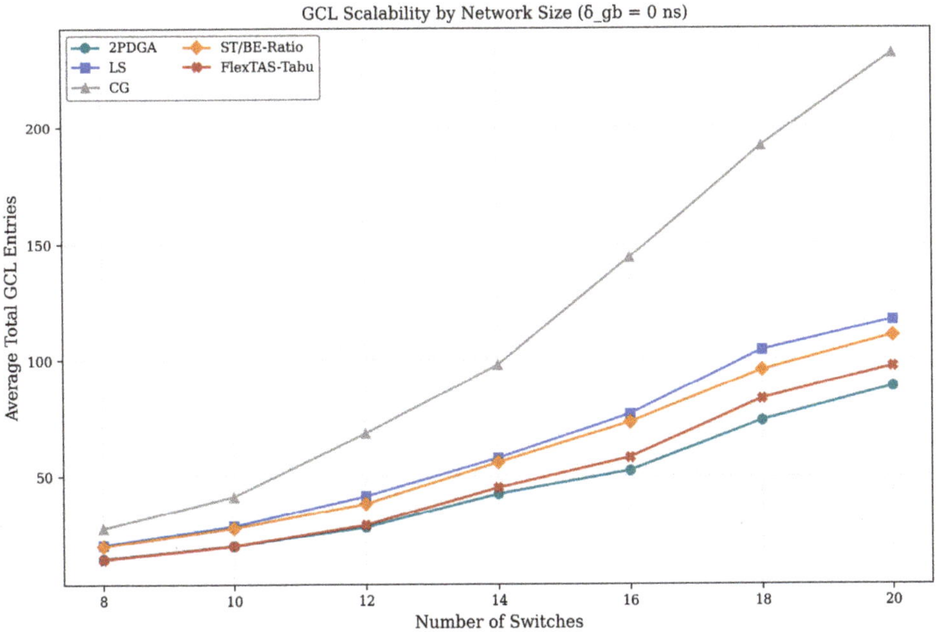

Figure 12. GCL Scalability by Network Size.

Table 8. Avg Total GCL by Network Size ($\delta_{gb} = 0$).

Switches	2PDGA	LS	CG	ST/BE-Ratio	2PDGA vs. CG
8	12.8	20.4	27.5	19.9	−53.50%
10	17.5	28.4	41.1	27.6	−57.40%
12	24.8	41.3	68.2	38	−63.60%
14	37.2	57.7	97.7	55.8	−61.90%
16	46.1	76.4	143.7	72.9	−67.90%
18	65.1	104.2	191.8	95.5	−66.10%
20	77.8	117.1	231.7	110.3	−66.40%

As illustrated in Figure 12, CG exhibits superlinear growth in GCL entries, escalating from 27.5 entries at 8 switches to 231.7 entries at 20 switches (8.4× increase). In contrast, 2PDGA demonstrates moderate growth from 12.8 to 77.8 entries (6.1× increase), while LS and ST/BE-Ratio show approximately linear growth with network size. The relative advantage of 2PDGA over CG remains stable at 53–68% across all network sizes.

The consistent advantage across network sizes confirms 2PDGA's suitability for large-scale ISN deployments where scalability is critical.

https://doi.org/10.3390/s26020377

6.6. Runtime Analysis

Table 9 presents runtime comparison across all algorithms. We report mean, P95, and max runtime for reference, while noting that direct runtime comparison can be misleading across heterogeneous solver implementations and environments. FlexTAS-Tabu does not support guard bands, so it is excluded from the runtime comparison.

Table 9. Runtime Comparison (all test cases).

Algorithm	Mean (ms)	P95 (ms)	Max (ms)
ST/BE-Ratio	586	2081	8890
CG	794	3002	126,536
LS	1195	7474	46,505
2PDGA	1557	6242	35,325

As shown in the phase breakdown Table 10, Phase I accounts for the largest share (45.5%), while Phase II and the fallback Rescue Search (Section 4.3) together contribute only about 10.8%, indicating that local refinement adds limited incremental cost. The remaining 43.6% is dominated by I/O and evaluation steps in the measurement pipeline (schedule serialization, metric aggregation, and latency replay), so the reported wall-clock time should be interpreted as a conservative upper bound; GA evaluation is also naturally parallelizable.

Table 10. 2PDGA Phase Runtime Breakdown.

Phase	Time (ms)	Percentage
Phase I (GA)	709	45.50%
Phase II (Local)	113	7.20%
Rescue Search	57	3.60%
Other overhead (I/O, eval)	678	43.60%

Runtime tables are provided for reference only; differences in solver choice and implementation details can dominate wall-clock time, making direct comparisons not strictly fair. The GA phase is population-based and amenable to parallel evaluation, so the reported wall-clock time is a conservative estimate of achievable runtime under parallel execution. Despite higher runtime, 2PDGA delivers significantly better GCL efficiency.

6.7. Communication Overhead Analysis

For practical distributed deployment, Phase II requires inter-switch coordination. We quantify the communication cost to validate deployment feasibility. Table 11 summarizes total bytes, messages, and Ethernet frames across percentiles, providing a compact view of both average and tail communication overhead.

Table 11. Phase II Inter-switch Coordination Overhead ($\delta_{gb} = 0$, $n = 504$).

Metric	Average	P50	P90	P99	Max
Total Bytes	545	240	656	7771	8616
Messages	16.7	10	20	226	226
Ethernet Frames	1.16	1	1	6	6

We distinguish two Phase II events: (i) local refinement executed, indicating that Phase II improves the max-per-port GCL entry count within at least one switch, and

https://doi.org/10.3390/s26020377

(ii) inter-switch coordination required, indicating that Phase II triggers cross-switch consensus/verification messages. Table 7 reports event (i) aggregated across all guard-band settings (231/1512 cases, 15.3%), whereas the communication statistics in this section quantify event (ii) for $\delta_{gb} = 0$ only (32/504 cases, 6.3%).

For $\delta_{gb} = 0$, the average coordination traffic is 545 bytes per case, which fits within a single Ethernet MTU (1500 bytes). When inter-switch coordination is required, the average volume is 4569 bytes (3–4 frames) with 136.4 messages over 5 refinement rounds. Notably, 93.7% of cases require no inter-switch coordination beyond the initial schedule broadcast, supporting practical distributed deployment with minimal bandwidth consumption.

7. Conclusions and Future Work

This paper introduced 2PDGA to address the scalability and efficiency challenges of IEEE 802.1Qbv [24] TAS scheduling. Our extensive empirical evaluation across 1512 configurations (spanning 3 guard band values, 3 topologies, and 7 network sizes) demonstrates that combining genetic algorithm optimization in the global phase with distributed local refinement yields substantial benefits over existing methods. Specifically, 2PDGA achieves 92.9% CAP@8 compliance rate under strict 8-entry hardware constraints ($\delta_{gb} = 0$), significantly outperforming LS (82.1%), ST/BE-Ratio (85.1%), FlexTAS-Tabu (78.6%), and CG (56.5%). The algorithm exhibits robust performance across guard band variations (0–200 ns), maintaining over 80% CAP@8 compliance even under conservative timing margins. Phase II refinement improves hardware feasibility by reducing avg max-per-port GCL from 6.02 to 5.55 (−7.7%), while communication overhead remains minimal at less than one Ethernet frame per case on average. The algorithm demonstrates particular strength in complex Grid topologies, achieving 100% CAP@8 compliance where CG achieves only 38.1%. This efficiency is achieved with median latency of 42.1 μs and P99 latency of 1409.8 μs, indicating improved tail behavior relative to LS (1694.9 μs) despite a modest median-latency trade-off. These findings confirm that integrating global genetic search with distributed local refinement is a highly effective strategy for deploying large-scale, hardware-constrained TSNs in Industry 4.0 applications.

Author Contributions: Conceptualization, R.-I.C. and T.-W.H.; methodology, R.-I.C. and T.-W.H.; software, T.-W.H.; validation, R.-I.C., T.-W.H. and Y.-T.C.; formal analysis, T.-W.H.; investigation, T.-W.H.; resources, R.-I.C. and Y.-T.C.; data curation, T.-W.H.; writing—original draft preparation, T.-W.H.; writing—review and editing, R.-I.C. and Y.-T.C.; visualization, T.-W.H.; supervision, R.-I.C. and Y.-T.C.; project administration, R.-I.C.; funding acquisition, R.-I.C. and Y.-T.C. All authors have read and agreed to the published version of the manuscript.

Funding: This research received no external funding.

Institutional Review Board Statement: Not applicable.

Informed Consent Statement: Not applicable.

Data Availability Statement: The original contributions presented in this study are included in the article. Further inquiries can be directed to the corresponding authors.

Acknowledgments: During the preparation of this manuscript, the authors used AI-assisted language editing tools to improve clarity and readability. The authors reviewed and edited the content and take full responsibility for the final version of the manuscript.

Conflicts of Interest: The authors declare no conflicts of interest.

https://doi.org/10.3390/s26020377

Abbreviations

The following abbreviations are used in this manuscript:

2PDGA	Two-Phase Distributed Genetic-Based Algorithm
AVB	Audio-Video Bridging
BE	Best Effort
CAP@N	Hardware compliance rate under a per-port GCL entry cap of N
CG	Conflict Graph
CNC	Centralized Network Configuration
CP	Constraint Programming
GA	Genetic Algorithm
GCL	Gate Control List
ISNs	Industrial Sensor Networks
ILP	Integer Linear Programming
IT	Information Technology
JRS	Joint Routing and Scheduling
LCM	Least Common Multiple
LS	List Scheduling
MEC	Multi-access Edge Computing
MTU	Maximum Transmission Unit
NP	Nondeterministic Polynomial Time
NW-PSP	No-wait Packet Scheduling Problem
OT	Operational Technology
PSO	Particle Swarm Optimization
RL	Reinforcement Learning
SMT	Satisfiability Modulo Theory
SMT-NW	Satisfiability Modulo Theory No-Wait
SR	Schedulability Rate
SR-A	Stream Reservation Class A
ST	Scheduled Traffic
TAS	Time-Aware Shaper
TSN	Time-Sensitive Networking
TT	Time-Triggered

References

1. Bello, L.L.; Steiner, W. A perspective on IEEE time-sensitive networking for industrial communication and automation systems. *Proc. IEEE* **2019**, *107*, 1094–1120. [CrossRef]
2. Nasrallah, A.; Thyagaturu, A.S.; Alharbi, Z.; Wang, C.; Shao, X.; Reisslein, M.; Elbakoury, H. Performance comparison of IEEE 802.1 TSN time aware shaper (TAS) and asynchronous traffic shaper (ATS). *IEEE Access* **2019**, *7*, 44165–44181. [CrossRef]
3. Sisinni, E.; Saifullah, A.; Han, S.; Jennehag, U.; Gidlund, M. Industrial internet of things: Challenges, opportunities, and directions. *IEEE Trans. Ind. Inform.* **2018**, *14*, 4724–4734. [CrossRef]
4. Stüber, T.; Osswald, L.; Lindner, S.; Menth, M. A survey of scheduling algorithms for the time-aware shaper in time-sensitive networking (TSN). *IEEE Access* **2023**, *11*, 61192–61233. [CrossRef]
5. Zhang, T.; Wang, G.; Xue, C.; Wang, J.; Nixon, M.; Han, S. Time-Sensitive Networking (TSN) for Industrial Automation: Current Advances and Future Directions. *ACM Comput. Surv.* **2024**, *57*, 1–38. [CrossRef]
6. Oliver, R.S.; Craciunas, S.S.; Steiner, W. IEEE 802.1 Qbv gate control list synthesis using array theory encoding. In Proceedings of the 2018 IEEE Real-Time and Embedded Technology and Applications Symposium (RTAS), Porto, Portugal, 11–13 April 2018; pp. 13–24.
7. Falk, J.; Dürr, F.; Rothermel, K. Exploring practical limitations of joint routing and scheduling for TSN with ILP. In Proceedings of the 2018 IEEE 24th International Conference on Embedded and Real-Time Computing Systems and Applications (RTCSA), Hakodate, Japan, 28–31 August 2018; pp. 136–146.
8. Vlk, M.; Hanzálek, Z.; Tang, S. Constraint programming approaches to joint routing and scheduling in time-sensitive networks. *Comput. Ind. Eng.* **2021**, *157*, 107317. [CrossRef]

9. Pahlevan, M.; Tabassam, N.; Obermaisser, R. Heuristic list scheduler for time triggered traffic in time sensitive networks. *ACM Sigbed Rev.* **2019**, *16*, 15–20. [CrossRef]
10. Falk, J.; Dürr, F.; Rothermel, K. Time-triggered traffic planning for data networks with conflict graphs. In Proceedings of the 2020 IEEE Real-Time and Embedded Technology and Applications Symposium (RTAS), Sydney, Australia, 21–24 April 2020; pp. 124–136.
11. Xue, C.; Zhang, T.; Zhou, Y.; Han, S. Real-time scheduling for time-sensitive networking: A systematic review and experimental study. *arXiv* **2023**, arXiv:2305.16772.
12. Dürr, F.; Nayak, N.G. No-wait packet scheduling for IEEE time-sensitive networks (TSN). In Proceedings of the 24th International Conference on Real-Time Networks and Systems, Brest, France, 19–21 October 2016; pp. 203–212.
13. Pahlevan, M.; Obermaisser, R. Genetic algorithm for scheduling time-triggered traffic in time-sensitive networks. In Proceedings of the 2018 IEEE 23rd International Conference on Emerging Technologies and Factory Automation (ETFA), Turin, Italy, 4–7 September 2018; pp. 337–344.
14. Kim, H.-J.; Lee, K.-C.; Kim, M.-H.; Lee, S. Optimal scheduling of time-sensitive networks for automotive Ethernet based on genetic algorithm. *Electronics* **2022**, *11*, 926. [CrossRef]
15. Zheng, Z.; Wu, Q.; Lv, W.; Gao, Q.; Weng, J.; Lin, P. TSN Traffic Scheduling and Route Planning Mechanism Based on Hybrid Genetic Algorithm. In Proceedings of the International Conference on Computer Engineering and Networks, Wuxi, China, 3–5 November 2023; pp. 269–280.
16. Lin, C.-K.; Zadorozhny, V.; Krishnamurthy, P.; Park, H.-H.; Lee, C.-G. A distributed and scalable time slot allocation protocol for wireless sensor networks. *IEEE Trans. Mob. Comput.* **2010**, *10*, 505–518. [CrossRef]
17. Tootoonchian, A.; Ganjali, Y. Hyperflow: A distributed control plane for openflow. In Proceedings of the 2010 Internet Network Management Conference on Research on Enterprise Networking, San Jose, CA, USA, 27 April 2010.
18. Zhong, C.; Jia, H.; Wan, H.; Zhao, X. Drls: A deep reinforcement learning based scheduler for time-triggered ethernet. In Proceedings of the 2021 International Conference on Computer Communications and Networks (ICCCN), Athens, Greece, 19–22 July 2021; pp. 1–11.
19. Geppert, H.; Dürr, F.; Bhowmik, S.; Rothermel, K. Just a second—Scheduling thousands of time-triggered streams in large-scale networks. *Comput. Netw.* **2025**, *264*, 111244. [CrossRef]
20. Lin, J.; Li, W.; Feng, X.; Zhan, S.; Ning, L.; Wang, Y.; Wang, T.; Wan, H.; Tang, B.; Tao, X. FlexTAS: Flexible Gating Control for Enhanced Time-Sensitive Networking Deployment. *IEEE Trans. Ind. Inform.* **2025**, *21*, 5390–5400. [CrossRef]
21. Varis, P. AM6442: Help to Choose Right Interface Between CPSW-RGMII & ICSSG-RGMIIs (TI E2E Forum Post). 2021. Available online: https://e2e.ti.com/support/processors-group/processors/f/processors-forum/1287262/am6442-help-to-choose-right-interface-between-cpsw-rgmii-icssg-rgmiis (accessed on 3 January 2026).
22. Analog, D. *ADIN6310 Hardware and TSN Switch Evaluation User Guide (UG-2280 Rev.B)*; Analog Devices, Inc.: Wilmington, MA, USA, 2025.
23. Moxa, I. *Moxa Managed Switch TSN-G5000 Series User Manual (Version 2.3)*; Moxa Inc.: New Taipei City, Taiwan, 2023.
24. *IEEE Std 802.1Qbv-2015*; IEEE Standard for Local and Metropolitan Area Networks—Bridges and Bridged Networks—Amendment 25: Enhancements for Scheduled Traffic. IEEE: New York, NY, USA, 2016.

https://doi.org/10.3390/s26020377

sensors

MDPI

Article

EdgeVidCap: A Channel-Spatial Dual-Branch Lightweight Video Captioning Model for IoT Edge Cameras

Lan Guo [1], Xuyang Li [1], Jinqiang Wang [1], Jie Xiao [1], Yufeng Hou [1], Peng Zhi [1], Binbin Yong [1], Linghuey Li [2], Qingguo Zhou [1] and Kuanching Li [2,*]

[1] School of Information Science and Engineering, Lanzhou University, Lanzhou 730000, China; guol2023@lzu.edu.cn (L.G.); lxuyang2023@lzu.edu.cn (X.L.); jqwang16@lzu.edu.cn (J.W.); xiaoj2024@lzu.edu.cn (J.X.); 120220909101@lzu.edu.cn (Y.H.); zhip21@lzu.edu.cn (P.Z.); yongbb@lzu.edu.cn (B.Y.); zhouqg@lzu.edu.cn (Q.Z.)

[2] Department of Computer Science and Information Engineering, Providence University, Taichung 43301, Taiwan; s1091858@gm.pu.edu.tw

* Correspondence: kuancli@pu.edu.tw

Abstract: With the deep integration of edge computing and Internet of Things (IoT) technologies, the computational capabilities of intelligent edge cameras continue to advance, providing new opportunities for the local deployment of video understanding algorithms. However, existing video captioning models suffer from high computational complexity and large parameter counts, making them challenging to meet the real-time processing requirements of resource-constrained IoT edge devices. In this work, we propose EdgeVidCap, a lightweight video captioning model specifically designed for IoT edge cameras. Specifically, we design a hybrid module termed Synergetic Attention State Mamba (SASM) that incorporates channel attention mechanisms to enhance feature selection capabilities and leverages State Space Models (SSMs) to efficiently capture long-range spatial dependencies, achieving efficient spatiotemporal modeling of multimodal video features. In the caption generation stage, we propose an adaptive attention-guided LSTM decoder that can dynamically adjust feature weights according to video content and auto-regressively generate semantically rich and accurate textual descriptions. Comprehensive evaluations of EdgeVidCap on mainstream datasets, including MSR-VTT and MSVD are analyzed. Experimental results demonstrate that our system demonstrated enhanced precision relative to existing investigations, and our streamlined frame filtering mechanism yielded greater processing efficiency while creating more dependable descriptions following frame selection.

Keywords: edge computing; video captioning; IOT; lightweight neural networks; attention mechanism; state space models

1. Introduction

With the flourishing development of short video platforms and the explosive growth of multimedia content, automatic video captioning technology has demonstrated broad application prospects in domains such as content retrieval, accessibility, and intelligent media processing [1,2]. Video captioning aims to automatically transform video content into accurate and fluent natural language descriptions. This task requires simultaneous understanding of visual content, temporal relationships, and semantic information, making it a significant research topic at the intersection of computer vision and natural language processing [3]. In recent years, with the rapid advancement of edge computing technology and significant improvements in deep neural network performance, intelligent edge devices have been widely deployed in video processing. These intelligent cameras equipped with edge computing capabilities (hereinafter referred to as edge cameras) possess more powerful local computational resources and can achieve real-time video analysis and processing, providing new technological pathways for the practical application of video captioning technology [4,5].

Video captioning technology has evolved from template-based approaches and statistical learning methods to deep learning paradigms. Early studies primarily relied on predefined templates and rules, where objects, actions, and scenes detected in videos were used to populate language templates [6]. Subsequently, statistical machine learning methods introduced more flexible language models, but these approaches struggled to handle complex visual-language associations [7]. In the deep learning era, the research paradigm for video captioning has undergone a fundamental transformation. The CNN-RNN architecture pioneered end-to-end caption generation [8], where Convolutional Neural Networks (CNNs) extract visual features and Recurrent Neural Networks (RNNs) perform sequence decoding. However, such methods often overlook the long-term temporal dependencies within videos. To better model temporal information, researchers have proposed various improvements: the introduction of attention mechanisms enables models to dynamically focus on essential parts of a video [9]; temporal attention networks further enhance the modeling of action and event evolution [10,11]; and hierarchical attention structures facilitate multi-scale feature extraction from frame-level to segment-level [12,13]. With the breakthrough progress of Transformers across various domains [14,15], video captioning methods based on self-attention mechanisms have gradually emerged as a research hotspot. Although these approaches demonstrate superior performance in modeling long-range dependencies, Vision Transformers (ViTs) are constrained by the quadratic computational complexity of their self-attention mechanisms, rendering them difficult to deploy in real-world scenarios with limited computational resources. Existing methodologies still suffer from the following critical issues: (1) redundant video information, high model computational complexity, and lack of targeted keyframe selection strategies; (2) insufficient multimodal feature fusion, suboptimal intermodal alignment, and excessive model parameters.

To address these aforementioned challenges, we propose EdgeVidCap, a channel-spatial dual-branch lightweight video captioning model for IoT edge cameras, incorporating cross-attention mechanisms into the keyframe selection process, enabling efficient extraction of salient information from video sequences. In terms of feature representation, the model integrates miniGPT-based visual object features, deep audio features, and 3D optical flow motion features to construct comprehensive multimodal representations. During the feature fusion stage, a hybrid module termed Synergetic Attention State Mamba (SASM) is designed, which introduces channel attention mechanisms to enhance feature selection capabilities while incorporating State Space Models (SSMs) to efficiently capture long-range spatial dependencies, thereby achieving efficient spatiotemporal modeling of multimodal video features. In the caption generation phase, an adaptive attention-guided sentence decoder is proposed, which dynamically adjusts feature weights according to contextual information to generate more accurate and natural descriptive text.

Our contributions are as follows.

- To propose a keyframe guidance mechanism that achieves precise localization and extraction of critical information in video sequences through cross-attention computation.
- To design a hybrid module called Synergetic Attention State Mamba (SASM), which incorporates channel attention mechanisms to enhance feature selection capabilities

while leveraging State Space Models (SSMs) to efficiently capture long-range spatial dependencies, enabling efficient spatiotemporal modeling of multimodal video features.

- Introduce adaptive attention mechanisms to construct a sentence decoder that achieves selective focus on fused features through dynamic adjustment of feature weights at different temporal instances.

2. Related Work

The research on video captioning began with the encoder–decoder framework. Venugopalan et al. [6] first proposed an end-to-end sequence-to-sequence learning model (S2VT), which utilized CNNs to extract video frame features and employed LSTMs for sequence decoding. Building on this, Yao et al. [16] introduced 3D convolutional networks to enhance the representation of spatiotemporal features. Pan et al. [17] designed a hierarchical LSTM network to separately model the temporal structure of videos and the language generation process. Although these methods established the basic paradigm for video captioning, they often faced challenges such as difficulties in modeling long-term dependencies and insufficient utilization of features.

To address these limitations, Krishna et al. [18] proposed a dense video captioning framework that improved the description of long videos through segment-wise processing. Wang et al. [19] designed a bidirectional LSTM structure to better leverage contextual information for guiding caption generation. The introduction of attention mechanisms significantly boosted the performance of video captioning. Early works primarily focused on temporal attention, such as the hierarchical temporal attention network proposed by Yu et al. [20], which adaptively focused on essential time segments in videos. With further advancements, spatial attention also gained attention. Zhang et al. [21] developed a spatiotemporal dual-attention mechanism to achieve fine-grained visual feature extraction.

With the successful application of the Transformer architecture in computer vision, recent research has increasingly focused on transferring the capabilities of large language models to video captioning tasks. Dai et al. [22] proposed a temporal-aware Transformer structure based on visual encoders, which improved the modeling of video dynamics while maintaining efficient inference. Guo et al. [23] proposed a semantic guidance network for video captioning, which effectively improved description accuracy and generalization ability by implementing a novel scene frame sampling strategy to address visual information redundancy and scene information omission. Yang et al. [24] introduced the VideoChat model, which significantly enhanced the naturalness and accuracy of captions by fine-tuning ChatGPT with video understanding instructions. Wang et al. [25] designed the Video-LLaMA framework, injecting video understanding capabilities into the LLaMA model, thereby enabling more flexible video–text interactions.

3. Problem Definition

3.1. Task Overview

Video captioning is a challenging multimodal task that aims to generate natural language descriptions for video content automatically. Given an input video sequence, the goal is to produce a coherent and semantically accurate textual description that captures the key visual events, objects, and their temporal relationships. This task is particularly challenging for IoT edge cameras due to computational constraints and the need for real-time processing.

3.2. System Pipeline Overview

The core objective of video captioning is to summarize and reinterpret video content using natural language. Due to the significant heterogeneity between video and natural language, the data processing involved in this task is highly complex. As such, video captioning represents a major challenge in computer vision. Having established the overall workflow, we now formally define the mathematical representations: Let the training dataset be represented as $Data = \{(Vi, Ti); 1 \leq i \leq N\}$, where V_i denotes the i-th video and T_i represents its corresponding ground-truth caption. Each video V_i is decomposed into a sequence of frames: $Frame = \{fi; 1 \leq i \leq S\}$, where S represents the total number of frames. According to the approach in [26], the dataset is divided into training, testing, and validation subsets in 65%, 30%, and 5%, respectively. These subsets are constructed as follows: The training set is as follows: $Data\_train = \{(V_i, T_i); 0 < i \leq \lfloor 0.65 \times N \rfloor\}$; the testing set is as follows: $Data\_test = \{(V_i, T_i); \lfloor 0.65 \times N \rfloor + 1 \leq i \leq \lfloor 0.95 \times N \rfloor\}$; and the validation set is as follows: $Data\_val = \{(V_i, T_i); \lfloor 0.95 \times N \rfloor + 1 \leq i \leq N\}$.

During the data preprocessing stage, each video is first decomposed into S frames using the FFmpeg tool, *i.e.*, $F_i = \{f_1, f_2, \ldots, f_s\}$. Subsequently, the audio information of each video is extracted to construct an audio set $A = \{a_1, a_2, \ldots, a_n\}$. Finally, cross-attention computation is used to obtain X keyframes as the input to the model, denoted as follows: $F = \{f_1, f_2, \ldots, f_x\}$. During the encoding stage, the sampled frame set F is input into 2D-CNN and 3D-CNN models. The 2D-CNN model outputs a P-dimensional feature vector, defined as $U_d = \{ud_1, ud_2, \ldots, ud_p\}$, while the 3D-CNN model outputs a Q-dimensional feature vector, $Z_d = \{zd_1, zd_2, \ldots, zd_q\}$. The corresponding audio information extracted from video A is input into Google's pre-trained audio model VGGish [27], which extracts an R-dimensional audio feature vector, $W_d = \{wd_1, wd_2, \ldots, wd_r\}$. The final textual description generated by the model is represented as follows: $Y = \{y_1, y_2, \ldots, y_m\}$.

4. Model Construction

4.1. Model Architecture

The architecture of our proposed algorithmic model is illustrated in Figure 1. The model takes a video as input, which is first decomposed into a sequence of image frames and a single-channel audio stream using FFmpeg. Given the high similarity between adjacent video frames, directly processing the complete frame sequence incurs substantial redundant computations, resulting in prolonged processing times and the potential introduction of extraneous information. To address this, we introduce a visual span-based keyframe selection mechanism (Section 4.2), which retains only the essential keyframes to supply visual features to the model, thereby effectively reducing computational overhead. In the feature extraction stage, we employ multiple methods to derive features from different modalities: static visual features of keyframes are extracted using a 2D CNN and a pruned miniGPT architecture; spatiotemporal 3D visual features of the video are captured via the I3D network [12]; and deep audio features are obtained from the video's audio component based on Google's pre-trained VGGish model [27]. Subsequently, we construct a multimodal fusion network (Section 4.3) to integrate the 2D and 3D visual features, while concatenating the audio features extracted by VGGish. Considering the distinct representational characteristics of visual and audio temporal features, we design the Synergetic Attention State Mamba Block (Section 4.4). This module adopts a dual-branch parallel architecture to achieve synergistic optimization between channel attention mechanisms and spatial state modeling. Finally, the fused encoding vector is fed into the adaptive sentence decoding module (Section 4.5). Within this module, the adaptive attention mechanism processes the hidden states output by the LSTM at each time step, dynamically adjusting the weights assigned to encoding vectors at different moments to enhance focus on critical content across multimodal features. A word probability distribution is then generated via the Softmax function, ultimately yielding a textual description corresponding to the input video.

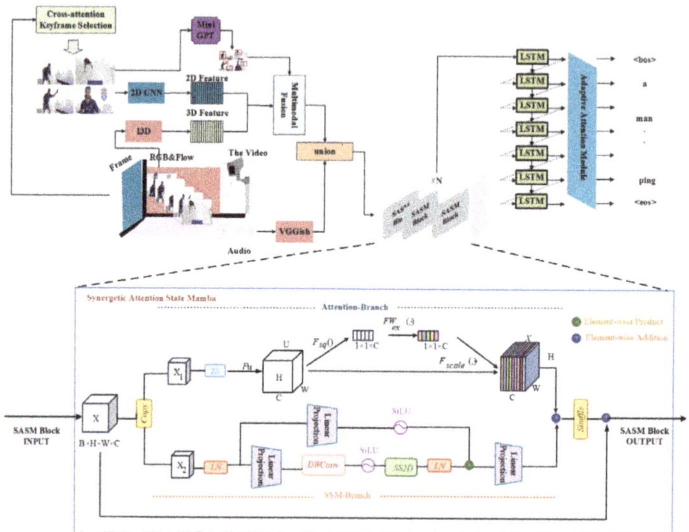

Figure 1. Channel-spatial dual-branch lightweight video description model for IoT edge cameras. Overview of the proposed algorithmic model for video description generation. The input video is decomposed into frames and audio using FFmpeg. Keyframes are selected via a visual span-based mechanism (Section 4.2) to reduce redundancy. Features are extracted using 2D CNN with pruned miniGPT for static visuals, I3D for spatiotemporal visuals, and VGGish for audio. These are fused in a multimodal network (Section 4.3), enhanced by the Synergetic Attention State Mamba Block (Section 4.4) for synergistic optimization, and decoded adaptively (Section 4.5) to produce textual descriptions.

4.2. Visual Span Video Keyframe Selection

In video content description generation tasks, processing all video frame sequences generates substantial computational redundancy, which is time-consuming and prone to producing partially extraneous information [28,29]. To mitigate these issues, we propose a novel video span keyframe selection methodology, as illustrated in Figure 2. Through the computation of attention weights between consecutive frames, scene transitions can be precisely captured [30]. When significant differences exist between two frames, the attention distribution exhibits greater dispersion; conversely, when two frames demonstrate high similarity, the attention becomes more concentrated. This mechanism facilitates the efficient identification and extraction of semantically significant frames within extended video sequences, thereby reducing computational overhead while preserving critical visual information.

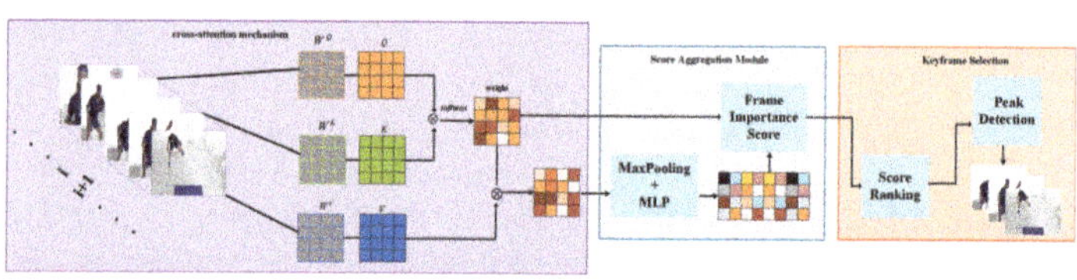

Figure 2. Visual-spanning keyframe selection. The framework processes input video sequences through attention-based mechanisms, computing attention weights between consecutive frames to precisely capture scene transitions. The architecture employs a sparse aggregation module to analyze temporal relationships: when significant differences exist between consecutive frames, the attention distribution exhibits greater dispersion, indicating potential scene transitions; conversely, when frames demonstrate high similarity, attention becomes more concentrated. Through similarity assessment, similar frames can be removed while retaining keyframes with greater differences.

The pseudocode of the algorithm is presented in Algorithm 1. Utilizing the cross-attention mechanism, the algorithm processes a given video comprising N sampled frames, denoted as $\{f_1, f_2, \ldots, f_N\}$.

Algorithm 1 Cross-attention keyframe selection

Input:

N video frames $\{I_1, I_2, \ldots, I_N\}$
Pre-trained visual model $\mathrm{Enc}(\cdot)$
Projection matrices W^Q, W^K, W^V
Threshold τ or desired number of keyframes M

Output: Keyframe set K

Steps:

For $i = 1$ to N do
$F_i \leftarrow \mathrm{Enc}(I_i)$
End for
For $i = 1$ to $N - 1$ do
$Q \leftarrow F_i W^Q$; $K \leftarrow F_{i+1} W^K$; $V \leftarrow F_{i+1} W^V$
$A_i \leftarrow \mathrm{softmax}\left(\frac{QK^T}{\sqrt{d}}\right)$
$s_i \leftarrow \mathrm{Pool}(A_i)$
$diff_i \leftarrow 1 - s_i$
end for
$K \leftarrow$ Select frames $\{I_{i+1}\}$ with $diff_i > \tau$ or top M $diff_i$
Return K

We first utilize a visual encoder to extract features from each frame, resulting in frame-level features $F_i \in \mathbb{R}^{L \times d}$, where L denotes the number of patches/tokens into which a frame is divided, and d represents the dimensionality of each token's feature vector. To evaluate scene changes, the differences between consecutive frames I_i and I_{i+1} are iteratively assessed.

In the Cross-Attention mechanism, to compute the attention distribution between frames I_i and I_{i+1}, we treat I_i as the Query (Q), and I_{i+1} as the Key (K) and Value (V). By applying learnable linear projection matrices W^Q, W^K, and W^V, the original features are mapped into the attention subspace, as formulated in Equation (1):

$$Q = F_i W^Q, \; K = F_{i+1} W^K, \; V = F_{i+1} W^V \tag{1}$$

The dimensions of Q, K, V are all $\mathbb{R}^{L \times d}$, matching the dimensions of the original features while incorporating a new learnable parameter space. Given Q and K, the attention weight matrix A_i can be computed as in Equation (2).

$$A_i = \mathrm{softmax}\left(\frac{QK^T}{\sqrt{d}}\right) \in \mathbb{R}^{L \times L} \tag{2}$$

Each element $A_i(p, q)$ of the matrix represents the association between the token and the qth token in the ith pair of frames. The use of the softmax operation ensures that the sum of attention weights for each row equals 1.

In the video keyframe selection task, our focus lies in the overall frame-level difference rather than the detailed output at the token level. To this end, an aggregation operation can be applied to the attention matrix A_i to derive a scalar representing the inter-frame similarity S_i. One of the most commonly used methods is to compute either the mean or the maximum value of the elements in A_i, as in Equation (3).

$$S_i = \mathrm{Pool}(A_i) \tag{3}$$

Here, Pool represents a pooling operator, such as average or max pooling. A larger S_i indicates a closer similarity between the two frames, whereas a smaller S_i reflects a more substantial content difference between the frames. As highlighted in this investigation, to emphasize the identification of keyframes with "the greatest changes", we define the difference function as depicted in Equation (4).

$$diff_i = 1 - S_i \tag{4}$$

The difference function d_i intuitively reflects the "magnitude of change" between frame I_i and frame I_{i+1}. When d_i takes a relatively large value (i.e., when similarity is very low), it indicates a significant visual transition at position i, often corresponding to a new scene or action turning point.

To select keyframes that best represent significant content changes, the difference sequence $\{d_1, d_2, \ldots, d_{N-1}\}$ can be sorted, or the values can be compared to a threshold τ. Frames with the highest scores or those exceeding the threshold are selected for further consideration. When τ is set as a reference threshold for identifying peaks of change in a video, the final keyframe set K is represented as in Equation (5).

$$K = \{I_{i+1} \mid diff_i > \tau\} \tag{5}$$

Here, K serves as the final set of selected keyframes, capturing the most significant scene changes.

We consider the relationships among all tokens within frames, rather than merely conducting comparisons at corresponding positions, which enables the capture of complex spatial variations. Through aggregation operations on the attention matrix A_i, the analysis can be elevated from token-level granular changes to frame-level holistic differences, thereby providing a more comprehensive understanding of temporal dynamics within the video sequence.

4.3. Multimodal Attention Fusion

A video is composed of a series of scenes or segments organized sequentially over time, and semantic relationships exist between these scenes or segment sequences. Specifically, the current segment may depend on information conveyed by the previous segment, or it may be highly correlated with subsequent segments. This reflects the interdependence of video segments and their contextual relationships [31–33]. In real-world scenarios, different types of representational information exhibit strong complementarity. Leveraging multi-source information can effectively uncover latent signals, offering both consistency and complementarity from various perspectives. Consistency refers to shared, common information, while complementarity represents independent or mutually exclusive types of information [34,35]. Therefore, we extract its 2D CNN features $\phi(V)$ using the ResNet152 network and its 3D CNN features $\psi(V)$ using the I3D network. Using the Self-Attention Embedding module, we capture the representational information of each individual modality, obtaining the single-modality feature representations F^{2D} and F^{3D} enhanced by Self-Attention. Since F^{2D} and F^{3D} are derived from the Self-Attention Embedding module, they inherently incorporate the contextual information of their respective modalities. To integrate these two types of visual representational information, we propose a dual-modality attention fusion mechanism. The structure of the proposed network is illustrated in Figure 3.

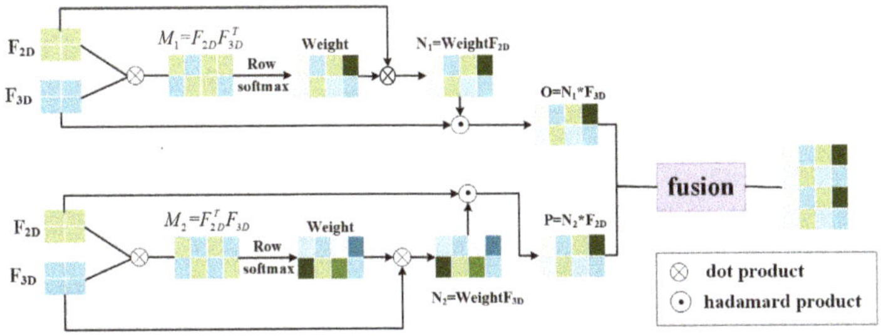

Figure 3. Multimodal attention fusion. The network architecture demonstrates our proposed dual-modality attention fusion mechanism designed to integrate 2D and 3D visual representational information. The architecture processes two input feature streams: F2D (2D CNN features extracted using ResNet152) and F3D (3D CNN features extracted using I3D network), both enhanced by the Self-Attention Embedding module. The fusion process employs attention weight computation through matrix operations, followed by row-wise softmax normalization to generate attention distributions. The mechanism utilizes both dot product and Hadamard product operations to capture different types of feature interactions between the two modalities. The final fused representation combines the contextual information from both 2D spatial features and 3D spatiotemporal features.

To achieve dual-modality fusion, we begin by calculating a pair of matching matrices M_1 and $M_2 \in \mathbb{R}^{u \times u}$ on the two single-modality representations to capture their interaction information. The matching matrices are computed as shown in Equation (6).

$$\begin{aligned} M_1 &= F_{2D} F_{3D}^T \\ M_2 &= F_{2D}^T F_{3D} \end{aligned} \tag{6}$$

Secondly, the attention distribution weights, denoted as *Weight*, are calculated for the matching matrices using the softmax function, as shown in Equation (7). *Weight* represents the correlation between the 2D CNN and 3D CNN features extracted from the video. A higher weight value indicates stronger interactions between different visual features, underscoring the significance of the fused information.

$$Weight = \text{softmax}(M) \tag{7}$$

Subsequently, the attention distribution weights *Weight* are multiplied with the single-modality feature matrices to obtain the final attention representation matrices N_1 and N_2, as defined in Equation (8).

$$\begin{aligned} N_1 &= Weight \cdot F_{2D} \\ N_2 &= Weight \cdot F_{3D} \end{aligned} \tag{8}$$

Finally, a multiplicative gating mechanism is employed to perform element-wise multiplication between the attention representation and the other single-modality representation, resulting in the intermodality attention matrices O and P, as defined in Equation (9). The matrices O and P are then combined to form the dual-modality attention fusion feature F_{Att}, as described in Equation (10).

$$\begin{aligned} O &= N_1 * F_{3D} \\ P &= N_2 * F_{2D} \end{aligned} \tag{9}$$

$$F_{\text{Att}} = \text{Concat}(O, P) \tag{10}$$

4.4. Synergetic Attention State Mamba

4.4.1. Preliminary

Recently developed SSM architectural models [36–38], including Structured State Space Sequence Models (S4) and Mamba, establish their core mechanisms upon the theoretical foundations of traditional continuous systems. The operational principle of such systems involves utilizing an intermediate latent state variable $h(t) \in \mathbb{R}^N$ as a bridge to achieve effective transformation from one-dimensional input functions or sequences $x(t) \in \mathbb{R}$ to corresponding outputs $y(t) \in \mathbb{R}$, as described in Equations (11) and (12). This aforementioned process can be mathematically represented as a linear Ordinary Differential Equation (ODE).

$$h'(t) = Ah(t) + Bx(t) \tag{11}$$

$$y(t) = Ch(t) \tag{12}$$

where $A \in \mathbb{R}^{N\times N}$ represents the state matrix, while $B \in \mathbb{R}^{N\times 1}$ and $C \in \mathbb{R}^{N\times 1}$ denote the projection parameters.

Given the inherent characteristics of deep neural networks in processing discrete sequence data, continuous-time systems must undergo appropriate numerical discretization processes. Based on the Zero-Order Hold approximation, matrix exponential functions are employed for precise discretization transformation, which is defined following Equations (13) and (14).

$$\bar{A} = \exp(\Delta A) \tag{13}$$

$$\bar{B} = (\Delta A)^{-1}(\exp(\Delta A) - \mathbf{I}) \cdot \Delta B \tag{14}$$

where the discretization time step Δ serves as a critical hyperparameter that directly influences the fidelity of system dynamics characteristics. The discretized state space equation is subsequently transformed into the following recurrence relation.

$$\begin{aligned} h_k &= \bar{A}h_{k-1} + \bar{B}x_k \\ y_k &= Ch_k \end{aligned} \tag{15}$$

Notably, modern SSM architectures achieve equivalent transformation between recursive and convolution computation through ingenious mathematical transformations. Specifically, the system's impulse response can be represented as a structured convolution kernel.

$$K = \left(C\bar{B}, C\bar{A}\bar{B}, \ldots, C\bar{A}^{L-1}\bar{B}\right) \tag{16}$$

4.4.2. SASM Block

Recent related studies have validated the exceptional performance of Mamba architecture across multiple critical application domains. Yang et al. proposed the SMamba framework [39], which effectively addresses real-time challenges in event-driven object detection through the introduction of sparsification mechanisms, providing novel technical pathways for high-frequency visual processing tasks. In the neuroimaging domain, Kannan et al. designed the BrainMT hybrid architecture [40] that ingeniously integrates Mamba's sequential modeling advantages with Transformer's attention mechanisms, successfully achieving precise modeling of long-range spatiotemporal dependencies in functional magnetic resonance imaging data. Xiao et al. constructed a frequency domain-enhanced Mamba model [41] that demonstrates significant performance improvements in remote sensing image super-resolution reconstruction tasks, providing compelling evidence for the effectiveness of combining frequency domain prior knowledge with State Space Models. Cui et al. proposed the MGCM framework [42] that achieves breakthrough progress in cancer prognosis analysis through deep integration of multimodal graph convolution with Mamba architecture.

Although the aforementioned studies demonstrate that SSMs achieve efficient long-sequence modeling through their elegant mathematical formulation, their fixed linear transformation mechanism constrains the model's adaptive processing capabilities for input features. In video content understanding scenarios, different visual feature channels carry heterogeneous semantic information. For instance, specific channels may focus on capturing object details, while others are more oriented toward scene layout or motion patterns. Traditional SSMs lack the perceptual capability for such feature heterogeneity, rendering them unable to achieve dynamic feature selection and weight allocation, thereby limiting their performance potential in complex visual tasks. Based on this observation, we propose the Synergetic Attention State Mamba (SASM) module, which achieves synergetic optimization of channel attention and spatial state modeling through a dual-branch parallel architecture. The pseudocode of the algorithm is presented in Algorithm 2.

Algorithm 2 Synergetic Attention State Mamba Block

Input:
Input tensor $X \in \mathbb{R}^{B \times C \times N}$ // Batch size B, Channels C, Sequence length N
Output: Output tensor $Y \in \mathbb{R}^{B \times C \times N}$
Steps:
// Step 1: Input Normalization
$X_{\text{norm}} \leftarrow \text{LayerNorm}(X)$
// Step 2: Attention Branch
$\text{Att} \leftarrow \text{Attention}(X_{\text{norm}})$ // Multi-head attention or similar
FC1_out ← FC1(Att) // Fully connected layer 1
GELU_out ← GELU(FC1_out) // GELU activation
FC2_out ← FC2(GELU_out) // Fully connected layer 2
$F_{\text{att}} \leftarrow$ AddNorm(FC2_out + Att) // Residual connection with normalization
// Step 3: State Branch (SSM-based)
SSM_out ← SSM(X_{norm}) // State Space Model (e.g., Mamba SSM)
LN_out ← LayerNorm(SSM_out)
$F_{\text{ssm}} \leftarrow$ FC(LN_out) // Fully connected layer
// Step 4: Synergetic Fusion
Prod ← ElementWiseProduct($F_{\text{att}}, F_{\text{ssm}}$) // Channel-wise multiplication for synergy
// Step 5: Output with Residual
$Y \leftarrow \text{Prod} + X$ // Add input residual for stability
Return Y

As illustrated in Figure 4, the SASM module receives input features $X \in \mathbb{R}^{B \times H \times W \times C}$ and simultaneously feeds them into the Attention-Branch and SSM-Branch for parallel processing. The Attention-Branch focuses on channel-level feature importance modeling, initially compressing the spatial dimensions through a global average pooling operation $F_{\text{sq}}(\cdot)$, which aggregates the spatial information of each channel into a single global descriptor.

$$z = F_{\text{sq}}(X) = \frac{1}{H \times W} \sum_{i=1}^{H} \sum_{j=1}^{W} X_{i,j} \in \mathbb{R}^{B \times 1 \times 1 \times C} \tag{17}$$

This global pooling strategy can effectively capture the statistical characteristics of each channel across the entire spatial domain, providing compact yet information-rich feature representations for subsequent channel importance assessment. Subsequently, a bottleneck structure is constructed through two-layer linear projections, incorporating SiLU activation functions to learn complex nonlinear dependencies among channels.

$$A = F_{\text{scale}}(F_{\text{sq}}(X)) = \sigma(W_2 \cdot \text{SiLU}(W_1 \cdot z)) \tag{18}$$

where $W_1 \in \mathbb{R}^{C/r \times C}$, $W_2 \in \mathbb{R}^{C \times C/r}$, and r represents the compression ratio. The first linear projection reduces parameter count and enhances generalization capability through dimensionality reduction operations (setting $r = 16$), while the SiLU activation function exhibits superior gradient flow characteristics and nonlinear expression capabilities compared to conventional ReLU. The second projection layer restores the feature dimensionality to the original channel count, ultimately constraining the output values within the $[0, 1]$ range through the Sigmoid activation function $\sigma(\cdot)$, thereby generating normalized channel attention weights. This approach not only effectively controls model complexity but also facilitates the network's learning of more robust and semantically rich inter-channel relational representations by introducing a moderate information bottleneck, thus achieving precise quantification and dynamic adjustment of feature importance across different channels.

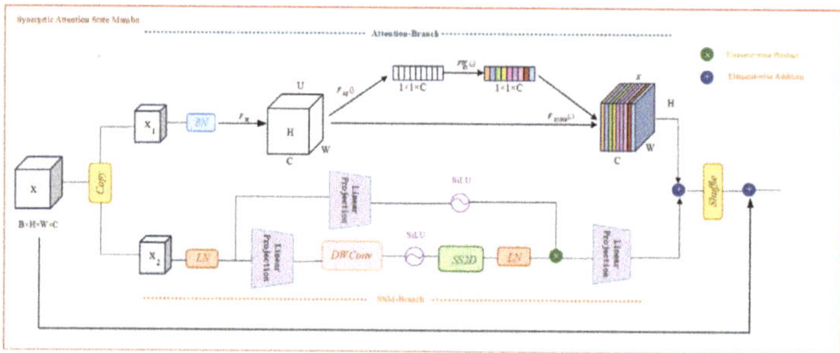

Figure 4. Synergetic Attention State Mamba block. This demonstrates the proposed Synergetic Attention State Mamba (SASM) module, which adopts a dual-branch parallel architecture to achieve synergetic optimization of channel attention and spatial state modeling. Unlike traditional SSMs with fixed linear transformation mechanisms, the SASM module integrates dynamic feature selection and weight allocation capabilities to handle heterogeneous semantic information across different visual feature channels.

The SSM-Branch focuses on efficient modeling of spatial long-range dependencies. Input features first undergo layer normalization (LN) for feature standardization, an operation that stabilizes the training process and alleviates gradient vanishing problems, ensuring numerical stability for subsequent state space modeling. The normalized features are then subjected to linear projection for feature transformation, mapping the input features to a representation space suitable for state space processing.

$$X_{\text{proj}} = \text{Linear}(\text{LN}(X)) \tag{19}$$

Subsequently, the local spatial receptive field is enhanced through depthwise separable convolution (DWConv):

$$X_{\text{local}} = \text{DWConv}(X_{\text{proj}}) \tag{20}$$

Depthwise separable convolution exhibits lower computational complexity compared to standard convolution while effectively capturing local spatial patterns, providing rich local contextual information for subsequent global state space modeling. This local–global hierarchical modeling strategy ensures that the model can perceive fine-grained spatial details while establishing long-range spatial dependencies. Subsequently, the transformed features are fed into the two-dimensional state space module (SS2D) for long-range spatial dependency modeling:

$$X_{\text{spatial}} = \text{SS2D}(X_{\text{local}}) \tag{21}$$

SS2D captures inter-frame temporal dependencies while inheriting the linear complexity of S6, which is crucial for generating accurate and coherent video captions. SS2D comprises three components: the Temporal Scanning and Merging operation (TSM), the visual S6 block, and the feature fusion operation. Figure 5 intuitively illustrates the internal mechanism of SS2D in video caption generation. Specifically, the temporal scanning and merging operation initially unfolds the video frame sequence into visual feature streams along four distinct directions (forward temporal, backward temporal, intra-scene keyframes, and scene transition points). Subsequently, the visual S6 block processes all sequences to extract spatiotemporal features, ensuring comprehensive capture of dynamic changes and scene information within the video content. Finally, the feature fusion operation integrates the output features from the four directions, constructing rich visual-semantic representations to generate accurate caption descriptions that are highly aligned with the video's visual content.

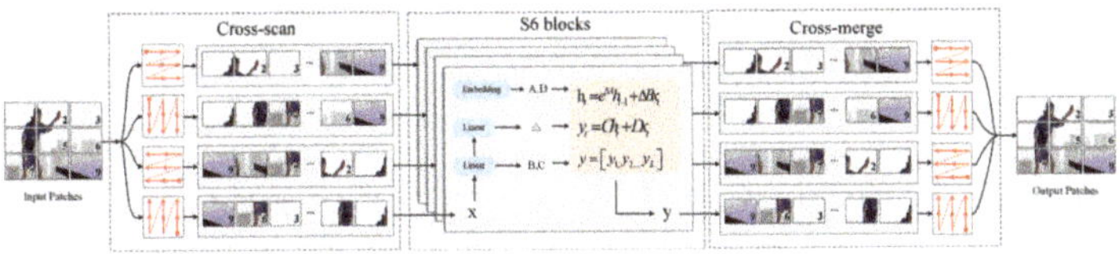

Figure 5. The internal modeling process of SS2D. This demonstrates the internal modeling process of the SS2D (two-dimensional state space) module, which extends traditional one-dimensional State Space Models to two-dimensional space to effectively capture long-range dependencies across spatial domains. The architecture demonstrates the cross-scan mechanism that processes input video frames in multiple directions, followed by S6 blocks that maintain recursive updates of hidden states in both horizontal and vertical directions. The process includes cross-merge operations that integrate features from different scanning directions. Unlike self-attention mechanisms with quadratic complexity O((HW)²), the SS2D design achieves linear time complexity O(HW), significantly reducing computational overhead and making it particularly suitable for rapid processing of large batches of video frames.

The SS2D module (Figure 5) represents an extension of traditional one-dimensional State Space Models to two-dimensional space, which effectively captures long-range dependencies across the entire spatial domain with linear time complexity $O(\text{HW})$ by maintaining recursive updates of hidden states in both horizontal and vertical directions. Compared to the quadratic complexity $O((\text{HW})^2)$ of self-attention mechanisms, this design significantly reduces computational overhead, making it particularly suitable for processing high-resolution video frames. The collaborative fusion mechanism achieves feature integration of the two branches through element-wise multiplication operations.

$$\mathbf{X}_{proj} = \text{Linear}(\text{LN}(\mathbf{X})) \tag{22}$$

where $\odot$ denotes the element-wise multiplication operation. This fusion strategy enables attention weights A to perform dynamic weighting of spatial features from the SSM-Branch along the channel dimension, achieving channel-sensitive spatial feature selection. Specifically, spatial features of important channels are amplified while contributions from redundant channels are suppressed, thereby enhancing the discriminative capability and semantic consistency of the overall feature representation. This gating mechanism effectively combines the selectivity of attention with the temporal modeling capability of State Space Models, achieving complementary advantages.

4.5. Adaptive Attention Module

The Adaptive Attention Module serves as the core component connecting multimodal video features with text generation in our video captioning framework. During the caption generation process, this module dynamically computes attention weights between the LSTM decoder's hidden states and the fused multimodal features F^{fused}, enabling context-aware text generation that adaptively focuses on relevant visual content at each decoding step. During the network decoding stage, an adaptive attention mechanism [43] is incorporated to extract attention-enhanced weights e_t by combining the attention-fused visual features F with the hidden state outputs h_t of the parallel LSTM decoder [44] at each time step. This mechanism adaptively adjusts the correlation ratio between the multimodal semantic hidden information g_t and the adaptive attention outputs e_t, focusing more effectively on the key contents of the multimodal representations encoded by the mul-feature. The adaptive attention computation process is as follows:

First, the enhanced information for the adaptive attention mechanism is calculated using Equations (23)–(25), providing attention information under the fusion mode for the adaptive attention module.

$$z_t = W_z^T \tanh\left(W_v F + (W_h h_t)\mathbf{1}^T\right) \tag{23}$$

$$\alpha_t = \text{softmax}(z_t) \tag{24}$$

$$e_t = \sum^{k} \alpha_{ti} f'_{ti} \tag{25}$$

At this point, $h_t \in \mathbb{R}^m$, $W_z \in \mathbb{R}^k$, $W_v \in \mathbb{R}^{k\times m}$, and $W_h \in \mathbb{R}^{k\times m}$ represent the weight parameters, and F denotes the output feature vector from the modality attention fusion. To ensure dimensional alignment during matrix addition in Equation (23), 1^T is employed for dimension adjustment; $1^T \in \mathbb{R}^k$, where α_{t_i} is a vector with all elements equal to 1; $\alpha_t \in \mathbb{R}^k$; and f'_{t_i} represents the ith feature of the dual-modality fused attention at time step t.

Secondly, the visual sentinel module λ_t in Equation (26) adaptively regulates the output r_t of the attention mechanism. During the adaptive regulation process, the determination of r_t depends on whether it is more influenced by the information e_t, reinforced through adaptive attention, or by the hidden information g_t captured based on dual-modality fused attention.

$$r_t = \lambda_t g_t + (1-\lambda_t)e_t \tag{26}$$

The computation of the visual sentinel λ_t is defined in Equation (27).

$$\lambda_t = \text{softmax}(\{z_i; \hat{z}_i\})[k+1] \tag{27}$$

Here, λ_t is obtained from the last element of the output result of the softmax function, while $\hat{z}_i$ is derived from the fusion of the multimodal fused hidden information h_t and the visual fused hidden information g_t.

Unlike static attention that treats all decoding steps uniformly, our adaptive attention considers the semantic evolution of the generated text sequence $w_1, w_2, \ldots, w_{t-1}$ to determine which visual aspects are most relevant for predicting the next word w_t. This is achieved by conditioning the attention computation on the decoder's hidden state h_t, which encodes the contextual information from previously generated words.

5. Experimental Analysis

5.1. Experimental Platform

The hardware configuration for our study involves training the model initially on a cloud server equipped with an Intel(R) Xeon(R) Gold 5118 CPU @ 2.30 GHz and an NVIDIA Tesla V100 GPU, followed by deployment of the final model to an edge camera utilizing the NVIDIA Jetson TX2 for evaluating runtime speed and performance. It has a dual-core Denver 2 64-bit CPU and a quad-core ARM A57 Complex graphics processor architecture with 256 CUDA cores for parallel computing and a Pascal graphics acceleration architecture.

In addition, the CPUs and the graphics processor share 8 GB of RAM. For model assessment, we employed the MSR-VTT and MSVD datasets, each comprising videos paired with their corresponding human-annotated descriptive sentences (ground truth). In terms of evaluation metrics, this work adopts the Bilingual Evaluation Understudy (BLEU) [45], the recall-oriented understudy for the evaluation of the girth with the longest common sequence (ROUGE-L) [46], the metric for the evaluation of translation with explicit ordering (METEOR) [47], and the Consensus-based Image Description Evaluation (CIDEr) [48]. The training platform and the experimental runtime environment for the model are given in Table 1.

Table 1. Experimental platform and environment configuration

Experimental Platform	Environment Configuration
RAM	128 GB
CPU	Intel(R) Xeon(R) Gold 5118 CPU @ 2.30 GHz (Intel Corporation, Santa Clara, CA, USA)
GPU_Memory	32 GB
GPU	NVIDIA Tesla V100 (NVIDIA Corporation, Santa Clara, CA, USA)
Driver	NVIDIA CUDA 11.0
Deep Learning Acceleration Library	cuDNN-V8.0.5
Deep Learning Framework	PyTorch 1.6
Inference device	NVIDIA Jetson TX2 (NVIDIA Corporation, Santa Clara, CA, USA)

5.2. Data Preprocessing

The proposed model utilizes the MSVD [49] and MSR-VTT [26] datasets. First, the extracted video frames are formatted and resized to 224 × 224 pixels. Then, 2D CNN features for each frame are extracted using the ResNet model, which incorporates channel attention. Additionally, 3D CNN features for the videos are extracted using the I3D pre-trained model, integrating optical flow and 3D spatial information. Finally, audio features corresponding to each video are extracted. The audio features are obtained using VGGish, a large-scale pre-trained model proposed by Google's Speech Understanding team. VGGish is trained on the extensive AudioSet dataset [10], offering strong generalization capabilities. For the textual descriptions in the datasets, the following steps are performed: First, sentences are tokenized using the Stanford NLP Toolkit, then truncated to 20 words, with punctuation removed and all words converted to lowercase. Next, the descriptions are tokenized, and all vocabularies are aggregated. A word frequency threshold is set to five, with words exceeding the threshold included in the vocabulary, while low-frequency words are excluded. Special tokens such as "<bos>", "<eos>", "<pad>", and "<nan>" are added to the vocabulary. Finally, the generated vocabulary is numerically indexed, and each textual description is vectorized into a format suitable for computation.

5.3. Experimental Parameter Settings

In the Self-Attention Embedding layer, the pooling kernel size is set to 3 × 3, and the output dimensions of the adaptive attention mechanism and other network components are all set to 1024.

During the model training, the Adam optimizer is utilized, and the batch size is set to 64. The initial learning rate is set to 0.0001, and it decays by a factor of 0.1 if the evaluation score on the validation set does not improve for 20 epochs after every 100 iterations. Gradient clipping is applied during backpropagation to prevent gradient explosion during training. During the description generation phase, the Dropout technique is employed, with a dropout rate of 0.5 to prune neurons in the network model. This approach reduces the interdependence among neurons in the video content description model, improving the generalization capability of the model while preventing overfitting.

5.4. Analysis of Experimental Results

To validate the effectiveness of the proposed video content description generation model, a comparative analysis was conducted against state-of-the-art models, including OA-BTG, POS + VCT, ORG-TRL (IRV2 + C3D), and SGN. The evaluation metrics used for comparison include BLEU, ROUGE, METEOR, and CIDEr. The detailed qualitative results are presented in Tables 2 and 3, while the quantitative results are illustrated in Figure 6.

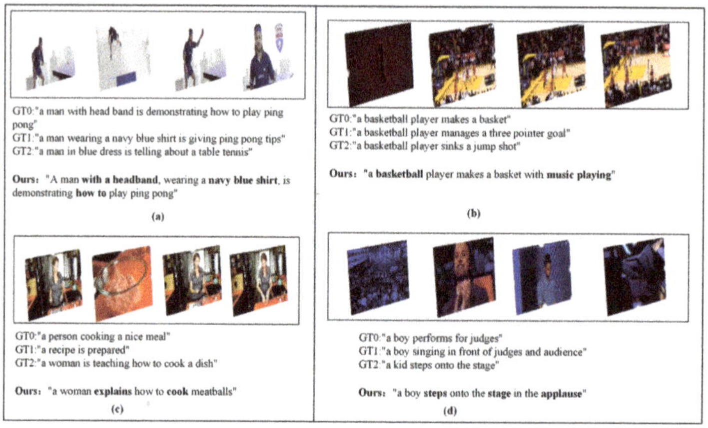

Figure 6. Test examples of the model. This demonstrates representative test examples of the model across different video content scenarios. Each example (**a–d**) displays sequential video frames, accompanied by multiple ground truth (GT) descriptions and the descriptions generated by the model for the videos. The comparison between ground truth annotations and model outputs demonstrates the system's capability to generate contextually appropriate and semantically accurate video descriptions across different domains and activity types.

Table 2. Comparative experiments of models on the MSVD dataset.

Model	BLEU-4	METEOR	ROUGEL	CIDEr
OA-BTG [21]	45.8	33.3	-	73.0
POS+VCT [50]	52.8	36.1	71.8	87.8
ORG-TRL (IRV2 + C3D) [51]	54.3	36.4	73.9	95.2
SGN [52]	52.8	35.5	72.9	94.3
TextKG [53]	60.8	38.5	75.1	105.2
MAN [54]	60.1	37.1	74.6	101.9
VIT/L14 [55]	60.1	41.4	78.2	121.5
GSEN [56]	58.8	37.6	75.2	102.5
STLF [57]	60.9	40.8	77.5	110.9
ours	**61.6**	**42.7**	**96.1**	**123.9**

From the perspective of the short video description generation task, although the MSVD dataset features shorter video durations and relatively simpler scenes, it still places high demands on the model's ability to generate accurate descriptions and capture core actions or scene elements. As shown in Table 2, the proposed model ("ours") achieves the highest or near-highest scores across BLEU-4, METEOR, ROUGE-L, and CIDEr metrics, surpassing advanced methods such as ViT/L14 and ORG-TRL. Notably, "ours" demonstrates a significant advantage in metrics like METEOR and CIDEr, which emphasize semantic and content matching more. This indicates the model's superior ability to comprehend video actions and semantic information, enabling precise descriptions of key content. Further comparisons reveal that compared to alternative methods requiring complex features or external knowledge augmentation; "ours" exhibits robust performance improvements under identical or similar feature conditions, suggesting that the multimodal feature fusion and temporal-context modeling strategies employed in "ours" effectively enhance the capture of core actions, events, and semantic information within short video scenarios.

Table 3. Comparative experiments of models on the MSR-VTT dataset.

Model	BLEU-4	METEOR	fROUGEL	CIDEr
OA-BTG [21]	41.4	28.2	-	46.9
POS+VCT [50]	42.3	29.7	62.0	49.1
ORG-TRL (IRV2 + C3D) [51]	43.6	28.8	62.1	50.9
SGN [52]	40.8	28.3	60.8	49.5
TextKG [53]	43.7	29.6	62.4	52.4
MAN [54]	42.5	28.6	62.2	50.4
VIT/L14 [55]	44.4	30.3	63.4	57.2
GSEN [56]	42.9	28.4	61.7	51.0
STLF [57]	**47.5**	30.3	63.8	54.1
ours	45.1	**30.6**	**63.8**	**58.6**

The MSR-VTT dataset encompasses more diverse scenes and multimodal information, with longer video durations and more complex content, imposing greater demands on a model's ability to integrate temporal modeling, action recognition, scene understanding, and language generation. As shown in Table 3, the proposed "ours" model also achieves top-tier or leading results across BLEU-4, METEOR, ROUGE-L, and CIDEr metrics. Particularly for BLEU-4 and CIDEr, where performance differences indicate a model's ability to capture critical semantic words and video attributes, "ours" outperforms other prominent methods, demonstrating its superiority in temporal dependency modeling and visual–semantic alignment. Compared to methods also reliant on visual features or knowledge graphs (e.g., ViT/L14, TextKG and STLF), the proposed model achieves more effective cross-modal information flow by improving multimodal feature fusion, temporal clue extraction, and language decoding strategies. It balances the diversity of video content with the accuracy of language expression during the generation process.

To validate the applicability and effectiveness of our proposed model in practical IoT edge computing environments, we deployed the trained model on edge devices for inference testing to evaluate its actual performance under resource-constrained conditions. Based on the performance comparison presented in Table 4, our proposed model demonstrates superior efficiency on the edge device platform (NVIDIA Jetson TX2) compared to existing state-of-the-art approaches. Specifically, our model achieves the lowest memory footprint of 2.97 GB, representing a reduction of 7.2% and 4.2% compared to Gated-ViGAT (3.2 GB) and SLSMedvc (3.1 GB), respectively. More importantly, our approach exhibits the fastest inference time of 0.3000 seconds, outperforming both Gated-ViGAT (0.3483 s) and SLSMedvc (0.3090 s) by 13.9% and 2.9%, respectively.

Table 4. Performance comparison of models on edge device NVIDIA Jetson TX2.

Model	Memory Usage	Inference Time(s)
Gated-ViGAT	3.2 GB	0.3483
SLSMedvc	3.1 GB	0.3090
ours	**2.97 GB**	**0.3000**

These improvements are particularly significant for edge deployment scenarios where computational resources are constrained and real-time processing is critical. Compared to Vision Transformer-based works, our Mamba-based architecture demonstrates superior computational efficiency and resource utilization on edge devices. While ViT architectures face significant computational and memory bottlenecks when processing long sequences due to their quadratic complexity in self-attention mechanisms, our Mamba-based approach effectively mitigates this issue through linear complexity state space modeling. The synergistic optimization achieved through our Synergetic Attention State Mamba Block not only maintains strong representational capabilities but also significantly reduces computational overhead, making it exceptionally well-suited for practical edge computing applications in video understanding tasks.

To comprehensively evaluate the performance of the proposed model, we implemented multiple network structure versions within the same experimental environment. These versions integrated different functional modules, including support for multimodal data, uniform frame sampling strategies, cross-attention frame selection mechanisms, miniGPT-based visual localization, and adaptive attention mechanisms. By conducting ablation experiments on the same dataset, we could independently examine each module's contribution to the overall performance and its impact on the quality of video descriptions. As depicted in Tables 5 and 6, experimental results demonstrate the performance of each module across various evaluation metrics, providing strong evidence for informed decisions in subsequent model selection and optimization.

Table 5. Ablation study of the model on the MSVD dataset.

Multimodal Features	Uniform Frame Sampling	Cross-Attention Frame Selection	miniGPT Visual Localization	Adaptive Attention	SASM	BLEU-4	METEOR	ROUGEL	CIDEr
✓	✓					58.1	40.3	93.7	115.4
✓		✓				59.2	41.0	94.1	118.3
✓	✓		✓			58.6	41.4	93.8	118.6
✓		✓	✓			60.2	41.7	95.2	120.8
✓	✓			✓		59.9	41.2	95.1	120.5
✓		✓		✓		60.5	41.8	95.4	121.3
✓	✓		✓	✓		61.1	42.2	95.7	121.6
✓			✓		✓	60.0	41.6	94.8	120.2
✓	✓	✓	✓		✓	60.9	42.1	95.5	122.4
✓	✓	✓	✓	✓	✓	**61.6**	**42.7**	**96.1**	**123.9**

Table 6. Ablation study of the nodel on the MSR-VTT dataset.

Multimodal Features	Uniform Frame Sampling	Cross-Attention Frame Selection	miniGPT Visual Localization	Adaptive Attention	SASM	BLEU-4	METEOR	ROUGEL	CIDEr
✓	✓					39.2	27.8	60.1	52.7
✓		✓				40.3	28.1	60.7	53.5
✓	✓		✓			39.5	27.9	60.0	54.3
✓		✓	✓			42.3	28.7	61.2	55.1
✓	✓			✓		42.0	29.1	60.4	55.8
✓		✓		✓		44.1	29.8	63.1	57.4
✓	✓		✓	✓		44.6	30.1	63.0	58.2
✓			✓		✓	41.8	29.0	61.8	55.7
✓	✓	✓	✓		✓	43.9	29.8	62.9	57.3
✓	✓	✓	✓	✓	✓	**45.1**	**30.6**	**63.8**	**58.6**

Component Contribution Analysis: The ablation study results demonstrate that the contribution of each component to model performance exhibits a distinct progressive pattern. The miniGPT method based on large-scale pre-trained language models outperforms traditional cross-attention mechanisms on both benchmark datasets (MSVD: BLEU-4 59.2 vs. 58.1; MSR-VTT: BLEU-4 40.3 vs. 39.2), fully demonstrating the inherent advantages of large-scale pre-trained language models. The combination of the visual localization frame selection strategy with the miniGPT framework produces significant synergistic effects (MSR-VTT: BLEU-4 improvement from 40.3 to 42.3), while the introduction of adaptive attention mechanisms further enhances model performance, particularly when combined with the miniGPT architecture (9.4% BLEU-4 improvement on MSR-VTT). Although the multi-component collaborative configuration already exhibits superior performance, the final integration of the proposed SASM module achieves optimal performance across all evaluation metrics, reaching BLEU-4 61.6 and CIDEr 123.9 on the MSVD dataset, and BLEU-4 45.1 and ROUGE-L 63.8 on MSR-VTT. That is, these results confirm the existence of significant positive synergistic effects among the proposed components.

Cross-Dataset Performance Analysis: The experimental results on two benchmark datasets reveal the adaptive characteristics of the proposed model in processing video content of different complexities. The model's overall performance on the MSVD dataset significantly exceeds that on MSR-VTT (baseline configuration BLEU-4: 58.1 vs. 39.2), reflecting the inherent differences in video–text alignment difficulty between the two datasets. Notably, advanced components demonstrate a greater relative contribution on MSR-VTT, the more challenging dataset. For instance, the combination of adaptive attention mechanism with miniGPT achieves a 9.4% BLEU-4 improvement on MSR-VTT compared to only 2.2% on MSVD, indicating that complex datasets better highlight the technical value of advanced components. Notably, the proposed SASM component under simplified configuration shows remarkable performance enhancement on MSR-VTT (3.7% BLEU-4 improvement compared to baseline miniGPT), further validating its superior capability in handling complex video content. The experimental results also demonstrate that SASM consistently provides stable performance gains across different configuration combinations, improving CIDEr by 1.9% on MSVD and ROUGE-L by 1.3% on MSR-VTT. This finding fully demonstrates the critical value of the proposed SASM module as the final refinement component of the model architecture, providing comprehensive and significant performance improvements for video description tasks.

6. Concluding Remarks

In this work, we present EdgeVidCap, a lightweight video captioning model tailored explicitly for resource-constrained IoT edge cameras. Our approach addresses the critical challenge of deploying sophisticated video understanding algorithms on edge devices while maintaining competitive performance. The key innovation lies in the Synergetic Attention State Mamba (SASM) module, which synergistically combines channel attention mechanisms with State Space Models to achieve efficient spatiotemporal feature modeling. Additionally, our adaptive attention-guided LSTM decoder dynamically adjusts feature weights to generate semantically rich and contextually accurate textual descriptions. Comprehensive experiments on MSR-VTT and MSVD datasets demonstrate that EdgeVidCap achieves competitive performance compared to state-of-the-art methods while significantly reducing computational complexity and parameter count, making it well-suited for real-time deployment on IoT edge devices. Looking ahead, extending our framework to multi-lingual caption generation and incorporating domain-specific knowledge for specialized applications such as surveillance or autonomous driving represents another valuable direction. Finally, developing more sophisticated attention mechanisms that can better capture fine-grained temporal dynamics and object interactions in complex video scenarios remains an important area for future exploration. These developments will continue to advance the practical deployment of intelligent video understanding systems in edge computing environments.

Nevertheless, several limitations warrant consideration. The lightweight architecture may struggle with highly complex scenes involving numerous objects or rapid transitions, and the model's ability to maintain contextual coherence across extremely long video sequences remains constrained by the inherent limitations of State Space Models for extended temporal modeling. Additionally, certain content types such as abstract videos or highly technical domains may challenge the current framework's representational capacity. Looking ahead, extending our framework to multi-lingual caption generation and incorporating domain-specific knowledge for specialized applications such as surveillance or autonomous driving represents another valuable direction. Finally, developing more sophisticated attention mechanisms that can better capture fine-grained temporal dynamics and object interactions in complex video scenarios remains an important area for future exploration. These developments will continue to advance the practical deployment of intelligent video understanding systems in edge computing environments.

Author Contributions: Methodology, writing—original draft, L.G. and X.L.; software, J.W., P.Z.; investigation, J.X., L.L. and Y.H.; writing—review and editing, B.Y., Q.Z. and K.L. All authors have read and agreed to the published version of the manuscript.

Funding: This research was funded by the National Key R&D Program of China, under Grant Nos. 2023YFB4503903 and 2020YFC0832500; the National Natural Science Foundation of China, under Grant Nos. U22A20261 and 61402210; the Gansu Province Science and Technology Major Project—Industrial Project, under Grant Nos. 22ZD6GA048 and 23ZDGA006; the HY-Project, under Grant No. 4E49EFF3; the Gansu Province Key Research and Development Plan—Industrial Project, under Grant No. 22YF7GA004; the Gansu Provincial Science and Technology Major Special Innovation Consortium Project, under Grant No. 21ZD3GA002; the Fundamental Research Funds for the Central Universities, under Grant Nos. lzujbky-2024-jdzx15, lzujbky-2022-kb12, lzujbky-2021-sp43, lzujbky-2020-sp02, and lzujbky-2019-kb51; the Open Project of Gansu Provincial Key Laboratory of Intelligent Transportation, under Grant No. GJJ-ZH-2024-002; and the Science and Technology Plan of Qinghai Province, under Grant No. 2020-GX-164; 2023 China Higher Education Institutions Industry-Academia-Research Innovation Fund for Digital Intelligence and Educational Projects No. 2023RY020.

Data Availability Statement: The raw data supporting the conclusions of this article will be made available by the authors on request.

Conflicts of Interest: The funders had no role in the design of the study; in the collection, analyses, or interpretation of data; in the writing of the manuscript; or in the decision to publish the results.

References

1. Aafaq, N.; Mian, A.; Liu, W.; Gilani, S.Z.; Shah, M. Video description: A survey of methods, datasets, and evaluation metrics. *ACM Comput. Surv.* **2019**, *52*, 1–37. [CrossRef]
2. Han, D.; Shi, J.; Zhao, J.; Wu, H.; Zhou, Y.; Li, L.-H.; Khan, M.K.; Li, K.-C. LRCN: Layer-residual Co-Attention Networks for visual question answering. *Expert Syst. Appl.* **2025**, *263*, 125658. [CrossRef]
3. Chen, S.; Jin, Q. Multi-modal conditional attention fusion for dimensional emotion prediction. In Proceedings of the 24th ACM International Conference on Multimedia, Amsterdam, The Netherlands, 15–19 October 2016; pp. 571–575.
4. Huang, S.-H.; Lu, C.-H. Sequence-Aware Learnable Sparse Mask for Frame-Selectable End-to-End Dense Video Captioning for IoT Smart Cameras. *IEEE Internet Things J.* **2023**, *11*, 13039–13050. [CrossRef]

5. Lu, C.-H.; Fan, G.-Y. Environment-aware dense video captioning for IoT-enabled edge cameras. *IEEE Internet Things J.* **2021**, *9*, 4554–4564. [CrossRef]
6. Venugopalan, S.; Rohrbach, M.; Donahue, J.; Mooney, R.; Darrell, T.; Saenko, K. Sequence to sequence-video to text. In Proceedings of the IEEE International Conference on Computer Vision, Santiago, Chile, 7–13 December 2015; pp. 4534–4542.
7. Zhao, B.; Gong, M.; Li, X. Hierarchical multimodal transformer to summarize videos. *Neurocomputing* **2022**, *468*, 360–369. [CrossRef]
8. Pan, Y.; Yao, T.; Li, Y.; Mei, T. X-linear attention networks for image captioning. In Proceedings of the IEEE/CVF Conference on Computer Vision and Pattern Recognition, Seattle, WA, USA, 13–19 June 2020; pp. 10971–10980.
9. Zhu, D.; Chen, J.; Shen, X.; Li, X.; Elhoseiny, M. Minigpt-4: Enhancing vision-language understanding with advanced large language models. *arXiv* **2023**, arXiv:2304.10592.
10. Gemmeke, J.F.; Ellis, D.P.W.; Freedman, D.; Jansen, A.; Lawrence, W.; Moore, R.C.; Plakal, M.; Ritter, M. Audio set: An ontology and human-labeled dataset for audio events. In Proceedings of the 2017 IEEE International Conference on Acoustics, Speech and Signal Processing (ICASSP), New Orleans, LA, USA, 5–9 March 2017; pp. 776–780.
11. Hou, Y.; Zhou, Q.; Lv, H.; Guo, L.; Li, Y.; Duo, L.; He, Z. VLSG-net: Vision-Language Scene Graphs network for Paragraph Video Captioning. *Neurocomputing* **2025**, *636*, 129976. [CrossRef]
12. Carreira, J.; Zisserman, A. Quo vadis, action recognition? A new model and the kinetics dataset. In Proceedings of the IEEE Conference on Computer Vision and Pattern Recognition, Honolulu, HI, USA, 21–26 July 2017; pp. 6299–6308.
13. Liu, Y.; Sun, Y.; Chen, Z.; Feng, C.; Zhu, K. Global spatial-temporal information encoder-decoder based action segmentation in untrimmed video. *Tsinghua Sci. Technol.* **2024**, *30*, 290–302. [CrossRef]
14. Zhang, B.; Gao, J.; Yuan, Y. Memory-enhanced hierarchical transformer for video paragraph captioning. *Neurocomputing* **2025**, *615*, 128835. [CrossRef]
15. Jiang, K.; Wang, Z.; Chen, C.; Wang, Z.; Cui, L.; Lin, C.-W. Magic ELF: Image deraining meets association learning and transformer. *arXiv* **2022**, arXiv:2207.10455. [CrossRef]
16. Yao, L.; Torabi, A.; Cho, K.; Ballas, N.; Pal, C.; Larochelle, H.; Courville, A. Describing videos by exploiting temporal structure. In Proceedings of the IEEE International Conference on Computer Vision, Santiago, Chile, 7–13 December 2015; pp. 4507–4515.
17. Pan, P.; Xu, Z.; Yang, Y.; Wu, F.; Zhuang, Y. Hierarchical recurrent neural encoder for video representation with application to captioning. In Proceedings of the IEEE Conference on Computer Vision and Pattern Recognition, Las Vegas, NV, USA, 27–30 June 2016; pp. 1029–1038.
18. Krishna, R.; Hata, K.; Ren, F.; Fei-Fei, L.; Niebles, J.C. Dense-captioning events in videos. In Proceedings of the IEEE International Conference on Computer Vision, Venice, Italy, 22–29 October 2017; pp. 706–715.
19. Wang, X.; Chen, W.; Wu, J.; Wang, Y.-F.; Wang, W.Y. Video captioning via hierarchical reinforcement learning. In Proceedings of the IEEE Conference on Computer Vision and Pattern Recognition, Salt Lake City, UT, USA, 18–23 June 2018; pp. 4213–4222.
20. Yu, H.; Wang, J.; Huang, Z.; Yang, Y.; Xu, W. Video paragraph captioning using hierarchical recurrent neural networks. In Proceedings of the IEEE Conference on Computer Vision and Pattern Recognition, Las Vegas, NV, USA, 27–30 June 2016; pp. 4584–4593.
21. Zhang, J.; Peng, Y. Object-aware aggregation with bidirectional temporal graph for video captioning. In Proceedings of the IEEE/CVF Conference on Computer Vision and Pattern Recognition, Long Beach, CA, USA, 15–20 June 2019; pp. 8327–8336.
22. Wang, Y.; Li, K.; Li, Y.; He, Y.; Huang, B.; Zhao, Z.; Zhang, H.; Xu, J.; Liu, Y.; Wang, Z.; et al. Internvideo: General video foundation models via generative and discriminative learning. *arXiv* **2022**, arXiv:2212.03191. [CrossRef]
23. Guo, L.; Zhao, H.; Chen, Z.; Han, Z. Semantic guidance network for video captioning. *Sci. Rep.* **2023**, *13*, 16076. [CrossRef]
24. Li, K.; He, Y.; Wang, Y.; Li, Y.; Wang, W.; Luo, P.; Wang, Y.; Wang, L.; Qiao, Y. Videochat: Chat-centric video understanding. *arXiv* **2023**, arXiv:2305.06355.
25. Zhang, H.; Li, X.; Bing, L. Video-llama: An instruction-tuned audio-visual language model for video understanding. *arXiv* **2023**, arXiv:2306.02858.
26. Xu, J.; Mei, T.; Yao, T.; Rui, Y. Msr-vtt: A large video description dataset for bridging video and language. In Proceedings of the IEEE Conference on Computer Vision and Pattern Recognition, Las Vegas, NV, USA, 27–30 June 2016; pp. 5288–5296.
27. Hung, Y.-N.; Lerch, A. Feature-informed Latent Space Regularization for Music Source Separation. *arXiv* **2022**, arXiv:2203.09132. [CrossRef]
28. Guo, K.; Zhang, Z.; Guo, H.; Ren, S.; Wang, L.; Zhou, X.; Liu, C. Video super-resolution based on inter-frame information utilization for intelligent transportation. *IEEE Trans. Intell. Transp. Syst.* **2023**, *24*, 13409–13421. [CrossRef]
29. Liao, J.; Yu, C.; Jiang, L.; Guo, L.; Liang, W.; Li, K.; Pathan, A.-S.K. A method for composite activation functions in deep learning for object detection. *Signal Image Video Process.* **2025**, *19*, 362. [CrossRef]
30. Xiao, Y.; Yuan, Q.; Jiang, K.; Chen, Y.; Wang, S.; Lin, C. Multi-Axis Feature Diversity Enhancement for Remote Sensing Video Super-Resolution. *IEEE Trans. Image Process.* **2025**, *34*, 1766–1778. [CrossRef]

31. Zhang, S.; Liu, J.; Jiao, Y.; Zhang, Y.; Chen, L.; Li, K. A Multimodal Semantic Fusion Network with Cross-Modal Alignment for Multimodal Sentiment Analysis. In *ACM Transactions on Multimedia Computing, Communications and Applications*; ACM: New York, NY, USA, 2025.
32. Liu, Z.; Dang, F.; Liu, X.; Tong, X.; Zhao, H.; Liu, K.; Li, K. A Multimodal Fusion Framework for Enhanced Exercise Quantification Integrating RFID and Computer Vision. *Tsinghua Sci. Technol.* **2025**. [CrossRef]
33. Xia, C.; Sun, Y.; Li, K.; Ge, B.; Zhang, H.; Jiang, B.; Zhang, J. Rcnet: Related context-driven network with hierarchical attention for salient object detection. *Expert Syst. Appl.* **2024**, *237*, 121441. [CrossRef]
34. Xu, G.; Deng, X.; Zhou, X.; Pedersen, M.; Cimmino, L.; Wang, H. Fcfusion: Fractal componentwise modeling with group sparsity for medical image fusion. *IEEE Trans. Ind. Inform.* **2022**, *18*, 9141–9150. [CrossRef]
35. Zhao, H.; Guo, L.; Chen, Z.; Zheng, H. Research on video captioning based on multifeature fusion. *Comput. Intell. Neurosci.* **2022**, *2022*, 1204909. [CrossRef]
36. Gu, A.; Dao, T. Mamba: Linear-time sequence modeling with selective state spaces. *arXiv* **2023**, arXiv:2312.00752. [CrossRef]
37. Liu, Y.; Tian, Y.; Zhao, Y.; Yu, H.; Xie, L.; Wang, Y.; Ye, Q.; Jiao, J.; Liu, Y. Vmamba: Visual state space model. *Adv. Neural Inf. Process. Syst.* **2024**, *37*, 103031–103063.
38. Wang, F.; Wang, J.; Ren, S.; Wei, G.; Mei, J.; Shao, W.; Zhou, Y.; Yuille, A.; Xie, C. Mamba-Reg: Vision Mamba Also Needs Registers. In Proceedings of the Computer Vision and Pattern Recognition Conference, Nashville, TN, USA, 11–15 June 2025; pp. 14944–14953.
39. Yang, N.; Wang, Y.; Liu, Z.; Li, M.; An, Y.; Zhao, X. SMamba: Sparse Mamba for Event-based Object Detection. *Proc. Aaai Conf. Artif. Intell.* **2025**, *39*, 9229–9237. [CrossRef]
40. Kannan, A.; Lindquist, M.A.; Caffo, B. BrainMT: A Hybrid Mamba-Transformer Architecture for Modeling Long-Range Dependencies in Functional MRI Data. *arXiv* **2025**, arXiv:2506.22591.
41. Xiao, Y.; Yuan, Q.; Jiang, K.; Chen, Y.; Zhang, Q.; Lin, C. Frequency-Assisted Mamba for Remote Sensing Image Super-Resolution. *IEEE Trans. Multimed.* **2025**, *27*, 1783–1796. [CrossRef]
42. Cui, J.; Li, Y.; Shen, D.; Wang, Y. MGCM: Multi-modal Graph Convolutional Mamba for Cancer Survival Prediction. *Pattern Recognit.* **2025**, *169*, 111991. [CrossRef]
43. Yan, C.; Hao, Y.; Li, L.; Yin, J.; Liu, A.; Mao, Z. Task-adaptive attention for image captioning. *IEEE Trans. Circuits Syst. Video Technol.* **2021**, *32*, 43–51. [CrossRef]
44. Jin, N.; Yang, F.; Mo, Y.; Zeng, Y.; Zhou, X.; Yan, K.; Ma, X. Highly accurate energy consumption forecasting model based on parallel LSTM neural networks. *Adv. Eng. Inform.* **2022**, *51*, 101442. [CrossRef]
45. Papineni, K.; Roukos, S.; Ward, T.; Zhu, W. Bleu: A method for automatic evaluation of machine translation. In Proceedings of the 40th Annual Meeting of the Association for Computational Linguistics, Philadelphia, PA, USA, 6–12 July 2002.
46. Lin, C.-Y. Rouge: A package for automatic evaluation of summaries. *In Text Summarization Branches Out*; Association for Computational Linguistics: Barcelona, Spain, 2004; pp. 74–81.
47. Banerjee, S.; Lavie, A. METEOR: An automatic metric for MT evaluation with improved correlation with human judgments. In Proceedings of the ACL Workshop on Intrinsic and Extrinsic Evaluation Measures for Machine Translation and/or Summarization, Ann Arbor, MI, USA, 25–30 June 2005; pp. 65–72.
48. Vedantam, R.; Zitnick, C.L.; Parikh, D. Cider: Consensus-based image description evaluation. In Proceedings of the IEEE Conference on Computer Vision and Pattern Recognition, Boston, MA, USA, 7–12 June 2015; pp. 4566–4575.
49. Chen, D.; Dolan, W.B. Collecting highly parallel data for paraphrase evaluation. In Proceedings of the 49th Annual Meeting of the Association for Computational Linguistics: Human Language Technologies, Portland, OR, USA, 19–24 June 2011.
50. Hou, J.; Wu, X.; Zhao, W.; Luo, J.; Jia, Y. Joint Syntax Representation Learning and Visual Cue Translation for Video Captioning. In Proceedings of the 2019 IEEE/CVF International Conference on Computer Vision (ICCV), Seoul, Republic of Korea, 27 October–2 November 2019.
51. Zhang, Z.; Shi, Y.; Yuan, C.; Li, B.; Wang, P.; Hu, W.; Zha, Z.J. Object Relational Graph with Teacher-Recommended Learning for Video Captioning. Computer Vision and Pattern Recognition. *arXiv* **2020**, arXiv:2002.11566.
52. Ryu, H.; Kang, S.; Kang, H.; Yoo, C.D. Semantic Grouping Network for Video Captioning. In National Conference on Artificial Intelligence. *arXiv* **2021**, arXiv:2102.00831.
53. Gu, X.; Chen, G.; Wang, Y.; Zhang, L.; Luo, T.; Wen, L. Text with knowledge graph augmented transformer for video captioning. In Proceedings of the IEEE/CVF Conference on Computer Vision and Pattern Recognition, Vancouver, BC, Canada, 17–24 June 2023; pp. 18941–18951.
54. Jing, S.; Zhang, H.; Zeng, P.; Gao, L.; Song, J.; Shen, H.T. Memory-based augmentation network for video captioning. *IEEE Trans. Multimed.* **2023**, *26*, 2367–2379. [CrossRef]
55. Shen, Y.; Gu, X.; Xu, K.; Fan, H.; Wen, L.; Zhang, L. Accurate and fast compressed video captioning. In Proceedings of the IEEE/CVF International Conference on Computer Vision, Paris, France, 1–6 October 2023; pp. 15558–15567.

56. Luo, X.; Luo, X.; Wang, D.; Liu, J.; Wan, B.; Zhao, L. Global semantic enhancement network for video captioning. *Pattern Recognit.* **2024**, *145*, 109906. [CrossRef]
57. Ma, Y.; Zhu, Z.; Qi, Y.; Beheshti, A.; Li, Y.; Qing, L.; Li, G. Style-aware two-stage learning framework for video captioning. *Knowl.-Based Syst.* **2024**, *301*, 112258. [CrossRef]

sensors

MDPI

Article

DRL-Driven Intelligent SFC Deployment in MEC Workload for Dynamic IoT Networks

Seyha Ros [1], Intae Ryoo [2,*] and Seokhoon Kim [1,3,*]

[1] Department of Software Convergence, Soonchunhyang University, Asan 31538, Republic of Korea; rosseyha003@gmail.com
[2] Department of Computer Engineering, Kyung Hee University, Yongin-si 17104, Republic of Korea
[3] Department of Computer Software Engineering, Soonchunhyang University, Asan 31538, Republic of Korea
* Correspondence: itryoo@khu.ac.kr (I.R.); seokhoon@sch.ac.kr (S.K.)

Abstract: The rapid increase in the deployment of Internet of Things (IoT) sensor networks has led to an exponential growth in data generation and an unprecedented demand for efficient resource management infrastructure. Ensuring end-to-end communication across multiple heterogeneous network domains is crucial to maintaining Quality of Service (QoS) requirements, such as low latency and high computational capacity, for IoT applications. However, limited computing resources at multi-access edge computing (MEC), coupled with increasing IoT network requests during task offloading, often lead to network congestion, service latency, and inefficient resource utilization, degrading overall system performance. This paper proposes an intelligent task offloading and resource orchestration framework to address these challenges, thereby optimizing energy consumption, computational cost, network congestion, and service latency in dynamic IoT-MEC environments. The framework introduces task offloading and a dynamic resource orchestration strategy, where task offloading to the MEC server ensures an efficient distribution of computation workloads. The dynamic resource orchestration process, Service Function Chaining (SFC) for Virtual Network Functions (VNFs) placement, and routing path determination optimize service execution across the network. To achieve adaptive and intelligent decision-making, the proposed approach leverages Deep Reinforcement Learning (DRL) to dynamically allocate resources and offload task execution, thereby improving overall system efficiency and addressing the optimal policy in edge computing. Deep Q-network (DQN), which is leveraged to learn an optimal network resource adjustment policy and task offloading, ensures flexible adaptation in SFC deployment evaluations. The simulation result demonstrates that the DRL-based scheme significantly outperforms the reference scheme in terms of cumulative reward, reduced service latency, lowered energy consumption, and improved delivery and throughput.

Keywords: deep reinforcement learning; multi-access edge computing; network functions virtualization; service function chaining; internet of things

1. Introduction

1.1. Background and Motivation

The Internet of Things (IoT) has been widely used for digitalization to expose the potential of utilizing network sensing and data gathering from citizen environments [1,2]. IoT device communication with several interface technologies (i.e., Wi-Fi, Bluetooth, ZigBee, LoRaWAN, NFC, and 6LoWPAN) through physical modulation [3–5] is used to access and communicate with network servers via fronthaul physical networks for diverse application scenarios. Thus, the increasing amount of data generated by IoT sensor networks leads to inefficient computation and resource utilization, resulting in the inability to conserve energy and reduce processing time on devices. IoT continues to generate tasks that require computing, with varying types of processing time, computing resources, and battery life. However, IoT generates massive traffic requests that often exacerbate bottlenecks and irregular fluctuations due to mobility and spatiotemporal variations in service usage patterns [6,7].

On the other hand, multi-access edge computing (MEC) can provide a solution for managing and orchestrating the resource utilization of computation from IoT sensing [8,9]. MEC has the potential to facilitate resource-intensive computation, which involves chaining virtualization resource capabilities and aims to reduce latency in communication protocols and network aspects [10–12]. However, MEC has the responsibility of addressing computational needs, leading to challenges in balancing execution delay and energy consumption. Additionally, the integration of MEC with software-defined networks/network function virtualization (SDN/NFV) controllers enhances the agility needed to reduce computation time and manage resource complexity, steering traffic patterns from ingress to egress. Service function chaining (SFC) provides instances of sequential virtual network functions (VNFs) to host virtual machines (VMs), allowing the order of VNFs to be propagated in the specified order for the required application. Consequently, MEC-enabled SDN/NFV offers lower latency and increased computational resources to manage the high demands of IoT services. Furthermore, the time needed to process resource allocation and placement for heterogeneous service functions poses a significant challenge for MEC, making real-time determination and adjustments essential for effective and efficient state transition decisions within this complex system.

To address these limitations, Deep Reinforcement Learning (DRL) has gained attention as a powerful agent for making intelligent, adaptive decisions in highly dynamic networking [13,14]. By considering various system interactions, DRL-driven approaches can continuously learn from the network environment and SFC placements [15–19]. As shown in Figure 1, leveraging the DRL-integrated MEC framework can intelligently allocate VNFs to ensure SFCs are deployed to maximize resource efficiency, minimize latency, and maintain high reliability, even amid unpredictable traffic fluctuations as the workload changes.

Furthermore, the timely and efficient advancement of MEC and SFC technologies remains challenging due to the optimal placement and resource allocation of VNFs in IoT-driven network environments. On the other hand, they have delegated the computing capacities for real-time orchestration and resource management needed to instantiate VNFs to meet the workload. Moreover, the trade-offs between critical performance metrics, such as latency, energy efficiency, cost, and resource utilization, further complicate the issue. Achieving an optimal balance between these factors is difficult due to the limited resources available at edge nodes and the unpredictable demand from IoT devices. In traditional approaches, SFC deployment often relies on predetermined rules or heuristic methods that cannot adjust efficiently in real-time, leading to inefficient resource usage and poor service quality. As the scale of IoT networks continues to grow and the demands of applications become more complex, there is a clear need for intelligent, adaptive strategies that can dynamically optimize SFC placement, resource allocation, and workload distribution across the edge network. Moreover, DRL is used to determine the policy for charging SFC deployment in the MEC server, enabling adaptive allocation of optimal decisions for instance resources in fluctuating IoT networks.

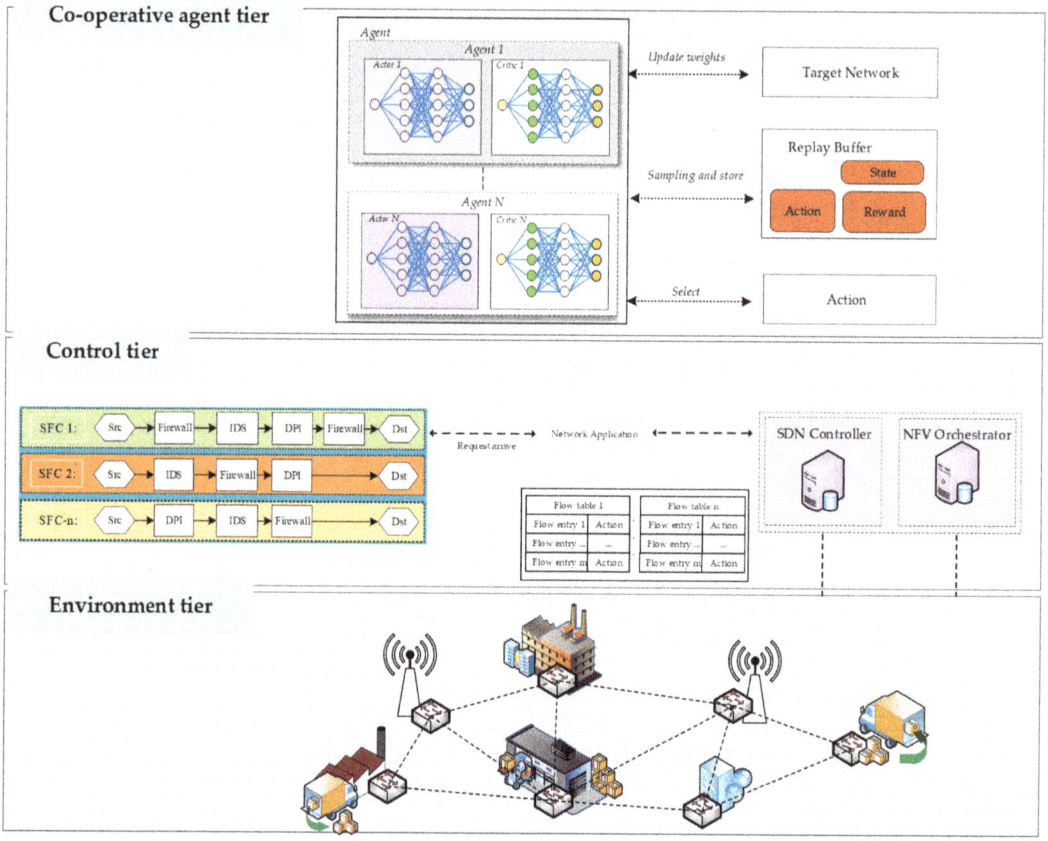

Figure 1. Multi-agent enabled in NFV for policy charging on resource utilization.

1.2. Motivation and Contributions

This paper addresses these challenges by proposing a DRL-driven framework for intelligent and efficient SFC deployment in MEC environments, capable of learning optimal placement policies that adapt to fluctuating workloads and network conditions. The following recapitalization is the main contribution of this paper:

- We formulated the VNF placement and resource allocation problem as a multi-objective optimization task, where conflicting performance goals are considered to minimize latency, conserve energy, and optimize resource utilization.
- By intelligently distributing workloads across geographically distributed edge nodes based on real-time system states, the model ensures balanced resource utilization and reduces service degradation in high-density IoT deployments. Our scheme can proactively reallocate resources to avoid and minimize overload risks, thereby improving the long-term sustainability of edge nodes.
- We design a joint optimization algorithm for task offloading and resource allocation based on the Deep Q-Network, with the optimization objectives of assisting the NFVO in instantiating resources according to the workload requirements of IoT devices.
- The reward provides comprehensive network performance. Our proposed scheme leverages DRL frameworks and the network environment to highlight significant

existing solutions across various aspects, including energy, latency, packet delivery ratio, packet drop ratio, and throughput.

1.3. Paper Organization

The remaining section of our study is organized as follows: Section 2 provides a literature review of existing work. Section 3 discusses network modeling using DRL to optimize the VNF resource allocation and placement. Section 4 outlines the performance metrics and compares the proposed methods with reference methods, concluding with a discussion in Section 5.

2. Related Work

In response to the current trend of utilizing IoT devices efficiently, many researchers have focused on resource and energy consumption to handle resource-intensive computing workloads. However, many studies investigating computing in the IoT network are still challenging due to the vast amount of big data and latency required to orchestrate resources and achieve real-time efficiency.

Many research scholars aim to optimize resource allocation and placement on MEC to enhance resource utilization concerning communication and computation-intensive resources [20–22]. Moreover, reducing latency for delay-sensitive tasks on MEC servers poses a significant challenge in this effort. Traditionally, resource allocation techniques rely on heuristic or optimization-based approaches, which struggle to adapt to the real-time and unpredictable nature of IoT traffic patterns. For example, centralized methods such as Mixed Integer Linear Programming (MILP) and convex optimization have been employed to optimize latency and bandwidth utilization [23,24]. In their work, Ref. [25] presented efficient task offloading and profit maximization in MEC-enabled 5G Internet of Vehicles (IoV). This study proposed a Lyapunov-Based Profit Maximization (LBPM) algorithm to optimize the time-averaged profit of MEC providers while ensuring timely and effective task execution from vehicles.

Additionally, the previous study on resource management in VNF placement still faces the problem of duplicates in the form of chaining and overwhelming resource utilization. For instance, refs. [26–28] study VNF placement and traffic routing simultaneously, dividing the methods into two phases: first, VNF placement, and then establishing the executing links. To achieve optimal resource utilization, ref. [27] consider the tradeoff between resource consumption and links, providing a two-phase VNF placement methodology that uses constrained depth-first search algorithms (CDFSAs) and path-based greedy algorithms to assign VNFs with minimum resource consumption [28]. The authors proposed two methods, hybrid SFC and a heuristic algorithm, to solve the dynamic SFC embedding for chaining VNF nodes. However, their utilization of the shortest path or greedy algorithms could not achieve network load balancing.

In recent years, some researchers have started applying machine learning to tackle various optimization problems [29–31], with a focus on resource allocation, resource placement, scheduling, traffic routing, resource offloading, and SFC orchestration. For instance, ref. [32] proposed PPO-ERA to provide a real-time, adaptive, and dynamic strategy for VNFs, addressing task delays and resource utilization. Meanwhile, SFC deployment over MEC servers shares idle computing resources that utilize the same SFC. In [33], VNF cooperative scheduling with priority-weighted delay is examined. Their work incorporated DRL with a target Q-network to enhance solutions for the optimal problem related to VNF scheduling, while supporting multidimensional resources in edge nodes. In [34], a multi-objective SFC mapping technique based on DQN is proposed to achieve delay and load balancing targets. In their work, Ref. [35] leverages the DQN and MQDR-based method for the dynamic deployment of customized SFCs, including dynamic adjustments of SFCRs. Furthermore, in [36], the VNF formulation problem is addressed using integer nonlinear programming to minimize bandwidth costs and ensure service execution for end-to-end delays.

Through their strategies and significant efforts, they enhance resource efficiency and effective resource utilization. However, computation and resource allocation to idle VNFs present challenges and drawbacks, particularly in terms of reallocating resources and placement. This can lead to overwhelming utilization in real time within the same SFC.

To clarify the significance of our research, we present the utilization of VNF resource placement and allocation approaches compared to the previous studies mentioned above. We develop a novel dynamic resource allocation and placement based on diverse SFR in NFVO. VNFs are monitored by NFVI to control resource adjustments that respond to real-time changes in VNFs within SFCs, coordinating with DQN variance methods. Furthermore, we consider the priority of SFC for managing resources based on workload in computing tasks.

3. Model and Problem Formulation

This system model section discusses our system simulation and represents the complete VNF and SFC related to MEC servers and the IoT sensing network. Regarding the resource allocation issue in the VNF of the SFC, the optimization goal of this paper is to address resource placement and facilitate cost-effective application deployments by considering the services required for managing end devices.

3.1. Network Model

In the network section, we examined the allocation and placement of NFV resource utilization to align with the computation and communication demands of MEC workloads. In this paper, we illustrate the physical infrastructure resource instantiation involved in creating several Network Functions Requests (NFRs) to support multiple Service Functions (SFs) in terms of requirements and monitoring resource workload. IoT contributes to resource-intensive network data traffic, which escalates resource-heavy computation and complex workloads in edge networks, as depicted in Table 1.

In the system model, the undirected graph is leveraged to represent network function resources, where G is a set of MEC servers and V is the subset of MEC nodes that connect to the link denoted as E. The task process can be defined in the primary phase as follows:

- Offloading task from IoT to MEC server for computing task: In each *timeslot-t*, IoT devices offload $task - j$ to $MEC - m$. Equation (1) indicates the communication model that is associated between end-devices and the MEC-server for data rate, denoted as ED^t_{n-m} for the state of allocated bandwidth $bw^t_{n\to m}$, channel gain $g^t_{n\to m}$, transmission power p^t_n, and noise $\forall\aleph$.

$$ED^t_{n-m} = bw^t_{n\to m}\log_2\left(1 + \frac{p^t_n g^t_{n\to m}}{\forall\aleph}\right) \tag{1}$$

In this scenario, we assume that the IoT fully offloads the $task - j$ to MEC $-m$ for computation in every $timeslot - t$, and all the MEC servers are supposedly equipped in every single device.

Table 1. Notation system model in the network model.

Notation	Description
G	Set of MEC servers
E	Set of links
V	Set of VNFs
J	A set of number tasks
N	The set of IoT devices
T	Number of timeslots
$\mathcal{R}_m$	Resources of MEC servers
P_j	Set all the VNFs by *IoT-R_j*
$C_{up,m}$	Upper-bound capacity of MEC servers on (CPU, RAM, Disk)
BW	Maximum of Bandwidths
d_e	Propagation delay between nodes on *link e*
F	Number of service requests
$BW^t_{up,m}$	Upper-bound bandwidth of *MEC-m* at *timeslot-t*
$C^t_{re,m}$	Remaining resources of *MEC-m* at *timeslot-t*
	Decision variable
$x^v_{j,f}(t)$	Equals one if the VNF of the service request that is deployed at *node-v* at *timeslot-t*, otherwise
$y^e_j(t)$	Selecting the virtual link between *node-j* at *timeslot-t*, otherwise

3.2. SFC Requests

The set IoT-R is denoted by F. The $\mathrm{j}-\mathrm{th}$ IoT denotes IoT-R_j, responding to a 5-tuple $(S_j, D_j, P_j, R_{bw,j}, R_{delay,j}, R^f_{cpu,j})$. In this tuple, S_j and D_j represent the source IoT device and destination MEC server, respectively. The set P_j denotes the sequence of VNF requirements by IoT-R_j. $R_{bw,j,}$ and $R_{delay,j}$ denote the bandwidth consumption required by IoT-R_j and maximum tolerated E2E delay of IoT-R_j, respectively.

3.2.1. Resource Constraints

We ensure sufficient MEC servers' resource to host VNFs and bandwidth for handling all the IoT-R_j:

$$\sum_{i\in J}\sum_{f\in F_j} R^f_{cpu,j}\cdot x^m_{j,f} \leq C^t_{re,m} \quad \forall m\in G, \forall t\in T \tag{2}$$

where $R^f_{cpu,j}$ indicates CPU demand of VNF-f in request-j, and $C^t_{re,m}$ demonstrates the remaining resource capacity of MEC-m at time-t.

$$\sum_{i\in J} y^e_j(t)\cdot R_{bw,j,} \leq C^t_{re,m} \tag{3}$$

where $y^e_j(t)$ indicates whether link e is traversed by IoT-R in request-$j \in R$ and equals 1 if the traffic of IoT-R travers physical link; 0 otherwise.

3.2.2. Delay Constraint

We use $\mathcal{P}D_j$ to indicate the total propagation delay of IoT-R not exceeding the maximum total of service requests:

$$\mathcal{P}D_j = \sum_{e\in E} y^e_j(t)\cdot d_e \leq R_{delay,j} \quad \forall j\in J, \forall t\in T \tag{4}$$

3.3. Optimization Modelling Designs

Improve resource allocation and placement of VNF over the MEC server. This paper aims to improve the system to maximize successful placement resources in service requests while maintaining effectiveness by minimizing energy consumption and delay for each application under computational and networking resources constraints.

$$Max\sum_{t=1}^{T}\sum_{j=J}\left(\sum_{f\in F_j}\sum_{v\in V} x^{v}_{j,f}(t) - \lambda_1.E_j - \lambda_2.\mathcal{P}D_j\right) \tag{5}$$

s.t. (2)–(4)

3.3.1. State Space

To address the network formulation for resource utilization in orchestration and management, the state is gathered from network components with critical states, as shown in Figure 2. The process proceeds by computing resource allocation, gathering resources from the network, and orchestrating for SFR. The Markov decision process is utilized to interact within the NFVO environment.

- $\mathcal{R}_m$ represents the coordination of resources in the MEC server to preserve the ability to handle the computation tasks during IoT and offload the tasks to MEC-m.
- $C_{up,m}$ represents the upper-bound resource utilization in MEC-m at timeslot-t.
- BW is communication from the local device to $MEC - m$, state of total bandwidth, observed from a total bandwidth allocation and channel gain between environments.
- $BW^{t}_{up,m}$ represents how much bandwidth is allocated between nodes to $MEC - m$ during the paging tasks at $timeslot - t$.
- A subset of a tuple $j^{comp}_{j-m}(t)$, which consists of processing tasks, including the consumed resources/energy, and time spent from experience.

$$S_t = \left\{\mathcal{R}_m, C_{up,m}, BW, BW^{t}_{up,m}, j^{comp}_{i-m}(t)\right\} \tag{6}$$

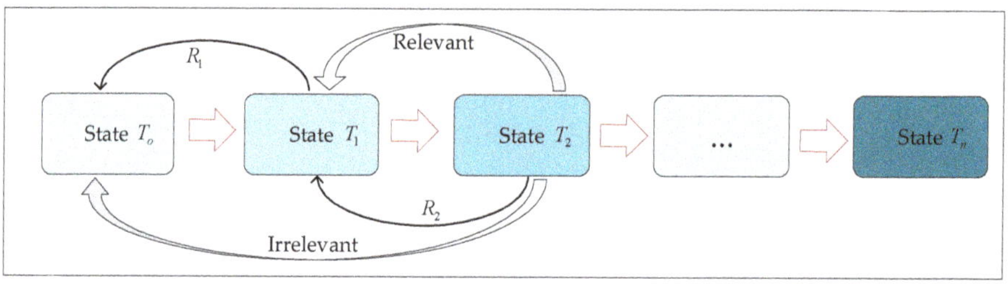

Figure 2. State space flow execution on an interval.

3.3.2. Action Space

The offloading task from IoT devices to the MEC server, whose backbone SDN controller has a global view of the flow entity, consists of the routing table synchronized as an action from the agent space. On the other hand, the mechanism of SDN-MEC enables DRL to empathize with the experienced batch of resource allocation and resource placement for performance patterns in each observation state iteration. $a^{off}_{j}(t)$ is set to determine the connection between IoT devices and MEC servers for offloading tasks. Additionally, $a^{Plac}_{mec|F}(t)$ is the optimal MEC selection for VNF placement to align the ordering of SFC forms in computing the task based on SFR. The corporation proposed by the agent and SDN controller is to optimize the flow rule of routing execution in installation and alleviation for the effective execution of tasks in terms of completion time within maximum tolerance delays.

$$a_t = \left\{a^{off}_{j}(t),\ a^{Plac}_{mec|F}(t)\right\} \tag{7}$$

3.3.3. Reward Based on Policy Charging Selection

In this proposed SDN-NFV, DRL aims to deal with the efficiency of applying the action a_t into the MEC-IoT environment state s_t by gaining the reward r_t to show the impact of the action that transitions the following states: s_{t+1}. In this study, the primary reward by dented R^t_{env} is to sum the total of two sub-rewards, reduced service latency and lowered energy consumption, denoted as r^t_{Lat} *and* r^t_{Ene}, respectively.

$$R^t_{env} = \lambda_{lat}(t) \cdot r^t_{Lat} + \lambda_{Ene}(t) \cdot r^t_{Ene} \tag{8}$$

where $\lambda_{lat}(t)$ and $\lambda_{Ene}(t)$ are time-varying weights $(\lambda_{lat}(t) + \lambda_{lat}(t) = 1)$ that adapt based on current conditions. When the network load is high or delay-sensitive service requests are prioritized, $\lambda_{lat}(t)$ is increased to focus on reducing latency. Conversely, under lower loads or when energy conservation is critical, $\lambda_{Ene}(t)$ is emphasized to minimize energy consumption.

The optimal policy is set to NFVO to orchestrate the resources from the overall batch that maximizes the long-term reward expectation by following Equation (9). On the other hand, Equation (10) presents an optimal policy selection for the state by following the Bellman equation.

$$\pi(t)^* = \underset{\pi}{\operatorname{argmax}} \mathbb{E}_\pi \left[\sum_{t \in T} \gamma^t R^t_{env} \right] \tag{9}$$

$$Q^*(s,a) = \mathbb{E}_{\sim s'} \left[R^t_{env} + \gamma \underset{a'}{\operatorname{argmax}} Q^*(s',a') \right] \tag{10}$$

3.4. *Pseudo DQN Algorithm Designs*

To effectively address the dynamic and resource-constrained nature of IoT-MEC, we leverage DQN-based algorithms to ensure proper VNF placement and resource allocation utilization. In this section, Algorithm 1 presents the DQN algorithms with embedding of VNF resource placements. The DQN-based VNF placement algorithm operates in two phases: the learning phase and the execution phase. From the learning phase, input the state from the IoT-MEC environment, such as $\left(V,\ E, \mathcal{R}_m,\ C_{u,m}, \mathrm{BW}, BW^t_{up,m}, C^t_{re,m}\ (t)\right)$. The algorithm begins by initializing the experience replay buffer and the online and target Q-network parameters. It then initializes the system state based on incoming SFRs, which include the resource requirements and the structure of the VNFFG. A batch of candidate MEC servers is sampled without repetition for potential VNF placement. At each *timestep* $-$ t, a random value is generated to determine the action-selection strategy. If the value is greater than a threshold ϵ-epsilon, the algorithm selects an action randomly to encourage exploration. Otherwise, it chooses the action with the maximum Q-value, computed by the online network, to exploit the learned policy. The selected action involves deploying a VNF on a chosen MEC server and computing the shortest communication path within the VNFFG. The algorithm then observes the resulting reward and transitions to the next state, storing the experience tuple as a result (s_t, a_t, r_t, s_{t+1}) in memory from which mini-batches are randomly sampled during training. For each sample, the algorithm computes a target Q-value using the Bellman equation and updates the network parameters by minimizing the mean squared error between predicted and target Q-values. The network parameter update process includes both the online Q-network update via gradient descent and the periodic synchronization of the target network to ensure stable learning. Furthermore, time complexity, training involves the sampling of a batch of size N, with each forward and backward pass costing Ψ, yielding $\mathcal{O}(N{\cdot}\Psi)$ per training step; the inference, which only required going forward through the network, has a complexity $\mathcal{O}(\Psi)$ per decision step. The training is looped continuously until VNFs in SFR are successfully placed in order of requirement. In the execution phase, the trained Q-network is used to make placement decisions. The action with the maximum Q-value is selected and executed at each time step, updating the placement strategy and transitioning the environment state accordingly. This process repeats until the complete VNF chain is placed, at which point the algorithm outputs the final placement strategy P^j_{MEC}. This approach enables the algorithm to make efficient and scalable placement decisions in a resource-constrained MEC-NFV/SDN, thereby optimizing system-level performance metrics such as delay, energy consumption, and load balancing.

Algorithm 1: Pseudo-code of DQN-based VNF placement algorithms

Input State $= \left(V,\ E, \mathcal{R}_m,\ C_{u,m}, \mathrm{BW}, BW^t_{up,m}, C^t_{re,m}\ (t)\right)$
Output VNF placement and allocation in MEC servers P^j_{MEC}
Learning process:
Initialize the experience reply.
For each
  Initialize the state s of VNF from SFR
  Sample a batch of $MEC\ Server - m$ without repetition
  For each time $step - t$ do
  Generate randomly value
  If random value, $\geq \epsilon$ **then**
    Randomly select an action $a(t)$
  Else
    Select of actions with the $MAX\ Q - value$
    $a_t = argmax_{a_t} Q(s_t, a_t, \theta)$ based on online_net
  End if
    Enforce the action that deploys VNF and calculates the shortest path of VNFFG
    Calculate the reward r_t and new state s_{t+1}
    Store the state transition sample (s_t, a_t, r_t, s_{t+1})
    $r(s_t, a_t, s_{t+1}) + \gamma \max_{a_{t+1}} Q(s_t, a_t, \theta^-)$
    Get updating the value of $\theta^- = \theta$ for every C steps
  If the VNF placement and deployment has yet completed;
  Then
  End if
End for
Execution process:
Read the online_net and target_net
For each $step - t$
  Do
  Select the action with Max Q_value;
  Execute the action and update the placement scheme:
  $P^j_{MEC} = s_t$
  Update the state : $s_t = s_{t+1}$
  If the VNF placement is completed, then.
  End if
End for
Return

4. Performance Evaluation

To conduct the network simulation [11,21], the network environment utilizes the NetworkX library to create network topologies for all network components. As depicted in Table 2, all simulations are executed on a computer with an AMD Ryzen (R) 7 5700X CPU, 3.0 GHz, 32 GB (Advanced Micro Devices, Inc., Santa Clara, CA, USA), NVIDIA RTX 4080 GPU (NVIDIA, Santa Clara, CA, USA), and Python programming. A network topology is instantiated to reveal the network for setting the network topology. Once the network-tolerant delay is set, the number of IoT devices is set to 100 to be attributed across five MEC servers. We utilize the DRL agent function with the OpenAI library within the DRL framework, initialized with PyTorch.

Table 2. Parameter configuration in the network and DRL framework.

Parameters	Specifications
Hosting infrastructure	Ryzen(R) 7 5700x3d CPU @ 3.0 GHz, 32 GB, NVIDIA RTX 4080 GPU
Number of IoT	100
Number of MEC servers	5
Service request configuration	NF (types = 5) SFC type of length (2–5) Flow rate (64 Kbps–4 Mbps) Tolerable time (100–500)
Task complexity and sizes	Random set (Low, normal, high)—(256 Kbits, 512 Kbits, 1024 Kbits)
Learning rate	0.001
Discount factor	0.95
Batch size	Random set (32, 64, 128, 256)
Exploration	0.5
Number of episodes	400
Python platform	PyTorch

4.1. Comparison of Proposed and Reference Schemes

Our study conducts network evaluation and sets up three comparison schemes to illustrate how the proposed approach differs from the baseline approach. This comparison illustrates the performance differences in terms of various computation resource workloads for IoT-MEC task offloading, leading to enhanced energy efficiency and reduced overhead latency.

- DQN-MIoT is our proposed method, which utilizes DRL algorithms combined with NFVO in MEC to allocate resources for VNF placement. Our proposed DRL-based NFV control leverages a DQN architecture to approximate the Q-value function, enabling collaborative configuration of SDN/NFV flow rules for optimized placement and resource allocation. This method effectively trains the function approximator to manage high-dimensional state observations and representations. As detailed in Section 3, the approach incorporates experience replay, neural network training, and synchronization with the SDN/NFV controller to learn sophisticated policies.
- DQL-MIoT is set to leverage the Deep Q-learning approach, which enables learning from the network environment and applying action to control policy; however, DL achieves low performance in the complex network topology and can only handle lightweight network topology cases.
- Greedy-MIoT represents the traditional SDN/NFV for IoT-MEC servers in computing task management. This baseline approach addresses a centralized MANO that manages resources and controls the characteristics of IoT, adhering to the definition of standard NFV rules. The resource management controller is based on topology,

traffic conditions, service requirements, and offloading policies. Greedy-MIoT relies on network-level optimization, efficient resource management, and resource allocation for non-complex applications.

- Random-MIoT indicates that the algorithm stochastically chooses an MEC service to an ingress source from traversing a VNF resource instance and a routing path to commonly chaining two adjacent VNF instances for every incoming IoT-R.

4.2. Results and Discussion

In this section, we present the results for the proposed DQN-MIoT and reference schemes, namely DQL-MIoT, Greedy-MIoT, and Random-MIoT, in terms of cumulative reward, sub-rewards for latency and energy, packet drop ratio, packet delivery ratio, throughput, and delay in services. The measurement of this performance metric significantly showcases how our system setting integrates with the DQN framework, ensuring the reliability of chaining VNFs and adjusting for resource differences under diverse applications and workloads. The same topology and task size are used in this simulation, but the controller and agent differ in terms of performance metrics. The result demonstrates the total reward throughout each significant scheme's DQN phase for exploration and exploitation within 400 episodes. Figure 3 illustrates the results of the proposed method, showing the total reward over 400 episodes, as defined in Equation (8). During the early learning phase (episodes 0–100), all approaches begin with negative cumulative rewards due to random policy exploration and ineffective action selection. As training progresses, DQN-MIoT shows a rapid improvement, achieving a positive cumulative reward after approximately 150 episodes, steadily increasing to 32.89 at episode 400. Meanwhile, DQL-MIoT gradually improves and achieves a final cumulative reward of 19.74, which is approximately 40% lower than DQN-MIoT. The Greedy-MIoT method shows minimal improvement, ending with a cumulative reward of only 2.53, which is approximately 92% lower than that of DQN-MIoT. The Random-MIoT baseline performs the worst, consistently maintaining negative rewards and ending at −26.48, indicating no effective learning or adaptation.

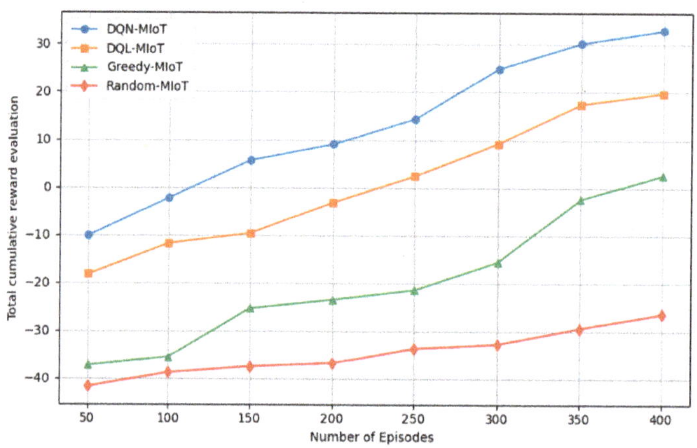

Figure 3. Result of cumulative reward evaluation.

In Figure 4a, initially, all methods exhibit negative sub-rewards, indicating poor latency performance due to random or sub-optimal policy actions during early learning phases. However, by episode 200, the DQN-MIoT approach begins to yield positive sub-reward values, signaling a successful adaptation to the MEC workload dynamics in IoT scenarios. As learning continues, DQN-MIoT and DQL-MIoT demonstrate robust convergence behavior, with DQN-MIoT consistently achieving higher sub-reward values than DQL-MIoT. By episode 400, DQN-MIoT achieves a latency sub-reward of 29.57, compared to 26.51 for DQL-MIoT, only 5.17 for Greedy-MIoT, and −30.31 for random-MIoT. This substantial gap underscores the benefits of employing a value-based Q-value with optimized exploration strategies for latency-sensitive SFC placement. Figure 4b illustrates the efficiency of energy score points as DQN-MIoT's training process transitions the agent into a more stable policy regime, resulting in a higher immediate reward score. DQN-MIoT demonstrated a steady improvement, eventually peaking as the training progressed due to its adaptive learning strategy, which optimized energy consumption under network constraints. In contrast, DQL-MIoT showed more gradual progress, reflecting its slower convergence in handling energy efficiency within the MEC-enabled IoT environment. The Greedy-MIoT and Random-MIoT consistently underperformed with negative energy sub-rewards throughout most episodes, as they lacked adaptive mechanisms to manage resource allocation effectively. From the reward efficiency perspective, the proposed DQN-MIoT scheme dynamically adjusts resource allocation and offloading decisions, effectively balancing computational capacity and energy constraints. This adaptability enables improved handling of resource-constrained and computation-intensive tasks within the network, demonstrating strong suitability for MEC-enabled IoT scenarios where energy efficiency and task completion are crucial.

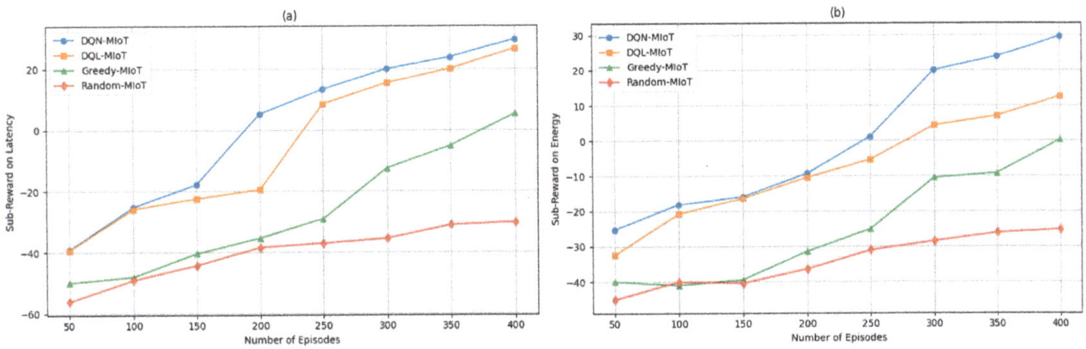

Figure 4. Performance metrics on sub-rewards of (**a**) latency and (**b**) energy.

The results are demonstrated in Figure 5a,b for task delivery and drop ratios, where network states are configured consecutively by setting different network conditions, congestion levels, and application tasks every 400 simulation intervals. We evaluate the agent based on the fluctuation of investment results in the network parameter setting compared to the diversity of state observation. In high traffic fluctuations and computation-intensive environments, DQN-MIoT maintains its advantage with a PDR of 99.9681%, whereas DQL-MIoT drops to 99.9145%, and Greedy-MIoT declines further to 99.7568%. These results demonstrate the robustness and reliability of the DQN-MIoT framework in maintaining high data delivery rates even under increasing network loads. Meanwhile, at shorter simulation durations (20 s), DQN-MIoT achieves a notably low packet drop ratio of 0.05%, outperforming DQL-MIoT (0.09%), Greedy-MIoT (0.14%), and Random-MIoT (0.24%). As the simulation time increases to 380 s, DQN-MIoT maintains its performance advantage, recording a drop ratio of 0.18%, while DQL-MIoT, Greedy-MIoT, and random-MIoT reach 0.245%, 0.3401%, and 0.3513%, respectively. This consistent performance trend underscores the superior decision-making and adaptability of the DQN-MIoT framework in managing network traffic, confirming its suitability for real-time, data-sensitive applications.

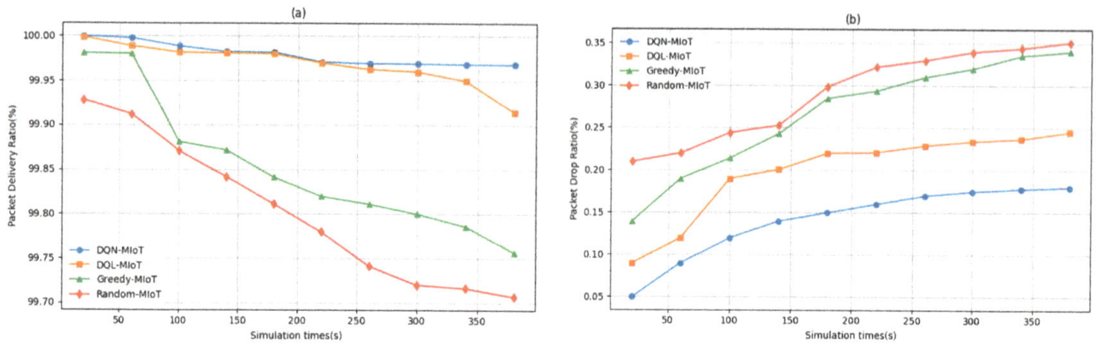

Figure 5. Performance metrics of (**a**) packet delivery and (**b**) packet drop ratio.

The throughput results presented in Figure 6, across different simulation times, further reinforce the superior performance of the DQN-MIoT approach compared to DQL-MIoT and Greedy-MIoT. At 20 s, DQN-MIoT achieves the highest throughput of 805.94 units, slightly surpassing DQL-MIoT (803.12) and notably outperforming Greedy-MIoT (799.28). DQN-MIoT maintains a stable throughput at 801.75, while DQL-MIoT, Greedy-MIoT, and random-MIoT drop to 798.11, 780.82, and 772.63, respectively. This steady trend indicates the DQN-MIoT model's efficiency in handling data traffic under varying load conditions.

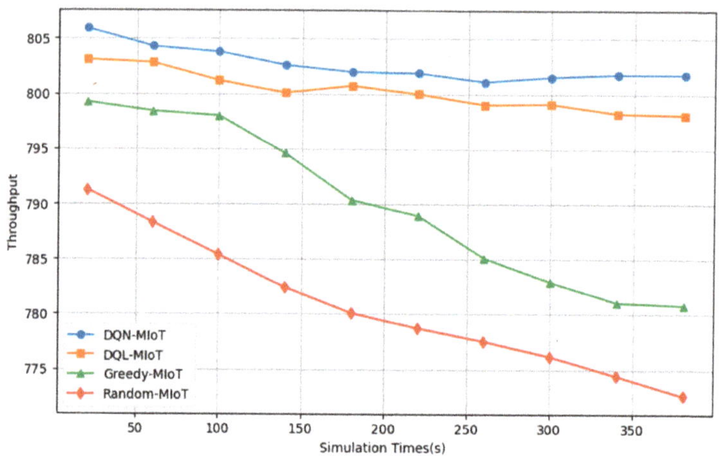

Figure 6. Result on throughput.

A thorough evaluation of performance metrics reveals that DQN-MIoT significantly outperforms reference schemes in terms of convergence speed, final reward value, and overall learning efficiency. Specifically, DQN-MIoT achieves a 66.7% higher final cumulative reward than DQL-MIoT, over 12 times higher than Greedy-MIoT, and vastly superior performance compared to Random-MIoT. This substantial improvement in DQN-MIoT's strong ability to learn effective policies for balancing latency and energy trade-offs in dynamic MEC-enabled IoT environments leads to more intelligent and robust SFC deployment.

5. Conclusions

In this paper, we proposed the DQN-based NFV in IoT-MEC to handle resource computation for diverse services. We designed an intelligent task offloading and resource orchestration framework for dynamic IoT-MEC environments. The framework integrates SFC for VNF placement, dynamic route path selection, and workload distribution through MEC-based task offloading. By leveraging DRL, specifically a DQN-based Markov Decision Process, the system learns to make adaptive decisions for task offloading and resource allocation. Our simulation results indicate that DQN-MIoT outperforms baseline approaches in terms of sub-rewards on latency, energy consumption for MEC workloads within heavy fluctuating traffic changes, packet delivery ratio, packet drop ratio, and throughput in various network conditions and resource allocation values. In the future, we aim to incorporate memory-augmented and graph-enhanced learning models to overcome the limitations of LLMs in capturing long-term, multi-stage attack patterns. Moreover, future simulations will consider federated and edge-aware deployments to handle resource constraints in real-time environments. We will explore lightweight, explainable AI (XAI)-driven frameworks to improve interpretability and transparency in task orchestration.

Author Contributions: Conceptualization, S.R., I.R. and S.K.; methodology, S.R.; software, S.R.; validation, S.R.; formal analysis, S.R.; investigation, S.K.; resources, S.K.; data curation, S.R.; writing—original draft preparation, S.R. and S.K.; writing—review and editing, S.R.; visualization, S.R.; supervision, I.R. and S.K.; project administration, S.K.; funding acquisition, S.K. All authors have read and agreed to the published version of the manuscript.

Funding: This work was supported by the Institute of Information and Communications Technology Planning and Evaluation (IITP) grant, funded by the Korean government (MSIT) (No. RS-2022-00167197, Development of Intelligent 5G/6G Infrastructure Technology for The Smart City); in part by BK21 FOUR (Fostering Outstanding Universities for Research) under Grant 5199990914048; and in part by the Soonchunhyang University Research Fund.

Institutional Review Board Statement: Not applicable.

Informed Consent Statement: Not applicable.

Data Availability Statement: Derived data supporting the findings of this study are available from the corresponding author on request.

Conflicts of Interest: The authors declare no conflicts of interest.

References

1. Anitha, P.; Vimala, H.S.; Shreyas, J. Comprehensive Review on Congestion Detection, Alleviation, and Control for IoT Networks. *J. Netw. Comput. Appl.* **2024**, *221*, 103749. [CrossRef]
2. Alsharif, M.H.; Kelechi, A.H.; Jahid, A.; Kannadasan, R.; Singla, M.K.; Gupta, J.; Geem, Z.W. A Comprehensive Survey of Energy-Efficient Computing to Enable Sustainable Massive IoT Networks. *Alex. Eng. J.* **2024**, *91*, 12–29. [CrossRef]
3. Ma, H.; Tao, Y.; Fang, Y.; Chen, P.; Li, Y. Multi-Carrier Initial-Condition-Index-Aided DCSK Scheme: An Efficient Solution for Multipath Fading Channel. *IEEE Trans. Veh. Technol.* **2025**, 1–14. [CrossRef]
4. Yu, Q.; Wang, H.; He, D.; Lu, Z. Enhanced Group-Based Chirp Spread Spectrum Modulation: Design and Performance Analysis. *IEEE Internet Things J.* **2025**, *12*, 5079–5092. [CrossRef]
5. Li, J.; Sun, G.; Wu, Q.; Niyato, D.; Kang, J.; Jamalipour, A.; Leung, V.C.M. Collaborative Ground-Space Communications via Evolutionary Multi-Objective Deep Reinforcement Learning. *IEEE J. Sel. Areas Commun.* **2024**, *42*, 3395–3411. [CrossRef]
6. Mijumbi, R.; Serrat, J.; Gorricho, J.-L.; Bouten, N.; De Turck, F.; Boutaba, R. Network Function Virtualization: State-of-The-Art and Research Challenges. *IEEE Commun. Surv. Tutor.* **2016**, *18*, 236–262. [CrossRef]
7. Aboubakar, M.; Kellil, M.; Roux, P. A Review of IoT Network Management: Current Status and Perspectives. *J. King Saud Univ. Comput. Inf. Sci.* **2021**, *34*, 4163–4176. [CrossRef]
8. Liyanage, M.; Porambage, P.; Ding, A.Y.; Kalla, A. Driving Forces for Multi-Access Edge Computing (MEC) IoT Integration in 5 G. *ICT Express* **2021**, *7*, 127–137. [CrossRef]

9. Singh, R.; Sukapuram, R.; Chakraborty, S. A Survey of Mobility-Aware Multi-Access Edge Computing: Challenges, Use Cases and Future Directions. *Ad Hoc Netw.* **2023**, *140*, 103044. [CrossRef]
10. Wang, H.; Chen, P. Parallelism-Aware Service Function Chain Placement for Delay-Sensitive IoT Applications with VNF Reuse in Mobile Edge Computing. In Proceedings of the 2024 IEEE International Conference on Web Services (ICWS), Shenzhen, China, 7–13 July 2024; pp. 968–973. [CrossRef]
11. Ros, S.; Tam, P.; Song, I.; Kang, S.; Kim, S. Handling Efficient VNF Placement with Graph-Based Reinforcement Learning for SFC Fault Tolerance. *Electronics* **2024**, *13*, 2552. [CrossRef]
12. Tam, P.; Kim, S. Graph-Based Deep Reinforcement Learning in Edge Cloud Virtualized O-RAN for Sharing Collaborative Learning Workloads. *IEEE Trans. Netw. Sci. Eng.* **2024**, *12*, 302–318. [CrossRef]
13. Wang, H.; Guo, R.; Ma, P.; Ruan, C.; Luo, X.; Ding, W.; Zhong, T.; Xu, J.; Liu, Y.; Chen, X. Towards Mobile Sensing with Event Cameras on High-Agility Resource-Constrained Devices: A Survey. *arXiv* **2025**, arXiv:2503.22943. [CrossRef]
14. Ullah, S.A.; Bibi, M.; Hassan, S.A.; Abou-Zeid, H.; Qureshi, H.K.; Jung, H.; Mahmood, A.; Gidlund, M.; Hossain, E. From Nodes to Roads: Surveying DRL Applications in MEC-Enhanced Terrestrial Wireless Networks. *IEEE Commun. Surv. Tutor.* **2025**, 1–42. [CrossRef]
15. Ding, H.; Zhao, Z.; Zhang, H.; Liu, W.; Yuan, D. DRL-Based Computation Efficiency Maximization in MEC-Enabled Heterogeneous Networks. *IEEE Trans. Veh. Technol.* **2024**, *73*, 15739–15744. [CrossRef]
16. Wu, J.; Yin, J.; Zhao, X.; Liu, Y. DRL-Driven Adaptive SFC Deployment with GCN in Distributed Cloud Networks. In Proceedings of the 2025 IEEE 4th Information Technology and Mechatronics Engineering Conference (ITOEC), Chongqing, China, 14–16 March 2025; pp. 1269–1273. [CrossRef]
17. Onsu, M.A.; Lohan, P.; Kantarci, B.; Janulewicz, E.; Slobodrian, S. A New Realistic Platform for Benchmarking and Performance Evaluation of DRL-Driven and Reconfigurable SFC Provisioning Solutions. *arXiv* **2024**, arXiv:2406.10356. [CrossRef]
18. Liu, Y.; Lu, Y.; Li, X.; Qiao, W.; Li, Z.; Zhao, D. SFC Embedding Meets Machine Learning: Deep Reinforcement Learning Approaches. *IEEE Commun. Lett.* **2021**, *25*, 1926–1930. [CrossRef]
19. Escheikh, M.; Taktak, W. Online QoS/QoE-Driven SFC Orchestration Leveraging a DRL Approach in SDN/NFV Enabled Networks. *Wirel. Pers. Commun.* **2024**, *137*, 1511–1538. [CrossRef]
20. Golec, M.; Khamayseh, Y.; Melhem, S.B.; Alwarafy, A. LLM-Driven APT Detection for 6G Wireless Networks: A Systematic Review and Taxonomy. *arXiv* **2025**, arXiv:2505.18846. [CrossRef]
21. Ros, S.; Kang, S.; Iv, T.; Song, I.; Tam, P.; Kim, S. Priority-Aware Resource Allocation for VNF Deployment in Service Function Chains Based on Graph Reinforcement Learning. *Comput. Mater. Contin.* **2025**, *83*, 1649–1665. [CrossRef]
22. Xu, Y.; He, Z.; Li, K. Resource Allocation and Placement in Multi-Access Edge Computing. *Stud. Big Data* **2024**, *151*, 39–62. [CrossRef]
23. Tomassilli, A.; Giroire, F.; Huin, N.; Pérennès, S. rovably Efficient Algorithms for Placement of Service Function Chains with Ordering Constraints. In Proceedings of the IEEE INFOCOM 2018—IEEE Conference on Computer Communications, Honolulu, HI, USA, 16–19 April 2018. [CrossRef]
24. Guérout, T.; Gaoua, Y.; Artigues, C.; Costa, G.D.; Lopez, P.; Monteil, T. Mixed Integer Linear Programming for Quality of Service Optimization in Clouds. *Future Gener. Comput. Syst.* **2017**, *71*, 1–17. [CrossRef]
25. Sun, G.; Wang, Z.; Su, H.; Yu, H.; Lei, B.; Guizani, M. Profit Maximization of Independent Task Offloading in MEC-Enabled 5G Internet of Vehicles. *IEEE Trans. Intell. Transp. Syst.* **2024**, *25*, 16449–16461. [CrossRef]
26. Pei, J.; Hong, P.; Xue, K.; Li, D. Efficiently Embedding Service Function Chains with Dynamic Virtual Network Function Placement in Geo-Distributed Cloud System. *IEEE Trans. Parallel Distrib. Syst.* **2019**, *30*, 2179–2192. [CrossRef]
27. Jin, P.; Fei, X.; Zhang, Q.; Liu, F.; Li, B. Latency-aware VNF Chain Deployment with Efficient Resource Reuse at Network Edge. In Proceedings of the IEEE Conference on Computer Communications (IEEE INFOCOM), Toronto, ON, Canada, 6–9 July 2020; pp. 267–276.
28. Zheng, D.; Peng, C.; Liao, X.; Cao, X. Toward Optimal Hybrid Service Function Chain Embedding in Multiaccess Edge Computing. *IEEE Internet Things J.* **2020**, *7*, 6035–6045. [CrossRef]
29. Tam, P.; Ros, S.; Song, I.; Kang, S.; Kim, S. A Survey of Intelligent End-To-End Networking Solutions: Integrating Graph Neural Networks and Deep Reinforcement Learning Approaches. *Electronics* **2024**, *13*, 994. [CrossRef]
30. Mao, M.; Hong, M. YOLO Object Detection for Real-Time Fabric Defect Inspection in the Textile Industry: A Review of YOLOv1 to YOLOv11. *Sensors* **2025**, *25*, 2270. [CrossRef]
31. Sun, R.; Cheng, N.; Li, C.; Chen, F.; Chen, W. Knowledge-Driven Deep Learning Paradigms for Wireless Network Optimization in 6G. *IEEE Network* **2024**, *38*, 70–78. [CrossRef]
32. Zhai, X.; He, Z.; Xiao, Y.; Wu, J.; Yu, X. Dynamic VNF Deployment and Resource Allocation in Mobile Edge Computing. In Proceedings of the 2024 IEEE International Symposium on Parallel and Distributed Processing with Applications (ISPA), Kaifeng, China, 30 October–2 November 2024; pp. 573–581. [CrossRef]

33. Yao, J.; Wang, J.; Wang, C.; Yan, C. DRL-Based VNF Cooperative Scheduling Framework with Priority-Weighted Delay. *IEEE Trans. Mob. Comput.* **2024**, *23*, 11375–11388. [CrossRef]
34. Xu, S.; Li, Y.; Guo, S.; Lei, C.; Liu, D.; Qiu, X. Cloud-Edge Collaborative SFC Mapping for Industrial IoT Using Deep Reinforcement Learning. *IEEE Trans. Ind. Inform.* **2021**, *18*, 4158–4168. [CrossRef]
35. Zhu, R.; Wang, P.; Geng, Z.; Zhao, Y.; Yu, S. Double-Agent Reinforced VNFC Deployment in EONs for Cloud-Edge Computing. *J. Light. Technol.* **2023**, *41*, 5193–5208. [CrossRef]
36. Gao, X.; Liu, R.; Kaushik, A.; Zhang, H. Dynamic Resource Allocation for Virtual Network Function Placement in Satellite Edge Clouds. *IEEE Trans. Netw. Sci. Eng.* **2022**, *9*, 2252–2265. [CrossRef]

sensors

MDPI

Article

Radio Coverage Assessment and Indoor Communication Enhancement in Hospitals: A Case Study at CHUCB†

Óscar Silva [1,2], Emanuel Bordalo Teixeira [1,2], Ana Corceiro [2], Antonio D. Reis [3] and Fernando J. Velez [1,2,*]

1. Instituto de Telecomunicações, Faculdade de Engenharia, Universidade da Beira Interior, Calçada Fonte do Lameiro, 6201-001 Covilhã, Portugal; oscar.silva@ubi.pt (Ó.S.); emanuelt@ubi.pt (E.B.T.)
2. Departamento de Engenharia Eletromecânica, Faculdade de Engenharia, Universidade da Beira Interior, Calçada Fonte do Lameiro, 6201-001 Covilhã, Portugal; ana.corceiro@ubi.pt
3. Departamento de Física, Faculdade de Ciências; Universidade da Beira Interior, Rua Marquês d'Ávila e Bolama, 6201-001 Covilhã, Portugal; adreis@ubi.pt

* Correspondence: fjv@ubi.pt

† This article is revised and expanded version of the paper entitled "Monitoring the Provision of Ubiquitous Cellular Coverage in a Hospital Environment: Radio Spectrum Measurements at CHUCB" (in Portuguese), which was presented at ICEUBI 2024—International Conference on Engineering, University of Beira Interior, Covilhã, Portugal, 27–29 November 2024.

Highlights:

What are the main findings?

- Long Term Evolution showed better overall performance in terms of coverage and signal quality in the received power measurements conducted at CHUCB.
- Critical areas with poor coverage were identified, especially at points 17, 19, and 21, where there was an absence or weak signal quality in various technologies.

What is the implication of the main finding?

- The identification of areas with poor coverage allowed for the proposal of targeted solutions, such as strategically setting up femtocells or DAS, to improve coverage and connectivity in critical areas.
- The improvement of cellular coverage is essential for efficient networking of health professionals, connected medical devices, and wireless patient monitoring systems.

Abstract: The adoption of wireless medical technologies in hospital environments is often limited by cellular coverage issues, especially in indoor areas with complex structures. This study presents a detailed radio spectrum measurement campaign conducted at the Cova da Beira University Hospital Center (CHUCB), using the NARDA SRM-3006 and R&S®TSME6 equipment. The signal strength and quality of 5G NR, LTE, UMTS, and NB-IoT technologies were evaluated. Critical coverage gaps were identified, particularly at points 17, 19, and 21. Results revealed that operators MEO and NOS dominate coverage, with MEO providing better 5G NR coverage and NOS excelling in LTE signal quality. Based on the results, the localized installation of femtocells is proposed to improve coverage in these areas. The approach was designed to be scalable and replicable, with a planned application at Cumura Hospital (Guinea-Bissau), reinforcing the applicability of the solution in contexts with limited infrastructure. This work provides both technical and clinical contributions to achieving ubiquitous cellular coverage in healthcare settings.

Keywords: WBAN; wireless communications; mobile networks; ubiquitous cellular coverage; NB-IoT; radio spectrum measurements; ICT

1. Introduction

We live in an era witnessing unparalleled scientific and technological advancements in telecommunications, particularly in the development of wireless networking, leading to the emergence of solutions that transform social and professional interaction [1]. In the healthcare sector, wireless body area networks (WBANs) have emerged as an innovative solution for remote patient monitoring [2]. These networks use low-energy devices capable of wireless communication [3]. In general, these devices include sensors, actuators, and microcontrollers, positioned around or inside the human body, to monitor, collect, and transmit specific data, such as heart rate, blood oxygen levels, body temperature [3,4], blood pressure/24-h monitoring, and Holter. These data, along with clinical analysis (including blood tests) results, cardiac monitoring data/ECG, ultrasound outcomes, EEG, clinical imaging, or sleep apnea monitoring tests, among other ones, are then processed and diagnosed by healthcare professionals. This technological advancement, together with advanced telemonitoring of at-risk patients, is important because it allows healthcare professionals to monitor patients' health status in real-time, thereby improving the provision of high-quality care [5].

Simultaneously, the increasing average life expectancy of human beings has led to a higher demand for hospital services, putting greater pressure on underlying human and financial resources. Many hospitalized patients present complex conditions, requiring constant monitoring to prevent serious health episodes. Studies show that warning signs, such as changes in heart rate and respiratory rate, can appear six to eight hours before critical events, such as cardiorespiratory arrests, being observed in 60% to 85% of cases. The early detection of these signs is essential to prevent worsening of the patient's health condition and save lives.

Although current monitoring systems allow for the tracking of vital parameters in real-time, their effectiveness depends on the constant presence of healthcare professionals, which is often unfeasible due to the shortage of human resources. To overcome this challenge, the Cova da Beira University Hospital Center (CHUCB), through the Telemonitoring of at-Risk Patients (TERI) project, implemented a telemonitoring system that combines preventive, continuous, and retrospective monitoring, optimizing available resources and ensuring faster and more effective responses. However, for the efficient operation of these technological solutions, a robust communication infrastructure is vital. The effectiveness of WBANs and system setups, like the ones from TERI, depends on reliable cellular coverage capable of ensuring the continuous and secure transmission of patient data.

Despite advances in information and communication technologies (ICTs) and their applications to healthcare, many hospitals still face significant challenges in ensuring suitable cellular and wireless local area networking coverage [6]. As demonstrated by Ahmed et al. [7], hospitals require minimum QoS thresholds that are not universally met due to the impact of buildings structural aspects in the signal propagation. Our study advances this field by empirically evaluating these metrics across multiple technologies (LTE, 5G NR, NB-IoT), complementing previous theoretical approaches. Previous studies indicate that the complexity of hospital structures and environmental interferences can compromise signal quality, leading to communication failures. These coverage gaps not only hinder the effective operation of WBANs but can also directly affect patient safety and well-being, especially in critical areas such as intensive care units and emergency rooms, since in the healthcare sector, data needs to be as complete as possible. Given the importance of ubiquitous communication, the effectiveness of networks in hospital environments fundamentally depends on the quality and availability of cellular coverage [8], as hospitals are very complex environments with various sources of interference and signal obstructions.

Thus, it is essential to identify the areas that need improvement in cellular coverage to ensure the continuity and quality of service provision [9]. Recent research highlights the importance of wireless technologies, such as ZigBee, Wi-Fi, ultra-wideband (UWB), and Bluetooth/BLE (i.e., IEEE 802.25.4, 802.11, 802.3, and 802.1, respectively), in conjunction with mobile networks, e.g., narrow-band Internet of Things (NB-IoT), as well as the use of small cells, such as femtocells, in indoor environments, to improve coverage, as described by authors from [3,4].

Despite the advances observed in the integration of mobile technologies into healthcare systems, two gaps persist in the scientific literature regarding the evaluation of cellular coverage in hospital environments. The first pertains to the scarcity of empirical studies conducting comparative measurement campaigns involving multiple technologies—namely 5G, LTE, UMTS, and NB-IoT—within the same hospital setting. Most existing works adopt theoretical approaches or are limited to the isolated analysis of a single technology. Even the seminal study by Chen et al. [10], which describes the implementation of a standalone 5G network in a hospital in China, focuses exclusively on this technology, without addressing coexistence or comparison with other network layers.

The second gap relates to the near-total absence of applied studies in African contexts, particularly concerning the technical analysis of cellular coverage in healthcare facilities. Although investigations such as those by Bétila [11] and Achieng and Ogundaini [12] highlight the fragility of digital infrastructures and insufficient coverage as critical obstacles to the modernization of healthcare systems in Africa, these approaches are centered on macrostructural perspectives, without incorporating empirical measurements or multitechnological comparative analysis in clinical environments.

This study thus aims to contribute to bridging these two gaps: firstly, by conducting a multitechnological technical measurement campaign in a real hospital context; and secondly, by establishing a solid methodological foundation for the future replication of this study in a resource-limited environment, specifically at the Hospital of Cumura in Guinea-Bissau.

The aim of this study is to evaluate the quality of cellular coverage at the CHUCB, identifying areas where cellular coverage improvements are needed. This study will serve as the basis for future work to be carried out at the Cumura Hospital in Guinea-Bissau, where telecommunications infrastructures are significantly more limited. For this purpose, measurements of the radio spectrum were carried out at more than 20 points in the hospital, using measurement devices, such as the NARDA SRM-3006 spectrum analyzer and the R&S®TSME6 scanner, encompassing the sub-6 GHz bands, thus including the range of frequencies, up to 2.6 GHz, from this study [13]. Data obtained has allowed for a detailed analysis of coverage quality, enabling the proposal of handy solutions, such as the installation of femtocells or DAS in critical areas, to ensure ubiquitous, efficient, and seamless communication. Carrying out this study is essential to ensure that all sectors of the hospital have the required coverage to operate safely and effectively, thereby enhancing the quality of the healthcare provided to patients.

The remaining sections of the paper are organized as follows. Section 2 addresses the applied methodology, outlining the context and objectives of the measurement procedures and of the equipment used. In Section 3, the measurements conducted with the Narda SRM-3006 and the R&S®TSME6 scanner at the identified measurement points are addressed together with a comparison with cellular coverage maps in the region of CHUCB, followed by the analysis of the results in Section 4. In Section 5, the importance of ubiquitous cellular coverage in the support of easy-to-use telemedicine wireless devices in hospital environments is discussed, along with the discussion of a proposal for the deployment of femtocells or DAS and future expansion, and prospects for international expansion in developing countries. Finally, the conclusions are presented in Section 6 along with suggestions for further work.

2. Methodology

2.1. Context and Objectives

Measurements of the radioelectric spectrum were carried out at the Centro Hospitalar Universitário Cova da Beira (CHUCB) to evaluate the quality of the signal available in different areas of the hospital and its surroundings, as well as identifying zones with coverage deficiencies that could compromise the effectiveness of WBANs and other wireless communication-dependent systems [1]. This study was motivated by the need to explore possibilities for providing ubiquitous cellular coverage in the hospital and surrounding context, thus ensuring that all sectors of the hospital, especially the critical ones, have ubiquitous coverage that guarantees the continuity of operations and the safety of patients [13].

2.2. Radio Monitoring Equipment

For the measurement campaigns, two main measurement devices were used:

- The NARDA SRM-3006 (Narda Safety Test Solutions GmbH, Pfullingen, Germany) is a spectrum analyzer that allows selective frequency measurements for safety analysis and environmental measurements in high-frequency electromagnetic fields, with a range from 9 kHz to 6 GHz [1]. The complete SRM-3006 measurement system consists of a Basic Unit SRM-3006 and a three-axis antenna, which enables quick and simple isotropic measurements, with automatic determination of the three spatial components of the electromagnetic field, as illustrated in Figure 1 [13]. The NARDA SRM-3006 is widely used to monitor the coverage of cellular mobile networks and local wireless networks [1]. As signals in this frequency range of such magnitude are very difficult to sample digitally [13], this equipment combines analogue and digital signal processing to ensure absolute values, and limits high-frequency electromagnetic fields.

Figure 1. Narda SRM-3006 spectrum analyzer.

- The R&S®TSME6 scanner (Rohde & Schwarz GmbH & Co. KG, Munich, Germany) is used for the analysis and optimization of mobile networks, as shown in Figure 2. This scanner, combined with the R&S®ROMES4 unit test software, version 21 (64-bit), can detect all available mobile network technologies across a frequency range from 9 kHz to 6 GHz, such as 5G NR, LTE, NB-IoT, and GSM, among others [1]. In addition to identifying the available mobile network technologies, the R&S®TSME6 can perform essential tasks involved in coverage measurements, such as detecting external interferences, measuring performance, and conducting quality analysis in mobile networks, e.g., bandwidth, total power received within the operator's bandwidth [1,10].

Figure 2. R&S®TSME6 drive test scanner.

The combination of the scanner with R&S®ROMES4 software allows viewing the available mobile networks, and which frequencies they are available on, while indicating the bandwidth and central frequency. The scanner supports various protocols such as 5G NR, GSM, LTE, NB-IoT, LTE-M, and TETRA. R&S®TSMA6 offers a detailed and comprehensive analysis of various parameters, performs an automated and reliable analysis, provides the view graphs of all detected technologies (with information to analyze various components of the cellular mobile network), with reduced energy consumption. The scanner combined with the R&S®ROMES4 unit test software also facilitates visualizing the timeline (with transmissions detected by the scanner) in graphical format. At the bottom of the homepage shown in Figure 3, in the lower horizontal bar, various menus with different functionalities are offered by the software: Welcome, Automatic Channel Detection (ACD), Navigation, 3GPP2 (CDMA200) Scanner, GSM Scanner, LTE Scanner, NB-IoT Scanner, and UMTS Scanner. Details are as follows: the Welcome menu lists all previously mentioned menus, while the ACD menu displays the frequency range and detected technologies, as shown in Figure 3.

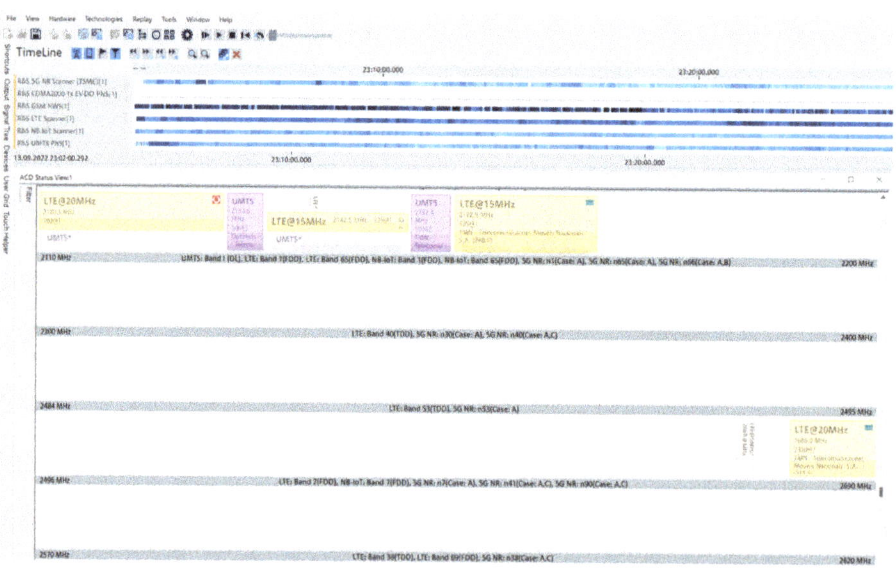

Figure 3. View of the automatic channel detection menu.

The Navigation menu allows users to check the estimated route of data collection and estimate the geographic positions of base stations (with the indicated transmission directions), as shown in Figure 4. The 5G NR Scanner presents technologies detected in 5G NR, including received signal strength indicator, RSSI [dBm], graphs, and related parameters (e.g., Physical Cell ID). The LTE Scanner allows users to view detected technologies, power [dBm] graphs, and associated parameters.

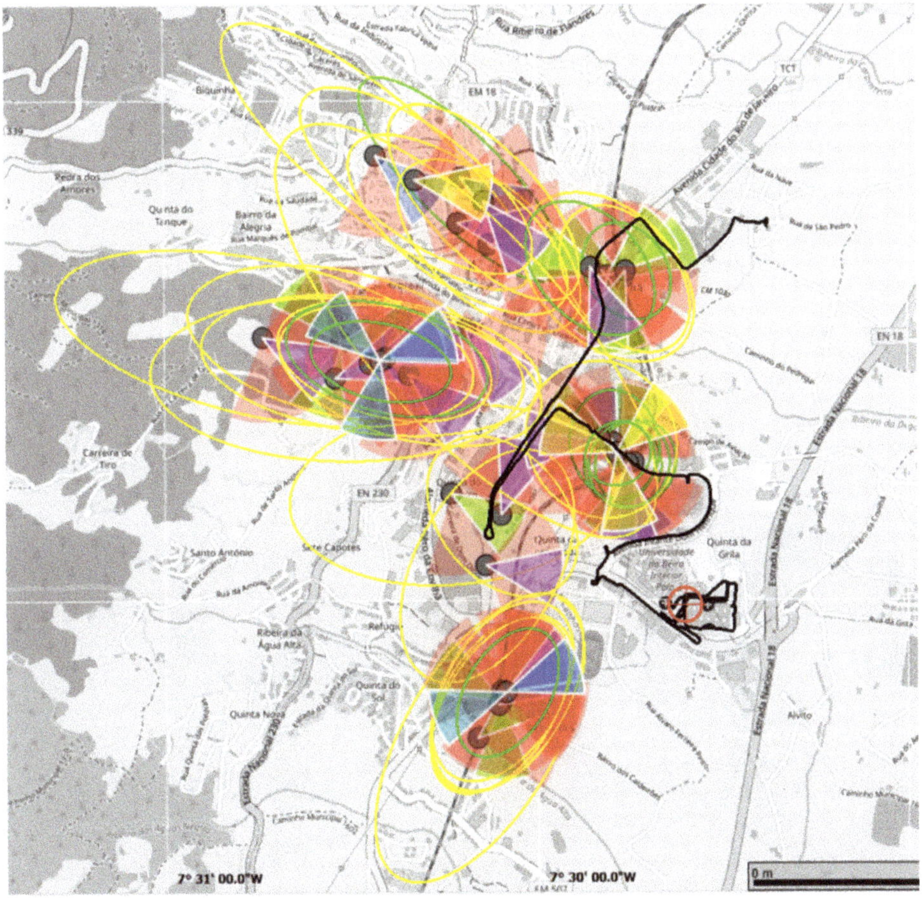

Figure 4. Navigation map obtained during the measurement campaign using the R&S®TSME6 scanner and ROMES4 software. Each coloured shape represents a detected cell, and the triangular segments within them indicate the antenna sectors or beams. The colours are automatically generated by the software to distinguish between sectors and do not reflect signal quality, frequency, technology, or operator.

The NB-IoT Scanner shows the detected operators' networks in NB-IoT, including New Radio Signal Strength, NRSS [dBm], view graphs (through NRSSI), and related parameters. The 3GPP2 Scanner displays the operators (i.e., CDMA2000) at any point. The UMTS Scanner allows users to view detected UMTS operators, display received signal code power, RSCP [dBm], view graphs (providing information on which operator has the most reliable signal coverage), and associated parameters. Although the R&S®ROMES4 software displays TMN and Optimus as the names of the mobile operators, from now on, in this work, their current names, MEO and NOS, respectively, will be adopted.

2.3. Measurement Procedures

The measurements were conducted both inside and around the hospital, covering critical areas such as wards, the emergency department, imaging, the helipad, and parking lots (Figure 5). According to [14], the Hospital should provide ubiquitous access to mobile and wireless communications for the use of relevant applications and patient databases. It is recommended that the base stations be located closer to the users, thus reducing the level of electromagnetic fields. The farther the base station is from its users, the higher the power required to transmit; consequently, the higher the electromagnetic field strength.

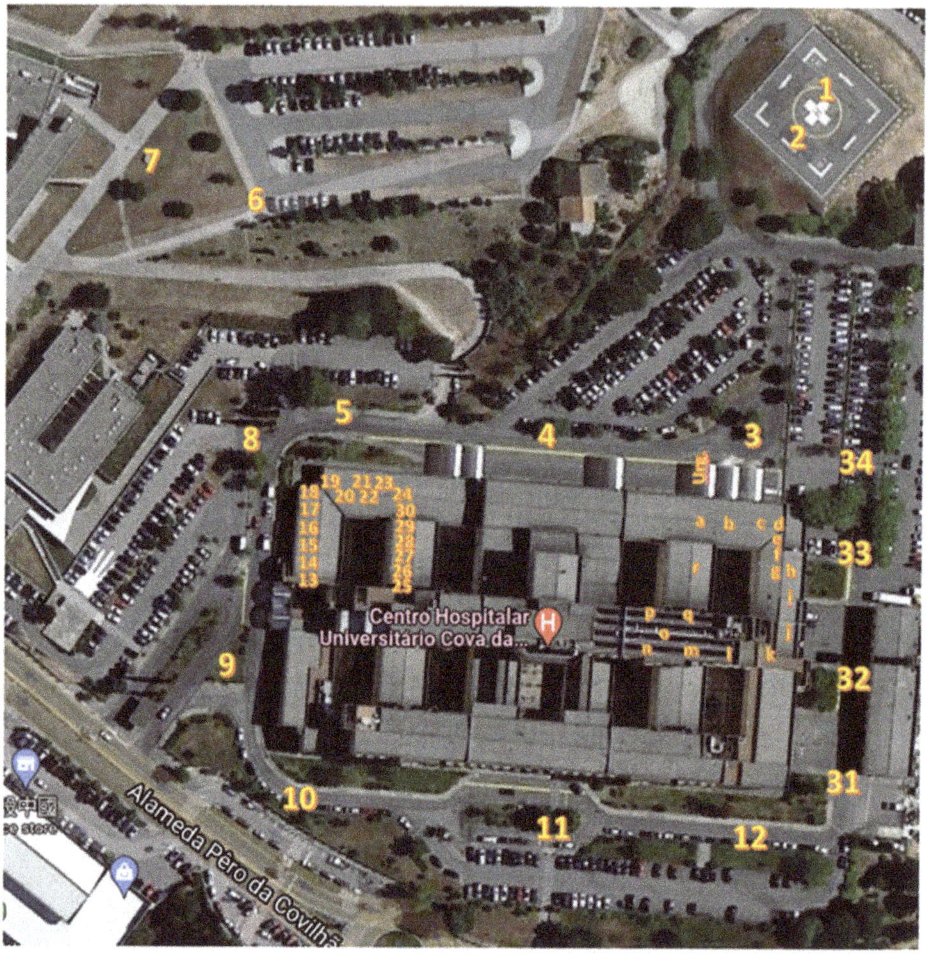

Figure 5. Map of measurement points at the Centro Hospitalar Universitário Cova da Beira. The numbered (1–34) and lettered (a–p) labels indicate spatial locations for possible measurements.

Signal strength and connection quality were analyzed at each measurement point. Although the most used theoretical parameters in modern mobile networks include RSSI, RSRP, RSRQ, and SINR [1] in this study, the specific metrics available in the measurement tool by technology were considered: NRSSI for NB-IoT, RSCP for UMTS, Power for LTE, and RSSI for 5G NR. Measurements have been taken at different times of the day to capture temporal variations in signal quality.

The collected data were subsequently analyzed to identify the quality of coverage in each area, considering the following sectors of the Hospital:

(i) Wards MEDICINE 1;
(ii) Wards SURGERY 1;
(iii) General emergency;
(iv) Imaging;
(v) Complementary exams.

The collected data were processed and compared to identify trends and patterns in the extension and quality of the mobile phone signal. Results were presented in graphs illustrating signal strength for different technologies at each measurement point, allowing for a clear visualization of areas where coverage is insufficient. Based on these results, specific recommendations were made for improving cellular coverage, including the proposal to install femtocells or DAS in critical areas.

3. Results

Although all the results have been obtained and analyzed, to maintain the conciseness of the manuscript, only the most relevant data are presented in the body of the text. The complete and detailed results of the measurements can be found in [13].

Measurements were undertaken in various areas inside and outside the CHUCB. For the measurements conducted with the NARDA SRM-3006, we present the results of six selected points for analysis. On the other hand, in the measurements taken with the R&S®TSME6 scanner, we analyze the worst measurement point for the four (4) technologies (LTE, UMTS, 5G NR, and NB-IoT), point 17. Furthermore, the summary with all six measurement points will be presented in Table 1. These points were carefully selected for analysis, considering their correspondence with the possible locations of the asset tracking system being designed to operate in the context of CHUCB.

Table 1. Table with the designation of the measurement points.

Point/Location	Narda SRM-3006	Scanner R&S®TSME6
Front door	325	45 s
13	328	1:18 min
17	332	2:10 min
19	333	2:32 min
21	334	2:47 min
23	337	3:05 min

The selected points are the same for both the NARDA SRM-3006 measurements and the scanner measurements. The R&S®ROMES4 unit test software, combined with the scanner, allowed us to record the time at each measurement point, which greatly facilitated the analysis of the results. Through the software, at each measurement point, it was possible to select a specific time to analyze the results. On the other hand, in the measurements undertaken with NARDA SRM-3006, each point has its corresponding measurement number, as presented in Table 1, thus facilitating the extraction of the data collected at each measurement point. Table 2 presents a listing of the frequency bands assigned to various operators for each available technology, which allowed for correlating the measurement results with the specific technologies and their respective operators [13].

Table 2 is essential for understanding the distribution of frequencies used by the main Portuguese operators, namely MEO, NOS, and Vodafone.

Table 2. Frequency bands of the Portuguese operators, based on the information provided by ANACOM.

Operator	Frequency Interval—Downlink [MHz] https://www.anacom.pt/render.jsp?categoryId=382989 (accessed on 4 February 2022)		Frequency Band [MHz]	Technology
MEO	791.0	801.0	800	Technological Neutrality
MEO	950.9	958.9	900	GSM/UMTS/WIMAX/LTE
MEO	1845.0	1865.0	1800	GSM/UMTS/WIMAX/LTE
MEO	2149.9	2169.7	2100	UMTS
MEO	2670.0	2690.0	2600	Technological Neutrality
NOS	811.0	821.0	800	Technological Neutrality
NOS	943.1	950.9	900	GSM/UMTS/WIMAX/LTE
NOS	1825.0	1845.0	1800	GSM/UMTS/WIMAX/LTE
NOS	2130.1	2144.9	2100	UMTS
NOS	2650.0	2670.0	2600	Technological Neutrality
Vodafone	801.0	811.0	800	Technological Neutrality
Vodafone	930.0	935.0	900	GSM/UMTS/WIMAX/LTE
Vodafone	935.1	943.1	900	GSM/UMTS/WIMAX/LTE
Vodafone	1805.0	1825.0	1800	GSM/UMTS/WIMAX/LTE
Vodafone	2110.3	2130.1	2100	UMTS
Vodafone	2570.0	2595.0	2600	Technological Neutrality
Vodafone	2630.0	2650.0	2600	Technological Neutrality

To facilitate the interpretation of the measurement results, typical thresholds for each technology and the considered metrics are shown in Table 3.

Table 3. Thresholds for each wireless technology and signal quality metric, expressed in dBm. The thresholds in Table 3 are based on 3GPP standards (TS 36.133; TS 25.133), R&S®TSME6 equipment documentation, and Rohde & Schwarz guidelines for 5G NR, LTE, and NB-IoT network analysis.

Technology	Metric	Unit	Typical Thresholds	Interpretation
5G NR	RSSI	dBm	$>-85 \cdot -85/-100 \cdot \leq -100$	Good · Fair · Poor
LTE	Power	dBm	$>-85 \cdot -85/-95 \cdot \leq -95$	Good · Fair · Poor
NB-IoT	NRSSI	dBm	$>-90 \cdot -90/-105 \cdot \leq -105$	Good · Fair · Poor
UMTS	RSCP	dBm	$>-85 \cdot -85/-95 \cdot \leq -95$	Good · Fair · Poor

3.1. Measurement Results with the Narda SRM-3006

Graphs in Figures 6–11 present the results of the measurements conducted with the NARDA SRM-3006 at the six selected points mentioned in Table 1.

The analysis of detected frequency bands in Figure 6 was made possible by providing a list of the frequency bands assigned to various mobile telecommunications operators, presented in Table 2.

Based on the data from Table 2, the following frequencies and their associated technologies were identified at point 13:

A—760 MHz 5G NR F—1977 MHz UMTS
B—819 MHz Technological Neutrality G—2132 MHz UMTS
C—945 MHz GSM/UMTS/LTE H—2415 MHz Technological Neutrality
D—1754 MHz GSM/UMTS/LTE I—2568 MHz Technological Neutrality
E—1837 MHz GSM/UMTS/LTE J—2687 MHz Technological Neutrality

Similar lessons can be learned at the entrance to the outpatient consultations, which is not far from point 13. However, in point 13, other relevant technologies were identified, given that, due to the existence of a large, glazed surface next to the door, measurements were taken of technologies that are present only outside.

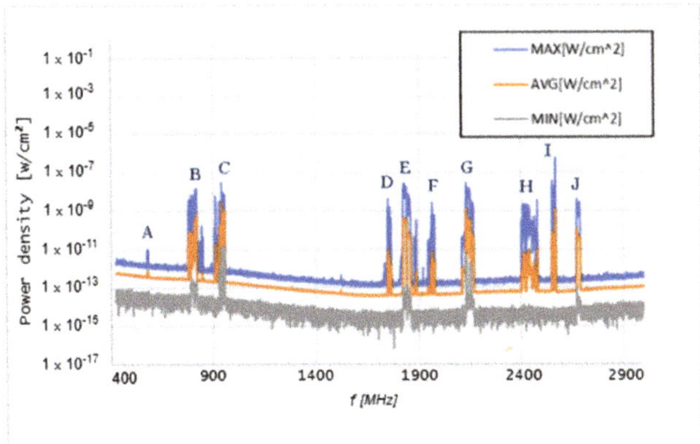

Figure 6. Graph of the measurement performed at point 13. Letters A–J indicate the detected frequency bands, which correspond to the allocations presented in Table 2.

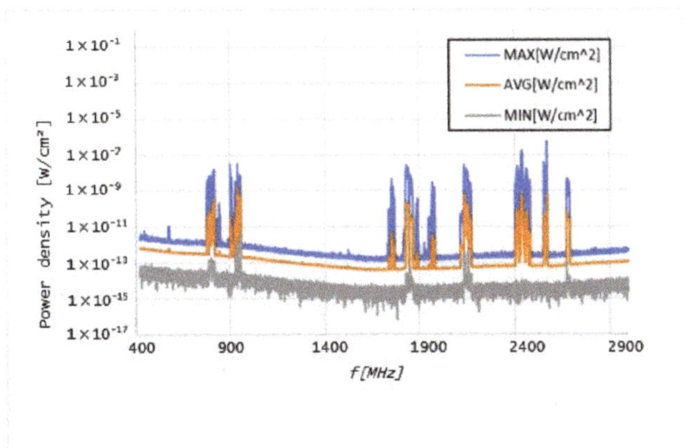

Figure 7. Graph of measurements at the entrance to the outpatient consultations.

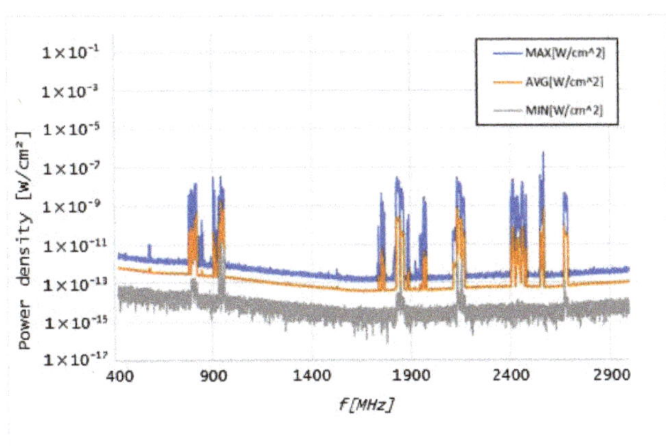

Figure 8. Graph of the measurements undertaken at point 17.

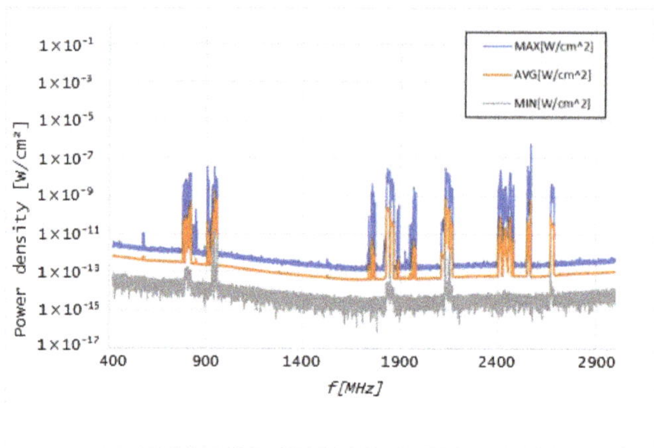

Figure 9. Graph of the measurements undertaken at point 19.

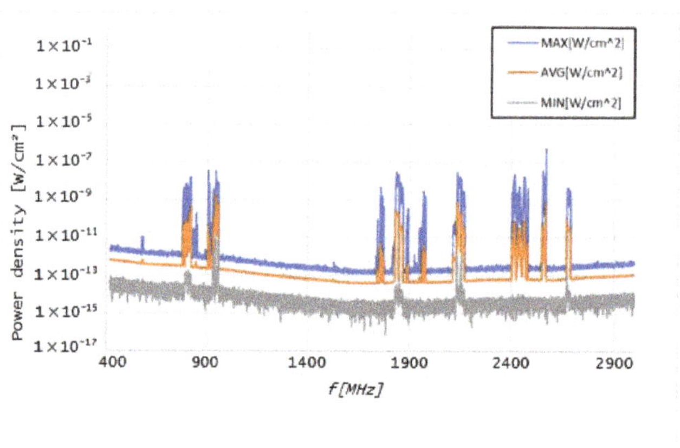

Figure 10. Graph of the measurements undertaken at point 21.

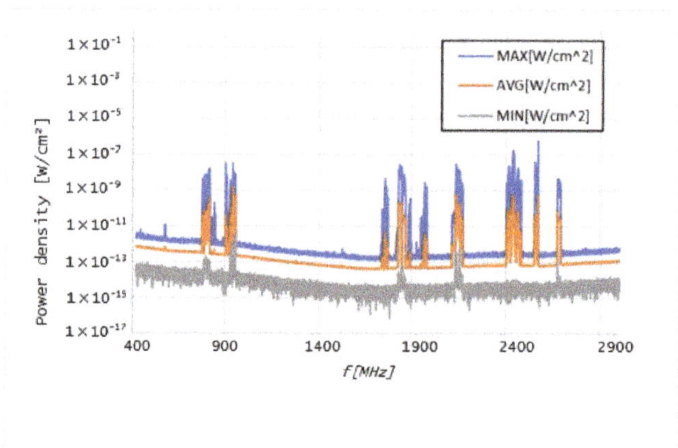

Figure 11. Graph of the measurements undertaken at point 23.

nPerf is a collaborative source of data on mobile network performance across different regions [15]. The nPerf platform gathers this data through crowdsourcing, by collecting geolocated signal strength and network performance information from mobile devices of end users who have installed the nPerf mobile application. Based on coverage maps obtained with nPerf, as shown in Figures 12–14 (for MEO, NOS, and Vodafone, respectively), within the hospital, we consider cellular coverage maps for the region of CHUCB, which are complementary to the point-based measurements conducted by us.

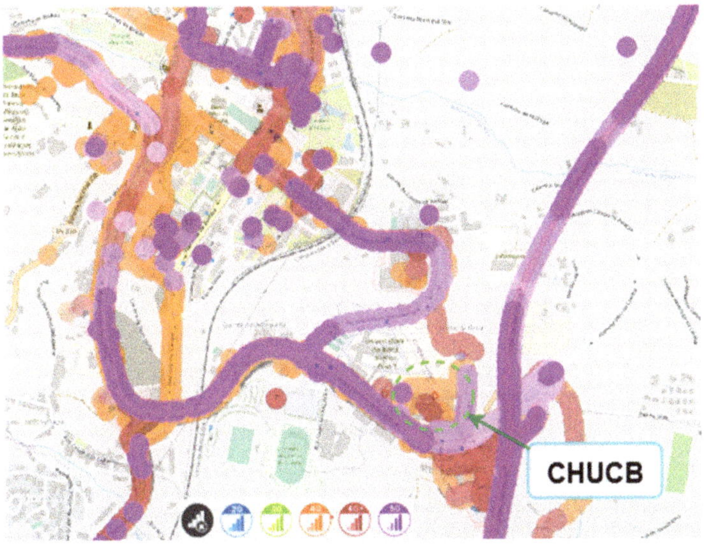

Figure 12. Outdoor cellular coverage map for the MEO operator in the vicinity of CHUCB. Colours represent different mobile network technologies: blue—2G, green—3G, orange—4G, red—4G+, and purple—5G. Source: nPerf platform, July 2025.

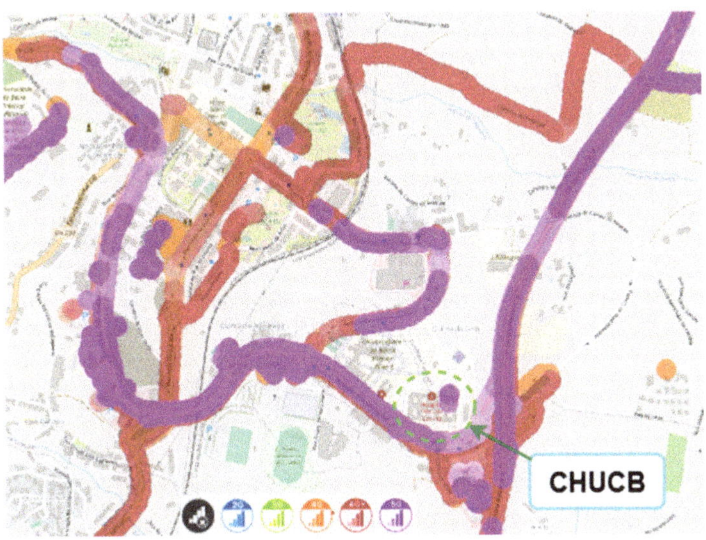

Figure 13. Outdoor cellular coverage map for the NOS operator in the vicinity of CHUCB. Colours represent different mobile network technologies: blue—2G, green—3G, orange—4G, red—4G+, and purple—5G. Source: nPerf platform, July 2025.

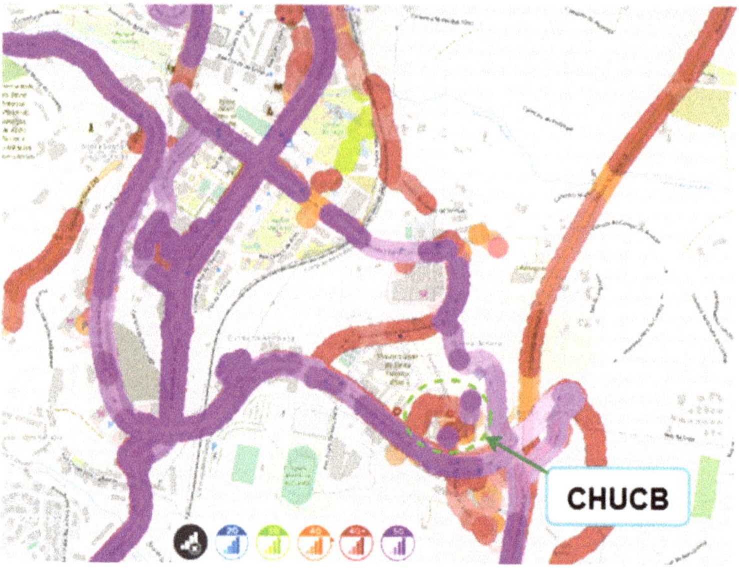

Figure 14. Outdoor cellular coverage map for the Vodafone operator in the vicinity of CHUCB. Colours represent different mobile network technologies: blue—2G, green—3G, orange—4G, red—4G+, and purple—5G. Source: nPerf platform, July 2025.

As it was not possible to obtain coverage maps from September 2022, the exact period during which the indoor measurements were carried out, results for July 2025 are presented here.

3.2. Measurement Results with the R&S®TSME6 Scanner

The measurements for this study were conducted in January 2022. The R&S®TSME6 scanner, in combination with the R&S®ROMES4 software, provided a detailed and real-time analysis of the technologies available at each measurement point. The measurements recorded the exact moment each point was evaluated, allowing for a temporal analysis that complements the spatial assessment of coverage. Figures 15–18 present the coverage graphs, representing the available received power for the four technologies detected in the measurements taken with the R&S®TSME6 scanner at measurement point 17 (mentioned in Table 1). These figures highlight specific characteristics that facilitate the interpretation and analysis of the data. The horizontal axis represents the signal peaks identified, indicating the different sub-measurement points within each main point. The vertical axis displays the corresponding unit values of the analyzed technology, reflecting the intensity of the measured signal in each case. To assist with visual interpretation, the signals are represented by three distinct colors: red, indicating a weak signal; pink, representing a medium signal; and yellow, which refers to a good or very good signal. Additionally, the analyzed operators are identified on the right side of the figures, highlighting the mobile networks measured at each point. It is important to note that, although the objective is to present multi-technology results, in some cases only one technology was detected or, in other cases, no technology was detected. Thus, in certain graphs, the representation may consist of a single bar or, in other cases, where no technology was detected, there are no bars, with each view graph having that meaning.

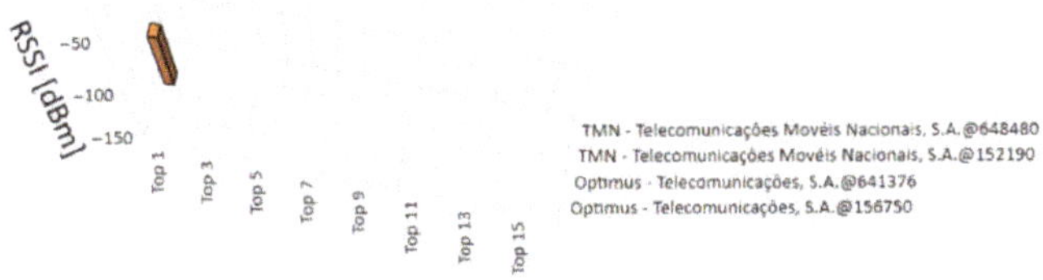

Figure 15. RRSI graph for 5G NR measurements at point 17.

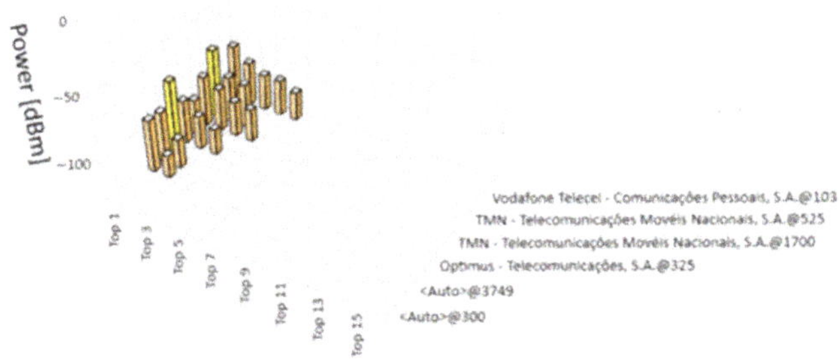

Figure 16. Graph of the received power for LTE measurements at point 17.

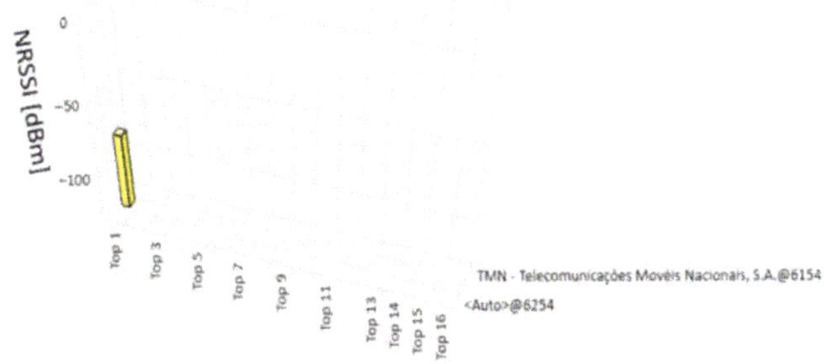

Figure 17. NRSSI Graph for NB-IoT measurements at point 17.

For each measurement point, the signal values (RSSI, Power, NRSSI, RSCP) were recorded for the 5G NR, LTE, NB-IoT, and UMTS technologies, enabling the immediate identification of the operator that offers the best signal quality for each technology. The meaning of the quantities is as follows:

RSSI (received signal strength indicator)—Indicates the strength of the received signal, in dBm, with ranges from −120 dBm (very weak signal) to 0 dBm (very strong signal).

Power—Refers to the signal strength, measured in dBm, usually between −30 dBm (very strong) and −110 dBm (weak).

NRSSI (NR signal strength indicator)—Indicates the signal strength, ranging from −140 dBm (very weak signal) to −40 dBm (strong signal).

RSCP (received signal code power)—Measures the average power of the received signal, in the range of −120 dBm (weak signal) to −40 dBm (strong signal).

Figure 18. RSCP Graph for UMTS measurements at point 17.

Table 4 presents a summary of these best signal coverage values for each operator and different measurement points/technologies. A clear representation of the coverage of each of the four technologies (5G NR, LTE, NB-IoT, and UMTS) at different measurement points is provided, highlighting which operator (MEO, NOS, or Vodafone) provided the best coverage for each technology.

Table 4. Summary of the best received power values for each operator at different measurement points for different technologies. (RSSI, Power, NRSSI, RSCP) for 5G NR, LTE, NB-IoT, and UMTS, respectively, highlighting the operator with the best coverage at each measurement point.

Measurement Points	Technology	Operator		
		MEO	NOS	Vodafone
13	5G NR (RSSI)	−100.22		
	LTE (Power)		−78.23	
	NB-IoT (NRSSI)	−104.34		
	UMTS (RSCP)		−89.2	
17	5G NR (RSSI)	−100.21		
	LTE (Power)		−74.02	
	NB-IoT (NRSSI)			
	UMTS (RSCP)			
19	5G NR (RSSI)		−100.52	
	LTE (Power)	−78.43		
	NB-IoT (NRSSI)	−92.15		
	UMTS (RSCP)		−95.4	
21	5G NR (RSSI)	−97.70		
	LTE (Power)	−83.11		
	NB-IoT (NRSSI)	−98.22		
	UMTS (RSCP)			
23	5G NR (RSSI)	−97.70		
	LTE (Power)	−80.88		
	NB-IoT (NRSSI)	−98.74		
	UMTS (RSCP)	−102.1		
Entrance to the outpatient consultations	5G NR (RSSI)		−94.5	
	LTE (Power)	−98		
	NB-IoT (NRSSI)	−100.31		
	UMTS (RSCP)	−98.6		

4. Analysis of the Cellular Coverage Results

The results of the measurements conducted with the NARDA SRM-3006 revealed important details about the distribution of cellular coverage at CHUCB. Several power peaks were identified at different frequencies, indicating the presence of some technologies, such as 5G NR and LTE, in various areas of the hospital. For example, the frequency of 760 MHz, associated with 5G NR technology, showed a significant peak, suggesting adequate coverage of this technology, in some of the considered measurement points. However, at higher frequencies, such as 2568 MHz, the coverage proved to be irregular.

Although the data obtained with the NARDA SRM-3006 allowed mapping some areas of the hospital that present significant coverage challenges, the level of detail was not sufficient. It became necessary to conduct additional measurements, with greater coverage, to more accurately determine the received power levels, frequencies, and available operators at CHUCB. Thus, new measurements were carried out using the R&S®TSME6 scanner, allowing for a more expedient identification of the operating frequencies and their respective operators.

Upon conducting a more detailed analysis of the measurement points, based on the new results, it was found that, at points 21, 23, and the entrance to the outpatient consultations, the 5G NR technology provided the best signal coverage. In contrast, at points 13, 17, and 19, it was the LTE technology that demonstrated better coverage. Overall, the LTE technology showed the best performance regarding power values and signal indicators (RSSI, NRSSI, RSCP). Moreover, both LTE and 5G NR technologies were present at all six measurement points analyzed, with LTE technology achieving the best coverage, except at the entrance to the outpatient consultations, where 5G NR showed superior coverage.

Regarding the operators, the results indicate that MEO and NOS were present at all six measurement points analyzed, while the Vodafone operator was absent at some of these points. In a comparative analysis between the two most frequently present operators (MEO and NOS), it was found that MEO provided better signal coverage at more points, for the four tested technologies (5G NR, LTE, NB-IoT, and UMTS).

Based on these results, for the analyzed technologies (LTE, UMTS, 5G NR, and NB-IoT), the zones requiring coverage improvement are mainly points 13, 17, and 21. These points recorded more frequent occurrences of weak signal, with points 17 and 21 showing the absence of some technologies, namely NB-IoT and UMTS at point 17, and UMTS at point 21. The analysis of results from this study reveals significant implications for hospital connectivity reliability. In multiple measurements, signal strength indicators for certain technologies fell below −85 dBm, which is beneath the generally recommended threshold for reliable communications in clinical environments. As emphasized by Ahmed et al. [7], hospital networks require consistent coverage to support proper operation of connected medical devices, while Niyato et al. [16] underscore how connectivity failures can compromise remote patient monitoring. These coverage gaps reinforce the need for targeted solutions such as the use of femtocells.

Although the data extracted from nPerf coverage maps do not fully represent the indoor environment of the hospital, they provide a complementary perspective on the evolution of cellular coverage in its surroundings. From the results obtained in 2025, MEO continues to have a considerably good coverage, with evidence of 5G coverage in the entrance to the outpatient consultations. For NOS, there is now evidence of good 5G coverage in the Emergency Service entrance, not well covered in our 2022 field tests. Vodafone also improved its coverage (4G, 4G+ in the entrance to the outpatient consultations), and clear evidence of good 5G coverage in the entrance of the Emergency Service.

5. Importance of Ubiquitous Cellular Coverage in Hospitals

Hospitals are dynamic and complex environments where seamless communication is essential for delivering high-quality patient care and ensuring operational efficiency. Cellular coverage plays a pivotal role in enabling the functionality of medical technologies, supporting telemedicine, and facilitating real-time data transmission. This section explores the critical importance of robust cellular coverage in hospital settings, highlighting its impact on medical systems, telemedicine, and proposed solutions for coverage improvement [17].

5.1. Impact on Medical Technologies

Modern hospitals increasingly rely on wireless systems to monitor patients, manage medical devices, and access electronic health records (EHRs). These technologies are indispensable for ensuring timely interventions and efficient workflows. However, their effectiveness is directly tied to the availability of reliable cellular coverage.

Wireless Body Area Networks (WBANs)—WBANs are a ground-breaking innovation that enables continuous monitoring of patients through wireless sensors. These sensors transmit vital signs such as heart rate, blood pressure, and oxygen levels in real-time, allowing healthcare professionals to respond quickly to changes in a patient's condition [18–20]. For example, early detection of abnormal heart rhythms can prevent cardiac arrest. However, coverage gaps can lead to delays or interruptions in transmitting this critical data, potentially compromising patient safety and outcomes.

Connected Medical Devices—Many hospital devices, such as infusion pumps, ventilators, and vital signs monitors, rely on wireless networks to operate seamlessly [21,22]. These devices often transmit data to centralized systems for analysis and decision-making. Weak or inconsistent cellular signals can result in data transmission errors, delayed readings, or even device malfunctions. In critical areas such as intensive care units or operating rooms, such disruptions can have life-threatening consequences.

Electronic Health Records (EHRs)—The digitization of medical records has transformed healthcare by enabling doctors and nurses to access patient histories, test results, and prescriptions from anywhere within the hospital. This facilitates faster decision-making and improves the quality of care [23]. However, any failure in cellular coverage can hinder access to these records, delaying treatment and increasing the risk of medical errors.

In summary, robust cellular coverage is essential to ensure the uninterrupted operation of these technologies, which are integral to modern healthcare delivery.

5.2. Role in Telemedicine

Telemedicine has emerged as a transformative tool in healthcare, enabling remote consultations, patient monitoring, and real-time collaboration among specialists. Its adoption has accelerated in recent years, driven by the need to reduce patient flow in physical facilities and optimize hospital resources. However, the success of telemedicine depends heavily on reliable cellular coverage.

Remote Consultations—Telemedicine allows patients to consult with healthcare providers from the comfort of their homes, reducing the burden on hospital infrastructure. For example, patients with chronic conditions can receive regular check-ups without traveling to the hospital. Weak cellular coverage can disrupt video calls, cause delays in data sharing, or lead to dropped connections, undermining the effectiveness of remote consultations.

Continuous Patient Monitoring—Telemedicine enables healthcare professionals to monitor patients recovering from surgery or managing chronic illnesses. Devices such as wearable sensors transmit data to remote monitoring systems, allowing doctors to track patient progress in real-time. Poor coverage can result in gaps in monitoring, delaying interventions, and increasing the risk of complications.

Collaborative Care—Telemedicine facilitates real-time collaboration among specialists, even when they are in different locations. For instance, a surgeon in one hospital can consult with a radiologist in another during a complex procedure. Reliable cellular coverage ensures seamless communication and data sharing, enabling better decision-making and improved patient outcomes.

In areas with poor coverage, telemedicine services can be severely compromised, leading to delayed diagnoses, reduced access to care, and diminished patient satisfaction. Reliable connectivity is essential to ensure uninterrupted video calls and real-time data transmission [24], and can be severely compromised, leading to delayed diagnoses, reduced access to care, and diminished patient satisfaction. Addressing these coverage gaps is critical for hospitals aiming to expand their telemedicine capabilities.

5.3. Proposed Solutions for Coverage Improvement

To address the challenges posed by coverage gaps, hospitals can adopt targeted solutions such as femtocells and distributed antenna systems (DAS). These technologies are designed to enhance indoor cellular coverage, ensuring reliable connectivity in all areas within CHUCB.

Femtocells—Femtocells are small, low-power indoor base stations that provide localized cellular coverage. They are particularly effective in areas with high user density, such as wards, emergency rooms, and imaging departments. Femtocells can be deployed strategically to address coverage gaps without requiring extensive modifications to existing infrastructure. For example, installing femtocells in critical areas identified during the measurement campaign (e.g., points 13, 17, and 21) can significantly improve signal strength and reliability. In contrast to approaches focused exclusively on 5G networks, such as that proposed by Kumar et al. [25], our study advocates femtocell deployment as a more cost-effective and adaptable solution for hospital environments like CHUCB. Unlike 5G-only infrastructure, femtocells support multiple additional cellular technologies (e.g., LTE, UMTS, NB-IoT), aligning with the multi-technology signal environment observed in our measurements. Furthermore, this strategy is consistent with the recommendations of Singh et al. [17], who emphasize the importance of scalable and economically viable solutions for healthcare facilities operating under budget constraints. By enabling localized coverage across heterogeneous radio access technologies, femtocells provide a practical balance between service quality and deployment costs.

Distributed Antenna Systems (DAS)—DAS consists of multiple antennas distributed throughout a building, connected to a central base station. This system provides uniform coverage across large spaces, making it ideal for hospitals with complex layouts. While DAS is more expensive to install and maintain, it offers excellent scalability and can complement femtocells in areas with lower traffic density. Although their efficiency in terms of mobility and homogeneous coverage is recognized, their applicability in contexts with localized needs and limited budgets is less advantageous [26].

Hybrid Solutions—A combination of femtocells and DAS can be employed to optimize coverage. For instance, femtocells can be used in high-density areas, while DAS can cover transition zones or large open spaces [27,28]. This hybrid approach ensures cost-efficient and technically robust coverage tailored to the specific needs of the hospital.

The use of radiating cable, a technology traditionally applied in indoor coverage of specific environments, was also considered. However, in the particular context of the Centro Hospitalar Universitário Cova da Beira (CHUCB), its implementation faces substantial practical and operational barriers, compromising the feasibility of its adoption [29]. The installation of radiating cable presents considerable technical requirements, as it necessitates precise positioning to avoid contact with walls or metallic supports, which implies the use of specific support structures. The calibrated grooves along the cable, responsible for the gradual emission of the signal, must be appropriately oriented to prevent significant losses, making the installation process even more delicate. Additionally, this type of cable experiences progressive attenuation with increasing distance, requiring the use of amplifiers or segmentations [30]. This solution, nonetheless, proves particularly effective in linear environments, such as tunnels or long corridors [31]. Hence, despite its technical value in certain specialized scenarios, the application of radiating cable is not suitable for the punctual, dispersed, and localized coverage needs observed in the present study.

The comparative economic analysis conducted by [32] further supports this decision, demonstrating that in small to medium-sized buildings with high traffic demands, as is the case in hospitals, femtocells present a significantly lower total cost of ownership (TCO) compared to DAS systems. As long as the cost per FAP remains below EUR 440, femtocells are consistently the most economical solution. The advantage of DAS systems only becomes evident in very large buildings with low traffic density and when installation and infrastructure costs can be amortized over extensive areas [32].

Implementing these solutions will not only enhance connectivity but also support the growing demand for wireless medical systems and telemedicine services, ultimately improving patient care and operational efficiency in CHUCB.

5.4. Applications of NB-IoT in Sensor-Based Hospital Monitoring

Although the planned strategy for asset monitoring at CHUCB involves the use of Bluetooth Low Energy (BLE) tags integrated with more than 300 existing Aruba (Meridian) access points capable of integrating BLE and supporting BLE beacons, allowing real-time device location through internal georeferencing solutions. Among the software compatible with these BLE solutions, Aruba Meridian and Cisco DNA Spaces stand out, allowing real-time tracking of devices and people, with simple integration into the existing infrastructure. Narrowband Internet of Things (NB-IoT) emerges as a promising technology for hospital monitoring and tracking applications in contexts where there is no dense Wi-Fi infrastructure or effective BLE coverage. Although NB-IoT coverage at CHUCB has been limited, this technology offers technical advantages such as long range, efficient building penetration, and low energy consumption, making it suitable for devices that reliably report data sporadically [33–35]. However, as Ahad et al. [36] caution, implementing NB-IoT networks in hospital environments introduces critical security challenges, including vulnerabilities in data interception, medical device spoofing, and authentication protocols. These concerns become particularly relevant as our measurement results identify unreliable NB-IoT coverage at CHUCB's points 17 and 21. In these areas, weak or absent signals not only impair communication reliability but also undermine the implementation of essential security measures. This dual challenge of connectivity and security underscores the necessity for future research addressing both coverage optimization and context-aware protection mechanisms for healthcare environments with constrained connectivity. The application of NB-IoT could be considered in outdoor areas, ambulances, or remote areas where such infrastructures are not available. This hybrid approach can extend the reach of tracking solutions, ensuring continuous coverage throughout the hospital perimeter.

There are already specific proposals in the literature for the use of NB-IoT for asset tracking in hospital environments, showing the feasibility of this approach [37]. Its integration with cloud-based IoT management platforms can enable functionalities such as real-time location, predictive analysis, and alert generation, with a direct impact on the efficiency of hospital services. Not only is asset management envisaged but also localization of patients will be explored (e.g., timely guiding patients to the most convenient service during their visit to the Hospital or localizing vulnerable patients).

Thus, although BLE continues to be the most promising technology in the hospital context, NB-IoT represents a relevant complementary technical solution, especially in future projects aimed at environments with limited indoor infrastructure or irregular coverage.

5.5. Future Expansion of the Study

The study conducted at the Centro Hospitalar Universitário Cova da Beira (CHUCB), as originally presented in [38], provides a solid foundation for future research and practical application of communication technologies in hospital environments, both locally and internationally. The expansion of this work will aim to address connectivity challenges in diverse healthcare settings, particularly in resource-limited environments.

A list of suggestions comprises the following aspects:

1. **Asset Tracking Solution at CHUCB**—The study is exploring the implementation of a Bluetooth Low Energy (BLE)-based asset tracking system integrated with the hospital's existing infrastructure. BLE tags will be paired with over 300 Aruba (Meridian) access points, which support BLE beacons and georeferencing solutions. The applications are as follows:
    (i) Medical Equipment Management—Real-time tracking of devices such as infusion pumps, ventilators, and monitors to optimize their usage and availability;
    (ii) Patient and Staff Tracking—Monitoring the location of patients and healthcare professionals to improve safety and operational efficiency;
    (iii) Dynamic Orientation—Guiding patients to the most convenient services during their hospital visit, enhancing their experience, and reducing delays.

This solution is expected to improve operational efficiency, safety, and the organization of workflows within CHUCB.

2. **International Expansion**—Aiming at targeting contexts in developing countries, the study will be extended to a case Study in the Hospital of Cumura in Guinea-Bissau, a reference unit for leprosy treatment in West Africa. Identified challenges are two-fold:
    (i) Connectivity Limitations—The hospital faces severe communication infrastructure challenges, including the absence of Internet access for healthcare professionals and manual recording of clinical data.
    (ii) Risks—These limitations pose significant risks to the quality of care provided, highlighting the need for accessible technological solutions.

In this context, the study identifies the need to investigate the feasibility of deploying low-cost and scalable technological interventions tailored to the local context. Specifically, the implementation of cellular coverage enhancement mechanisms, such as femtocells or distributed antenna systems (DAS), will be considered contingent upon the outcomes of a comprehensive radio spectrum measurement campaign to be conducted during the forthcoming phase of the research. Concurrently, the persistent reliance on paper-based medical records underscores the critical need to assess the potential transition to electronic health records (EHRs) as a means to improve clinical data accessibility, integrity, and continuity of care. Moreover, given the limited availability of local information technology infrastructure, the adoption of cloud-based platforms for clinical data management and decision support will also be evaluated, with particular attention to scalability, data security, and operational sustainability.

In the Hospital of Cumura in Guinea-Bissau, the same measurement and analysis approach (considered at CHUCB) will be applied, including radio spectrum assessments and cellular coverage evaluations. The study will compare the deployments at CHUCB

(Portugal) and Cumura Hospital (Guinea-Bissau) to assess indoor communications enhancement and adapt solutions to local constraints, such as energy availability, reliability of network access provision, and financial limitations.

The ultimate goal is to develop a replicable technological model capable of enhancing internal communication, safeguarding clinical data, and supporting medical decision-making in resource-limited environments. Accordingly, the study will examine how solutions such as femtocells, BLE, and NB-IoT can be tailored to the specific technical and economic conditions of developing countries. The research to be conducted in Guinea-Bissau will thus serve as a natural and innovative extension of this work, with the potential to modernize hospital infrastructure in low-income settings, assess public policy and regulation enhancements, and help reduce global disparities in access to digital healthcare.

The relevance of this expansion is also demonstrated by recent studies addressing healthcare challenges across Africa. Bétila [11] demonstrated that the development of information and communication technologies (ICTs) significantly enhances the impact of public health investment, improving indicators such as life expectancy and infant mortality. However, the study also underscores that these benefits are contingent on the availability of reliable communication infrastructure, the focus of the interventions proposed here. Likewise, Achieng and Ogundaini [12] emphasize that fragile digital health infrastructure and poor data governance are critical barriers to implementing big data analytics for infectious disease surveillance in sub-Saharan Africa. Hence, improving cellular coverage for ICT availability enhancement in hospitals directly aligns with the recommendations of [11,12]. The Guinea-Bissau case study will benefit from incorporating these relevant lines of research.

Mobile network coverage maps for the area surrounding Cumura Hospital, based on publicly available data from the nPerf platform, are prospectively addressed in Figures 19 and 20, even before performing the indoor coverage assessment. They illustrate the estimated signal coverage provided by the local MTN and Orange operators, respectively. Although these maps are not based on in situ measurements, they offer an overview of the existing coverage conditions in the region, and justify the relevance of this study.

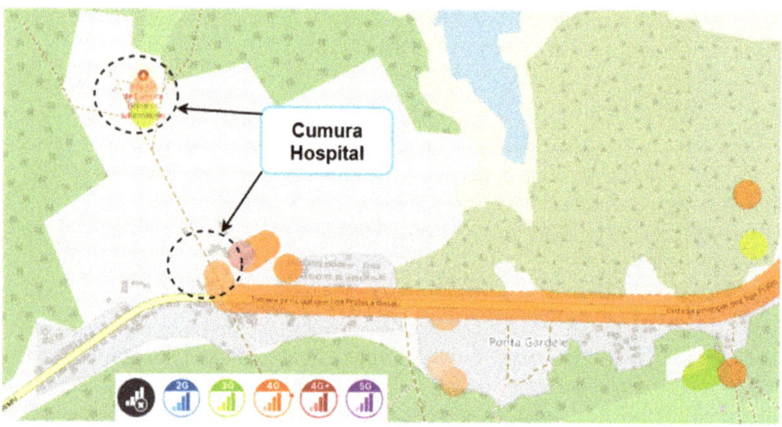

Figure 19. Mobile network coverage in the Cumura region (MTN operator), Guinea-Bissau. Colours represent different mobile network technologies: blue—2G, green—3G, orange—4G, red—4G+, and purple—5G. Source: nPerf platform, July 2025.

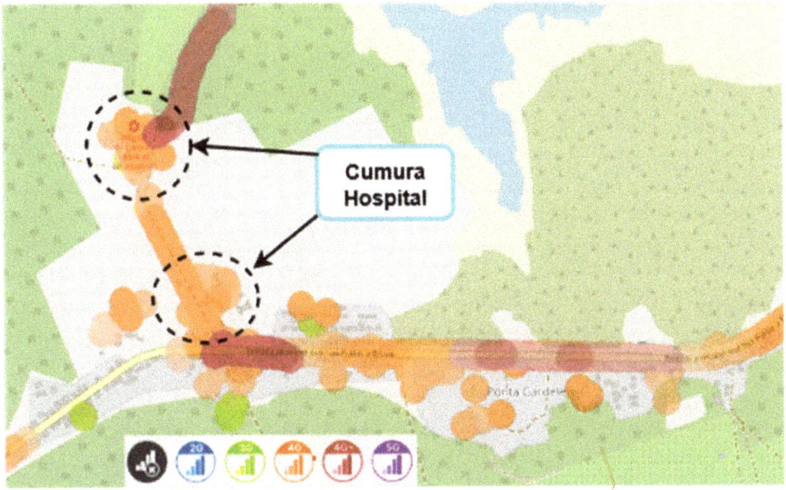

Figure 20. Mobile network coverage in the Cumura region (Orange operator), Guinea-Bissau. Colours represent different mobile network technologies: blue—2G, green—3G, orange—4G, red—4G+, and purple—5G. Source: nPerf platform, July 2025.

Nevertheless, it is important to note that nPerf data does not distinguish indoor measurements. The apparent display of results within the building results from its geolocation accuracy, which is limited to approximately 50 m.

Hence, in situ measurements carried out in this work were essential to rigorously assessing signal quality. These maps will also serve as reference material for planning the next phase of fieldwork in Guinea-Bissau.

6. Conclusions

In this work, the cellular coverage at the Cova da Beira University Hospital Center (CHUCB) was evaluated. Based on the results obtained from the measurements carried out using the R&S®TSME6 scanner in combination with the R&S®ROMES4 software and comparing them with the previous measurements made with the NARDA SRM-3006, it was possible to achieve a greater level of detail regarding the distribution of different communications technologies in the hospital.

The analysis of the results allowed identifying specific areas that require coverage improvements. It was found that, at measurement points 21, 23, and at the entrance gate of external consultations, the 5G NR technology showed the best signal coverage. Whereas, at points 13, 17, and 19, it was the LTE technology that demonstrated superior coverage. The LTE and 5G NR technologies were present at all six measurement points analyzed, with LTE providing better signal coverage, except at the entrance to the outpatient consultations, where 5G NR showed superior coverage. In general, the LTE technology showed the best performance regarding power values and signal indices (RSSI, NRSSI, RSCP). It was found that, regarding the operators, the results indicated that MEO and NOS were present at all six measurement points analyzed, while the absence of the Vodafone operator was recorded at some of these points. MEO provided the best signal coverage in more locations and for the four technologies analyzed (5G NR, LTE, NB-IoT, and UMTS). The identified areas that require coverage improvements include points 13, 17, and 21. To address these shortcomings, the implementation of femtocells in areas with insufficient signal is proposed. This solution will optimize the quality of communication at CHUCB, ensuring robust and uninterrupted coverage, essential for the proper functioning of hospital systems, especially in critical areas.

Implementing these improvements will have a significant impact on the efficiency of hospital services, particularly in supporting health monitoring systems and wireless communication networks, facilitating telemonitoring of patients at risk, and ensuring that mobile technologies can be fully utilized to provide high-quality and safe healthcare. As emphasized by Ahad et al. [36], network security must form a cornerstone of healthcare's digital transformation. In future extensions of this study, particularly at Cumura Hospital (Guinea-Bissau), where infrastructure limitations may increase risks, such as sensitive data interception, it will be essential to implement robust security protocols aligned with these authors' recommendations. The confidentiality and integrity of medical data transmitted via mobile networks thus become paramount for ensuring reliable telemonitoring solutions in resource-constrained environments.

In addition to the proposed improvements in cellular coverage, the relevance of emerging solutions for real-time tracking within the hospital is also highlighted in this study. It is expected that the tracking system based on BLE and Access Points, currently under evaluation at CHUCB, will not be limited to the management of medical equipment and devices, but will also allow for the real-time location of patients. This functionality opens up new possibilities in terms of dynamic orientation of patients during their hospital journey and monitoring of vulnerable patients, contributing to enhanced safety and efficiency in the hospital environment.

In addition to the conclusions obtained based on the measurements carried out at CHUCB, this work aims to serve as a basis for a future international extension of the study to be conducted in a hospital in Guinea-Bissau. The choice of this new location is driven by the urgent need to understand the challenges associated with cellular coverage enhancement in hospital environments of developing countries, where telecommunications infrastructures are significantly more limited. The same measurement and analysis methodology will be applied in order to compare connectivity realities, identify critical areas, and propose viable solutions adjusted to local technical and economic constraints. This expansion of the study will not only validate the applicability of the proposed solutions but also contribute to the development of more accessible and scalable strategies to improve healthcare in contexts with limited resources.

nPerf is a valuable tool for providing a broad overview of cellular coverage, especially in outdoor environments, as demonstrated by recent publicly available data gathering in 2025. Its effectiveness is maximized when used in conjunction with detailed, real-time measurements for critical indoor areas, as demonstrated in the CHUCB field tests.

Author Contributions: Conceptualization, Ó.S., E.B.T. and F.J.V.; methodology, Ó.S., E.B.T. and A.C.; software, Ó.S. and A.C.; validation, Ó.S., E.B.T. and A.C.; formal analysis, Ó.S. and E.B.T.; investigation, A.C. and F.J.V.; resources, A.C. and A.D.R.; data curation, A.D.R. and F.J.V.; writing—original draft preparation, Ó.S. and E.B.T.; writing—review and editing, E.B.T. and F.J.V.; visualization, E.B.T. and F.J.V.; supervision, F.J.V.; project administration, Ó.S.; funding acquisition, F.J.V. All authors have read and agreed to the published version of the manuscript.

Funding: The completion of this work was financially supported by the Telemonitoring of Patients at Risk (TERI) project under the System for Supporting the Modernization and Capacity Building of Public Administration (SAMA 2020), co-financed by COMPETE 2020 through the European Regional Development Fund (FEDER)—Public Administration Capacity Building Operations (PI 11.1). The authors thank Fundação para a Ciência e a Tecnologia, I.P. (Portuguese Foundation for Science and Technology), FCT/MECI, for the support through national funds and, when applicable, cofounded EU funds under UID/50008: Instituto de Telecomunicações. Óscar da Silva also thanks FCT/MECI for the support granted through the doctoral scholarship PALOP/BD/155059/2024 (PALOP and Timor

Leste). Emanuel Teixeira also thanks FCT/MECI for the support through national funds and, when applicable, co-funded EU funds under UI/BD/150923/2021, and through the Bolsas de Incentivo ao Doutoramento (BID) program of the Instituto Coordenador da Investigação (ICI)—Faculdade de Engenharia (FE), Santander Universidades—UBI, under the 2016–2017 scholarship.

Data Availability Statement: The original contributions presented in this study are included in the article. Further inquiries can be directed to the corresponding author(s).

Conflicts of Interest: The authors declare no conflict of interest.

Abbreviations

The following abbreviations are used in this manuscript:

5G NR	5G New Radio
ANACOM	Autoridade Nacional de Comunicações
BLE	Bluetooth Low Energy
CDMA2000	Code Division Multiple Access 2000
CHUCB	Centro Hospitalar Universitário Cova da Beira
DAS	Distributed Antenna Systems
EHRs	Electronic Health Records
FAP	Femtocell Access Point
FCT/MCTES	Fundação para a Ciência e a Tecnologia/Ministério da Ciência, Tecnologia e Ensino Superior
FEDER	European Regional Development Fund
ICTs	Information and Communication Technologies
LTE	Long Term Evolution
NB-IoT	Narrow-band Internet of Things
NRSSI	NR Signal Strength Indicator
ROMES4	Drive Test Software
RSCP	Received Signal Codes Power
RSRP	Reference Signal Received Power
RSRQ	Reference Signal Received Quality
RSSI	Received Signal Strength Indicator
SAMA	System for Supporting the Modernization and Capacity Building of Public Administration
SINR	Signal-to-Interference-plus-Noise Ratio
TCO	Total Cost of Ownership
TERI	Telemonitoring of Patients at Risk
UMTS	Universal Mobile Telecommunications System
UWB	Ultra-Wideband
WBANs	Wireless Body Area Networks

References

1. da Óscar, S. Cellular and Wireless Mobile Communications Applied to E-Health in Hospital Environments. Master's Thesis, Universidade da Beira Interior, Covilhã, Portugal, 2022. (In Portuguese)
2. Majeed, J.H.; Aish, Q. A remote patient monitoring based on WBAN implementation with internet of thing and cloud server. *Bull. Electr. Eng. Inform.* **2021**, *10*, 1640–1647. [CrossRef]
3. Taleb, H.; Nasser, A.; Andrieux, G.; Charara, N.; Cruz, E.M. Wireless technologies, medical applications and future challenges in WBAN: A survey. *Wirel. Netw.* **2021**, *27*, 5271–5295. [CrossRef]
4. Hajar, M.S.; Al-Kadri, M.O.; Kalutarage, H.K. A survey on wireless body area networks: Architecture, security challenges and research opportunities. *Comput. Secur.* **2021**, *104*, 102211. [CrossRef]
5. Friend, T.H.; Jennings, S.J.; Copenhaver, M.S.; Levine, W.C. Implementation of the Vocera Communication System in a Quaternary Perioperative Environment. *J. Med. Syst.* **2017**, *41*, 6. [CrossRef] [PubMed]
6. Vyas, S.; Gupta, S. WBAN-based remote monitoring system utilising machine learning for healthcare services. *Int. J. Syst. Syst. Eng.* **2023**, *13*, 100. [CrossRef]

7. Ahmed, I.; Karvonen, H.; Kumpuniemi, T.; Katz, M. Wireless communications for the hospital of the future: Requirements, challenges and solutions. *Int. J. Wirel. Inf. Netw.* **2020**, *27*, 4–17. [CrossRef]
8. Anbarasan, H.S.; Natarajan, J. Blockchain Based Delay and Energy Harvest Aware Healthcare Monitoring System in WBAN Environment. *Sensors* **2022**, *22*, 5763. [CrossRef]
9. Manzo, B.F.; Brito, M.J.M.; Alves, M. Influence of communication on the hospital accreditation process. *Rev. Bras. Enferm.* **2013**, *66*, 46–51. (In Portuguese) [CrossRef]
10. Elendu, I.C.; Onwuzuruigbo, I.C.; Okereke, C.E. 5G-enabled smart hospitals: Innovations in patient care and facility management. *Medicine* **2024**, *103*, e37957. [CrossRef] [PubMed]
11. Bétila, R.R. Public health expenditure and health outcomes in Africa: The Moderating effect of ICT development. *J. Knowl. Econ.* **2024**, *16*, 2719–2750. [CrossRef]
12. Achieng, M.S.; Ogundaini, O.O. Big data analytics for integrated infectious disease surveillance in sub-Saharan Africa. *S. Afr. J. Inf. Manag.* **2024**, *26*, 11. [CrossRef]
13. Velez, F.J.; Teixeira, E.B.; Corceiro, A.; Silva, Ó. *Radiofrequency Spectrum Measurement Campaign at Pero da Covilhã Hospital*; TERI Report UBI.3.1; Universidade da Beira Interior: Covilhã, Portugal, 2023.
14. Punj, R.; Kumar, R. Technological aspects of WBANs for health monitoring: A comprehensive review. *Wirel. Netw.* **2019**, *25*, 1125–1157. [CrossRef]
15. nPerf SAS. nPerf Is a French Company Leading the Provision of Accurate and Collaborative Data on Mobile Network Performance Worldwide. Through Its Innovative Platform, nPerf Collects and Analyses Data to Deliver Insights That Help both Consumers and Operators. Available online: https://www.nperf.com (accessed on 12 July 2025).
16. Niyato, D.; Hossain, E.; Camorlinga, S. Remote patient monitoring service using heterogeneous wireless access networks: Architecture and optimization. *IEEE J. Sel. Areas Commun.* **2009**, *27*, 412–423. [CrossRef]
17. Singh, R.; Ballal, K.D.; Nwabuona, S.C.; Berger, M.S.; Dittmann, L.; Ruepp, S.; Wienecke, T. Assessment of Cellular Coverage for a Smart Ambulance Use Case. In Proceedings of the 2022 IEEE International Conference on Advanced Networks and Telecommunications Systems (ANTS), Gandhinagar, India, 18–21 December 2022; pp. 369–374.
18. Herbst, J.; Bergkemper, L.; Fahldieck, C.; Lipps, C.; Jingu, A.; Steimle, J.; Schotten, H.D. One Step Towards Secure Identification in Wireless Body Area Networks (WBANs): Intelligent Insole Sensor Systems. In Proceedings of the 2024 IEEE International Conference on Flexible and Printable Sensors and Systems (FLEPS), Tampere, Finland, 30 June–3 July 2024; pp. 1–4.
19. Iniyan, M.; Banumathi, A. The WBANs: Steps towards a Comprehensive Analysis of Wireless Body Area Networks. *Sci. Temper.* **2024**, *15*, 2888–2898. [CrossRef]
20. Majeed, M.R.; Ali, I.T. An Enhancement for Wireless Body Area Network Using Adaptive Algorithms. *Int. J. Comput. Exp. Sci. Eng.* **2024**, *10*, 388–396. [CrossRef]
21. Manjula, V.; Chillara, V.L.N.S.P.V.; Rao, T.P.R.C.; Varma, N.S.V.A.; Kumar, P.S.; Reddy, B.S. Cyber Threats and Vulnerabilities in Connected Medical Devices: A Review. In *Cybersecurity and Data Management Innovations for Revolutionizing Healthcare*; IGI Global: Hershey, PA, USA, 2024; Chapter 7; pp. 148–174.
22. Singh, J. Challenges with Medical Devices Connected to Hospital Network. *Int. J. Res. Appl. Sci. Eng. Technol.* **2024**, *12*, 735–749. [CrossRef]
23. Moura, S.A. Electronic Patient Medical Record: A Proposal. *Revista UNIFA* **2001**, *14*, 8–15. (In Portuguese)
24. Petroni, A.; Salvo, P.; Cuomo, F. On Cellular Networks Supporting Healthcare Remote Monitoring in IoT Scenarios. *Front. Commun. Netw.* **2021**, *2*, 610182. [CrossRef]
25. Kumar, A.; Albreem, M.A.; Gupta, M.; Alsharif, M.H.; Kim, S. Future 5G network based smart hospitals: Hybrid detection technique for latency improvement. *IEEE Access* **2020**, *8*, 153240–153249. [CrossRef]
26. Fudaba, N.; Nakamura, T.; Seki, H. Investigation of a Femto-DAS Hybrid System for In-Building Wireless Solutions. In Proceedings of the 2016 IEEE 83rd Vehicular Technology Conference (VTC Spring), Nanjing, China, 15–18 May 2016; pp. 1–5.
27. Rianti, P.; Alfin, A.R.; Pakpahan, D.H. Analysis of Indoor Coverage Performance in 5G Networks at 3500 MHz Using Femtocell. *J. Ilm. Teknol. Inf. Terap.* **2024**, *7*, 37–45.
28. Adekogba, G.V.; Adedeji, K.B.; Olasoji, Y.O. Development of an Interference Reduction Scheme for Femtocell Network. *J. Eng. Adv.* **2024**, *5*, 114–122. [CrossRef]
29. De la Roche, G.; Zhang, J. Chapter 2—Indoor Coverage Techniques. In *Femtocells: Technologies and Deployment*; De la Roche, G., Zhang, J., Eds.; Wiley: Hoboken, NJ, USA, 2010; pp. 27–30.
30. Li, K.; Hui, L.; Zhu, G. Research on Improving the Radiation Performance of Leaky Coaxial Cable. In Proceedings of the 2024 9th International Conference on Computer and Communication Systems (ICCCS), Nyingchi, China, 26–29 April 2024; pp. 158–162.
31. Blaszkiewicz, O.; Sadowski, J.; Stefanski, J. Position Estimation in Corridors Along the Coupled Mode of Radiating Cables. *Sensors* **2020**, *20*, 5064. [CrossRef] [PubMed]

32. Liu, Z.; Kolding, T.; Mogensen, P.; Vejgaard, B.; Sorensen, T. Economical Comparison of Enterprise In-Building Wireless Solutions Using DAS and Femto. In Proceedings of the 2012 IEEE Vehicular Technology Conference (VTC Fall), Quebec City, QC, Canada, 3–6 September 2012; pp. 1–5.
33. Sapra, P.; Pandey, A.K. NB-IoT-Based Healthcare Information Transmission. In Proceedings of the 2023 3rd International Conference on Advance Computing and Innovative Technologies in Engineering (ICACITE), Greater Noida, India, 12–13 May 2023; pp. 2282–2285.
34. Chu, J.; Wang, Y.; Li, X.; Yun, X. NB-IoT-Based Health Monitoring System for COVID-19. *Wearable Technol.* **2021**, *2*, 24–32. [CrossRef]
35. Vishalatchi, S. An Intelligent Medical Monitoring System using Narrow Band–IoT. *Int. J. Multidiscip. Res.* **2024**, *6*, 24–29.
36. Ahad, A.; Ali, Z.; Mateen, A.; Tahir, M.; Hannan, A.; Garcia, N.M.; Pires, I.M. A comprehensive review on 5G-based smart healthcare network security: Taxonomy, issues, solutions and future research directions. *Array* **2023**, *18*, 100290. [CrossRef]
37. Kumar, A.; Sharma, R.; Gupta, N. NB-IoT-Based Smart Healthcare Monitoring System. In Proceedings of the 2024 International Conference on Smart Electronics and Communication (ICOSEC), Trichy, India, 10–12 October 2024; pp. 1–6.
38. da Silva, Ó.; Teixeira, E.; Corceiro, A.; Reis, A.; Velez, F.J. Monitoring the Provision of Ubiquitous Cellular Coverage in a Hospital Environment: Radio Spectrum Measurements at CHUCB. In Proceedings of the ICEUBI—International Congress on Engineering 2024, Covilhã, Portugal, 27–29 November 2024. (In Portuguese)

sensors

MDPI

Article

A Cluster Head Selection Algorithm for Extending Last Node Lifetime in Wireless Sensor Networks

Marcin Lewandowski † and Bartłomiej Płaczek *,†

Institute of Computer Science, University of Silesia, Będzińska 39, 41-200 Sosnowiec, Poland; marcin.lewandowski@us.edu.pl
* Correspondence: bartlomiej.placzek@us.edu.pl; Tel.: +48-32-3689760
† These authors contributed equally to this work.

Abstract: This paper introduces a new cluster head selection algorithm for wireless sensor networks (WSNs) to maximize the time until the last sensor node depletes its energy. The algorithm is based on a formal analysis in which network lifetime is modeled as a function of node energy consumption. In contrast to existing energy-balancing strategies, this analytical foundation leads to a distinctive selection rule that prioritizes the node with the highest transmission probability and the lowest initial energy as the initial cluster head. The algorithm employs distributed per-cluster computation, enabling scalability without increasing complexity relative to network size. Unlike traditional approaches that rotate cluster heads based on time or equal energy use, our method adapts to heterogeneous energy consumption patterns and enforces a cluster head rotation order that maximizes the lifetime of the final active node. To validate the effectiveness of the proposed approach, we implement it on a real-world LoRaWAN-based sensor network prototype. Experimental results demonstrate that our method significantly extends the lifetime of the last active node compared to representative state-of-the-art algorithms. This research provides a practical and robust solution for energy-efficient WSN operation in real deployment scenarios by considering realistic and application-driven communication behavior along with hardware-level energy consumption.

Keywords: wireless sensor network; lifetime of sensor network; cluster head rotation; transmission reduction; internet of things

1. Introduction

Wireless sensor networks (WSNs) are essential components of the IoT that enable data collection through multiple sensor nodes located in different areas. Data collected by WSNs can be processed for various purposes, including process monitoring, decision-making, event recognition, control, and others [1]. The design and development of WSNs encounters a range of specific constraints that do not exist in traditional computer networks. Sensor nodes are usually powered by an embedded battery with limited capacity. In many cases, replacing or recharging batteries in sensor nodes is impractical [2] and the sensor nodes with discharged batteries are no longer used. For these reasons, operations performed within a WSN should consider the need for efficient energy use and ensure sufficiently long operational times for sensor nodes. Addressing these constraints requires the development of dedicated data transmission algorithms to extend the lifetime of WSNs. While the need for energy conservation applies to all aspects of sensor node operation, data transmission has the most significant impact on energy consumption [3–5]. Previous works have suggested that the energy consumption of the data transmission module is significantly higher than the energy consumption of the microcontroller that manages sensor node operations [6].

To ensure the possibility of effective data acquisition from many sensor nodes and reduce the number of transmissions, WSNs can be clustered, as shown in Figure 1. Clustering of WSNs was introduced to achieve effective energy and transmission management by grouping network nodes into clusters in which one node acts as the cluster head [7,8]. The cluster head node is responsible for coordinating communication with both its cluster members and the base station. Due to the tasks it performs, the cluster head node consumes energy resources faster than the remaining nodes (cluster members). Therefore, the role of the cluster head must be transferred (rotated) between those nodes belonging to the cluster [9–11]. The concept of cluster head rotation is illustrated in Figure 1. The network consists of two clusters, each containing four sensor nodes and a single base station located externally. In Figure 1a, which represents the n-th round, one sensor node in each cluster is designated as the cluster head, while the remaining nodes act as cluster members, sending their data to the respective cluster head for aggregation and subsequent transmission to the base station. In Figure 1b, corresponding to the (n + 1)-th round, the roles have rotated, with new cluster heads selected in each cluster. In this paper, we propose a new algorithm for selecting the cluster head node. Our proposed algorithm effectively extends the time until the last node in the WSN cluster dies, i.e., depletes its energy resources.

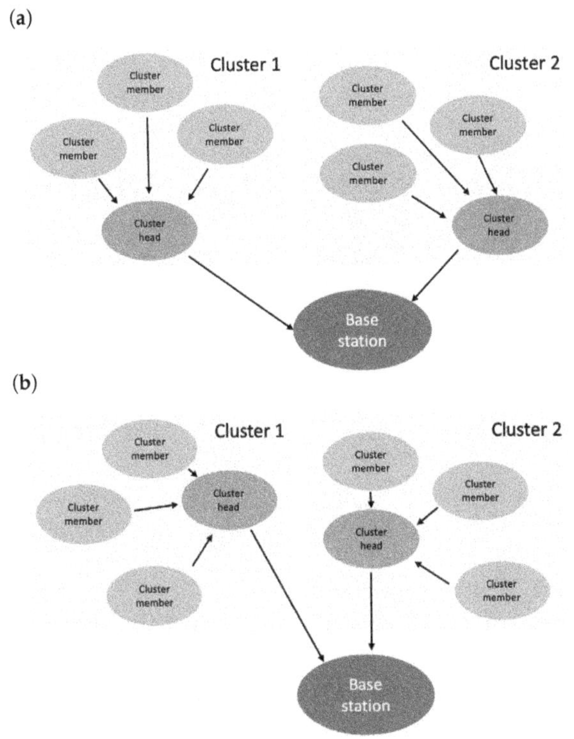

Figure 1. Operation of the sensor network: (**a**) in the n-th round and (**b**) in the (n + 1)-th round.

Currently, available algorithms for selecting the cluster head and rotating the role of cluster head node focus mainly on extending the time until the available energy in one of the sensor nodes is discharged (i.e., until the first node dies) [12–14]. These algorithms usually delay the time until the first node in a WSN cluster dies by evenly distributing the energy consumption. Such approaches are ineffective when the aim is to prolong the time until all nodes deplete their energy resources (i.e., until the last node dies). Therefore, we introduce a new algorithm to prolong the last node lifetime. The considered time to death of the last node is essential in applications where it is necessary to obtain data on the monitored process for as long as possible, even if the death of subsequent nodes limits the scope of these data [15]. For instance, extending the time to death of the last node is a more meaningful metric for applications where WSN data serve as input for machine learning models that can handle missing values. By ensuring that at least one node remains active for as long as possible, the system can continue to provide valuable data for decision-making, classification, or prediction.

Another motivation for our work is that available cluster head rotation algorithms do not allow for fully efficient use of energy resources when nodes in a WSN autonomously decide on the need for transmission based on current sensor readings. In modern energy-aware sensor nodes, sensor readings are analyzed locally and transmission only occurs if the data are useful for a given application. Thus, data transmission is performed irregularly (with different probabilities) and nodes use their energy resources at different rates. The new method presented in this paper takes into account the transmission probabilities of individual sensor nodes when selecting the cluster head, leading to extended network lifetime.

The new challenge we address in this paper is the design of a cluster head rotation method that explicitly considers the non-uniform transmission probabilities of nodes. This approach more accurately reflects real-world deployments that involve event-driven or application-aware sensing. The proposed method aims to maximize the lifetime of the last node by integrating these heterogeneous transmission behaviors into the cluster head selection process.

The main contributions of this work are summarized as follows:

- We show that the last node lifetime in a WSN cluster strongly depends on the order in which the sensor nodes take on the role of cluster head.
- We demonstrate that the most effective order can be found by taking into account the initial energy levels and transmission probabilities of sensor nodes. We propose an algorithm for selecting the cluster head which ensures a longer time to death of the last node.
- We provide results of experimental lifetime evaluations using a real-world WSN prototype based on LoRaWAN technology, and compare the results achieved by our proposed algorithm to those achieved by state-of-the-art solutions.

The rest of this paper is structured as follows. Section 2 includes a review of the current state of science and technology in methods for extending the lifetime of sensor networks, particularly through the selection of cluster head nodes. Based on the conducted literature review, we identify the advantages, limitations, and drawbacks of the available methods. Section 3 includes a presentation of the proposed method which enables the extension of the lifetime of the sensor network. Section 4 presents a model for determining the lifetime of a wireless sensor network. This model is then used to conduct a qualitative experimental evaluation of cluster head node selection methods. The key elements of the model are the data transmission algorithms implemented by individual nodes and the parameters describing the energy consumed by the sensor nodes at different stages of network operation. Section 5 presents the conducted experiments and results confirming the usefulness of the developed solutions. It should be noted that the proposed algorithms were implemented in real sensor network nodes. This is particularly important for evaluating the proposed algorithms, as it confirms their feasibility for practical implementation. Finally, a summary of the obtained results, conclusions, and future research directions on methods for extending the lifetime of sensor networks is provided in Section 6.

2. Related Works

Various cluster head selection and rotation approaches have been proposed in the literature to extend the lifetime of WSNs. These approaches are based on different definitions of network lifetime and take into account the specific applications and topologies of WSNs. In this section, we characterize the main categories of the existing approaches and discuss our proposed cluster head rotation scheme in this context.

The simplest method of organizing data exchange in WSNs is direct transmission. This method assumes that all sensor nodes play the same role and that their task is to send collected data directly to the base station [16]. With such assumptions, there is no division of the network into clusters, and consequently no distinction in the role of the cluster head. It should be noted that direct transmission of all collected data to the base station results in high energy consumption and short sensor node lifetimes. In addition, the direct transmission method has low scalability, as the base station in this approach must receive and process large portions of data from all sensor nodes. If the base station's capacity is exceeded, data from the sensor nodes may be lost. The complexity of this method is low and its hardware implementation is straightforward; however, the disadvantages mentioned above mean that the direct method is very rarely used in practice.

The limitations of direct transmission have led to the development of more advanced data collection methods taking into account the division of nodes in the sensor network into clusters. These methods reduce the number of data transmissions to the base station and lower the energy consumption of the sensor nodes. Nodes belonging to a cluster transmit data to the cluster head. Then, the cluster head aggregates the received data and for transmission to the base station. As mentioned in the Introduction, the role of the cluster head must be transferred between nodes in order to balance the energy consumption and avoid a situation in which a node acting as the cluster head for a long time would quickly deplete its energy resources.

The existing algorithms for rotating the role of cluster head can be divided into two categories. The first category includes time-based algorithms, in which sensor nodes act as cluster heads for a predefined period, while the second category consists of algorithms considering the level of consumed or available energy in a node. An example is an algorithm which changes the role after a predefined energy consumption threshold is exceeded [17,18].

A distributed algorithm for organizing sensor nodes into clusters has been implemented in the hierarchical routing protocol known as the Low-Energy Adaptive Clustering Hierarchy (LEACH) [19]. In this approach, the role of cluster head is rotated among the nodes, with a new cluster head randomly selected after a predefined period. The responsibilities of the cluster head include creating a Time Division Multiple Access (TDMA) schedule that allocates access to the transmission medium for multiple cluster members. Each cluster member transmits data during the time slots assigned by the cluster head. The cluster head collects these data for forwarding to the base station. The operation of the LEACH protocol is divided into rounds, each consisting of two phases: the setup phase and the transmission phase. During the setup phase, the cluster head is changed and data containing information about the roles of individual nodes are disseminated. In the transmission phase, actual data transmission begins, which means that the sensor nodes send their data to the cluster head according to their assigned time slots. LEACH enables cluster heads to perform local data aggregation within each cluster, reducing the amount of data transmitted to the base station [20,21].

There are several well-known variants of the LEACH protocol, each designed to address specific limitations of the original approach by modifying the cluster head selection strategy, clustering mechanism, or communication scheme. These extensions aim to improve energy efficiency, load balancing, or adaptability to network conditions such as node mobility or non-uniform energy distribution. Table 1 summarizes the key characteristics of selected LEACH-based protocols, including LEACH, LEACH-C [22], LEACH-D [23], and LEACH-F [24], based on their design principles and operational differences.

Table 1. Comparison of LEACH-based protocols.

Protocol	CH Selection Method	Clustering Type	Rotation Mechanism	Advantages	Limitations
LEACH	Random probabilistic	Distributed	Random per round	Local data aggregation	Unbalanced CH distribution
LEACH-C	Centralized (based on energy and location)	Centralized	Recomputed per round	Balanced CH placement	Additional overhead to BS
LEACH-D	Nearest neighbor of current CH (if energy > threshold)	Distributed	Localized CH handover	Smooth transitions	Fails if neighbors lack energy
LEACH-F	Fixed clusters, round-robin CH	Centralized (initial only)	Round-robin	No re-selection needed	Not suited for mobile networks

In the HEED (Hybrid Energy-Efficient Distributed Clustering) protocol [25], new cluster heads are also selected after a predetermined duration of one round. This approach is similar to the operation of the LEACH protocol described earlier; however, in the HEED protocol, selection of the cluster head takes into account the remaining energy of each sensor node. The probability of a given sensor node being selected as the cluster head is proportional to the amount of energy available at that node. A distributed procedure is used to select the head of the cluster, which is based solely on local information about neighboring nodes. Nevertheless, this process incurs additional energy costs during data exchange between nodes.

Another method of rotating the role of the cluster head among the sensor nodes is ANTCLUST [26]. As in previous approaches, this method selects the cluster head at the beginning of each round. In order to improve the network lifetime, the ANTCLUST algorithm selects a new cluster head depending on the battery charge level and the distance to neighboring sensor nodes. A specific feature of this method is the use of a clustering algorithm based on a nature-inspired ant colony model.

An alternative approach is the Stable Election Protocol (SEP) [27], which was developed for heterogeneous sensor networks in which the sensor nodes have different initial energy levels. Similar to the LEACH protocol, the SEP protocol randomly selects new cluster heads at the beginning of each round. The advantage of this approach is that sensor nodes with higher available energy are more frequently chosen as cluster heads compared to those with lower energy resources. This method prolongs the time until the first node dies.

A variation of the protocol discussed above is Prolong-SEP (P-SEP) [28], which was developed to extend the lifespan of sensor networks that operate based on fog computing. This algorithm aims to balance the energy consumption of all nodes in order to maximize the lifetime of the network. Nodes with an energy level above a specified threshold are nominated as candidates for the role of cluster head, then the cluster head is randomly selected from among these candidates while considering their distance to other nodes. It is important to note that in both the SEP and P-SEP, the selection of the cluster head is part of a complex clustering procedure; consequently, SEP and P-SEP may be inefficient when frequent changes in node roles within the network are necessary.

Another solution is the Hamilton Energy-Efficient Routing (HEER) protocol [29]. The HEER protocol utilizes a greedy algorithm to establish a Hamiltonian path among sensor nodes within each cluster. This path dictates the organization of data transmissions. The sensor nodes positioned along the path take turns serving as the cluster head. Similar to the other methods mentioned above, the role of cluster head is rotated after a predetermined amount of time.

The energy consumption of the sensor nodes is taken into account in the Energy-Distance Aware Clustering method (EDAC) [30]. In this method, the cluster head is selected based on two key parameters: the remaining energy in the node, and the energy used to send data from other nodes to the potential cluster head. Based on these two parameters, a metric is developed to facilitate uniform energy consumption among sensor nodes. This metric also aids in determining the optimal timing for changing the cluster head.

In the case of the Energy-Distance Aware Clustering Scheme (E-DACS) for wireless sensor networks [31], the rotation of node roles is determined by considering the remaining energy of each node, the mutual distances between nodes, and the distance to the base station. A new cluster head is selected periodically when the energy level of the current cluster head falls below that of any other sensor node within the cluster.

Another algorithm for transferring the role of the cluster head is Energy-Driven Cluster Head Rotation (EDCR) [26]. This algorithm operates based on the relative levels of remaining energy in the nodes within a given cluster. The sensor node with the highest energy level is designated as the cluster head. A dynamically determined threshold triggers the role rotation procedure. The threshold is calculated using the following formula: $P \cdot EC$, where $0 < P < 1$ is a constant and EC represents the remaining energy in the node. The EC parameter is measured at the moment when the node is selected as the cluster head. In this method, the selection of a new cluster head occurs when the remaining energy of the current cluster head falls below the threshold value. According to this algorithm, the lower the available energy in the nodes, the more frequently the cluster head role is switched. This strategy aims to balance energy consumption among sensor nodes.

The existing methods described above all have significant disadvantages. The primary issue is the assumption that all sensor nodes within a cluster transmit their data regularly at equal time intervals. However, it is important to note that each node may transmit data at different frequencies during specific network operation steps, for instance, to eliminate redundant or irrelevant information. This variability results in dynamic changes in energy consumption among the nodes, which can differ significantly; consequently, existing methods are ineffective in extending the network lifespan, as they do not account for the differences in energy consumption among individual nodes [11,32].

Our proposed method for rotating the role of the cluster head considers the probability of data transmission by specific sensor nodes. By taking into account the transmission probabilities of individual nodes, our algorithm achieves more accurate estimation of energy consumption and provides improved management of the energy resources available within the network.

Another disadvantage of current methods is that they are primarily designed to prolong the time to the death of the first sensor node; consequently, new approaches are needed for applications in which the goal is to extend the time to the death of the last node in the WSN.

In addition, the methods in the literature do not account for parameters that describe energy consumption, which varies depending on the radio transmission technology employed in a specific WSN. Our proposed method incorporates parameters from the energy consumption model that can be estimated based on the known characteristics of hardware solutions, including radio modules. These parameters enable more accurate prediction of energy consumption and node lifetime, which facilitates more appropriate cluster head selection and extends the overall network lifetime.

3. Proposed Method

In this paper, we examine the lifetime of a WSN, defined as the duration until the energy of all nodes in the network is depleted. Formally, the lifetime of the network (LT) can be expressed as follows:

$$LT = \max\{t : \max_{i \in I} \{e_i(t)\} > \epsilon\} \tag{1}$$

where $e_i(t)$ denotes the available energy for sensor node i at time step t, I is the set of identifiers for all nodes in the WSN, and ϵ stands for the minimum energy required by a sensor node to perform its operations during a single time step.

To discuss the underlying concepts of our cluster head selection method for extending the network's LT, we consider a network consisting of two nodes (Figure 2). Let us assume that the symbol i denotes the identifier of the sensor node that initially serves as the cluster head, while j represents the identifier of the node that takes over the role of cluster head after node i dies. Furthermore, we assume that the unit of time corresponds to the duration of a single operational step of the WSN. The time until the energy of node i is discharged can be determined as follows:

$$T_1 = \frac{EI_i}{EH} \tag{2}$$

where EI_i is the initial energy of node i and EH is the energy consumed in a single step (the amount of energy used per unit of time) when the node acts as the cluster head.

After time T_1, the energy of node j is

$$E_j(T_1) = EI_j - \frac{EI_i}{EH} \cdot EM_j, \tag{3}$$

where EI_j is the initial energy of node j and EM_j is the energy consumed per time step by node j when it acts as a cluster member.

After the death of node i, node j acts as the cluster head until its energy is depleted. The duration of this period can be calculated as follows:

$$T_2 = \frac{E_j(T_1)}{EH} = \frac{EI_j}{EH} - \frac{EI_i \cdot EM_j}{EH^2}. \tag{4}$$

As a result, for the case under analysis, the LT can be estimated using the following formula:

$$LT = T_1 + T_2 = \frac{EI_i + EI_j}{EH} - \frac{EI_i \cdot EM_j}{EH^2}. \tag{5}$$

It is important to note that when selecting node i, we do not alter the value of the sum $EI_i + EI_j$, nor do we change the value of EH.

Therefore, to extend the *LT*, it is essential to minimize the product $EI_i \cdot EM_j$ by appropriately choosing node *i*:

$$EI_i \cdot EM_j \rightarrow \min. \tag{6}$$

Based on Equation (6), we can conclude that node *i* should be the one with the smallest initial energy and that node *j* should be the one that consumes the least energy when acting as the cluster member. The selection of node *i* directly influences the choice of node *j*. Therefore, by modifying the rule for selecting node *j* as previously formulated, we can assert that node *i* should be the one that consumes the most energy when acting as a cluster member. For example, we can consider a scenario where nodes A and B both start with the same or very similar initial energy levels. However, node A transmits data more frequently due to its sensing conditions or application-specific role, resulting in higher energy consumption when acting as a cluster member. In contrast, node B transmits less frequently, meaning that it consumes less energy as a cluster member. In this scenario, we should prefer to assign the cluster head role to node A.

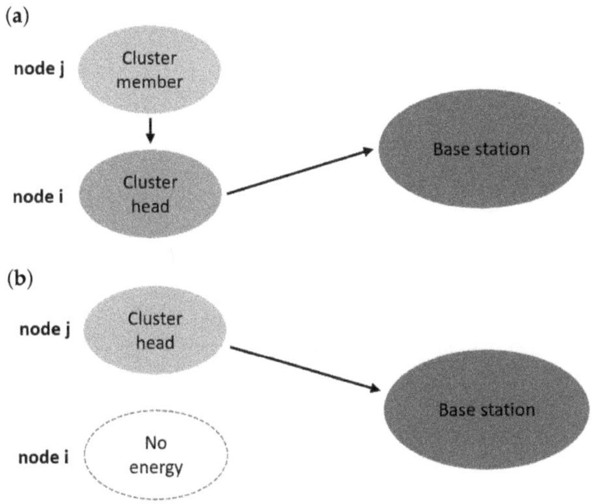

Figure 2. Example of a sensor network with two nodes: (**a**) sensor node *i* initially serves as the cluster head and (**b**) node *j* takes over the role of cluster head after node *i* dies.

In the considered WSN, the operations of sensor nodes are organized into rounds. Each round comprises a fixed number of time steps, denoted as *k*. During each round, sensor nodes may transmit data to the cluster head depending on sensed events or data importance. These transmissions occur irregularly (i.e., not at every time step) due to the nature of the sensed phenomena and the need to conserve energy. To model and anticipate the behavior of sensor nodes in future rounds, we define a transmission probability p_i for each node *i*, which represents the estimated probability that the node will transmit data to its cluster head during a single time step in the current round. This probability is computed based on the transmission activity observed in the previous round, employing a simple but effective prediction mechanism. For each node (*i*), we evaluate the so-called transmission probability p_i as follows:

$$p_i = E_i / k \tag{7}$$

where E_i is the number of time steps when transmission from node *i* was necessary during the previous round and *k* is the total number of time steps in one round.

The amount of energy consumed by the cluster member is proportional to the transmission probability p_i. Thus, according to the above-discussed cluster head selection rule, node i should be the one with the highest transmission probability.

The problem of extending the network lifetime LT defined by Equation (1) is illustrated in Figures 3–6. The examples presented in these figures relate to a network consisting of two nodes. In the scenarios depicted in Figures 3 and 4, nodes 1 and 2 both start with the same initial energy levels of $EI_1 = 100$ and $EI_2 = 100$. Additionally, it is assumed that $EH = 5$ and that the transmission probability for node 1 is lower than for node 2, resulting in $EM_1 = 1$ and $EM_2 = 2$. Figure 3 illustrates the scenario in which node 1 (the node with the lower transmission probability) is selected as node i. In this case, the LT is equal to 32 time steps. Conversely, in the example shown in Figure 4, node 2 (which has a higher transmission probability) is chosen as node i, extending the LT to 36 time steps.

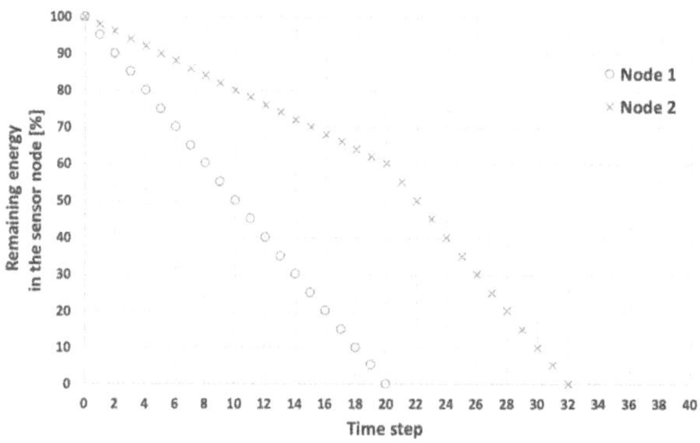

Figure 3. An example of energy consumption by sensor nodes. Node 1 is initially selected as the cluster head, initial energy level is the same for both nodes, $LT = 32$.

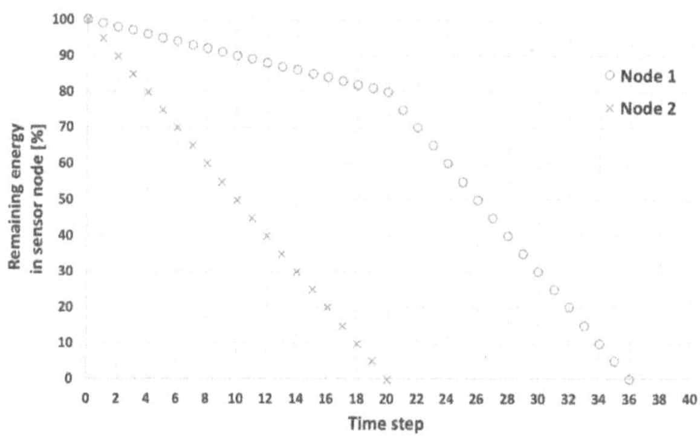

Figure 4. An example of energy consumption by sensor nodes. Node 2 initially selected as the cluster head, initial energy level is the same for both nodes, $LT = 36$.

An example involving sensor nodes with varying initial energy levels is illustrated in Figures 5 and 6. Here, it is assumed that the initial energy level of node 1 is 100, while node 2 has an initial energy level of 50. The other network parameters remain constant. When node 1 is selected as the initial cluster head ($i = 1$), the network lifetime is equal to 22 time steps (Figure 5). Conversely, when the node with the lower initial energy level (node 2) acts as the initial cluster head ($i = 2$), the network lifetime increases to 28 time steps (Figure 6).

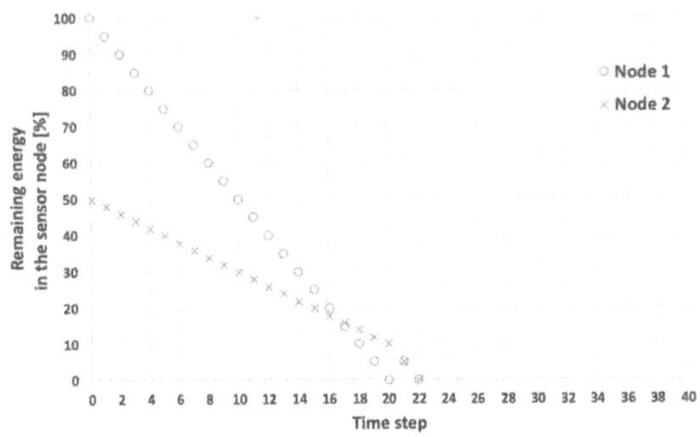

Figure 5. An example of energy consumption by sensor nodes. Node 1 is initially selected as the cluster head, the nodes have different initial energy levels, $LT = 22$.

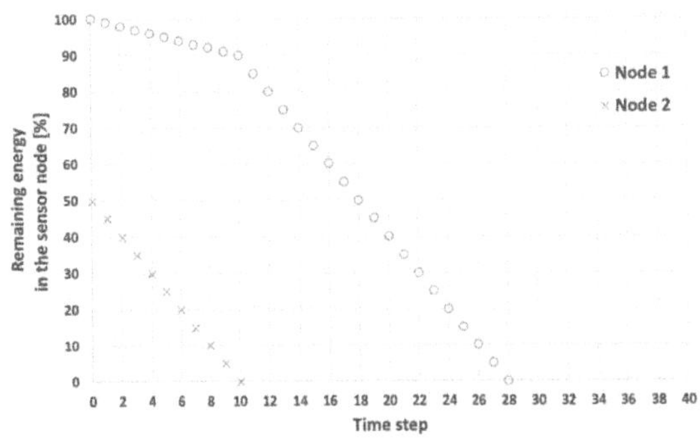

Figure 6. An example of energy consumption by sensor nodes. Node 2 is initially selected as the cluster head, the nodes have different initial energy levels, $LT = 28$.

The above analysis of a network with two sensor nodes allows us to observe that the selection of the cluster head has a significant impact on the last node's lifetime. Although real-world clusters typically contain multiple sensor nodes, the fundamental principles that govern efficient cluster head selection can be clearly illustrated in the case with two nodes. The insights gained from these examples are scalable, as the same decision metrics apply when extended to clusters with more nodes. Thus, our algorithm is designed based on the analysis presented above to incorporate scalable parameters and decision criteria, making it applicable and effective in clusters of arbitrary size.

The proposed Algorithm 1 consists of two main steps. In the first step, the nodes with the lowest initial energy are identified as candidates for the role of cluster head. In the second step, the candidate node with the highest transmission probability is selected.

The initial stage of the algorithm involves determining the transmission probabilities p_i. The transmission probabilities for all sensor nodes are stored in an array p. Next, the set of active nodes (those for which $W_i = 1$) is determined. It is important to note that a sensor node may be inactive ($W_i = 0$) due to energy depletion or other failures. Candidate nodes are selected from the set of active nodes. A sensor node is identified as a candidate if its initial energy E_i does not exceed the minimum initial energy of all nodes by more than 5%. The set of candidate nodes is represented in the pseudocode by the variable X. Finally, the candidate node with the highest transmission probability is chosen as the next cluster head.

By considering multiple candidate nodes, the proposed algorithm prevents situations in which minor variations in initial energy levels lead to exclusion of the transmission probability criterion during the cluster head selection process. An example of our algorithm's operation is illustrated in Figure 7.

Algorithm 1 The proposed cluster head rotation procedure.

Output: ID of the node that will serve as the cluster head in the next round.

function DETERMINECLUSTERHEADNODE(W, n, E, k, EI)
  Initialize array p ▷ transmission probabilities for all nodes
  for i $\leftarrow$ 0 to $n-1$ **do**
    $p_i \leftarrow E_i \,/\, k$
  end for
  $X \leftarrow$ identifiers of nodes i for which $W_i = 1$
  $X \leftarrow$ identifiers of nodes $i \in X$ for which $EI_i \leq 1.05 \cdot \min_{i \in X} EI_i$
  nextParentNode $\leftarrow$ identifier $i \in X$ for which $p_i = \max_{i \in X} p_i$
  return nextParentNode
end function

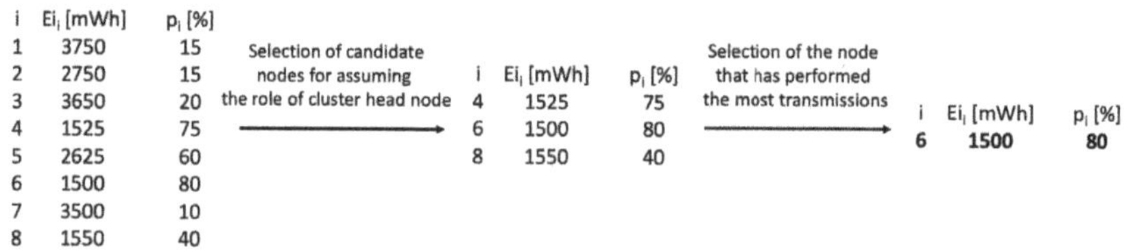

Figure 7. Example of cluster head selection using Algorithm 1.

The computational complexity of the proposed cluster head selection algorithm is O(n log n), where n is the number of sensor nodes. While most steps are linear, including computing the transmission probabilities and filtering the nodes, the selection processes for choosing the nodes with high transmission probability and minimum initial energy are performed using sorting, which dominates the overall complexity. Thus, sorting-based minima and maxima computations are the most computationally expensive operations.

4. Model Sensor Network

In this section, we present the model sensor network utilized to conduct experimental evaluations of the proposed cluster head rotation method. The primary components of the model include the data transmission algorithms employed by individual nodes and the parameters that characterize the energy consumption of a sensor node at various stages of network operation. The values of these parameters were determined through experiments conducted with the implemented prototype of the sensor network.

The operation of the considered WSN is designed to deliver valuable measurement data from the sensor nodes to the base station. In each operational step of the network, a selected sensor node serves as the cluster head, while the remaining nodes fulfill the roles assigned to cluster members. If a cluster member decides to transmit data to the cluster head during a given step, it activates its radio module to perform the transmission. If not, the transmission is skipped. The cluster head node analyzes measurements from its own sensors and additionally gathers information from the cluster members before forwarding the collected data to the base station.

Each round of the WSN operation consists of an equal number of steps. After the last step of a round, the algorithm selects the node that will act as the cluster head during the next round. Initialization and assignment of node roles are performed during the initial stage of network operation. During the configuration phase, each node is assigned a unique logical address (ID), allowing the identification of individual nodes in the WSN.

Each round of WSN operation consists of an equal number of steps. After the final step of each round, a node is selected to serve as the cluster head for the subsequent round.

During the WSN configuration phase, each node is assigned a unique ID, enabling the identification of individual nodes within the network. After the network is activated, the node with the lowest ID begins to transmit synchronization frames, thereby assuming the role of the cluster head. The higher the ID, the longer a node will wait to receive the synchronization frame. Consequently, the remaining nodes are assigned the role of cluster members, either due to their longer listening period for the synchronization frame or their later activation time. Following the initialization process, the sensor nodes enter a sleep mode, the duration of which depends on the objectives of the sensor network and the requirements regarding how frequently measurements must be taken.

The operations performed by the cluster members are outlined in Algorithm 2. When analyzing the provided pseudocode, it is important to note that it pertains to the operation of a node within a single operational time step. During a node's operation, a periodic increment of the step counter occurs. The next operation involves acquiring data from sensors, after which the node makes a decision regarding data transmission. The instruction labeled "decide whether data should be transmitted" represents a decision-making process that is dependent on the specific application. In practice, this may involve assessing whether the sensed data exceed a predefined threshold, indicate a significant event, or meet specific relevance criteria. In our experimental environment, this decision is modeled using a predefined transmission probability assigned to each node, which reflects the likelihood of the node generating useful data at any given time. This abstraction facilitates the emulation of application-aware or event-driven behavior in which nodes with higher transmission probabilities are more active, resulting in varying energy usage. If the sensor node determines that the data should be sent to the cluster head, then it proceeds with the transmission. To conserve energy, sensor nodes activate the communication module only when data transmission is necessary.

After the node has completed the predefined number of steps, the procedure for selecting the cluster head node is initiated. This process begins with the activation of the communication module, as the cluster member will be waiting for the synchronization frame to be transmitted by the cluster head at this stage. If the node does not proceed to the cluster head node selection procedure during a specific network operation step, then the communication module is deactivated for a defined period (*sleep time*).

Algorithm 3 describes the operation of the cluster head. The procedure begins with the increment of the time step counter. The next operation is to activate the communication module and transmit a synchronization frame to all nodes in the cluster. The synchronization frame contains data that are essential for new nodes to join the network, i.e., the current step counter state and the cluster head node identifier. This allows new nodes to join the network at any time during the round.

After transmitting the synchronization frame, the cluster head reads data from its sensors along with the other cluster members, then waits to receive data from the remaining nodes in the cluster. The value of the *data reception time* parameter is appropriately determined to ensure that the cluster head can collect data from all cluster members. After receiving the data, the transmission counter E is updated at each step of the node's operation. The value of E_i is incremented if cluster member i has reported its sensor readings to the cluster head at a given time step. Furthermore, for the cluster head (i.e., when i represents the ID of the current cluster head), the transmission counter E_i is incremented when the cluster head determines that its own sensor readings need to be transmitted to the base station.

Algorithm 2 Cluster member operation.

```
step ← step + 1
read data from sensors
decide whether data should be transmitted
if data should be transmitted then
    turn on communication module
    send data to cluster head
end if
if step = last step then
    if communication module is off then
        turn on communication module
    end if
    start cluster head selection procedure
end if
turn off communication module (sleep time)
```

The next operation involves data aggregation and transmission to the base station. If the node has completed the predefined number of steps, then the round concludes and the procedure for selecting the cluster head node begins. After this procedure is complete, the communication module is set to sleep mode.

Algorithm 3 Cluster head operation.

```
step ← step + 1
turn on communication module
send synchronization frame to all cluster member nodes
read data from sensors
wait for data from cluster member nodes (data reception time)
update transmission count E_i
aggregate data
send aggregated data to base station
if step = last step then
    start cluster head node selection procedure
end if
turn off communication module (sleep time)
```

After completing a specified number of steps in the operation of the sensor nodes (specifically, at the end of each round), the procedure for selecting the cluster head is initiated (Algorithm 4). The course of this procedure depends on the role that the node is currently performing. If the node is acting as the cluster head, then its task is to determine the ID of the node that will assume this role in the next round. In this context, the proposed cluster head rotation approach (Algorithm 1) can be utilized or an alternative state-of-the-art method may be employed. After a new cluster head is selected, a synchronization frame containing the newly assigned cluster head ID is transmitted to all nodes within the cluster. It is essential that all nodes listen to this frame simultaneously in order to prevent situations where only some nodes receive the correct cluster head identifier. Such errors could lead to improper node operation, frequent executions of the initialization algorithm, and negative impacts on the overall lifetime of the sensor network.

The operations performed by the cluster members during the selection of a new cluster head begin with listening for the synchronization frame. This process ends when the frame is received or when a specified timeout occurs, as defined by the variable *data reception time*. If a node does not receive the synchronization frame, then the initialization procedure is initiated. Conversely, when the synchronization frame is received, the node checks the ID of the cluster head contained within it. If the ID matches that of the node performing this operation, then that node assumes the role of the cluster head in the upcoming round. Otherwise, the node takes on the role of a cluster member, and the cluster head ID is interpreted as the recipient address to which data must be sent in the new round.

Algorithm 4 Procedure for selecting the cluster head.

```
if node role = cluster head then
    run the appropriate method for selecting the new cluster head
    send synchronization frame to all nodes in the cluster
    turn off communication module (sleep time)
else if node role = cluster member then
    start listening for the synchronization frame
    repeat
        wait
    until received synchronization frame or data reception time has passed
    if synchronization frame received then
        if cluster head node ID = own ID then
            node role = cluster head node
        else
            node role = cluster member node
        end if
        turn off communication module (sleep time)
    else
        start initialization procedure
    end if
end if
step = 0
```

The procedure for determining the lifetime of the WSN is outlined in Algorithm 5. The process begins with the initialization of all sensor nodes and the assignment of their initial roles. The next step involves executing a single round of sensor network operations, which consists of performing k operational steps for the nodes. In each operational step, a designated sensor node acts as the cluster head and consumes energy defined by the variable S_{CH}. The remaining nodes are designated as cluster members. The energy consumption of a cluster member accounts for two scenarios. If, a cluster member transmits data to the cluster head in a particular step, then it consumes an amount of energy, represented by the variable S_{TRANS}; otherwise, no transmission occurs and the node consumes an amount of energy determined by the variable $S_{NOTRANS}$. Upon completing the round, the cluster head selection procedure is executed. After this procedure is finished, the variable *round counter* is incremented by one. In the subsequent step, the number of active nodes is assessed. If there are no active nodes, the WSN operation terminates, and the algorithm returns the total number of rounds during which the network performed its tasks.

Algorithm 5 Procedure for determining the lifetime of a sensor network.

```
Output: Sensor network lifetime (number of rounds)
  function DETERMINENETWORKLIFETIME(W, s, n, k, S_CH, S_TRANS, S_NOTRANS)
      perform node initialization
      while true do
          for j ← 0 to k − 1 do                              ▷ LoRaWAN technology, k = 60
              for i ← 0 to n − 1 do
                  if role of the i-th node = cluster head node then
                      perform a cluster member node operation step
                      s_i ← s_i − S_CH
                  end if
                  if role of the i-th node = cluster member then
                      perform a cluster head node operation step
                      if i-th node transmitted data in the current step then
                          s_i ← s_i − S_TRANS
                      else
                          s_i ← s_i − S_NOTRANS
                      end if
                  end if
              end for
              execute cluster head node selection procedure
          end for
          round counter ← round counter + 1
          activeNodes ← 0
          for i ← 0 to n − 1 do
              if s_i > ϵ then
                  activeNodes ← activeNodes + 1
              end if
          end for
          if activeNodes = 0 then
              break
          end if
      end while
      return round counter
  end function
```

It is important to note that all variables in Algorithms 1–4 are considered local to individual sensor nodes and are not shared between nodes. Each node operates independently based on its own state and sensor readings. However, in Algorithm 5, which describes the global simulation of the entire WSN, all variables used in the pseudocode should be treated as global, meaning that they represent the current state of all nodes in the network and are accessible for evaluating the network lifetime.

To validate the algorithms presented in this section, we implemented and tested them in a prototype WSN. Details of the experimental testbed are described in Section 5. These tests confirmed the feasibility of practically implementing the proposed approach and allowed us to determine the amount of energy consumed by sensor nodes under conditions that closely resemble real-world scenarios. Next, we calibrated our WSN model based on the physical implementation. The calibration process included measurements that enabled us to determine the parameters S_{CH}, S_{TRANS}, and $S_{NOTRANS}$. Detailed results are presented in the following section.

5. Experiments

The experimental testbed was established using LoRaWAN technology [33,34]. A LoRaWAN sensor network can comprise nodes (including both cluster heads and cluster members), gateways (concentrators), a network server (base station), and application servers. In designing a sensor network that employs this technology, it was assumed that the data transmitted by the cluster head could be received by multiple gateways [35]. The software operating on the gateway is responsible for forwarding incoming traffic to the network server. This process can be executed using cellular networks, Ethernet, WiFi, or satellite technology. Subsequently, the network server facilitates the transmission of LoRaWAN messages by relaying data to the primary application servers. In addition to the aforementioned data transmission scheme, direct communication between end nodes is also feasible, which was utilized during our research.

The WSN prototype was constructed using modules based on the Arduino MKR WAN 1310 board (Arduino S.r.l., Monza, Italy), which provides connectivity to the IoT Cloud along with existing LoRaWAN infrastructure such as The Things Network and other boards through direct communication mode. The prototype board comprised three independent components: a 32-bit SAMD21 microcontroller based on the ARM Cortex-M0 core, the Murata wireless communication module, and the ECC508 integrated circuit, which facilitates hardware support for data transmission encryption. Notably, the manufacturer also supplied a power supply stabilization block. In battery-powered systems it is possible to disconnect this block from the rest of the circuit, which positively impacts the reduction of energy consumption by the node.

When the microcontroller and the LoRaWAN radio module are in deep sleep mode, the current consumption is measured at 16.6 μA, which allows for an extended operational time for the sensor node. Given the relatively long initialization time of the LoRaWAN radio module, it was determined that the network operation step would be set to one second, with synchronization conducted at one-minute intervals.

The communication module (Murata CMWX1ZZABZ, Murata Investment Co., Ltd., Shanghai, China) operates in accordance with the LoRaWAN 1.0.x specification, implementing a pure ALOHA-based uncoordinated medium access protocol at the MAC layer and supporting Class A functionality, which is typical for ultra-low-power devices. In LoRaWAN Class A, following each uplink transmission (from the device to the gateway), the device opens two predefined receive windows (RX1 and RX2), during which it may receive a downlink response from the network.

The algorithms for rotating the cluster head role were implemented on the SAMD21 microcontroller and the STM32 family circuit along with the LTC4150 module, which measures energy consumption for a given network node, as illustrated in Figure 8 (modules integrated into a single sensor node are indicated with a dashed line). Each node was equipped with the ALS-PT19 (Everlight Electronics Co., Ltd., Taipei, Taiwan) analog light sensor. During the research, a Mean Well APV-12-5 (Mean Well Enterprises Co., Ltd., New Taipei City, Taiwan) stabilized power supply and a step-down converter based on the

XL4015 (XLSemi Microelectronics Co., Ltd., Shanghai, China) circuit were utilized to reduce the supply voltage to the 3.3 V level required for the prototype board. Energy consumption was measured over a period encompassing 43,200 operational steps for each node.

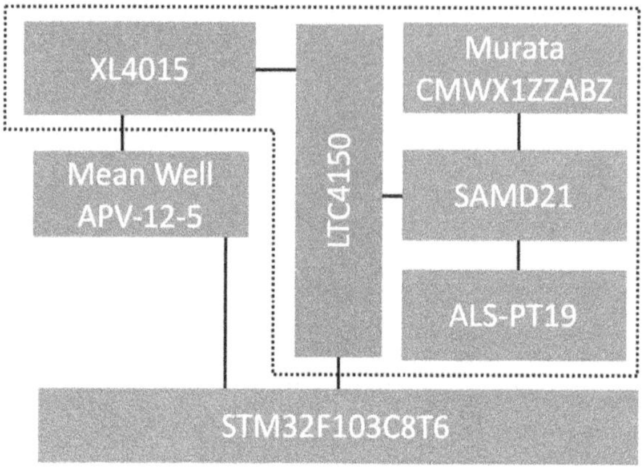

Figure 8. Part of the experimental testbed for a single sensor node.

The energy consumption measurements were conducted using the LTC4150 module [36], which generates a pulse on a dedicated output each time the sensor node consumes 0.1707 mAh. By analyzing the recorded number of pulses generated by the LTC4150 module and the known measurement duration, it was possible to determine the energy consumption per operational step of the sensor node. The energy measurements reflect the raw module usage only. Losses due to power regulation are not included in the reported values. These measurements focused on the energy consumption of the sensor node in the following scenarios: when the node acts as a cluster head (S_{CH}), when it functions as a cluster member and transmits data to the cluster head (S_{TRANS}), and when it operates as a cluster member but does not transmit data to the cluster head ($S_{NOTRANS}$).

Energy consumption measurements were carried out over a period of six hours for each of the node's operating scenarios. Based on the conducted studies, it was observed that the master node consumed energy equal to 838 mWh. When the node performed the role of a cluster member without transmitting data to the cluster head, the measurement system recorded an energy consumption of 655 mWh. In situations where the cluster member did not engage in data transmission, it consumed 40 mWh of energy. By dividing the obtained measurement results by the number of steps during which the measurements were taken, the values for the parameters S_{CH}, S_{TRANS}, and $S_{NOTRANS}$ required for the simulation algorithm were determined. A summary of the energy consumption measurements by the sensor nodes is presented in Table 2.

Table 2. Energy consumption per step of a sensor node's operation in different operational scenarios.

Parameter	Energy Consumption [mWh]
S_{CH}	0.019403
S_{TRANS}	0.015178
$S_{NOTRANS}$	0.000939

After determining the parameters that describe energy consumption in the sensor nodes, we used the procedure described in Algorithm 5 to assess the lifetime of the WSN. Algorithm 5 was employed to determine the network lifetime for each method under comparison. The operation "execute cluster head node selection procedure" in Algorithm 5 was implemented separately for each method examined during the experiments. Dedicated implementations were developed for the basic approach, LEACH, EDCR, and the proposed method.

It should be noted that each round in the examined WSN lasts for one minute. The ϵ parameter was set to the S_{CH} value. The network's lifetime was determined as the total number of rounds counted from the network's initialization until the last node ceased to function. For example, if the network operated for 3330 rounds, the resulting network lifetime would be 55 min and 30 s.

For the purpose of the experiments, a WSN consisting of ten nodes was considered. The experiments were conducted with constant and variable transmission probabilities. In the case of time-varying transmission probability, changes occurred every 5 min within 15-min cycles. In the second scenario, the transmission probability remained constant throughout the duration of the experiment, as presented in Table 3. The transmission probabilities were arbitrarily selected to represent a variety of possible node behaviors in WSNs. These values are not derived from real-world measurements but were defined to simulate both static and dynamic transmission scenarios. The data transmission behavior was simulated probabilistically in both constant and time-varying transmission probability scenarios. At each time step of WSN operation, a random number uniformly distributed in the interval [0, 1] was generated independently for each sensor node. A node was assumed to transmit data to the cluster head if the generated number was less than or equal to its current transmission probability. In the time-varying case, the probability thresholds were updated every 5 min according to the pattern shown in Table 3.

For the first series of experiments, it was assumed that each node was equipped with a fully charged battery with a capacity of 2310 mWh.

Table 3. Transmission probabilities considered during determination of network lifetime.

Sensor Node Identifier									
1	2	3	4	5	6	7	8	9	10
Constant probability of transmission									
10%	30%	40%	10%	30%	40%	10%	30%	40%	10%
10%	30%	40%	10%	30%	40%	10%	30%	40%	10%
10%	30%	40%	10%	30%	40%	10%	30%	40%	10%
Variable probability of transmission (changing every 5 min)									
30%	30%	30%	40%	70%	30%	30%	30%	40%	70%
10%	20%	20%	70%	10%	10%	20%	20%	70%	10%
20%	50%	40%	50%	50%	20%	50%	40%	50%	50%

Figure 9 presents the results obtained from the basic approach, in which the node with the lowest identifier is designated as the cluster head. After its battery is depleted, the role is successively transferred to the next active node in ascending order of identifiers. In this scenario, the network lifetime was recorded at 122 h and 39 min. Figure 10 illustrates the situation with a variable transmission probability, resulting in a reduced lifetime of 96 h and 25 min. A significant drawback of this approach is that the assignment of identifiers to individual nodes within the sensor network critically influences the overall lifetime. The network lifetime declines sharply when nodes that transmit the least data are depleted first. This method has considerable limitations, as it is challenging to predict the number of transmissions each node will perform and how to assign their identifiers—which determine the order in which they assume the cluster head role—so as to maximize the network lifetime.

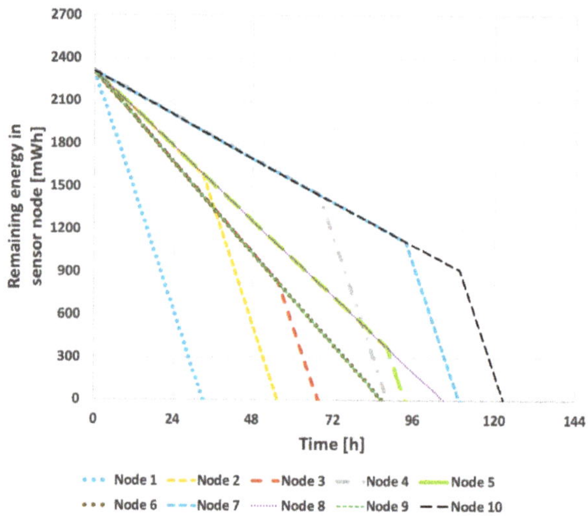

Figure 9. Energy consumption by sensor nodes for the basic approach and the EDCR algorithm (constant data transmission probability).

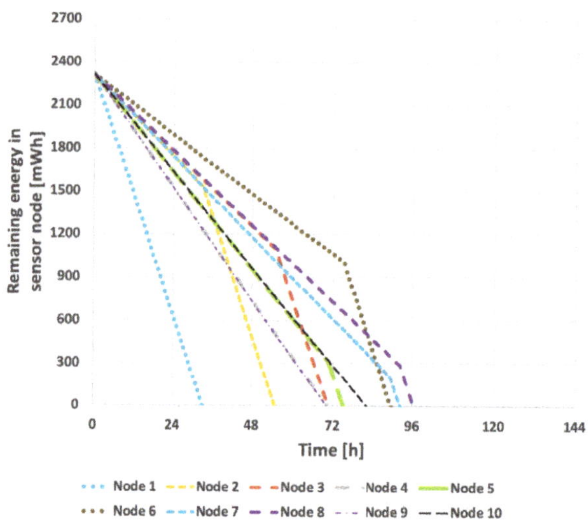

Figure 10. Energy consumption by sensor nodes for the basic approach and the EDCR algorithm (variable transmission probability).

Figures 11 and 12 illustrate the results obtained using the LEACH method. In the case of constant transmission probability, the network lifetime was 111 h and 43 min. In the second scenario, this was reduced to 91 h and 51 min. The conducted studies indicate that the effectiveness of extending the network's lifetime with this approach is relatively low.

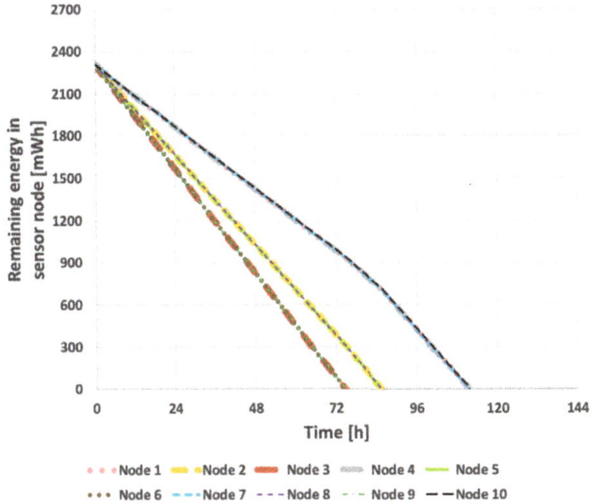

Figure 11. Energy consumption by sensor nodes for the LEACH method (constant transmission probability).

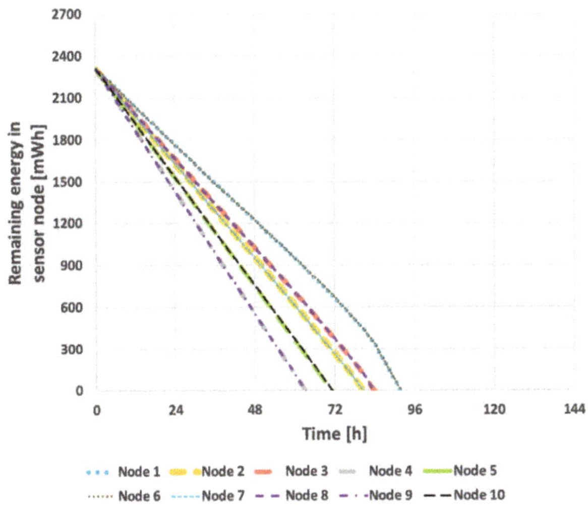

Figure 12. Energy consumption by sensor nodes for the LEACH method (variable transmission probability).

Experiments were conducted to compare the lifetimes achieved using the state-of-the-art methods described in Section 2, which aim to achieve uniform energy consumption among sensor nodes. As anticipated, these methods resulted in a shorter time to the death of the last node compared to the proposed approach, as they were specifically designed to prolong the time until the first node dies. A representative example of the aforementioned state-of-the-art methods is EDCR.

For the EDCR protocol, the initial step involves determining the energy threshold, after which the algorithm transfers the role of the cluster head to the subsequent node. Following the calibration process for both constant and variable transmission probabilities, an energy threshold of 0% was established, as illustrated in Figures 13 and 14. This indicates that the transfer of the parent role occurs only after the node is completely discharged, effectively reducing the method to the basic approach in which nodes are sequentially discharged based on the identifiers assigned to them during the design phase. As shown in Figures 9 and 10, it can be observed that the network lifetime was 122 h and 45 min in the case of constant transmission probability, whereas for periodic changes in transmission probability the lifetime was 96 h and 21 min.

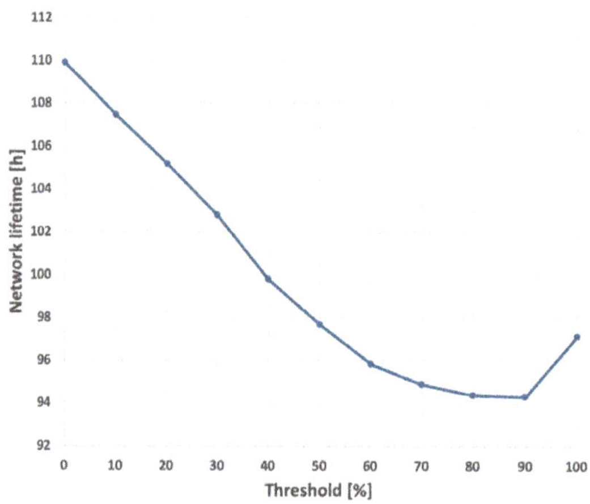

Figure 13. Calibration of the EDCR algorithm (constant data transmission probability).

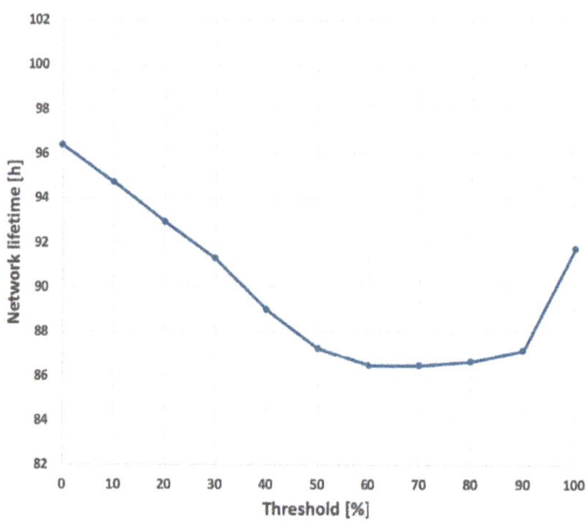

Figure 14. Calibration of the EDCR algorithm (variable data transmission probability).

The results obtained for the proposed method are presented in Figures 15 and 16. In the scenario where the transmission probability is constant, the proposed method extended the network lifetime to 130 h and 15 min. Because the proposed method accounts for the current transmission probabilities, which are calculated in each round, the response to changes that necessitate selection of a new cluster head occurs much more rapidly. Consequently, the network lifetime in the case of variable transmission probability was also extended, reaching 105 h and 7 min.

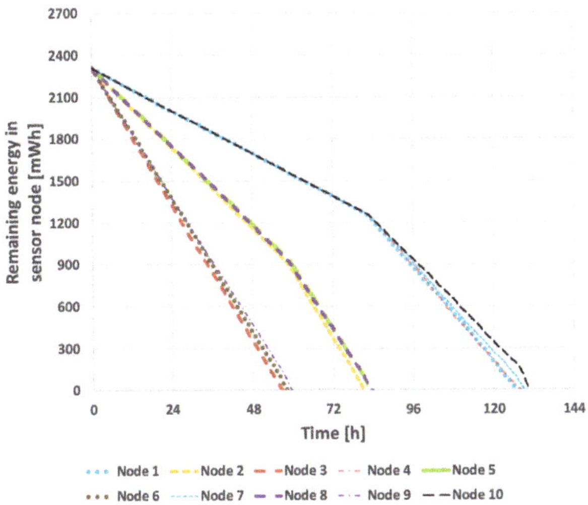

Figure 15. Energy consumption by sensor nodes for proposed method (constant data transmission probability).

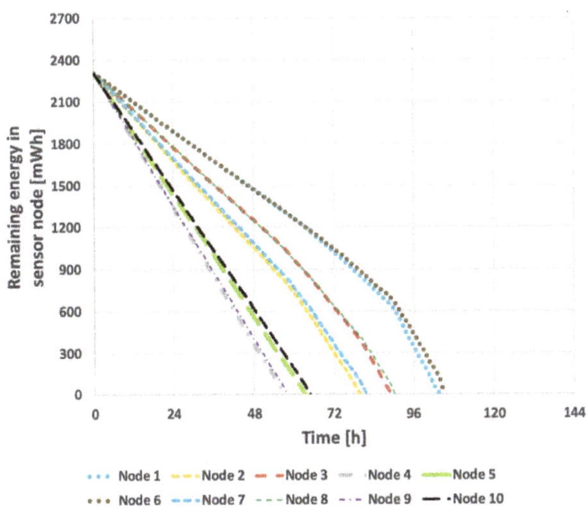

Figure 16. Energy consumption by sensor nodes for proposed method (variable data transmission probability).

Table 4 presents the aggregated results obtained for both the proposed approach and other available methods, assuming the same initial energy level for all nodes under both constant and variable data transmission probabilities. Furthermore, the Wilcoxon statistical test was conducted to demonstrate the statistical significance of the results, with a significance level of $p < 0.05$. The symbol ↑ indicates that the indicated algorithm is statistically superior to all other algorithms examined in this test. Lifetimes achieved for the variable data transmission probability are also illustrated in Figure 17.

Based on the above results, it can be observed that the longer time to death of the last node in the WSN when using the proposed algorithm is primarily attributed to its ability to handle transmission probabilities in the cluster head selection process. The proposed algorithm selects the node with the highest current transmission probability as the cluster head in each round. This design ensures that nodes which are expected to transmit data more frequently (i.e., that consume energy at a higher rate) are prioritized to perform the cluster head role earlier. Consequently, nodes with lower transmission probabilities (which consume less energy as cluster members) are left to perform the cluster head role at the end of the sequence. The final cluster head retains a higher energy reserve compared to the others; after all other nodes deplete their energy while serving as cluster heads, this last node can continue to operate as the cluster head for longer, extending the network lifetime. In contrast, the compared existing approaches (EDCR and LEACH) aim to equalize energy consumption among nodes, preventing any single node from depleting too early. This strategy tends to distribute energy usage more uniformly, limiting the possibility of preserving a reserve of energy to sustain network operation at later stages.

Table 4. Network lifetime for the compared methods (equal initial energy levels of nodes).

Data Transmission Probability	Method	Network Lifetime
Constant	Basic approach	122 h 39 m
	LEACH	111 h 43 m
	EDCR	122 h 45 m
	Proposed method	130 h 15 m ↑
Variable	Basic approach	96 h 25 m
	LEACH	91 h 51 m
	EDCR	96 h 21 m
	Proposed method	105 h 7 m ↑

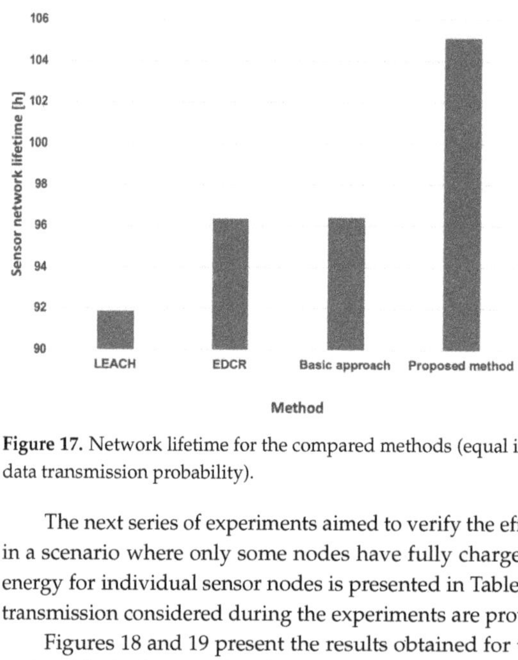

Figure 17. Network lifetime for the compared methods (equal initial energy levels of nodes, variable data transmission probability).

The next series of experiments aimed to verify the effectiveness of different algorithms in a scenario where only some nodes have fully charged batteries. The initial available energy for individual sensor nodes is presented in Table 5, while the probabilities of data transmission considered during the experiments are provided in Table 3.

Figures 18 and 19 present the results obtained for the basic approach, in which the node with the lowest identifier is designated as the cluster head. When its battery is depleted, the role is successively transferred to the next active node in ascending order of identifiers.

Figure 18 illustrates the network lifetime when the transmission probability was held constant, resulting in the lifetime of 107 h. In contrast, when the data transmission probability fluctuated, the recorded network lifetime was 83 h and 33 min, as depicted in Figure 19.

Table 5. Assumed initial available energy in sensor nodes during the experiments.

Sensor Node Identifier									
1	2	3	4	5	6	7	8	9	10
Initial available energy in sensor node [mWh]									
1155	1155	1155	1155	2310	2310	2310	2310	2310	2310

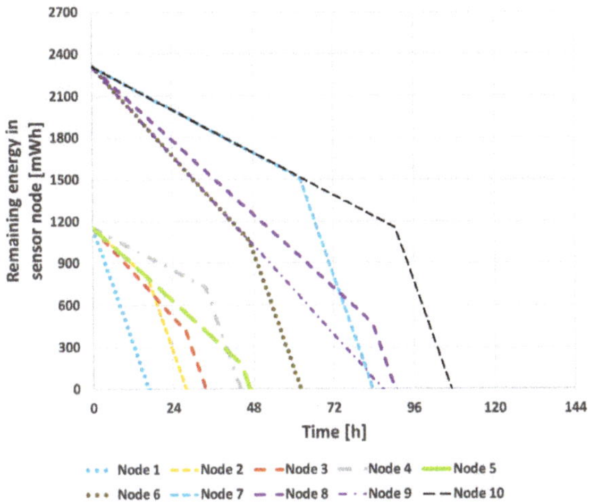

Figure 18. Energy consumption by sensor nodes for the basic approach and the EDCR algorithm (different initial energy levels of nodes, constant data transmission probability).

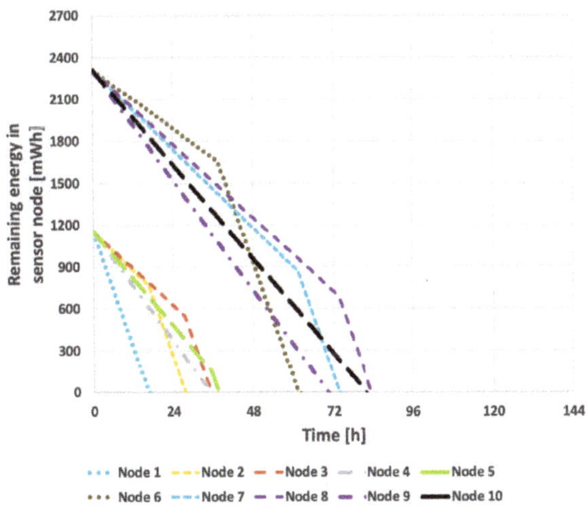

Figure 19. Energy (different initial energy levels of nodes, variable transmission probability).

Figures 20 and 21 present the results obtained for the LEACH method. In the scenario where the data transmission probability remained constant, the network lifetime was 94 h and 52 min. When the data transmission probability varied over time, the network lifetime decreased to 80 h and 54 min. These results indicate that the LEACH algorithm is not well-suited for use in a network where individual nodes are equipped with batteries of varying capacities.

The results for the EDCR algorithm are presented in Figures 18 and 19. This approach necessitates a calibration process, as illustrated in Figures 22 and 23. Based on these results, it is evident that the longest network lifetime was achieved with a threshold of 0%, indicating that the cluster head node should be replaced only after the current node is completely discharged. This aligns with the basic approach; therefore, the results in Figures 18 and 19 are identical for both methods.

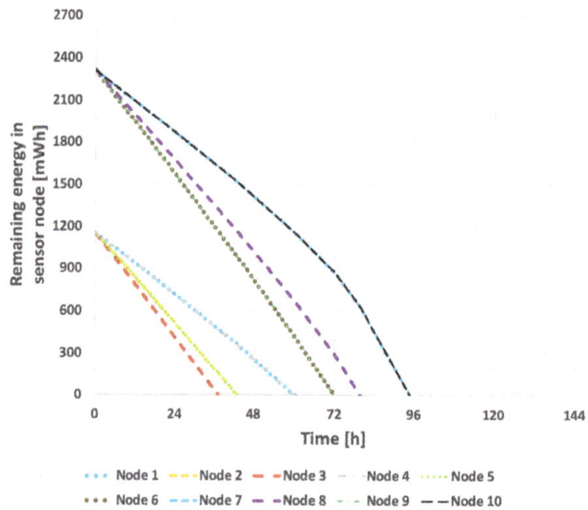

Figure 20. Energy consumption by sensor nodes for the LEACH method (different initial energy levels of nodes, constant transmission probability).

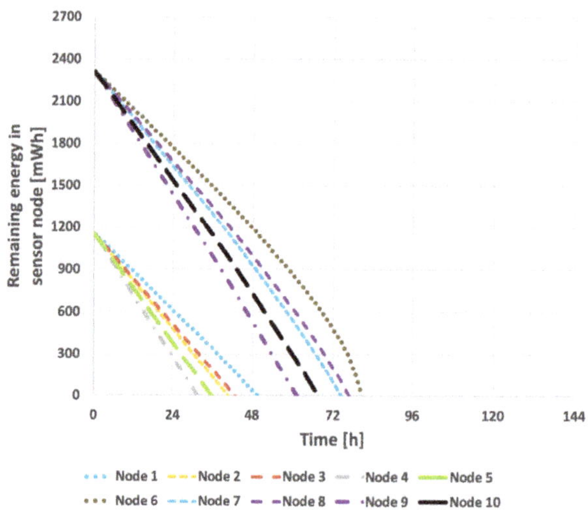

Figure 21. Energy consumption by sensor nodes for the LEACH method (different initial energy levels of nodes, variable transmission probability).

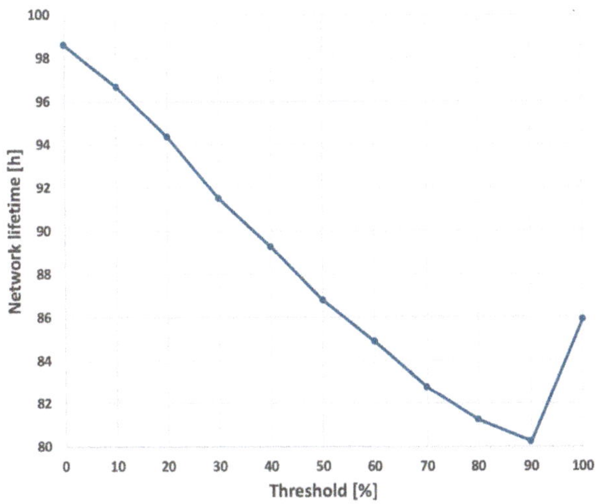

Figure 22. Calibration of the EDCR algorithm (different initial energy levels of nodes, constant data transmission probability).

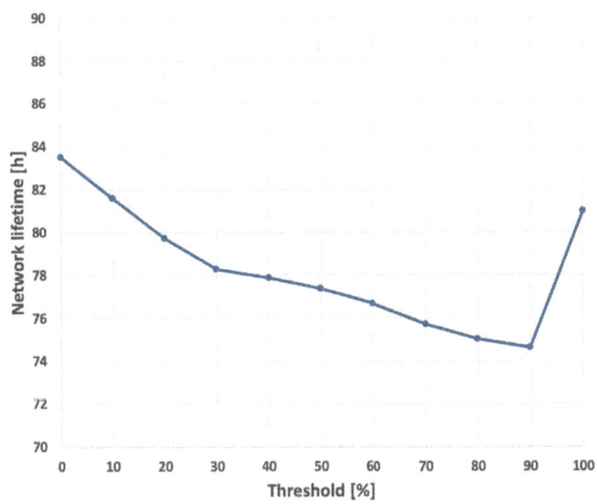

Figure 23. Calibration of the EDCR algorithm (different initial energy levels of nodes, variable data transmission probability).

Implementing the EDCR algorithm to extend network lifetime makes the assignment of node identifiers even more critical to the results. This is due to the necessity of considering two key parameters when configuring the network, namely, the number of transmissions recorded by each node and its battery charge level. The network lifetime is comparable to that achieved with the basic approach, reaching 106 h and 57 min for a constant transmission probability and 83 h and 28 min in the second scenario.

The results obtained when applying the proposed method are presented in Figures 24 and 25. By taking the initial battery charge level into account, the proposed solution effectively extends the network's lifetime. In the scenario with a constant data transmission probability, the network's lifetime reached 111 h and 57 min. It is important to note that the proposed solution accommodates situations in which a node transmits data only during selected operational steps. Consequently, in the scenario where the data transmission probability experiences cyclic variations, the network's lifetime was extended to 94 h and 33 min.

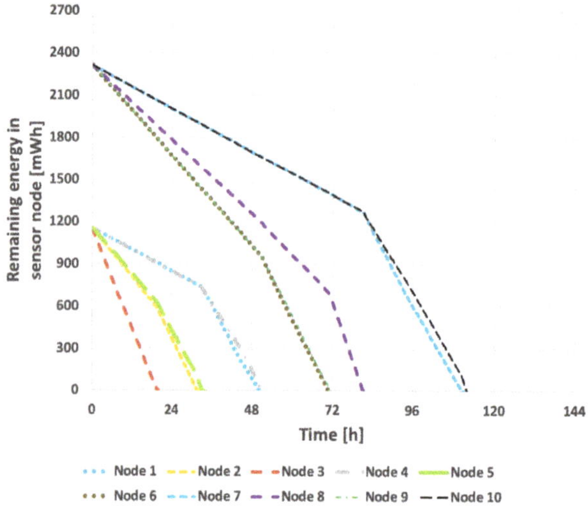

Figure 24. Energy consumption by sensor nodes for the proposed method (different initial energy levels of nodes, constant data transmission probability).

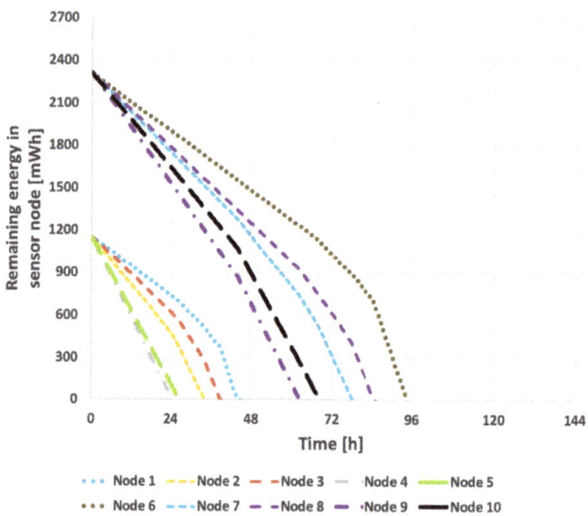

Figure 25. Energy consumption by sensor nodes for the proposed method (different initial energy levels of nodes, variable data transmission probability).

Table 6 and Figure 26 present the aggregated results obtained for the proposed approach and the other methods considering different initial energy levels in all nodes for both constant and variable data transmission probabilities. The conducted experiments demonstrate that the lifetime of the prototype sensor network is significantly extended when using our proposed method when compared to the network lifetime achieved using the other algorithms. To confirm the statistical significance of the results, an additional Wilcoxon statistical test was performed, with a significance level of $p < 0.05$.

Table 6. Network lifetime for the compared methods (different initial energy levels of nodes).

Data Transmission Probability	Method	Network Lifetime
Constant	Basic approach	107 h
	LEACH	94 h 52 m
	EDCR	106 h 57 m
	Proposed method	111 h 57 m ↑
Variable	Basic approach	83 h 33 m
	LEACH	80 h 54 m
	EDCR	83 h 28 m
	Proposed method	94 h 33 m ↑

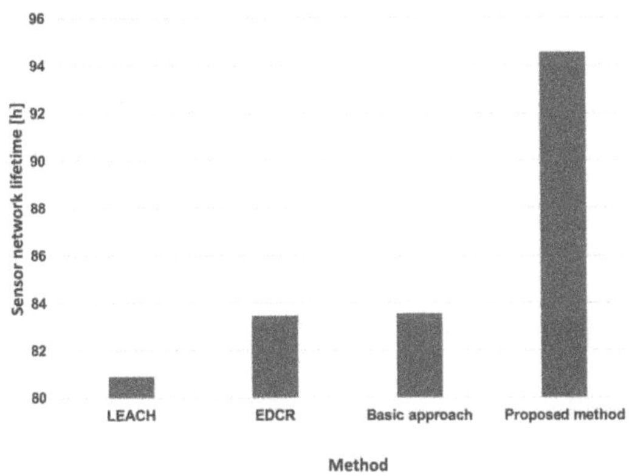

Figure 26. Network lifetime for the compared methods (different initial energy levels of nodes, variable data transmission probability).

Based on the results obtained in the second series of experiments where the sensor nodes had different initial energy levels, it was observed that the improvement in extending the time to death of the last node is primarily due to the proposed algorithm selecting the node with the lowest initial energy as the initial cluster head. This decision has a critical impact on the network lifetime. By initially assigning the most energy-constrained node to the cluster head role, the proposed algorithm ensures that this node contributes to network operation while it still has sufficient energy. In other methods, a low-energy node kept in the network as a cluster member during early rounds may expend its energy passively and become depleted before being assigned the cluster head role. The EDCR method prioritizes the selection of nodes with the highest available energy for the cluster head role. Although this approach is effective in balancing energy consumption, it is not well suited for maximizing the time to the last node's death. By continuously assigning the cluster head role to high-energy nodes, low-energy nodes are left to consume their energy slowly in the cluster member role, and may never be utilized as cluster heads before becoming depleted.

6. Conclusions and Future Work

In this paper, we have proposed a novel cluster head selection algorithm for WSNs that extends the time until the last sensor node depletes its energy. The proposed algorithm is based on a formal analysis for the minimal setup that considers network lifetime as a function of energy consumption in sensor nodes. By examining a two-node network scenario, we derive a cluster head selection rule that applies to larger clusters and prioritizes the node with the highest transmission probability and lowest initial energy as the cluster head.

Although the proposed cluster head selection algorithm is initially developed based on detailed analysis of a network with only two sensor nodes, is inherently scalable and is designed for application in clusters with many sensor nodes. The key decision metrics (initial energy and transmission probability) remain valid and critical in larger clusters. The proposed algorithm operates using distributed per-cluster computations. In a WSN that is partitioned into clusters, the cluster head selection process is executed independently within each cluster. This ensures that the algorithm's complexity does not grow significantly with the overall size of the network. As a result, the proposed algorithm is scalable and can be applied to WSNs with an arbitrary numbers of nodes, provided that the network is appropriately clustered.

Experimental validation of our method using a sensor network prototype demonstrated that the proposed algorithm significantly extends the operational lifetime of the last active node. Our results indicate that existing algorithms which focus on balancing energy depletion among nodes are ineffective in maximizing the time until the last node dies. Instead, our research shows that sensor nodes should be depleted in a specific order that can be determined using the proposed method. By adhering to this depletion sequence, the last sensor node remains operational for a longer duration, effectively extending the useful lifetime of the WSN.

In addition, we implemented an experimental WSN model that accurately reflects real-world WSN behavior. The results obtained with the experimental model confirm that our method consistently achieves longer network lifetimes compared to traditional approaches that do not consider transmission probabilities during cluster head selection.

Based on the experiments conducted in this research, the lifetime of the last sensor node in our prototype WSN was significantly extended when using the proposed method. Our experiments included a comparison between the proposed method and representative existing algorithms from the literature that consider both the time and the available energy of nodes when rotating the role of cluster head.

The results of our experiments demonstrated that algorithms in which the role of the cluster head is transferred after a specific period provide suboptimal utilization of energy resources. This inefficiency arises because the sensor nodes in the WSN consume energy at varying rates. Our research confirms that methods which determine the next cluster head based on available energy levels in order to balance energy consumption among individual nodes are ineffective when the objective is to extend the time until the last node dies.

While most cluster head selection algorithms in the literature are evaluated primarily through simulations, our research distinguishes itself by validating the proposed algorithm using real-world prototypes of sensor nodes based on LoRaWAN technology. This practical evaluation allowed us to capture real environmental influences such as hardware-specific energy consumption patterns and transmission delays. Testing on physical sensor nodes ensures the feasibility and robustness of our algorithm in realistic deployment scenarios.

The outcome of this study also includes recommendations for future research directions concerning cluster head rotation algorithms in WSNs. One potential direction is the development of methods that account for redundant nodes, which could assume the responsibilities of a given node in the event of battery depletion. Another avenue for exploration is the consideration of nodes equipped with various energy sources and the ability to harvest energy from their environment [37,38]. Additionally, the proposed method can be further refined and enhanced by incorporating suitable algorithms for predicting transmission probabilities from individual nodes as well as by mechanisms for managing more complex node hierarchies that involve nodes equipped with different sets of sensors.

Author Contributions: Conceptualization, M.L. and B.P.; data curation, M.L. and B.P.; formal analysis, M.L. and B.P.; funding acquisition, M.L. and B.P.; investigation, M.L. and B.P.; methodology, M.L. and B.P.; project administration, B.P.; resources, M.L. and B.P.; software, M.L.; supervision, B.P.; validation, M.L. and B.P.; visualization, M.L.; writing—original draft, M.L. and B.P.; writing—review and editing, M.L. and B.P. All authors have read and agreed to the published version of the manuscript.

Funding: This research received no external funding.

Institutional Review Board Statement: Not applicable.

Informed Consent Statement: Not applicable.

Data Availability Statement: Data are contained within the article.

Conflicts of Interest: The authors declare no conflicts of interest.

References

1. Kandris, D.; Anastasiadis, E. Advanced wireless sensor networks: Applications, challenges and research trends. *Electronics* **2024**, *13*, 2268. [CrossRef]
2. Carsancakli, M.F.; Al Imran, M.A.; Yildiz, H.U.; Kara, A.; Tavli, B. Reliability of linear WSNs: A complementary overview and analysis of impact of cascaded failures on network lifetime. *Ad Hoc Netw.* **2022**, *131*, 102839. [CrossRef]
3. Bouguera, T.; Diouris, J.F.; Chaillout, J.J.; Jaouadi, R.; Andrieux, G. Energy consumption model for sensor nodes based on LoRa and LoRaWAN. *Sensors* **2018**, *18*, 2104. [CrossRef] [PubMed]
4. Casals, L.; Mir, B.; Vidal, R.; Gomez, C. Modeling the energy performance of LoRaWAN. *Sensors* **2017**, *17*, 2364. [CrossRef] [PubMed]
5. Liando, J.C.; Gamage, A.; Tengourtius, A.W.; Li, M. Known and unknown facts of LoRa: Experiences from a large-scale measurement study. *ACM Trans. Sens. Netw. (TOSN)* **2019**, *15*, 1–35. [CrossRef]
6. Pukrongta, N.; Kumkhet, B. The relation of LoRaWAN efficiency with energy consumption of sensor node. In Proceedings of the 2019 International Conference on Power, Energy and Innovations (ICPEI), Pattaya, Thailand, 16–18 October 2019; pp. 90–93.
7. Rawat, P.; Chauhan, S. A survey on clustering protocols in wireless sensor network: Taxonomy, comparison, and future scope. *J. Ambient. Intell. Humaniz. Comput.* **2023**, *14*, 1543–1589. [CrossRef]
8. Shafique, T.; Soliman, A.H.; Amjad, A.; Uden, L.; Roberts, D.M. Node Role Selection and Rotation Scheme for Energy Efficiency in Multi-Level IoT-Based Heterogeneous Wireless Sensor Networks (HWSNs). *Sensors* **2024**, *24*, 5642. [CrossRef]
9. Rawat, P.; Chauhan, S. Clustering protocols in wireless sensor network: A survey, classification, issues, and future directions. *Comput. Sci. Rev.* **2021**, *40*, 100396. [CrossRef]
10. Lewandowski, M.; Płaczek, B. An event-aware cluster-head rotation algorithm for extending lifetime of wireless sensor network with smart nodes. *Sensors* **2019**, *19*, 4060. [CrossRef]
11. Mostarda, L.; Navarra, A.; De Leone, R. Optimal vs rotation heuristics in the role of cluster-head for routing in IoT constrained devices. *Internet Things* **2023**, *22*, 100757. [CrossRef]
12. Hassan, A.; Anter, A.; Kayed, M. A survey on extending the lifetime for wireless sensor networks in real-time applications. *Int. J. Wirel. Inf. Netw.* **2021**, *28*, 77–103. [CrossRef]
13. Lata, S.; Mehfuz, S.; Urooj, S.; Alrowais, F. Fuzzy clustering algorithm for enhancing reliability and network lifetime of wireless sensor networks. *IEEE Access* **2020**, *8*, 66013–66024. [CrossRef]
14. Prasad, D.; Hassan, A.; Verma, D.K.; Sarangi, P.; Singh, S. Disaster management system using wireless sensor network: A review. In Proceedings of the 2021 International Conference on Computational Intelligence and Computing Applications (ICCICA), Nagpur, India, 26–27 November 2021; pp. 1–6.
15. Yao, C.; Yang, Y.; Yin, K.; Yang, J. Traffic anomaly detection in wireless sensor networks based on principal component analysis and deep convolution neural network. *IEEE Access* **2022**, *10*, 103136–103149. [CrossRef]
16. Shahraki, A.; Taherkordi, A.; Haugen, Ø.; Eliassen, F. Clustering objectives in wireless sensor networks: A survey and research direction analysis. *Comput. Netw.* **2020**, *180*, 107376. [CrossRef]
17. Gamwarige, S.; Kulasekere, E. An algorithm for energy driven cluster head rotation in a distributed wireless sensor network. In Proceedings of the International Conference on Information and Automation, Colombo, Sri Lanka, 15–18 December 2005; pp. 354–359.

18. Gamwarige, S.; Kulasekere, C. Application of the EDCR algorithm in a cluster based multi-hop wireless sensor network. In Proceedings of the 2006 International Symposium on Communications and Information Technologies, Bangkok, Thailand, 18–20 October 2006; pp. 1118–1123.
19. Qubbaj, N.; Taleb, A.A.; Salameh, W. Review on LEACH protocol. In Proceedings of the 2020 11th International Conference on Information and Communication Systems (ICICS), Irbid, Jordan, 7–9 April 2020; pp. 414–419.
20. Heinzelman, W.R.; Chandrakasan, A.; Balakrishnan, H. Energy-efficient communication protocol for wireless microsensor networks. In Proceedings of the 33rd Annual Hawaii International Conference on System Sciences, Maui, HI, USA, 4–7 January 2000; p. 10.
21. Daanoune, I.; Abdennaceur, B.; Ballouk, A. A comprehensive survey on LEACH-based clustering routing protocols in Wireless Sensor Networks. *Ad Hoc Netw.* **2021**, *114*, 102409. [CrossRef]
22. Mishra, P.; Alaria, S.; Dangi, P. Design and comparison of LEACH and improved centralized LEACH in wireless sensor network. *Int. J. Recent Innov. Trends Comput. Commun.* **2021**, *9*, 34–39. [CrossRef]
23. Liu, D.; Liang, C.; Mo, H.; Chen, X.; Kong, D.; Chen, P. LEACH-D: A low-energy, low-delay data transmission method for industrial internet of things wireless sensors. *Internet Things Cyber-Phys. Syst.* **2024**, *4*, 129–137. [CrossRef]
24. Ihsan, A.; Saghar, K.; Fatima, T.; Hasan, O. Formal comparison of LEACH and its extensions. *Comput. Stand. Interfaces* **2019**, *62*, 119–127. [CrossRef]
25. Ullah, Z. A survey on hybrid, energy efficient and distributed (HEED) based energy efficient clustering protocols for wireless sensor networks. *Wirel. Pers. Commun.* **2020**, *112*, 2685–2713. [CrossRef]
26. Dergaoui, O.; Baddi, Y.; Hasbi, A. Introduce the CH Role Rotation Mechanism in the Multilayered Deterministic WSN Clustering to Achieve Long-Term Load Balancing. In Proceedings of the International Conference on Signal Processing and Information Communications, Singapore, 25–27 February 2023; pp. 41–49.
27. Mittal, N.; Singh, U. Distance-based residual energy-efficient stable election protocol for WSNs. *Arab. J. Sci. Eng.* **2015**, *40*, 1637–1646. [CrossRef]
28. Naranjo, P.G.V.; Shojafar, M.; Mostafaei, H.; Pooranian, Z.; Baccarelli, E. P-SEP: A prolong stable election routing algorithm for energy-limited heterogeneous fog-supported wireless sensor networks. *J. Supercomput.* **2017**, *73*, 733–755. [CrossRef]
29. Kamel, S.E.; Ghanem, T.F.; Amin, K.M.; Abdelkader, H. Efficient energy management technique for WSNs. In Proceedings of the 12th International Conference on Computer Engineering and Systems (ICCES), Cairo, Egypt, 19–20 December 2017; pp. 122–126.
30. Ababneh, A.A.; Al-Zboun, E. EDAC: A Novel Energy-Aware Clustering Algorithm for Wireless Sensor Networks. *Int. J. Adv. Comput. Sci. Appl.* **2016**, *7*, 333–338.
31. Alkalbani, A.S.; Mantoro, T.; Degala, S. Energy-Distance Aware Clustering Scheme (E-DACS) for Wireless Sensor Networks. In Proceedings of the 12th International Conference on Computing and Information Technology (IC2IT), Bangkok, Thailand, 8–9 July 2016; pp. 277–292.
32. Selvi, G.V.; Anbarasan, A.B.; Murthy, B.A.; Prabavathy, S. An Application Oriented Integrated Unequal Clustering Algorithm for Wireless Sensor Network. In *Underwater Vehicle Control and Communication Systems Based on Machine Learning Techniques*; CRC Press: Boca Raton, FL, USA, 2023; pp. 140–154.
33. Almuhaya, M.A.; Jabbar, W.A.; Sulaiman, N.; Abdulmalek, S. A survey on Lorawan technology: Recent trends, opportunities, simulation tools and future directions. *Electronics* **2022**, *11*, 164. [CrossRef]
34. Tong, S.; Wang, J.; Yang, J.; Liu, Y.; Zhang, J. Citywide lora network deployment and operation: Measurements, analysis, and implications. In Proceedings of the 21st ACM Conference on Embedded Networked Sensor Systems, Istanbul, Turkiye, 12–17 November 2023; pp. 362–375.
35. Ndukwe, C.; Iqbal, T.; Liang, X.; Khan, J.; Aghenta, L.O. LoRa-based communication system for data transfer in microgrids. *AIMS Electron. Electr. Eng.* **2020**, *4*, 303–325. [CrossRef]
36. Shafiq, Z.; Egger, W. Study of charging strategies of lithium batteries and their effect on the batteries technologies. In Proceedings of the 2022 IEEE 13th Annual Information Technology, Electronics and Mobile Communication Conference (IEMCON), Vancouver, BC, Canada, 12–15 October 2022; pp. 0540–0546.
37. Singh, J.; Kaur, R.; Singh, D. Energy harvesting in wireless sensor networks: A taxonomic survey. *Int. J. Energy Res.* **2021**, *45*, 118–140. [CrossRef]
38. Sharma, P.; Singh, A.K. A survey on RF energy harvesting techniques for lifetime enhancement of wireless sensor networks. *Sustain. Comput. Inform. Syst.* **2023**, *37*, 100836. [CrossRef]

sensors

MDPI

Article

Cross-PLC: An I3oT Cross Platform to Manage Communications for Applications in Real Factories

Antonio Lacasa [1], Javier Llopis [1], Nicolás Montés [2,*,†], Ivan Peinado-Asensi [2] and Eduardo Garcia [1,†]

1 Ford Spain, Poligono Industrial Ford S/N, 46440 Almussafes, Spain; alacasa1@ford.com (A.L.); jllopis4@ford.com (J.L.); egarci75@ford.com (E.G.)
2 Department of Mathematics, Physics and Technological Sciences, University CEU Cardenal Herrera, C/San Bartolome 55, 46115 Alfara del Patriarca, Spain; ivan.peinadoasensi@uchceu.es
* Correspondence: nicolas.montes@uchceu.es
† These authors contributed equally to this work.

Abstract: Recently, a new concept has emerged for the development of Industrial Internet of Things (IIoT) applications, the Industrializable Industrial Internet of Things (I3oT). As a criterion for the design of industrial applications, the I3oT imposes the exclusive use of pre-installed elements in the company such as PLCs, sensors, IT/OT networks, etc., trying to minimize the impact on the factories and guaranteeing a cheap and assumable scalability for companies, something that cannot be implemented with the vast majority of IIoT applications available in the market. In our previous work, we have used I3oT applications for predictive maintenance on different components: cylinders, presses, welding clamps and also energy-saving tools, detection of bottlenecks and sub-bottlenecks, etc., all of them generalized for the entire factory. However, the main drawback comes from the flow of data through the IT/OT network. This article presents the Cross-PLC, a tool to allow massive data extraction using the company's IT/OT network by communicating with any type of PLC or brand existing in the market. The Cross-PLC performs passive listening, and through different communication criteria, the Cross-PLC becomes a virtual PLC containing all the parameters necessary for the I3oT applications developed. This article presents the design of this tool, its implementation and use at Ford Factory in Almussafes (Valencia).

Keywords: IIoT; I3oT; cross platforms; Cross-PLC; Industry 4.0

1. Factory Conditions in the Fourth Industrial Revolution: Welcome to "The Jungle"

The governance of factories in the automotive sector is extremely complex. These factories use thousands of robots, clamps, cylinders, conveyor belts, etc., equipment with its components, electric motors, gears, chains, with each of the elements applied to different processes, such as welding, stamping, painting, etc. In addition, all this machinery interacts with the operators involved in different phases of the process, who work assembling the components, verifying the quality of the parts, and in some cases, they must modify machine parameters to guarantee the productivity and quality of the parts. The goal of automation is none other than to try to eliminate dependence on that human factor. However, some machines are not able to adapt to all plant situations, which calls into question whether a complete automation of a factory without human presence would be the most efficient approach, see, for example, [1,2]. With the emergence of Industry 4.0 and its technologies: Industrial Internet of Things (IIoT), Big Data, Digital and Hybrid Twins, etc., a significant improvement in factory governance is expected in which data will become a lens through which Industry 4.0 can be constructed [3]. The Industrial Internet of Things (IIoT) is one of the most relevant enabling technologies of the Industry 4.0 (I4.0), [4,5] and consists of the application of the IoT in the industry. Namely, the IIoT is applied to connect machines and devices in industrial environments, focusing on machine-to-machine communication; any failure can lead to high-risk losses and the amount of data collected in IIoT is much larger than in IoT [6]. Furthermore, IIoT is also considered an I4.0 equivalent concept in some of the literature [7].

When the industry or the responsible managers have to decide whether to install IIoT applications in their company on a massive level, they are often discouraged by several factors and these are as follows:

- Energy efficiency: since most IIoT devices are powered by batteries [8–10].
- *Interoperability*: since connecting so many devices is usually a serious challenge for the IIoT [9].
- *Safety*: since information and privacy are vital at the corporate level [6,8–10].
- *Scalability*: since the massification of IIoT solutions implies the use of a huge number of devices connected to each other in hierarchical subdomains [9].
- *Maintenance and updates*: since system operators will not only have to manage the original system but also all the new ones, and therefore, many engineers will have to be trained for this [6,9].
- *IT/OT integration*: IIoT systems require the convergence of OT and IT for the integration of data from both parties [6].
- *Cultural change*: Most of the industries resist change because they are afraid and do not understand the technology associated with IIoT [6].

There is an important effort in the literature to overcome the previous issues. The research on functional architectures is a trend in automation and supervision applied to I4.0- and IIoT-enabled factories [11–18]. An interesting conclusion was obtained in [11] because experiment-based architectures are increasing over time to overcome the actual problems. In ref. [18], states that implemented IIoT applications are scarce, and most of the architectures are hypothetical, studied using software simulations, virtual environments or use cases providing scarce implementation information, which are scenarios that are far from real applications for industrial processes.

The transition from the current installation configuration of industrial production governed by traditional industrial control systems (ICS) to a configuration of Industry 4.0 requires a progressive transformation. It involves an adaptation of the devices and architectures used in ICS to adapt to the new paradigm in order to achieve both vertical and horizontal integration of devices at all levels [16]. One of the industrial elements that has been key throughout the automation revolution is the programmable logic controller. Its role has been mainly to command low-level configurations providing a first layer of control for the processes and being the closest interlocutor to both the sensors and the actuators. Recently, proposals have been made for the development of new PLCs for Industry 4.0. such as IoT-PLC, see [19], or PLC 4.0, see [20]. The first PLC for IIoT was developed by the company Phoenix Contact, Telford, Shropshire.

However, the updating of the existing elements in the factories is usually slow. In automotive factories, we can find thousands of robots, grippers, welding clamps, conveyors, elevators, etc., that are part of the manufacturing lines, each one of them sensorized and governed mostly by PLCs. Companies have, as one of their objectives, to make their assets profitable, and for this reason, old and new technologies of the last 20/30 years had to coexist within large factories, and therefore, the update is only carried out when obsolete elements stop working or there is an urgent need to update them. This mixture of technologies and brands, together with the unpredictability of breakdowns, the consequent line stops, loss of production and the need to guarantee the daily production ratio, is what makes today's factories known as "the jungle".

1.1. Previous Works: I3oT (Industrializable Industrial Internet of Things)

In order to generate IIoT solutions that are able to adapt to the reality of the factories and the needs of the IIoT tools described, we have proposed in our previous works, see [21], a new concept: the Industrializable Industrial Internet of Things (I3oT). The approach of this new concept is the use of the installations available in the factories to develop IIoT applications from them. The machines installed in the industry operate automatically and have sensors that provide the information received by the PLC to control the lines. The factories have an IT/OT network through which the machines communicate and the factory is managed. Under this paradigm the *I3oT* applications could be easily extrapolated and scalable to the rest of the systems at a very low cost, allowing the definitive establishment of Industry 4.0 and its technologies. The following sub-sections show the different tools developed so far.

1.1.1. Miniterms

One of the first I3oT applications developed were the so-called *Mini-terms,* and these were described in ref. [22]. The mini-terms are based on programming a timer in the PLC or PC-Line so that through the sensors installed for the normal operation of the line, we can measure the time it takes for the line elements to perform their task. These data are sent through the OT and IT networks for analysis and processing. Deterioration over time is an indicator that the component is near the end of its useful life and it may produce a line stoppage. The great advantage of using the *mini-terms* is that there is no need to install new sensors, and their industrialization is immediate. Currently, at Ford factory in Almussafes (Valencia), there are more than 46,000 elements or components under surveillance with this technology that detect anomalies in pneumatic and electrical welding clamps, screwdrivers, clamps, elevators, etc. The use of mini-terms to anticipate machine failure is generating important benefits at an industrial level, such as the increase in technical availability (TAV), >6%, see [22].

1.1.2. Criterion C-360

In ref. [21], it is proposed to use the *I3oT* concept in the stamping process through the so-called *Criterion C-360*. With this criterion, 360 values per cycle are generated from the variables or sensors available in the stamping process. Unlike the use of *mini-terms*, there are 360 values per cycle, while in the *mini-term*, there was one value used per cycle, which allows us to evaluate the possibilities of the *I3oT* philosophy when applied to other industrial processes. Many applications that the (*I3oT*) system may have in the stamping process, and in particular, of *Criterion C-360*, are yet to be discovered. Based on this criterion, many applications have been developed for predictive maintenance based on tonnage sensors [23], another tool used for energy saving [24] and finally, the feasibility of developing a digital twin for the stamping process is explored through the *I3oT* philosophy of the stamping process [25]. The following sub-sections show more information about these applications.

1.1.3. Predictive Maintenance on Presses: Gravity Center (GC)

One of the ways to monitor the press health is checking that the effort made by the press is carried out in the most balanced way. In the tool developed in ref. [23], the tonnage variables are used to calculate the gravity center of the moving part of the press; the slide and the die that move through the guides located in the four columns of the press. The system calculates the 360 values of the gravity center for each stroke, and when the center goes out of the set limits, an alarm is generated to alert the maintenance operators that something anomalous is happening, see [23].

1.1.4. Manufacturing Maps

In ref. [26], the use of the Petri Nets together with *mini-terms* is proposed to model the factory by layers in order to build a factory model through the *manufacturing maps*. These maps are considered the "Google Maps" of a factory. On the top level we have the *commodity view*, a complete view of the factory whose level would be more focused on senior managers and then, we go down layer by layer, passing through the *line view* and *station view* until reaching the machine level, where we will directly have the *mini-terms*. The *manufacturing maps* have two fundamental components, Big Data based on *mini-terms* and Petri nets. Big Data provide the sub-cycle time data of the components and Petri nets provide the complete modeling of the factory that allows us to reconstruct the information based on *mini-terms* at any level, see [26]. In ref. [27], the author uses *manufacturing maps* to detect bottlenecks and sub-bottlenecks and propose improvements to the production line in order to reduce energy consumption and/or increase jobs per hour (JPH).

1.1.5. Secondary Wear Detection on Welding Clamps by Virtual Sensors

Another I3oT application developed in our previous work was the detection of secondary wear in welding clamps. This is critical for maintaining the efficiency and quality of welding operations. The secondary part, which is responsible for transferring the electrical energy from the transformer to the electrode, is subject to constant wear due to the heat and pressure during the welding process. The detection of secondary component wear is therefore essential to avoid potential issues such as increased energy consumption, decreased quality and frequent downtime. In ref. [28], the author discusses the importance of monitoring secondary wear, highlighting the importance of keeping accurate records of secondary wear, and replacing parts when necessary to avoid unexpected downtime.

1.1.6. Energy Savings on Production Lines

As mentioned in the introduction, the pressure to which the operators are subjected limits them from optimizing certain parameters of the lines because they prefer not to take a risk in order to avoid consequences. We can find a clear example of this problem when choosing the speed of industrial robots. In large factories such as Ford Valencia, there are thousands of robot arms that are usually placed by default at 100% of their maximum speed, which generates unnecessary energy consumption. In ref. [29], the author seeks to develop an algorithm to reduce the speed of the robot arms automatically so that energy saving will be generated. The level of energy savings depends on several factors, but the most influential one is line imbalance, something that is usually more common in the lines that produce different car models and variants. In ref. [29], the simulation of the manufacturing lines was used to estimate energy savings managing to reduce consumption by 57%. Moreover, in ref. [29], this simulation was used with a real mono-model line achieving a saving of 11%.

1.2. Cross Platforms

The cross-platform software (also called multi-platform or platform-independent software) is a computer software designed to work across multiple computing platforms. Some cross-platform programs require a separate compilation for each platform, but others can run directly on any platform without any special preparation. It is mainly used for the development of applications for mobile phones, and it is important that a particular app can be used for any platform. In ref. [30], a study was carried out on the apps available in the Google Play Store in order to determine how many of them had been developed with cross-platform software. The study indicates that 15% of the total has been developed using this technology. The advantages of working with this software is the use of uniform designs, the reduction in time and cost in production and the implementation of faster and more flexible updates. Conversely, we find performance limitations as we do not have access to native features and we always have platform dependency [31].

The development of cross-platform applications is also extended to other areas of engineering. For example, we can find cross-platform applications for programming robots [32–34] or also for programming computer numerical control machines (CNC) [33] and even developing a cross-platform application to manage communications at the industrial level [35] or programing PLCs with a cross-platform application such as PLC-PROG [36].

1.3. Purpose of This Article

The objective of this article is to develop a cross-platform *I3oT* tool to extract information from various PLCs and their variants and generations co-existing in a factory in the least intrusive way possible. This tool has been called *Cross-PLC* and will be the tool to which all *I3oT* applications will be connected to manage their communication with the factory PLCs.

The main handicap for the *I3oT* philosophy to grow in more monitored elements and new developments lies in the IT/OT networks available in the companies and in the diversity of programmable elements (PLCs) that we can find in factories of the automotive sector. In order to be less intrusive but more efficient and scalable, the passive method and the actuator model will be used to communicate with the PLCs.

As seen in our previous works, the *I3oT* concept and then *Cross-PLC* allows us to develop IIoT applications with low cost and industrial impact, eliminating or minimizing all the problems reported in the literature about the IIoT applications regarding energy efficiency, security, scalability, maintenance and updates, IT/OT integration and cultural change [6,8–10].

The organization of the remainder of the paper is as follows. The *Cross-PLC* platform design is defined in Section 2. Section 3 defines the implementation of the *Cross-PLC* platform, and Section 4 shows some experimental results in the Ford Factory in Valencia with PLC's in Siemens and Rockwell. Sections 5 and 6 show the discussion and conclusion, respectively.

2. Design of the Cross-Platform *I3oT* Tool, *Cross-PLC*

The objective of the *I3oT* cross-platform design, *Cross-PLC*, is the development of an application that facilitates communication with the programmable logic controllers (PLCs) that allows information to be extracted from them with the least possible impact on the pre-installed systems in the factory. Figure 1 shows the concept of *Cross-PLC*.

2.1. Choosing the Communication Method

Communication in computer systems can be classified into two main types; active and passive. In active communication, the sender initiates and controls the communication, sending data to a receiver on a regular basis or when necessary according to a predefined schedule. For example, in a temperature monitoring system in a warehouse, the temperature sensor is checked every minute by a monitoring application. The advantages of active communication are as follows:

1. *Precise control*: the sender has complete control over when and what data are sent.
2. *Regular updates*: the sender provides regular updates, which can be useful for applications that require frequently updated data.

Disadvantages of active communication:

1. *Network saturation*: when there are too many devices sending data frequently, it can cause network congestion.
2. *Power consumption*: on mobile devices or embedded systems, constant active communication can consume more battery power.
3. *Potential latency*: data may not be immediately available when needed as they depend on the predefined time interval for querying the data.

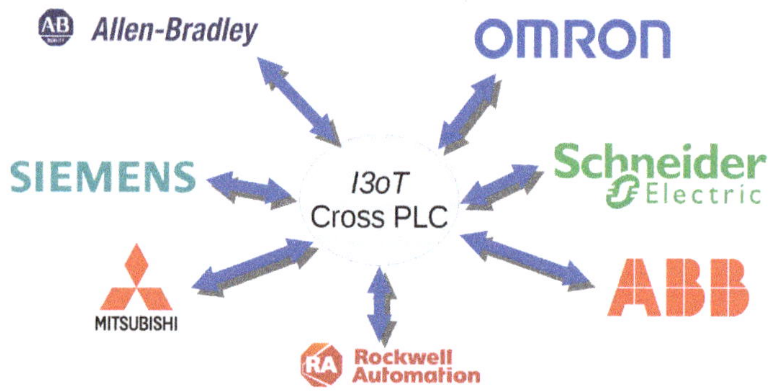

Figure 1. *I3oT* cross platform, *Cross-PLC*.

In contrast, in passive communication, the receiver initiates communication when it is ready to send data and the sender simply detects and responds to requests. For example, in a sensor system in a production plant the sensors will only send data when they detect a significant change in plant conditions. The advantages of passive communication are as follows:

1. *Network efficiency*: avoids network saturation by sending data only when needed.
2. *Energy saving*: reduces energy consumption by avoiding constant communication.
3. *Quick response*: provides a quick response to requests as data are sent immediately when available.

For the communication development of the *I3oT Cross-PLC* tool, passive communication is better than active communication in several crucial aspects. First, its efficiency in managing network resources is remarkable. By sending information only in response to specific events, passive communication minimizes data traffic, thus avoiding network congestion and ensuring optimal use of available resources. On the other hand, active communication has to make continuous requests at regular time intervals until it can obtain the expected value, which can generate a greater volume of traffic, which, in turn, could potentially saturate the network and slow down the performance of the system. Another point to note is that passive communication demonstrates superior responsiveness to specific events and large frames. By allowing the devices to respond only to relevant events, the waiting time is significantly reduced and the responsiveness of the system is improved; if, for example, 5000 data per frame are to be sent, it is more effective if the data source sends them when it knows that its data have changed, and therefore, it does not need to be requesting every x time interval if any of those 5000 data have changed. This is in contrast to active communication that has a predefined response time and is less flexible.

2.2. Cross-PLC Actuator Model

The actuator model was proposed by Carl Hewitt in 1973 as a way to address concurrency in distributed applications. This paper proposes an approach to modeling systems as a collection of interacting actuators.

In the actuator model, the actuators are independent computational entities that can run concurrently and asynchronously. Each actuator has its own internal state and can communicate with other actuators by sending them messages. This ability to communicate between actuators is essential to build distributed systems in which multiple components must interact with each other efficiently and scalably. In distributed applications with a high demand for connections, the actuator model offers a flexible and modular architecture. Actuators can process messages independently, allowing for non-blocking concurrency. This means that an actuator does not have to wait for another actuator to finish its task before continuing with its own, which avoids blockages and bottlenecks in the execution of the program. In addition, actuators can be easily scaled by adding more instances of actuators to distribute the workload, ensuring high scalability of the system.

The actuator model offers several key advantages for distributed applications with a high demand for connections. First, it provides effective isolation and modularity as each actuator is an independent entity with its own internal state and behavior. This facilitates the construction of modular systems and the management of the status in a clear and controlled manner. Second, non-blocking concurrency enables efficient message processing, ensuring optimal performance even under heavy workloads. Third, the inherent scalability of the actuator model allows the system to easily grow and handle a higher volume of connections without sacrificing performance. In addition, fault tolerance is improved due to the ability to monitor and recover between actuators, which guarantees the robustness of the system. Finally, the flexibility of the actuator model allows for easy adaptation and evolution of the system as user requirements and demands change.

2.3. Network Architecture in Cross-PLCs

Cross-PLCs focus on efficient and versatile communication with PLCs, taking advantage of the native communications of the different PLCs available on the market: Rockwell, Siemens, OMRON, ABB, Schneider, Allan Bradley, etc., using specific protocols of each of them to maximize compatibility and efficiency in communication. The actuator model allows the Cross-PLC application to develop according to the communication needs and the different brands existing in the factory. By way of example, the following subsections show how communication has been carried out for the two most used PLCs, Rockwell and Siemens, at the Ford factory in Almussafes, (Valencia, Spain).

2.3.1. Communication with Rockwell PLCs in Cross-PLCs

Communication with Rockwell PLCs is performed using the common industrial protocol (CIP), an industry communication standard widely used in Rockwell devices. CIP is an object-oriented, ethernet-based protocol that provides a common platform for data communication, control and configuration in industrial environments. This protocol offers a wide range of services including process data exchange, remote programming and device status monitoring. CIP is designed to be scalable and flexible, allowing the integration of devices from different manufacturers within the same system and facilitating interoperability among industrial automation equipment.

2.3.2. Communication with Siemens PLCs in Cross-PLCs

Communication with Siemens PLCs is carried out through the ISO protocol (https://www.rfc-editor.org/rfc/inline-errata/rfc1006.html, accesed on 28 April 2025) over transmission control protocol (TCP), a choice that guarantees compatibility with the devices of this manufacturer. The ISO protocol over TCP is an implementation of the ISO 8073 standard, which defines a set of rules for communication between distributed systems over TCP/IP networks. This protocol provides a mechanism for the reliable and efficient exchange of data using TCP connections to ensure the orderly and error-free delivery of messages. ISO over TCP offers features such as message segmentation and reassembly, flow control and error detection and recovery, making it suitable for industrial applications where reliability and data integrity are critical.

2.3.3. Bases and Fundamentals of the Implemented Network Architecture

The architecture of this application is based on fundamental principles of industrial communication and modular and scalable design approaches that make the application simulate a virtual PLC. This is achieved through an object-oriented design that encapsulates the logic of communication and control in reusable and easily configurable components. This allows seamless integration with different devices and systems regardless of their manufacturer or communication protocol. The different components of the application such as communication modules, data management services and user interfaces are implemented as independent actuators that can be scaled and adapted according to the needs of the system.

2.3.4. Sending Data to MQTT Architecture

Message queuing telemetry transport (MQTT) is a lightweight, open-source messaging protocol designed for communication between devices on networks with limited bandwidth or unstable connections. The MQTT version used in the present paper is V 3.1.1.1. This protocol is based on the publish/subscribe model, where devices can post messages on a "topic" and subscribe to topics to receive relevant messages. RFC9431 https://www.rfc-editor.org/rfc/rfc9431.pdf, (accessed on 28 April 2025), RFC 9431 https://www.rfc-editor.org/rfc/rfc9431.pdf, (accessed on 28 April 2025) RFC 7252, https://www.rfc-editor.org/rfc/pdfrfc/rfc7252.txt.pdf, (accessed on 28 April 2025). This model is chosen as the final part of the Cross-PLC architecture. Once the data are obtained from the PLCs, they are sent through this protocol, which has three main components: the client, the broker and the publisher/subscriber, with Cross-PLC being the publisher. Some of the main advantages of using MQTT are as follows:

1. *Bandwidth usage efficiency:* MQTT uses a compact message format, minimizing bandwidth consumption and enabling efficient communication even on networks with bandwidth limitations.
2. *Scalability:* MQTT's publish/subscribe model allows for flexible scalability, as clients can subscribe to multiple topics, and brokers can handle a large number of clients and messages simultaneously.
3. *Reliability:* MQTT offers integrated delivery confirmation and quality of service (QoS) mechanisms to ensure the reliability of message delivery, making it suitable for applications in which data integrity is critical.
4. *Flexibility:* MQTT is highly adaptable and can be deployed on a wide variety of devices and platforms from resource-constrained embedded devices to high-capacity servers, making it suitable for a wide range of Internet of Things (IoT) applications, telemetry systems, instant messaging and more.
5. *Compatibility:* MQTT is a standard and open source protocol with implementations available in a variety of programming languages and platforms, ensuring interoperability and ease of integration with existing systems.

2.4. Cross-PLC Concept with PLC ControlLogix Communications

The developed Cross-PLC system accepts PLC communications and transforms them to a JSON structure to store and analyze data obtained from the factory. In the case of Rockwell, it exchanges PLC data via unconnected CIP (https://datatracker.ietf.org/doc/html/rfc2653, accessed on 28 April 2025) Data Write Tables Messages with MQTT Servers. empowering PLC as an event-driven model and reducing network bandwidth usage. The currently supported features are as follows:

- CIP Write Data Table. Only basic types SINT, INT, DINT, REAL.
- Accept any remote element. *Can be overwritten by any PLC.*
- Fragment CIP Write. More than 104 DINT elements.
- Simple CIP Read Data Table Messages. Only basic types SINT, INT, DINT, REAL.
- Simple CIP Write Data Table Messages for Structures parsed as SINT.
- Simple CIP Read Data Table Messages for Structures.
- API swagger-ui at api-docs.
- Web page.
- Metrics.

For this, a structure has been created in which we receive data from the connections of the PLCs to the server. An active connection from a PLC to the Cross-PLC is a network card that has sent data in the last 30 s. A card in Rockwell can be used to send data from multiple PLCs, and each connection has a TAG associated with it. A TAG refers to the "Destination Element" of the MSG instruction of the Rockwell PLCs. It is a variable of the virtual PLC so it cannot start with a number; it must start with letters or low dash.

In Figure 2, we can see a connection from a card with its IP address that has several TAGS associated with it that correspond to a PLC data sending block. TAGS are classified into two types, stored TAGs and active TAGs. Active tags are those that have received data within 30 s, while stored tags are those that have been written (and read) and may not be counted in active tags because they have not been sent again after 30 s.

Ip	Port	First Time Connection	Last Time Connection	Cip Type	Cip Session	Cip Last Service	Cip Tags
19.172.131.38	61394	2024-04-15T06:58:10.531Z	2024-05-03T19:15:33.596Z	UCMM	2045312332	WRITE_TAG	B2_6E_01.GATEWAY_6W B2_6E_1.ControlDesconexion B2_6E_1.WX0.STOCK_6E.B2_Stock_6E B2_6E_1.WX0.EQUIPO_ACTIVO.B2_ControlDesconexion B2_6E_1.yyPdM_Actual_03 B2_6E_1.yyPdM_Actual_01 B2_6E_1.yyPdM_Actual_02 B2_6E_1.yyPdM_Actual_27 B2_6E_1.yyPdM_Actual_27_1 B2_6E_1.RT.SMART._50_560_1 B2_6E_1.RT.SMART._50_655_1 B2_6E_1.WX0._6E_RACK32_PZA_SUPERIOR_LV4B_503418_AA.B2MissingPartsBApre_6W

Figure 2. Example of an active connection with its TAGS.

Figure 3 shows the active tags that have sent information to the server within the last 30 s, being able to know which links and connections are working. It also shows the number of elements associated with each tag and the type of data being received. For each tag, a parser or formatter is associated that indicates the method in which the structure blocks are decoded before having support and being sent to the MQTT user, see Figure 4.

Ip	Port	Tag	Timestamp	Number of elements	Decoder	Type
19.172.131.38	61394	B2_6E_01.GATEWAY_6W	2024-05-03T19:15:33.596Z	60	none	INT
19.172.131.38	61394	B2_6E_1.ControlDesconexion	2024-05-03T19:11:01.367Z	200	none	DINT
19.172.131.38	61394	B2_6E_1.WX0.STOCK_6E.B2_Stock_6E	2024-05-03T12:01:02.937Z	1	none	DINT
19.172.131.38	61394	B2_6E_1.WX0.EQUIPO_ACTIVO.B2_ControlDesconexion	2024-05-03T12:03:08.980Z	1	none	DINT
19.172.131.38	61394	B2_6E_1.yyPdM_Actual_03	2024-05-03T18:48:37.626Z	18	mtcriteria1_3	DINT
19.172.131.38	61394	B2_6E_1.yyPdM_Actual_01	2024-05-03T18:48:37.682Z	46	mtcriteria1_3	DINT
19.172.131.38	61394	B2_6E_1.yyPdM_Actual_02	2024-05-03T18:24:51.482Z	90	mtcriteria2_4	DINT
19.172.131.38	61394	B2_6E_1.yyPdM_Actual_27	2024-05-03T18:03:13.204Z	17	mtcriteria11_27	DINT
19.172.131.38	61394	B2_6E_1.yyPdM_Actual_27_1	2024-05-03T18:20:09.180Z	57	mtcriteria11_27	DINT
19.172.131.38	61394	B2_6E_1.RT.SMART._50_660_1	2024-04-30T08:55:20.395Z	1	none	DINT

Figure 3. List of active tags.

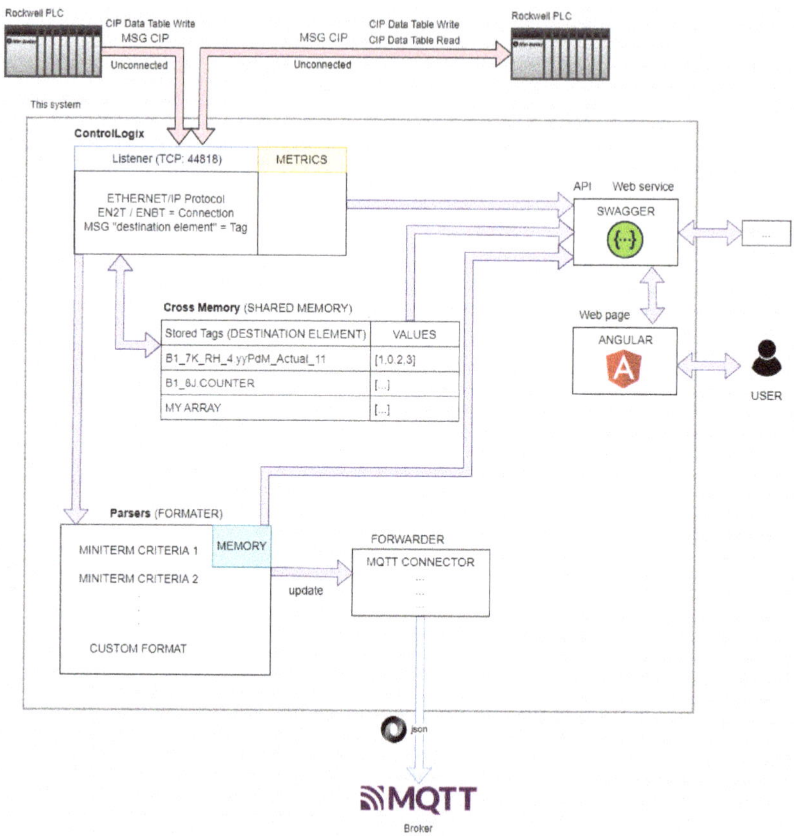

Figure 4. Cross PLC Architecture for ControlLogix.

2.4.1. Criteria Designed for Communication with Various Line Components

In order to adjust the data or requirements of the applications to the transfer of information, the Cross-PLC allows the creation of criteria that make up data packets. These criteria are programmed into the PLC that packages the information and transmits it with this specific criteria. There are currently six types of criteria defined to identify the behavior of mechanical elements in terms of movement time and the physical parameters measured on the machines. As the I3oT concept develops in more specific applications, it is expected that the number of criteria will increase. The criteria currently defined with the applications developed are as follows:

- **Criterion 01:** a device that requires a single measurement of the mini-term to capture the entire operation. For example, a robotic water gun, lifting device or safety window.
- **Criterion 02:** a device that requires multiple mini-term measurements to capture the entire operation. For example, a pneumatic valve that actuates multiple clamps.
- **Criterion 03:** a device that requires a single mini-term measurement and travels in only one direction within a given station. For example, a clamp on a pallet with a "docking" station so that it is closed in the first station but open in the last one.
- **Criterion 04:** a device that requires multiple mini-term measurements and travels in a single direction within a given station. For example, a group of grippers on a pallet with a "docking" station that is closed in the first station but open in the last one.

- **Criterion 11:** routine to collect a single measurement of the mini-term and the physical parameter. For example, a servo-actuated robotic welding gun. The robot measures time and current and then sends the results to the PLC (more accurate method).
- **Criterion 360:** specific to presses, requiring 360 measurements of a physical parameter of the press that are traveling in only one direction, for example, any physical parameter obtained from presses such as: tonnage, speed, pressures, temperatures, consumptions, strength, etc.

2.4.2. Memory Usage

All the numbers below are from a 1756-L73S processor running V20.18 firmware.

Loading all required routines, Tags, UDTs and with one (1) Criterion 01 and one (1) Criterion 02 module, then the memory usage is 27072 Bytes.

After the initial memory usage above, then each call/request for a Criteria 01 routine requires 272 Bytes.

After the initial memory usage above, then each call/request for a Criteria 02 routine requires 632 Bytes.

Scan Time All the numbers below are from a 1756-L73S processor running V20.18 firmware. Based on adding three (3) Criterion 01 devices, the scan time is increased by 3.174 milliseconds.

Then, adding one routine, it increases by 0.001 milliseconds.

3. Implementation

3.1. ControlLogix (Listener Driver)

The Cross-PLC accepts any ControlLogix CIP MSG Data Table Write Unconnected (fragmented or not) and parses the Tags or the destination element to a json. The system can respond to a limited CIP Data Table Read Unconnected Messages if the element to read exists in the shared memory. If the tag is not present in shared memory, an *"ERROR: EPATH Invalid Parameter (0x20) + destination not assigned (0x01)"* message is sent to the requester PLC.

The data types accepted are arrays (any size) of the following:

- SINT
- INT
- DINT
- REAL

If any other type or structure is sent, then an *"ERROR: EPATH Invalid Parameter (0x20) + destination unknown (0x00)"* message will be sent to the requester PLC. Connections will be dropped after the OS timeout TCP connection time is achieved (normally 30 s).

3.2. CrossMemory (Shared Memory)

In this part, all received tags (destination element) are stored on RAM memory. It is used to reply to the Read Data Table request and API services. This memory does not take care about who write the tags. It means that any write from any PLC to the same tag name will be overwritten and stored in the same place ("whiteboard").

3.3. Parsers (Transformation)

This part takes care to transform the array of data to a json structure. It receives any update of CrossMemory tags if then they match with the pattern of the tagname ("Destination element") of the parser. We also have to take care about duplicates and store our own dictionary of sent messages. The output of the parser is sent to the forwarder to be processed.

3.4. Sending (Forwarding)

This component sends the parser output ot the MQTT server/broker as a json message. An example for the mini-terms parser is as follows:

Routing key:

- mt.factory02.area01.(_a1_l8_1)_actual_02.114.1


```
{
''device_criteria'': 2,
''device_type'': 5,
''trigger_value'': 145279,
''value'': 867,
''job_id'': 1,
''tag_position'': 114,
''host'': ''host01'',
''plant'': ''area01'',
''date'': ''2024-09-03T07:12:05.009Z'',
''topic_id'': ''factory02.area01.(\_a1\_l8\_1)\_actual\_02.114.1'',
''mqtt_routing'': ''mt.factory02.area01.(\_a1\_l8\_1)\_actual\_02.114.1'',
''factory'': ''factory02''
}
```


An example for the generic parser is as follows:

Routing key:

- factory01.area15.manuf_line01.SCA_WARNING


```
{
''tagname'': ''manuf\_line01.SCA\_WARNING'',
''pos_dest'': 0,
''type'': 196,
''type_txt'': ''DINT'',
''type_size'': 4,
''number_of_elements'': 1,
''timestamp'': ''2024-10-26T14:19:14.983Z'',
''timestamp_end'': ''2024-10-26T14:19:14.983Z'',
''values'': [1],
''ip_form'': ''19.100.100.10'',
''port_form'': 1234,
''CIP_session'': 4023284046,
''CIP_context'': ''13aca2430000e414'',
''decoderMsgsEmitted'': 23,
''host'': ''host01'',
''factory'': ''factory01'',
''plant'': ''area15''
}
```


The "routing key" to the MQTT server is the combination of the information regarding the "factory", "plant" and "tagname".

- factory: is configured at config file.
- plant: is configured at config file.
- tagname: is the "Destination element".

- Example: 0145a.body1.B1_7X_LH_7.RT._010R2SCA_BARREL_WARNING

Also add "mt" as the first key if it is mini-terms parser activated and contains the special structure of *tagname.position.jobid* with adding brackets at the first part of tagname, taking out the dot.

- Example: mt.0097a.body1.(_b1_8c_c519_1)yypdm_actual_02.115.1

3.5. Config File

On the deploy process, a config file is placed at the same level of the binary file. It is a JS file with the next configurable parameters:

- EIP_PORT: TCP port for listening CIP commands (default 44818).
- HOST_EIP_BIND: IP of host network card to limit listening of CIP messages (0.0.0.0 to read on all network cards).
- PLANT: Prefix for MQTT topic routing.
- FACTORY: Prefix for MQTT topic routing.
- API_WEB_PORT: Port for listening to API web services and web page.
- HOST_API_WEB_BIND: IP of host network card to limit listening to API web services and web page (0.0.0.0 to read on all network cards, 127.0.0.1 to limit to the current host).
- MQTT_OPTIONS:
  - port: TCP port of the MQTT server.
  - port: TCP port of the MQTT server.
  - host: IP address of the MQTT server.
  - clientId: ID client to show on MQTT server.
  - username: user name to connect to the MQTT server.
  - password: password to connect to the MQTT server.
  - clean: clean connection start.

4. Experimental Application Examples

This section shows the experimental results of Cross-PLC in various applications developed at the Ford plant in Valencia. In all of them, Cross-PLC integrates Rockwell and Siemens PLCs. In particular, it integrates Rockwell PLCs from the ControlLogix family (1756, 5555 series, Series 6x, Series 7x, Series 8x, and CompactLogix), and for Siemens, the S7 family compatible with ISO-on-TCP (some, for example, are S7-1200, S7-1500, S7-300, and S7-400).).

4.1. Mini-Term 4.0

The Mini-term 4.0 application, see [22], is the most widely used today and is used to manage information using Cross-PLC. Figure 5 shows all the elements and components monitored by this platform. There are currently 39,036 monitored components. Figure 6 shows the details of the monitored components in the body plant. Elements like cylinders, lifter, pantograph, robots, roller door, screwdriver, motors, switch, welding guns, 7th Axis, etc., are elements that are under surveillance using Cross-PLC as a tool to extract the data using the IT/OT system installed in the factory.

4.2. Other I3oT Applications Developed Through Cross-PLCs

Since the Cross-PLC platform was put into operation, new I3oT applications have been developed to automate numerous tasks that before used to be carried out manually by technicians. The following sub-sections show some of them.

Figure 5. Distribution of Mini-terms installed in Ford factory (Almussafes, Valencia) 4.0. Connected elements.

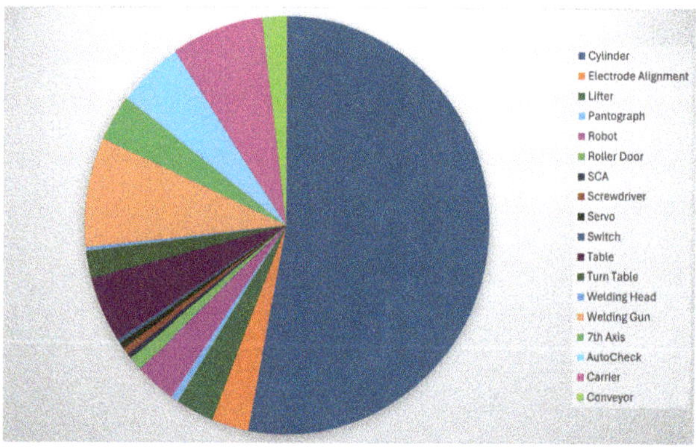

Figure 6. Elements monitored in body plant.

4.2.1. Smart Call Solution

The first solution is to eliminate the large number of push-button switches (exclusive hardware with batteries) located in each of the plant lines that are used to send a reminder to the warehouse when material is required for the assembly of the product. The push buttons have been replaced by a call from the PLC that notifies the warehouse through the Cross-PLC when more material is needed, whether it is screws, gears, hinges, etc., or any mechanical elements that robots use to assemble parts. A new routine has been designed in the PLC that allows counting the number of times the work is carried out compared to the amount of material available on the line so that when the number of boxes of material automatically end, a signal is sent from the PLC to the warehouse to replace the boxes. With this, we will also be able to know the amount of material orders made daily and monthly and keep an exhaustive count of the parts produced.

4.2.2. Automatic Production Line Status Monitoring

To carry out maintenance, repairs or any necessary action on the manufacturing lines, the first step is to remove the parts inside the line just before the stop. These gaps found in the line must be counted and calculated manually to subsequently communicate them to the previous processes so that the other lines are not blocked or full of parts, and thus, we will be able to perform the tasks safely and effectively, and therefore, at start-up, the lines will be filled again with the necessary material. Thanks to the Cross-PLC, this counting task has been automated, which allows more time to carry out the maintenance and start-up tasks of the line, improving these processes and above all, optimizing line stop preparation times.

4.3. Energy Consumption Monitoring

Another very useful tool developed has been the detection of work cells that are stopped or problems such as leaks in the supply systems by controlling the energy. In this case, we need to monitor the consumption of the different cells of a manufacturing area, and when an anomaly happens, it will be quickly detected where it is happening, reducing the time spent to solve the problems that may appear and improving energy efficiency.

5. Discussion

The presented tool, Cross-PLC, generates a significant improvement in information management when developing Industry 4.0 tools. As indicated in the introduction, there are numerous drawbacks to the massive implementation of IIoT tools in industry. The improvements generated by Cross-PLC from this perspective are described as follows:

- *Energy efficiency*: Since using the IT/OT network already available does not generate additional energy costs.
- *Interoperability*: Since it allows the interconnection and centralization of information available in different PLCs, making it transparent to the user.
- *Safety*: Since the Cross-PLC tool is only configured for data extraction, not for modifying production line information.
- *Scalability*: Since it does not present any limit on the brand of PLC or the control device to be connected.
- *Maintenance and updates*: Since using the devices already connected to the IT/OT network does not generate any additional maintenance or update costs.
- *IT/OT integration*: since the nature of the Cross-PLC proposal allows for this integration.
- *Cultural change*: Since for the user, and even for the developer, the IT part is opaque and does not generate any additional effort.

Communication between PLCs and crossPLC can be established in two main ways: natively, using the PLC's own language, or through HTTP requests using JSON formats. Native communication, by using the PLC's specific language, simplifies integration with that specific model. There are no issues with data translation or interpretation. However, compatibility between different versions of PLC firmware can be a challenge. If a new version introduces different data structures or commands, Cross-PLC would need to be updated to understand and interpret these changes. This requires constant maintenance of Cross-PLC to ensure compatibility with each version of each supported PLC model. The advantage is that performance is usually optimal as no format conversions are required. On the other hand, JSON-based communication offers greater flexibility and version compatibility. JSON is a lightweight and human-readable data exchange format widely used on the web. Its simple, standardized structure facilitates communication between different systems, regardless of the programming language or platform. This is the key to its robustness against version changes: as a PLC-independent data format, PLC firmware updates that do not modify the agreed-upon JSON structure do not affect communication with Cross-PLC. If new features or variables are added to the PLC, they simply need to be included in the JSON exchange without needing to modify the underlying structure. When interpreting the JSON, Cross-PLC would simply read the new data or ignore any data it does not need, maintaining compatibility. In other words, communication using JSON decouples the internal structure of the PLC from the Cross-PLC platform. While it is true that Cross-PLC does not support all PLC protocols, it does establish simple native communication for the main programmable controller protocols. For example, Rockwell only supports "unconnected" datagrams, but it simplifies PLC logic by allowing data to be transmitted as if it were another PLC. Currently, Cross-PLC supports http communication but it is only tested in Rockwell and Siemens PLC. Omron PLC also supports http communication but we have not tested it.

The *Cross-PLC* is compatible with other proposals, like, for instance, the new PLCs developed for Industry 4.0. such as IoT-PLC, see [19] or PLC 4.0, see [20] or the PLC for IIoT developed by the company Phoenix Contact, Germany. The *Cross-PLC* and then the *I3oT* concept only propose to use the installation setup first and then, when the installation setup is not enough, propose new devices

6. Conclusions

The creation of the Industrializable Industrial Internet of Things (I3oT) concept for the development of massively industrializable IIoT applications imposes the use of existing facilities in the company as a criterion. As seen in our previous work, this concept allows us to develop numerous tools capable of predicting a machine failure, detecting sub-bottlenecks and bottlenecks, rebalancing lines in real time, etc. The great drawback is that in order to continue maintaining the concept of I3oT, we need to use the IT/OT network to extract data from the PLCs installed in the factory. The Cross-PLC allows reading that information in a passive way with the PLCs sending the data when they have undergone a significant change. Cross-PLCs update the information in their memory, and the applications make use of this information for their operation using the Cross-PLC as a virtual PLC that provides it with information. This allows us, on the one hand, to extract plant information from the different PLC brands and, on the other hand, to standardize the I3oT application development process. In future works, we will continue with the research for new I3oT applications because the Cross-PLCs are very useful for solving the problems of communication through the IT/OT network of the factories.

Author Contributions: Conceptualization, A.L. and J.L.; methodology, A.L. and J.L.; software, A.L. and J.L.; validation, A.L., J.L. and E.G.; formal analysis, A.L., J.L., I.P.-A. and N.M.; investigation, A.L., J.L., I.P.-A. and N.M.; resources, E.G.; data curation, A.L. and J.L.; writing—original draft preparation, A.L., J.L., I.P.-A. and N.M.; writing—review and editing, A.L., J.L., I.P.-A., N.M. and E.G.; visualization, A.L., J.L., I.P.-A. and N.M.; supervision, N.M. and E.G.; project administration, A.L. and J.L.; funding acquisition, E.G. All authors have read and agreed to the published version of the manuscript.

Funding: This research received no external funding.

Institutional Review Board Statement: Not applicable.

Informed Consent Statement: Not applicable.

Data Availability Statement: Data are contained within the article.

Conflicts of Interest: The authors declare no conflicts of interest.

Abbreviations

The following abbreviations are used in this manuscript:

IT/OT	Information technology/operational technology

References

1. Haight, J.M.; Kecojevic, V. Automation vs. human intervention: What is the best fit for the best performance? *Process Saf. Prog.* **2005**, *24*, 45–51. [CrossRef]
2. Haight, J.M.; Caringi, R.G. Automation vs. human intervention: What is the best mix for optimum system performance? a case study. *Int. J. Risk Assess. Manag.* **2007**, *7*, 708–721. [CrossRef]

3. Abiodun, T.; Rampersad, G.; Brinkworth, R. Driving Industrial Digital Transformation. *J. Comput. Inf. Syst.* **2022**, *63* , 1345–1361 . [CrossRef]
4. Calderón, D.; Folgado, F.J.; González, I.; Calderón, A.J. Implementation and Experimental Application of Industrial IoT Architecture Using Automation and IoT Hardware/Software. *Sensors* **2024**, *24*, 8074. [CrossRef]
5. Mrabet, H.; Alhomoud, A.; Jemai, A.; Trentesaux, D. A Secured Industrial Internet-of-Things Architecture Based on Blockchain Technology and Machine Learning for Sensor Access Control Systems in Smart Manufacturing. *Appl. Sci.* **2022**, *12*, 4641. [CrossRef]
6. Babayigit, B.; Abubaker, M. Industrial Internet of Things: A Review of Improvements Over Traditional SCADA Systems for Industrial Automation. *IEEE Syst. J.* **2023**, *18*, 120–133. [CrossRef]
7. Nakagawa, E.Y.; Antonino, P.O.; Schnicke, F.; Capilla, R.; Kuhn, T.; Liggesmeyer, P. Industry 4.0 reference architectures: State of the art and future trends. *Comput. Ind. Eng.* **2021**, *156*, 107241. [CrossRef]
8. Soori, M.; Arezoo, B.; Dastres, R. Internet of things for smart factories in industry 4.0, a review. *Internet Things Cyber-Phys. Syst.* **2023**, *3*, 192–204. [CrossRef]
9. Wójcicki, K.; Biegańska, M.; Paliwoda, B.; Górna, J. Internet of Things in Industry: Research Profiling, Application, Challenges and Opportunities—A Review. *Energies* **2022**, *15*, 1806. [CrossRef]
10. Gosh, S.K.; Banerjee, A.; Aich, P.; Basu, D.; Gosh, U. Intelligent IoT for Automotive Industry 4.0: Challenges, Opportunities and Future Trends. In *Intelligent Internet of Things for Healthcare and Industry* ; Ghosh, U., Chakraborty, C., Garg, L., Srivastava, G., Eds.; Springer: Berlin/Heidelberg, Germany, 2023; pp. 327–352.
11. Mirani, A.A.; Velasco-Hernandez, G.; Awasthi, A.; Walsh, J. Key Challenges and Emerging Technologies in Industrial IoT Architectures: A Review. *Sensors* **2022**, *22*, 5836. [CrossRef]
12. Fraile, F.; Sanchis, R.; Poler, R.; Ortiz, A. Reference models for digital manufacturing platforms. *Appl. Sci.* **2019**, *9*, 4433. [CrossRef]
13. Serôdio, C.; Mestre, P.; Cabral, J.; Gomes, M.; Branco, F. Software and Architecture Orchestration for Process Control in Industry 4.0 Enabled by Cyber-Physical Systems Technologies. *Appl. Sci.* **2024**, *14*, 2160. [CrossRef]
14. Ungurean, I.; Gaitan, N.C. A software architecture for the industrial internet of things—A conceptual model. *Sensors* **2020**, *20*, 5603. [CrossRef] [PubMed]
15. Trunzer, E.; Calà, A.; Leitão, P.; Gepp, M.; Kinghorst, J.; Lüder, A.; Schauerte, H.; Reifferscheid, M.; Vogel-Heuser, B. System architectures for Industrie 4.0 applications: Derivation of a generic architecture proposal. *Prod. Eng.* **2019**, *13*, 247–257. [CrossRef]
16. Bangemann, T.; Riedl, M.; Thron, M.; Diedrich, C. Integration of classical components into industrial cyber-physical systems. *Proc. IEEE* **2016**, *104*, 947–959. [CrossRef]
17. Lombardi, M.; Pascale, F.; Santaniello, D. Internet of things: A general overview between architectures, protocols and applications. *Information* **2021**, *12*, 87. [CrossRef]
18. Oñate, W.; Sanz, R. Analysis of architectures implemented for IIoT. *Heliyon* **2023**, *9*, e12868. [CrossRef]
19. Mellado, J.; Núñez, F. Design of an IoT-PLC: A containerized programmable logical controller for the industry 4.0. *J. Ind. Inf. Integr.* **2022**, *25*, 100250. [CrossRef]
20. Azarmipour, M.; Elfaham, H.; Gries, C.; Epple, U. PLC 4.0: A Control System for Industry 4.0. In Proceedings of the IECON 2019—45th Annual Conference of the IEEE Industrial Electronics Society, Lisbon, Portugal, 14–17 October 2019; pp. 5513–5518.
21. Peinado-Asensi, I.; Montés, N.; Garcia, E. Industrializable industrial internet of things (I3oT) for a massive implementation of 568 industry 4.0 applications: A press shop case example. *Int. J. Prod. Res.* **2024**, *1*, 1–17.
22. Garcia, E.; Montés, N.; Llopis, J.; Lacasa, A. Miniterm, a Novel Virtual Sensor for Predictive Maintenance for the Industry 4.0 Era. *Sensors* **2022**, *22*, 6222. [CrossRef]
23. Peinado-Asensi, I.; Montés, N.; Garcia, E. Virtual sensor of gravity centres for real-time condition monitoring of an industrial stamping press in the automotive industry. *Sensors* **2023**, *23*, 6569. [CrossRef] [PubMed]
24. Peinado-Asensi, I.; Montés, N.; Garcia, E. A Framework to Reduce Energy Consumption in a Press Shop Floor based on Industrializable IIoT (I3oT). *Heliyon* **2024**, *10*, e29432. [CrossRef] [PubMed]
25. Peinado-Asensi, I.; Montés, N.; Garcia, E. Stamping process analysis in an industrial plant and its limitations to obtain an industrializable continuous twin. *Int. J. Mater. Form.* **2024**, *17*, 12. [CrossRef]
26. Llopis, J.; Lacasa, A.; Garcia, E.; Montés, N.; Hilario, L.; Vizcaíno, J.; Vilar, C.; Vilar, J.; Sánchez, L.; Latorre, J.C. Manufacturing Maps, a Novel Tool for Smart Factory Management Based on Petri Nets and Big Data Mini-Terms. *Mathematics* **2022**, *10*, 2398. [CrossRef]
27. Llopis, J.; Lacasa, A.; Garcia, E.; Montés, N. I3oT (Industrializable Industrial Internet of Things) Tool for Continuous Improvement in Production Line Efficiency by Means of Sub-Bottleneck Detection Method. *Machines* **2024**, *12*, 760. [CrossRef]
28. Ibáñez, D.; Garcia, E.; Soret, J.; Martos, J. Incipient Wear Detection of Welding Gun Secondary Circuit by Virtual Resistance Sensor Using Mahalanobis Distance. *Sensors* **2023**, *23*, 894. [CrossRef]
29. Garcia, E.; Montés, N. Real-Time Idle Time Cancellation by Means of Miniterm 4.0. *Energies* **2019**, *12*, 1230. [CrossRef]

30. Biorn-Hansen, A.; Grønli, T.-M.; Majchrzak, T.A.; Kaindl, H.; Ghinea, G. The Use of Cross-Platform Frameworks for Google Play Store Apps. In Proceedings of the 55th Annual Hawaii International Conference on System Sciences, Maui, HI, USA, 4–7 January 2022; Volume 1, pp. 7772–7781.
31. Biørn-Hansen, A.; Rieger, C.; Grønli, T.M.; Majchrzak, T.A.; Ghinea, G. An empirical investigation of performance overhead in cross-platform mobile development frameworks. *Empir. Softw. Eng.* **2020**, *25*, 2997–3040. [CrossRef]
32. Rendiniello, A.; Remus, A.; Sorrentino, I.; Murali, P.K.; Pucci, D.; Maggiali, M.; Natale, L.; Traversaro, S.; Villagrossi, E.; Polo, A.; et al. A Flexible Software Architecture for Robotic Industrial Applications. In Proceedings of the 2020 25th IEEE International Conference on Emerging Technologies and Factory Automation (ETFA), Vienna, Austria, 8–11 September 2020; Volume 1, pp. 1273–1276.
33. Martinova, L.; Fokin, N. Development of a Cross-Platform Software Application for Programming CNC Machine Tools. In Proceedings of the 2023 International Conference on Industrial Engineering, Applications and Manufacturing (ICIEAM), Sochi, Russia, 15–19 May 2023; Volume 1, pp. 616–622.
34. Focchi, M.; Roscia, F.; Semini, C. Locosim: An Open-Source Cross-Platform Robotics Framework. In *Synergetic Cooperation between Robots and Humans. CLAWAR 2023*; Lecture Notes in Networks and Systems, Volume 811; Oussef, E.S.E., Tokhi, M.O., Silva, M.F., Rincon, L.M., Eds.; Springer: Cham, Switzerland ; 2024; Volume 1, pp. 395–406.
35. Hsiao, C.-H.; Le, W.-P. OPIIoT: Design and Implementation of an Open Communication Protocol Platform for Industrial Internet of Things. *Internet Things* **2021**, *16*, 100441 [CrossRef]
36. Grosso, V. PLC-PROG (Improving PLC Programming Through a New Graphical, Object-Oriented and Brand-Independent Programming Framework). 2017. Available online: https://cordis.europa.eu/project/id/243484/reporting (accessed on 28 April 2025).

sensors

MDPI

Article

Overview of Embedded Rust Operating Systems and Frameworks

Thibaut Vandervelden [1], Ruben De Smet [2], Diana Deac [2,3], Kris Steenhaut [1,2,*] and An Braeken [1]

[1] Department of Engineering Technology (INDI), Vrije Universiteit Brussel, Pleinlaan 2, 1050 Brussels, Belgium; thvdveld@vub.be (T.V.); an.braeken@vub.be (A.B.)
[2] Department of Electronics and Informatics (ETRO), Vrije Universiteit Brussel, Pleinlaan 2, 1050 Brussels, Belgium; rubedesm@vub.be (R.D.S.); diana.deac@vub.be or diana.deac@campus.utcluj.ro (D.D.)
[3] Communications Department, Technical University of Cluj-Napoca, Memorandumului 28, 400114 Cluj-Napoca, Romania
* Correspondence: ksteenha@etrovub.be

Abstract: Embedded Operating Systems (OSs) are often developed in the C programming language. Developers justify this choice by the performance that can be achieved, the low memory footprint, and the ease of mapping hardware to software, as well as the strong adoption by industry of this programming language. The downside is that C is prone to security vulnerabilities unknowingly introduced by the software developer. Examples of such vulnerabilities are use-after-free, and buffer overflows. Like C, Rust is a compiled programming language that guarantees memory safety at compile time by adhering to a set of rules. There already exist a few OSs and frameworks that are entirely written in Rust, targeting sensor nodes. In this work, we give an overview of these OSs and frameworks and compare them on the basis of the features they provide, such as application isolation, scheduling, inter-process communication, and networking. Furthermore, we compare the OSs on the basis of the performance they provide, such as cycles and memory usage.

Keywords: rust; embedded operating systems; performance evaluation

1. Introduction

An embedded Operating System (OS) is a software layer that particularly manages scheduling of tasks and hardware resources of an embedded device. For many years, these OSs have been developed in the C programming language. The C language is a compiled language that provides low-level access to memory, making it suitable for embedded devices. Unfortunately, it does not prevent the programmer from writing unsafe operations, such as indexing an array out of its bounds. This can lead to security vulnerabilities, which is a big concern, especially with the increasing number of interconnected devices.

The goal of Google's "Project Zero" [1], which started in 2014, is to find security vulnerabilities in popular software. Each year, they publish a report with detected and reported zero-day vulnerabilities. They also keep track of these vulnerabilities in a publicly available dataset [2]. At the time of writing, this dataset contains 310 vulnerabilities, with 225 (72%) of them being caused by memory corruption, use-after-free, or type confusion. In a presentation at the BlueHat IL conference in 2019, Mat Miller, a security engineer at Microsoft said that the root cause of the vulnerabilities found in Windows products are from memory safety issues [3].

Tools that check for memory vulnerabilities do exist. However, software developers must know how to use them correctly and understand the reports that these tools generate. Designing a programming language that enforces safe memory manipulation would be a better solution.

In recent years, new programming languages suitable for embedded devices have emerged. The most prominent is the Rust programming language. It is a compiled language, providing safe low-level access to memory. The language has a strong type system and a set of rules that prevent unsafe memory operations. The compiler checks at compile time if the code follows these rules, and if not, the code will not compile.

Many papers discuss the performance of Rust programming language [4–8] and its safety [9–13]. The conclusion of these works is that Rust can be considered a good replacement for C, yielding comparable performance while providing safety.

Ayers et al. [14], Uzlu and Şaykol [15], and Noseda et al. [16] focus specifically on embedded systems programming in Rust. They show that the design concepts of Rust are a good fit for embedded systems. With the ownership model and borrowing rules, peripherals can only be accessed by one task at a time. This prevents misuse of the peripherals, and is checked at compile time. The zero-cost abstractions allow for high-level Application Programming Interfaces (APIs) to be written, without having to worry about the performance of the code. However, these papers also show that compared to C, Rust binaries are larger, which can be a problem for embedded devices. They pinpoint that the increased binaries' size is caused by generic code and by string formatting.

The structure of this work is as follows: in Section 2, we have a look at the recent literature on the Rust programming language, and in Section 3, we explain how the language is used in the embedded Rust ecosystem. We highlight core features of OSs. In Section 4, we discuss OSs and frameworks that are written in Rust and evaluate them in Section 5. Section 6 concludes the work.

2. Related Work

An important reference concerning the review and comparison of OSs for embedded devices is the work of Javed et al. [17]. The authors thoroughly examine eight OSs, designed specifically for Internet of Things (IoT) devices, written in C or C++. Their analysis covers a wide range of critical aspects, such as the type of kernel used by each OS, the scheduling mechanisms implemented, Inter-Process Communication (IPC) mechanisms, and the programming models and languages supported, as well as the network stack functionalities. Furthermore, the authors discuss memory management, energy efficiency, simulation tools, and application support provided by these OSs. We consider the same core features for our evaluation of Rust OSs for embedded systems.

Another work that discusses core features of OSs for embedded devices is [18]. In this work, the authors discuss the main features of eleven OSs. This discussion is given in the form of a table. However, the authors do not enter into detail beyond this table comparison.

The work of [19] provides a performance evaluation of three popular OSs for IoT devices. In their study, they benchmark Contiki-NG, RIOT-OS, and Zephyr, all written in C. They conduct a total of eight benchmarks, based on the Thread-Metric Benchmark Suite. These benchmarks evaluate OSs in various aspects, including context switching, interrupt processing, IPC, and memory management. They also analyze the memory footprint and energy consumption of each OS. We adopt a similar approach to evaluate the performance of Rust-based OSs. We consider interrupt processing, scheduling latency, and the memory footprint.

Of course, many other papers discuss and evaluate OSs for embedded devices. However, our work is the first to discuss and evaluate OSs entirely written in Rust.

3. Preliminaries

The first stable version of the Rust programming language [20] was released on 15 May 2015. One of the selling points of Rust is its compiler-guaranteed memory safety, enabled by its novel ownership model. This ownership model is a set of rules that defines what can and cannot be performed with memory. The compiler will check if the code follows these rules.

Rust has three ownership rules. (1) Each value in Rust has only one owner, e.g., a variable being the owner of stack memory. (2) There can only be one owner at a time. Two variables cannot share memory. (3) When an owner goes out of scope, the value is dropped, e.g., the memory is not in use any more and resources are freed. A variable's memory ownership can be transferred to another variable. This mechanism, called *moving* of ownership, restricts the original owner from doing anything with the memory. The *borrowing* rules address the inconvenience of moving ownership all the time. At any given time, (1) there can be any number of immutable references to a variable, or (2) there can only be one mutable reference. Whenever ownership of a value is borrowed, the owner cannot do anything with the memory until the borrow is released.

With the *ownership* and *borrowing* rules, many memory safety problems are addressed, such as null pointer dereferencing, dangling pointers, use-after-free, and data races. The rules are checked at compile time, which minimizes runtime performance overhead. Some checks, such as array bounds checking, are performed at runtime. However, the compiler can often optimize these away if it can prove that they are not necessary.

The Rust ecosystem for embedded devices, asynchronous Rust, and the core features of OS and frameworks are discussed in Section 3.3.

3.1. Embedded Rust Ecosystem

Rust comes with three built-in libraries. The *core* library provides fundamental types and functions that are available in all Rust programs, without relying on the standard library (*std*). The *alloc* library extends the functionality of the *core* library by adding features related to memory allocation, deallocation, and data structures such as dynamically sized arrays. The *alloc* library is only available on platforms that provide a memory allocator. This is usually the case on desktop platforms, but not necessarily on embedded platforms. Although memory allocators can be implemented for these platforms, they often entail reduced runtime performance. Finally, there is the standard library (*std*) with a wide range of functionality that makes it easier to work with various data types, perform I/O operations, and utilize higher-level abstractions. The standard library relies on the presence of an operating system, and is usually not available in resource-constrained platforms.

For embedded devices, the program entry point needs to be defined. This is the position in code where the program starts executing. The program starts with initializing static memory and vector tables, and sets up the stack pointer. This code needs to be explicitly written by the programmer, unless libraries are available that take care of this job. On ARM Cortex-M platforms, the `cortex-m-rt` [21] library can be used. It takes care of the aforementioned tasks and provides a macro to define the entry point. Libraries for MIPS-, RISC-V-, or ESP32-C-based microcontrollers also exist, being `mips-rt` [22], `riscv-rt` [23], and `esp32c-rt` [24], respectively. For Espressif-based microcontrollers, such as the ESP32 series, a fork of the Rust compiler is provided by Espressif Systems [25]. This modified Rust compiler is able to compile a modified standard library for these devices. This allows developers to write very-high-level code, without the trouble of handling the hardware. One downside is that it creates an Espressif-specific ecosystem, often incompatible with the rest of the embedded Rust ecosystem.

After the setup performed by `cortex-m-rt` or `mips-rt`, the microcontroller peripherals need to be initialized, such as UART, I2C, and SPI. This is conducted by accessing the registers of the microcontroller. The description of the registers available in a microcontroller is usually provided by the manufacturer in the form of an System View Description (SVD) file. Using the `svd2rust` [26] tool, a Rust Peripheral Access Crate (PAC) is created using the SVD file. A Rust "crate" is what a library is called in Rust. This PAC contains a type safe API to access the peripherals of the microcontroller. `svd2rust` supports the following architectures: ARM Cortex-M, MSP430, RISC-V, and Xtensa LX6.

Now that peripheral registers can be accessed using a type safe API, Hardware Abstraction Layers (HALs) can be used to abstract more parts of peripherals. The Rust Embedded Working Group has a set of common and recommended guidelines for writing HALs. One of their guidelines is that types in HALs should implement the traits defined in the `embedded-hal` crate. Traits allow for defining shared behavior without specifying how the behavior is implemented, much like interfaces in object-oriented programming. The `embedded-hal` crate contains traits for types that abstract over embedded hardware.

This crate offers an abstraction for building a platform-agnostic embedded ecosystem. Other crates provide traits for types that abstract over embedded hardware. Examples are `embedded-nal` and `embedded-storage`. The former contains traits for types that abstract over embedded networking, where the latter contains traits for types that abstract over storage such as EEPROM, NOR-flash, etc. Using these traits, HAL developers can enable the use of existing drivers for their platform for devices, such as sensors and actuators. For driver developers, the use of traits can make the driver generic and, thus, available for any platform that makes use of the `embedded-hal` crate. Although these abstraction layers seem to add a lot of overhead, it is often optimized away by the Rust compiler.

3.2. *Asynchronous Rust*

Asynchronous programming is a programming model where tasks are independently waiting for some resource to become available without blocking each other. An example is a task that makes use of hardware communication peripherals, e.g., I2C, SPI, or UART. Waiting for these peripherals to become available might block the microcontroller, wasting battery and time.

The Rust asynchronous model is built around the `Future` trait, representing an asynchronous computation. A *future* waiting for a resource will not block, but instead return and be scheduled to wake up again later. A future needs to be *polled* for it to be able to complete its computation. This is performed by calling the `poll` function on a future, which returns a `Poll` enum. The `Poll` enum has two possible values, either `Pending` or `Ready(T)`, with `T` being the value the future returns when ready. Continuously calling the `poll` function until it is ready is obviously not optimal. As an argument, the function receives a `Context`, with which it is able to notify a scheduler, called an `Executor` in Rust, when it should be polled again.

Figure 1 depicts the asynchronous model in Rust, showing an executor and two futures. The executor polls the first future, which is executed until it is ready, or until it needs to wait for a resource. To indicate that it is waiting, the future returns `Poll::Pending` to the executor. The executor then polls the second future, which is executed in the same way. An interrupt routine notifies the executor that the first future is ready to be polled, which makes the executor poll the first future again. The first future will then be ready and will return `Poll::Ready` to the executor, telling it not to poll that future anymore.

The asynchronous model is embedded in the Rust language which facilitates the writing of asynchronous code. With the `async` keyword, a function can be defined as asynchronous. This function returns a future, which can be awaited by calling `.await` on the future. Note that futures are lazy, meaning that they are not executed until they are polled. Scheduling and polling of futures is performed by an executor, which is a runtime that manages these futures. Without an executor, futures cannot be executed.

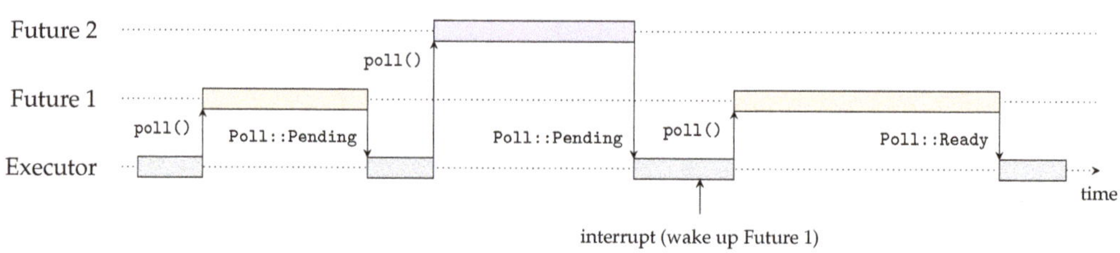

Figure 1. Asynchronous model in Rust with an executor and 2 futures. The executor polls the futures, which are executed until they are ready. A future returns `Poll::Pending` when it needs to wait for a resource, and `Poll::Ready` when it is ready. The executor is notified when a future is ready to be polled again.

3.3. Operating Systems and Frameworks

Using the HALs and PACs described in Section 3.1, one can develop an OS or framework. The primary function of an OS is to handle low-level tasks. In contrast, a framework typically offers a collection of libraries and tools designed to facilitate application development. An OS can be built using a framework as its foundation. The following sections go deeper into the core features of an OS: task scheduling, application isolation and memory protection, IPC, hardware interaction, and networking.

3.3.1. Task Scheduling

Task scheduling is an important part of an OS or framework. An OS usually runs multiple applications on a microcontroller, where each application is a separate task or a set of tasks. All these tasks need to be scheduled in such a way that each of them obtains its fair share of microcontroller time.

Tasks can be scheduled *preemptively* or *non-preemptively*. With preemptive scheduling, a scheduler can interrupt and stop the execution of a running task, such that the new task can be executed with the intention to continue the interrupted task later. In non-preemptive scheduling, a task runs until it completes or voluntarily yields control to allow other tasks to execute. Tasks that voluntarily yield control are called *cooperative* tasks. Whereas non-preemptive scheduling is simpler to implement, it is usually not suitable for real-time systems, as it cannot guarantee strict deadlines. The following scheduling algorithms are commonly used in embedded systems:

Priority-Base Each task is assigned a priority, and the task with the highest priority is scheduled first. Priorities are usually assigned by the developer.

Round-Robin Each task receives a time slice, after which the next task is scheduled. Tasks are always scheduled in the same order.

Rate-Monotonic Scheduling This is a priority-based scheduling algorithm where the priority of a task is determined by its period. The period of a task is defined by the time it takes until the task needs to yield control again. Tasks with shorter periods have higher priorities.

Earliest Deadline First This is a priority-based scheduling algorithm where the priority of a task is based on its deadline. Tasks with the earliest deadlines have the highest priority.

Multi-Level Feedback Queue (MLFQ) Tasks are grouped into different queues, e.g., based on their priority. Each queue has its scheduling algorithm, which is tailored to the tasks in that queue.

These scheduling algorithms can be combined, allowing a task to have both a priority and a deadline. In such cases, the task with the highest priority and the earliest deadline is scheduled first. There are many more scheduling algorithms, each with its use cases and advantages, but the ones mentioned above are the most common in embedded systems.

3.3.2. Application Isolation and Memory Protection

Application isolation and memory protection are essential security features in an OS, particularly in the IoT domain. They ensure that tasks cannot access memory outside their designated permissions for reading or writing. Isolation is typically achieved through virtual memory, where each task operates within its own protected virtual address space, mapped to physical memory by the OS. Hardware mechanisms, such as the Memory Protection Unit (MPU), enforce strict access controls by defining specific memory regions accessible to each task. If a task attempts to access unauthorized memory, the MPU triggers a fault to prevent the operation.

3.3.3. Inter-Process Communication (IPC)

IPC is the part of the OS that defines how tasks share data with each other. This is especially relevant when application isolation or memory protection is present. There are many ways to implement IPC, each with their use cases and advantages. Implementing IPC efficiently is crucial for the performance of the OS, providing responsive and reliable applications. This can be achieved in different ways:

Shared Memory Tasks can access and modify the same memory region, which can be managed safely through synchronization mechanisms like semaphores or mutexes.

Message Passing Tasks communicate with each other using message queues, mailboxes, or similar message passing systems, providing a structured approach to sharing information between tasks. This method ensures that synchronization is handled by the message passing system, reducing the likelihood of errors compared to shared memory.

Signals Signals are a special form of message passing, where the message is very simple. This mechanism enables efficient event notification between tasks.

Each method has its own advantages and is chosen based on factors such as the type of data being communicated, synchronization requirements, latency considerations, and system architecture.

3.3.4. Hardware Interaction

Embedded applications often require interaction with hardware peripherals such as sensors and actuators, which are controlled via registers. To facilitate the interaction with these registers, the OS or framework must offer an API that ensures type safety, ensuring that only appropriate registers are accessed, as verified by the compiler. As discussed in Section 3.1, the `svd2rust` tool can generate a PAC from an SVD file. This PAC provides a type-safe API for accessing the microcontroller's registers. HALs can then be developed on top of these PACs, abstracting more complex aspects of the peripherals. Some OSs and frameworks provide custom HALs tailored to their specific abstractions and requirements. This is often mandated by their IPC, application isolation, and memory protection design choices.

3.3.5. Networking

The Rust core library does not provide networking support, so network stacks must be implemented by the OS or framework. It is an essential component in the IoT domain, allowing devices to communicate with each other over wired or wireless networks. Most network stacks are implemented in the OS as part of the kernel, or in a separate library. Platforms that support the Rust standard library can utilize its networking stack.

For wired connections, network stacks typically support Internet Protocol version 4 (IPv4), whereas for wireless IoT connectivity, Internet Protocol version 6 (IPv6) is more common. However, IPv6 packets are often too large for low-power wireless networks, so the IPv6 over Low-power Wireless Personal Area Networks (6LoWPAN) protocol is used to run IPv6 over these networks. Common transport layer protocols are User Datagram Protocol (UDP) and Transmission Control Protocol (TCP), with UDP being more common in the IoT domain due to its lower resource requirements. Constrained Application Protocol (CoAP), Message Queuing Telemetry Transport (MQTT), and Matter are popular application layer protocols in the IoT domain.

The most important network stack in the Rust ecosystem is smoltcp [27]. It is a standalone network stack that targets bare-metal systems and supports common protocols like IPv4, IPv6, 6LoWPAN, UDP, and TCP. It can also process Ethernet and IEEE 802.15.4 frames. Smoltcp provides a `Device` trait, which defines how the network stack can interact with the hardware. Adding support for a device requires implementing this trait for the specific hardware. The smoltcp interface is polling-based, requiring the user to call the `poll` function on the network stack to process incoming and outgoing packets. This polling-based interface maps well to the asynchronous model in Rust.

4. Rust-Based Operating Systems and Frameworks

Since the start of the Rust project, many OSs and frameworks targeting embedded devices have been developed. In this section, we discuss features like scheduling mechanism, IPC, hardware interaction, and networking capabilities for some of these. We will evaluate four OSs and frameworks that are well known and used in the Rust ecosystem in detail.

4.1. Overview

For the selected OSs and frameworks, Table 1 shows the targeted platforms, licensing, number of contributors, git commits, lines of code, and GitHub stars. All four support ARM Cortex-M-based microcontrollers. We observe that some of them also start to support RISC-V-based microcontrollers. We also noticed that Tock [28] is the most popular OS in the Rust ecosystem, followed by Embassy [29] and RTIC [30]. Despite Hubris [31] being less popular, it still has an interesting approach for building a secure and robust OS.

Table 1. General overview of Operating Systems and frameworks in Rust for embedded systems.

	License	Targeted Platforms	Contr. [1]	Git Commits	kLOC	GitHub Stars
Tock (2.1.1) Operating System	Apache 2.0 or MIT	ARM Cortex-M RISC-V [2]	186	13,803	193.5	5271
Hubris (1.0.0) Operating System	Mozilla Public License 2.0	ARM Cortex-M	49	1840	89.2	2908
RTIC (2.0.0) Framework	Apache 2.0 or MIT	ARM Cortex-M	83	1707	13.7	1708
Embassy (0.1.0) Framework	Apache 2.0 or MIT	ARM Cortex-M RISC-V [2]	353	8393	134.3	4925

[1] Number of active contributors. [2] Experimental support.

4.1.1. Tock

Tock [32] is an OS targeting Cortex-M- and RISC-V-based embedded platforms. Its development started around 2015, with the start of Rust, and is available under Apache 2.0 or MIT license, at the user's choice. Licensing like this is common in the Rust ecosystem. Tock's primary objective is to execute multiple untrusted applications, with its emphasis on shielding against potentially malicious applications and device drivers. The Tock developers have written their own network stack, which has support for 6LoWPAN and Thread over IEEE 802.15.4 links.

4.1.2. Hubris

Hubris [31], developed by the Oxide Computer Company, is an OS that only targets 32-bit ARM Cortex-M microcontrollers. Although Hubris targets ARM Cortex-M microcontrollers, they have a limited set of supported boards. This is because they only support devices that they use themselves. Hubris is licensed under the Mozilla Public License Version 2.0. One of the goals of Hubris is to provide a robust and secure OS for embedded devices. They achieve this by using a strict task model, where each task is defined at compile time.

4.1.3. RTIC

RTIC [30], short for Real-Time Interrupt-driven Concurrency, is a hardware-accelerated Real-Time Operating System (RTOS) based on research from the Luleå University of Technology (LTU) Sweden. It is licensed under the Apache 2.0 license or the MIT license, at the user's choice. It targets ARM Cortex-M microcontrollers, with support for RISC-V in experimental stage. RTIC only provides an execution framework, meaning that it only provides the tools to write the execution and scheduling of tasks. HALs from other sources, such as the ones from the Rust ecosystem, should be used for interfacing with the hardware.

4.1.4. Embassy

Embassy [29], originally developed by Dario Nieuwenhuis, is a framework that provides an asynchronous runtime (see Section 3.2) for embedded devices. It is licensed under the Apache 2.0 license or the MIT license, at the user's choice. Embassy's asynchronous runtime has support for ARM Cortex-M, RISC-V, and AVR platforms. It can also be used on platforms that support the `std` library, such as Linux or Windows. Furthermore, it can also be used on a WebAssembly architecture, although its primary focus is on embedded devices.

4.1.5. Other Notable OSs and Frameworks

There are many more OSs and frameworks that are written in Rust. However, these are either not as well known or not as mature as the ones discussed above, or their development has halted. The following list does not aim to be exhaustive:

Aerugo (2023–2024) [33] was developed as part of the European Space Agency activity to evaluate Rust for space applications. It is a real-time OS for ARM Cortex-M microcontrollers, more specifically, the ATSAMV71Q21 microcontroller.

Bern RTOS (2021–2023) [34] is a real-time OS for ARM Cortex-M microcontrollers. It was developed by Stefan Lüthi during his master's thesis at the Bern University of Applied Sciences.

Drone OS (2017–2023) [35] Valentine Valyaeff started with the development of Drone OS in late 2017; targeting ARM Cortex-M and RISC-V microcontrollers. It was halted at the beginning of 2023.

lilos (2019–ongoing) [36] is a minimal async executor for embedded devices, even though it is presented as a real-time OS. It currently only supports the ARM Cortex-M architecture.

RIOT-rs (2024–ongoing) [37] is developed by the RIOT community. It is a port of the RIOT OS to Rust. It is built on top of the hardware abstractions and async programming framework provided by Embassy. It provides new abstractions such as threads, which are not available in Embassy. While RIOT is a mature OS for embedded devices, RIOT-rs is still in the early stages of development, and is, therefore, not included in our evaluation.

Wasefire (2023–ongoing) [38] is a research project of Google. Its goal is to provide a platform for embedded devices on which WebAssembly applications can run.

4.2. Discussion of Core Features

The following sections provide a detailed discussion on the core features of the four OSs and frameworks. Per key aspect, we provide the design decisions and architecture of each of the discussed projects.

4.2.1. Task Scheduling

Tock: Tasks that can be scheduled by the Tock kernel are defined in kernel- and user-space. In kernel-space, these tasks are called capsules. A capsule provides a specific service, such as a driver for a hardware peripheral. In user-space, these tasks are defined by the user as applications. Multiple applications can be loaded onto the microcontroller, each running in their own tasks. Tock defines the `Scheduler` trait, such that the kernel can be generic over different schedulers. Tock provides multiple different implementations, currently either round-robin, priority-based, cooperative, or MLFQ.

The scheduler is used in the main loop of the kernel. When an interrupt occurs, the currently running task is preempted by the kernel task. It is then up to the scheduler to decide which task to run next. Kernel capsules and interrupts are scheduled first. These are scheduled cooperatively, meaning that they need to yield control to allow other tasks to run. The scheduler trait allows deferring handling of interrupts, but none of the current schedulers make use of this feature. User-space tasks cannot preempt other user-space tasks.

If all tasks are ready or waiting for a resource, the kernel will enter a sleep mode. Depending on the platform, this mode enters a low-power state, where the microcontroller consumes less power. When an interrupt occurs, the kernel wakes up and the scheduler is run to determine the next task to run.

Hubris: Hubris focuses on robustness and security. To achieve this, tasks are defined at compile time in an application configuration file. This means that tasks are known at compile time, as it is not possible to create tasks at runtime. This reduces the risk of failure due to memory exhaustion when creating tasks.

Hubris uses a priority-based scheduler, where each task is assigned a priority. The task with the highest priority is scheduled first. Lower priority tasks are scheduled when no higher priority tasks are ready to run. Tasks with the same priority are scheduled cooperatively. When an interrupt occurs, the currently running task is preempted, but only when the preempting task has a higher priority.

Hubris has a *supervisor* task, which has the highest priority. It must take action when other tasks fail. When a task fails, e.g., because of an explicit crash, a hardware fault, or system call fault, the supervisor task is scheduled to run. The supervisor task asks the kernel to restart the failed task. If the supervisor task should fail, the full system is restarted.

Another important task is the *idle* task, which has the lowest priority. This task is scheduled when no other task needs to run. It will place the microcontroller in a low-power state, waiting for an interrupt.

RTIC: RTIC provides two kind of tasks: hardware tasks and software tasks. Hardware tasks are bound to a hardware interrupt and are executed as a reaction to a hardware event. These tasks, though not enforced, should always run to completion as they handle real hardware interrupts. Software tasks are not bound to any hardware event, but bound to a *dispatcher*. This dispatcher is acting as an async executor. This executor is driven by an unused hardware interrupt. For each unused hardware interrupt, an executor is assigned to it with a priority level. The list of executors should cover the list of priority levels defined by the application.

RTIC uses preemptive priority-based scheduling, optimized using a Stack Resource Policy (SRP) [39] based concurrency and resource management model. This model prevents deadlocks when sharing resources between tasks. Each task has a priority level and defines what resources it is sharing with other tasks. Using this information, the highest possible priority level is calculated for each resource. A running task raises the preemption level to the highest priority level of all resources it is using. This way, a task can only be preempted by a task with a higher priority level. Tasks sharing resources can, thus, not be preempted by each other. This analysis is performed at compile time, where the tasks are analyzed under this model and code is generated. The generated code creates async executors for each priority level. An example of how tasks are scheduled in RTIC is shown in Figure 2.

This mechanism maps well to the ARM Cortex-M BASEPRI register [40], when available on the microcontroller. It is used to mask interrupts with a lower priority level than the one set in this register. If the BASEPRI register is not available, interrupt source masking is used instead.

Embassy: Embassy heavily relies on Rust's asynchronous ecosystem. Tasks are asynchronous functions annotated with Embassy's `task` macro. This macro implements Embassy traits necessary for these asynchronous functions to be used by the Embassy executor. Using this macro, the size of the function is known at compile time, meaning that no heap allocations are needed.

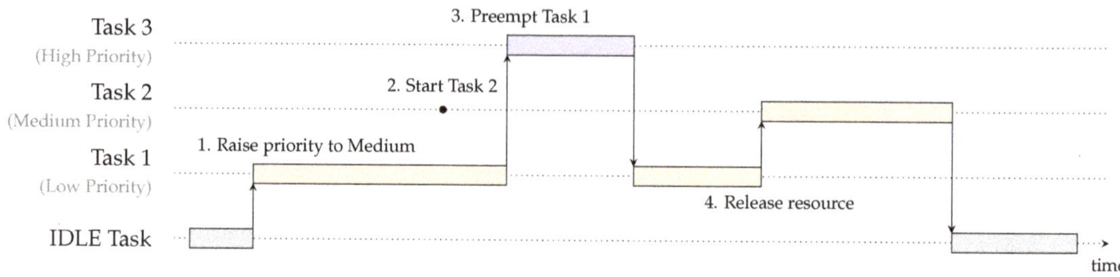

Figure 2. Example of Stack Resource Policy-based scheduling in RTIC with 3 tasks, with Task 1 having the lowest priority and Task 3 the highest. Task 1 and Task 2 share the same resource. When Task 1 is scheduled, it raises the running priority to medium, which is the highest priority of the resources it is using (shown in step 1). Task 2 is scheduled, but cannot preempt Task 1 as it requires the same resource (shown in step 2), preventing a deadlock where Task 2 would wait indefinitely for the occupied resource. Task 3 is scheduled, preempting Task 1 (shown in step 3) as it has a higher priority. When Task 3 is finished, the execution of Task 1 is resumed. Task 1 releases the resource and lowers the priority to its original level (shown in step 4). Task 2 can now preempt Task 1.

Embassy uses a cooperative scheduling model, where tasks need to yield control to allow other tasks to run. Yielding control is achieved by awaiting another `Future`, or by calling the `yield_now` function. Priority-based scheduling is also supported by Embassy. This is achieved by using different executors, where each executor has its own priority level. Executors are driven by interrupts. Using the hardware registers, interrupts can be prioritized. The interrupt with the highest priority level is used to drive the executor with the highest priority level. This way, the executor with the highest priority level is always scheduled first.

4.2.2. Application Isolation and Memory Protection

Tock: Tock uses a combination of language-based and hardware-based isolation mechanisms. The language-based isolation is achieved by using capsules, which are untrusted by default and are, as such, not allowed to use `unsafe` code. Only capsules that implement core kernel functionalities are trusted and are allowed to use `unsafe` code.

The hardware-based isolation is implemented using the MPU of the microcontroller. The MPU is used to isolate the memory of each process. When a process tries to access memory outside its designated memory region, the MPU triggers a fault, preventing the operation.

Hubris: Hubris has its own build system, called `xtask` (not to be confused with the `cargo-xtask` tool). This system builds every task defined in the application configuration file as a separate binary. Each task defines how much Random Access Memory (RAM) and flash it needs. When all tasks are built, they are linked together into a single binary. Since each task is built as a separate binary, the tasks are isolated from each other. Furthermore, Hubris makes use of the MPU to isolate the memory of each task at runtime.

The disadvantage of this approach is that tasks that use the same library, e.g., a library for some specific communication protocol, are duplicated in the binary. This can lead to a larger binary size.

RTIC and Embassy: RTIC and Embassy do not use any form of application isolation or memory protection. Memory protection could be achieved by using the MPU of the microcontroller. The control registers of the MPU are often accessible using an HAL or PAC libraries.

4.2.3. Inter-Process Communication (IPC)

Tock: Communication in Tock always occurs via the kernel using system calls. The system call triggers a context switch to the kernel, which then reads register values to determine how to handle the call. The context switch allows the kernel to switch to a privileged mode, allowing it to have full access to the system. There are seven system calls, split into two categories. The first category is for administrative purposes, containing three system calls: yielding control, requesting memory, and terminating the process. The second category is for interacting with capsules, containing four system calls. The *subscribe* command allows subscribing to an event, e.g., a specific interrupt. The *command* command allows invoking an action on a capsule. Finally, the *read-only allow* and *read-write allow* commands are for sharing data.

IPC between user applications is based on a client-server model. A process provides a service, implemented as a server, while other processes can share memory with the server to communicate. Sharing memory is conducted using the system calls. This shared memory is used to pass messages between the client and the server, or the other way around. The protocol of this communication is not specified by Tock, and is up to the developer to implement. The server and client can also communicate using the *subscribe* and *command* system calls.

Communication between user applications and capsules is achieved using the same system calls. Capsules often require dynamic memory, e.g., for storing metadata. Dynamic allocation is prohibited in the kernel, preventing a point of failure. Since capsules live in the kernel, they are not allowed to allocate memory. Instead, when capsules require dynamic memory, they can allocate memory from the process that invoked the capsule. This is implemented as *grants*, where the process provides a grant to the capsule using the *read-only allow* or *read-write allow* system calls.

IPC between capsules is not needed as they all live in the kernel space. Instead, they can directly call each other's functions.

Hubris: IPC is based around *synchronous* messages, where sending a message blocks the sender, while it is waiting for a response. A receiver waiting for a message is also blocked until a message is received. Both tasks need to *rendezvous* in the right state. It is the kernel that copies the message from the sender to the receiver.

Since both tasks are blocked, one task is blocked while listening and the other while transmitting, no message queue is needed. A task can only continue its execution when the message is fully transmitted and received. This has the benefit that tasks cannot flood each other with messages. On the other hand, this can potentially lead to deadlocks. To solve this issue, Hubris only allows a task to send a message to a task with a higher priority.

Messages have a maximum size of 256 bytes. For bigger messages, the sender can use *leases*. A lease is a shared memory region that is shared between the sender and the receiver, where the sender leases the memory to the receiver. While the sender is waiting for a reply, the receiver has exclusive access to the memory. When the receiver is finished with the memory, it releases the lease, allowing the sender to access the memory again. This is an abstraction that can be expressed using the Rust borrowing rules, allowing the compiler to check if the memory is used correctly. This method also allows for higher priority tasks to send messages to lower priority tasks.

The protocol used for communication between tasks is defined by an experimental interface definition language called *Idol*. The language defines the messages that can be sent between tasks. At compile time, the message definitions are transpiled to Rust structs. These structs are then used to serialize and deserialize the messages. This is achieved using the popular `serde` library, a high-performance framework for serializing and deserializing Rust data structures.

RTIC: To share data between tasks, RTIC uses *channels*. A channel consists of multiple *senders* and one *receiver*. Tasks that want to send data use the sender construction, while the task that wants to receive data uses the receiver construction. The channel uses statically allocated memory to store the data.

The channels can be used asynchronously by software tasks. A sender transmitting data might need to wait for space in the channel to become available. Additionally, the receiver might need to wait for data to be available.

Hardware tasks can also use channels, but should not use the async features of the channel. These tasks should be short and should not block for a long time. A synchronous channel is, therefore, available for hardware tasks. Sending data over the channel might return an error when the channel is full.

Embassy: Embassy provides four different ways of IPC. The first way is by using *channels*. These channels can have multiple senders and multiple receivers. However, only one receiver can receive the message. The second way is with *priority* channels, where messages have priorities. Messages with higher priorities are received first. The third way is by means of *broadcast* channels, where multiple receivers can receive the same message. The last way is by using *signals*, which is the same as a channel, but with a signal message. When a new message is sent, the old message is overwritten.

4.2.4. Hardware Interaction

Tock: Tock uses a Hardware Interface Layer (HIL) instead of the more commonly used `embedded-hal`, discussed in Section 3.1. This layer is hardware-agnostic and defines how components of the Tock OS interact with each other. Components can be hardware peripherals, such as SPI or I2C, but they can also be temperature sensors or buzzers. Hardware-specific Tock libraries implement the traits defined in the HIL. They also have board-specific libraries that initialize the microcontroller and board-specific Integrated Circuits (ICs) as well as the sensors or actuators.

Hubris: Interacting with hardware is achieved using driver abstractions, which are regular tasks that run in unprivileged mode, but can interact with the hardware. Hubris does not use the `embedded-hal` libraries for the hardware abstractions, as these libraries require privileged access. These drivers are usually split into two parts, platform-specific and platform-agnostic parts. However, this split is not well defined by Hubris. The platform-specific parts are written as driver crates and usually access the hardware. In some cases, these crates communicate using IPC with other driver crates, or a combination of both. The platform-agnostic parts are written as driver servers, which wrap the platform-specific crates and provide an IPC interface for other tasks.

RTIC: RTIC does not provide any hardware abstractions. The default way to interact with hardware is by using the HAL and PAC crates.

Embassy: Embassy provides its bespoke HALs, which are tailored to the asynchronous runtime of Embassy. Many hardware operations can be performed asynchronously, such as reading from a sensor or writing to a display. This makes the asynchronous runtime of Embassy a good fit for interacting with hardware. However, it is not necessary to use the HAL provided by Embassy, but then the hardware interaction will not be asynchronous. Embassy provides HALs for nRF microcontrollers from Nordic Semiconductor, STM32 microcontrollers from ST Microelectronics, and Raspberry Pi RP2040 microcontrollers.

4.2.5. Networking

Tock: The network stack of Tock is written as a capsule. For the data link layer, an `ieee802154` module provides the implementation of an IEEE 802.15.4 framer and a trait definition for an IEEE 802.15.4 device. The implementation of this trait is platform-specific and should provide buffers with the use of grants. Another capsule that is provided is the `net` capsule. This contains the implementation of IPv6 over 6LoWPAN, commonly used in IEEE 802.15.4-based networks. It supports compression for the Internet Control Message Protocol for IPv6 (ICMPv6) and UDP, with UDP the only supported transport layer protocol. Note that there is no support for Ethernet devices.

Hubris and Embassy: Hubris and Embassy use smoltcp as their network stack. For Hubris, the network stack is running in a dedicated task.

Embassy comes with a wrapper library, called `embassy-net`. It is a wrapper around the smoltcp library, running in its own Embassy task. At the time of writing, `embassy-net` only supports Ethernet over IPv4. Embassy does not contain an HAL implementation for devices using other physical media.

RTIC: RTIC does not provide a network stack. However, it is possible to use smoltcp with RTIC, as smoltcp is a standalone library.

4.3. Comparison Conclusion and Use Cases

Table 2 provides a summary of the features discussed in this section for Tock, Hubris, RTIC, and Embassy. For scheduling processes, we see that all of them provide a priority-based or round-robin-based scheduler. These are often relatively easy to implement compared to other scheduling mechanisms. Tock, however, provides more than one scheduling mechanism, such as purely cooperative-based scheduling or MLFQ scheduling.

Table 2. Summary of discussed key aspects for Tock, Hubris, RTIC, and Embassy.

	Scheduling	Inter-Process Communication (IPC)	App. Isolation	Hardware Interaction	Network Stack
Tock OS	One of: • Round-robin • Cooperative • Priority-based • MLFQ	• System calls • Shared memory	MPU	Bespoke HAL	Bespoke stack: • IEEE 802.15.4 framer • 6LoWPAN • ICMPv6 • UDP
Hubris OS	Priority-based and cooperative	Synchronous message-passing	MPU	Bespoke HAL	smoltcp based: • Ethernet framer • IEEE 802.15.4 framer • IPv4/IPv6 • 6LoWPAN • ICMPv4/ ICMPv6 • TCP/UDP
RTIC Framework	• Priority-based and preemptive • Hardware-accelerated	Channel based	-	`embedded-hal`	-
Embassy Framework	Priority-based and cooperative	Channel based	-	• Bespoke HAL (async) • `embedded-hal`	smoltcp based: • Ethernet framer • IEEE 802.15.4 framer • IPv4/IPv6 • 6LoWPAN • ICMPv4/ ICMPv6 • TCP/UDP

In terms of Application Isolation and Memory Protection, both Tock and Hubris have mechanisms in place to isolate applications from each other. Tock and Hubris both use a combination of language-based and hardware-based isolation mechanisms, by using the MPU of the microcontroller. Neither RTIC nor Embassy provide any form of application isolation or memory protection.

Both frameworks can use the standard HALs of the Rust ecosystem. This enables the frameworks to run on a wider range of microcontrollers. Developers of HALs are not restricted to a specific OS or framework. However, this is not the case for Tock, as this OS already existed before the Rust ecosystem was mature and gained popularity early on.

For networking, Tock has its own network stack, whereas Hubris and Embassy use smoltcp. Note that Tock lacks support for Ethernet devices. Relying on smoltcp allows Hubris and Embassy to support a wider range of protocols. However, Tock's network stack is more integrated with the OS.

In conclusion, real-time applications found in sensor networks, i.e., railway monitoring systems, disaster mitigation such as earthquake early warning systems, healthcare monitoring systems, and industrial automation systems, can benefit from the features provided by RTIC and Embassy. Both frameworks provide a lightweight runtime, suitable for real-time applications, with the latter providing a more complete library and network stack. For applications that require a more secure and full-fledged OS, Tock and Hubris are more suitable. Examples of such applications are automotive systems, threat monitoring systems, and privacy-sensitive applications.

5. Evaluation

In this section, we evaluate Tock, RTIC, and Embassy, discussed in Section 4. We do not evaluate Hubris, as it only supports a limited number of platforms, which are often developed by the Oxide Computer Company themselves. We evaluate this OS and these frameworks based on their scheduling latency and memory usage. The scheduling latency is crucial for real-time systems, where tasks need to be executed within a certain time frame. These measurements give an indication of how fast the OS can respond to external events. The memory usage is also important, as embedded devices often have limited resources.

Measurements are conducted on the nRF52840-DK development board from Nordic Semiconductor. It is based on a 32-bit ARM Cortex-M4 architecture, running at 64,MHz. For our measurements, we use the MSO2002B series mixed signal oscilloscope from Tektronix, OR, U.S., which has a resolution of 1,ns. We use the `rustc v1.73.0-nightly-2023-07-30` compiler for all our examples, as it is the version required by Tock.

5.1. Interrupt Latency and Task Scheduling

For measuring the interrupt latency, we set a General Purpose Input/Output (GPIO) pin high at the beginning of the Interrupt Service Routine (ISR). This ISR is triggered by an input signal. The interrupt latency is the time between the input signal triggering the interrupt and the start of the ISR. We can measure this using the logic analyzer. The interrupt duration can be measured by setting the GPIO pin low at the end of the ISR. To measure the task scheduling latency, we use a task that toggles a GPIO pin. The time between the end of the ISR and the start of the task is measured using the logic analyzer. Adding up the interrupt latency, the interrupt duration and the scheduling latency gives the total latency. An overview of the measurement setup is shown in Figure 3.

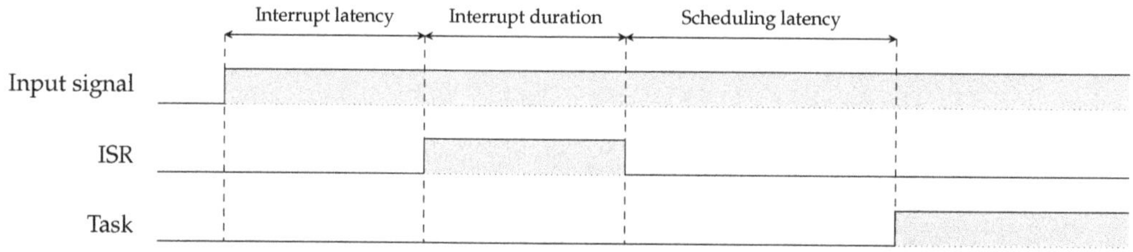

Figure 3. *Interrupt latency* and *scheduling latency* measurement setup. The interrupt latency is the time between the interrupt being triggered and the start of the ISR. The interrupt duration is the time it takes to handle the ISR. The scheduling latency is the time it takes to schedule a task. The microcontroller should be in an idle state such that the interrupt does not preempt a running task. Otherwise, the scheduling latency is not measured correctly, as after the interrupt handling, another task would resume its execution before task scheduling occurs.

The measurements are shown in Table 3. We perform the measurements for two different compiler optimization levels. The first half of the table shows the measurements when the software is compiled for speed optimization, while the second half shows the measurements when the software is compiled for size optimization. As input signal for the interrupt, we use a periodic signal such that multiple measurements can be conducted.

This allows us to compute confidence intervals for the measurements, which are shown in the table. They are calculated using the normal distribution with a confidence level of 95%.

As expected, the total latency of Tock is highest. When the interrupt is triggered, a running task is preempted by the kernel, which then schedules the ISR. This ISR runs all functions that are registered to the interrupt. Furthermore, the OS deals with setting up the MPU correctly. This results in a higher interrupt latency, interrupt duration, and scheduling latency. Note that we conducted measurements for all four scheduling mechanisms in Tock. For each of them, the interrupt latency and interrupt duration are almost the same. The scheduling latency is different, with the highest scheduling latency for the MLFQ scheduler. This is expected, as the MLFQ scheduler has the most complex scheduling mechanism. The lowest scheduling latency is for the cooperative scheduler.

Table 3. Interrupt latency, interrupt duration, and scheduling latency measurements. The measurements are conducted on the nRF52840-DK development board. The software is compiled once for speed optimization (`opt-level = 3`) and once for size optimization (`opt-level = "z"`). Confidence intervals are calculated using the normal distribution with a confidence level of 95%.

Optimized for Speed	Interrupt Latency (µs)	Interrupt Duration (µs)	Scheduling Latency (µs)	Total Latency (µs)
Embassy	0.822 (0.003)	4.844 (0.003)	4.164 (0.001)	9.830 (0.003)
RTIC	0.668 (0.003)	2.207 (0.001)	1.135 (0.003)	4.010 (0.004)
round-robin Tock	15.683 (0.005)	15.683 (0.002)	52.058 (0.003)	83.424 (0.005)
priority Tock	15.741 (0.006)	15.635 (0.004)	36.510 (0.003)	67.886 (0.005)
cooperative Tock	15.737 (0.005)	15.634 (0.004)	31.323 (0.003)	62.694 (0.005)
MLFQ Tock	15.596 (0.005)	15.652 (0.002)	72.166 (0.003)	103.414 (0.004)
Optimized for Size	**Interrupt Latency (µs)**	**Interrupt Duration (µs)**	**Scheduling Latency (µs)**	**Total Latency (µs)**
Embassy	1.03 (0.01)	6.573 (0.002)	5.7 (0.4)	13.3 (0.4)
RTIC	0.995 (0.003)	2.825 (0.002)	1.432 (0.005)	5.252 (0.006)
round-robin Tock	15.237 (0.005)	29.917 (0.007)	74.656 (0.003)	119.810 (0.006)
priority Tock	15.232 (0.006)	29.48 (0.02)	56.279 (0.004)	100.99 (0.02)
cooperative Tock	15.375 (0.006)	30.12 (0.02)	50.454 (0.004)	95.95 (0.01)
MLFQ Tock	15.422 (0.006)	28.871 (0.008)	84.33 (0.07)	128.63 (0.08)

The total latency is lowest for RTIC, as they use the hardware to its full potential. We see that the total latency for Embassy is slightly higher than RTIC. Embassy has a slight overhead compared to RTIC, because of its asynchronous runtime.

For measurements in Table 3, only one task is scheduled, which is the task that toggles the GPIO pin. The scheduling latency in these measurements is, therefore, the smallest possible. Figure 4 shows the relation between the number of tasks and the total latency. For these measurements, additional tasks are running concurrently with the task that toggles the GPIO pin. We see that for RTIC, Embassy, and Tock with the priority scheduler and the MLFQ scheduler, the total latency increases linearly with the number of tasks. They have an R^2 value of around 0.99 for a linear fit. For Tock with the round-robin scheduler and the cooperative scheduler, the total latency increases non-linearly.

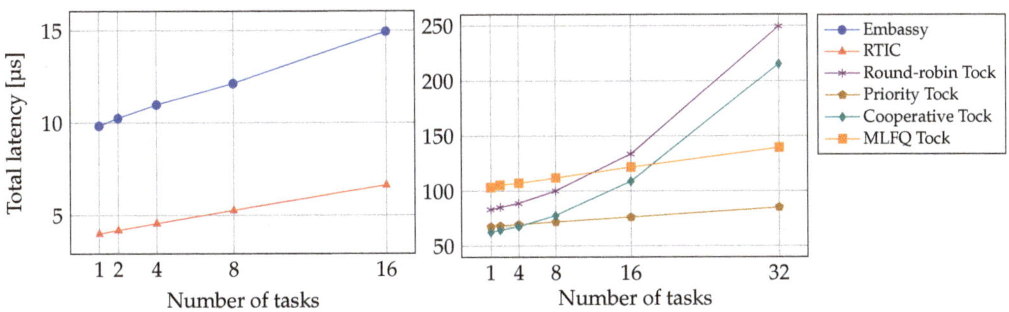

Figure 4. Total latency measurements for different number of tasks for Embassy, RTIC, and Tock. For Tock with the round-robin and cooperative scheduler, the total latency increases non-linearly with the number of tasks. All other schedulers show a linear increase in total latency.

5.2. Memory Requirements

The memory usage of an OS or framework is important, as embedded devices often have limited resources. We measure the memory usage of each OS or framework by looking at the binary size and the static memory usage. From the compiled binary, we extract the `.text` and `.bss` sections, which are the firmware size and the static memory usage, respectively. We use a simple application that blinks an LED for our measurement, as this is a very small application that shows the overhead of the OS or framework.

Table 4 shows the memory requirements of Tock, RTIC, and Embassy. The measurements show that RTIC has the smallest memory footprint, followed by Embassy. Embassy's memory footprint is higher than RTIC, as it provides an executor for running asynchronous tasks. It is also known that asynchronous functions in Rust have a higher memory overhead compared to synchronous functions [41].

Table 4. Memory requirements for an application blinking an LED every 250 milliseconds. The application is compiled for the nRF52840-DK development board, and optimized for size (`opt-level = "z"`).

	Text (byte)	Data (byte)	BSS (byte)	Total (byte)
Embassy	9588	112	34,264	43,964
RTIC	6864	0	40	6904
Kernel Tock	200,708	36	34,492	235,236
Simple kernel Tock	40,964	32	10,960	51,956
Application Tock	286	0	0	286

The memory footprint of Tock is split into two parts: the kernel and the application. The application part of Tock is very small, as it only contains system calls to the kernel. The kernel, however, is very large compared to RTIC and Embassy, as it contains many drivers and other functionalities. These drivers are potentially not used by applications, which is the case for our simple application. We tried to minimize the memory footprint of the Tock kernel by compiling without these drivers, which had a significant impact on the memory footprint.

6. Conclusions

In this work, we provide an introduction to embedded Rust and asynchronous programming in Rust. We discuss scheduling mechanisms, IPC, application isolation and memory protection, hardware interaction, and networking, and compare the design and implementation of these features in Tock, Hubris, RTIC, and Embassy. This comparison shows that each OS or framework has its own strengths and weaknesses. Tock is a full-fledged OS with support for networking and a wide range of microcontrollers. Hubris is a new OS that is still in development, but has a unique approach to application isolation. RTIC is a framework that is optimized for real-time systems, with a small memory footprint. Embassy is a framework that is optimized for asynchronous programming, with a slightly higher memory footprint compared to RTIC, but with a more flexible, asynchronous-capable HAL. We also provide a performance evaluation of Tock, RTIC, and Embassy, based on their scheduling latency and memory usage. The results show that RTIC has the lowest scheduling latency and memory footprint, followed by Embassy. Tock has the highest scheduling latency and memory footprint, as it is a full-fledged OS.

As future work, these Rust-based OSs and frameworks can be further evaluated on other aspects, such as energy consumption, scalability, or performance with more complex applications. They could also be compared to other OSs and frameworks, such as RIOT-OS, Zephyr, and Contiki-NG, written in other programming languages. Further studies could also explore their security features, ease of integration with hardware, and long-term maintenance requirements.

Author Contributions: Conceptualization, T.V. and A.B.; data curation, T.V.; funding acquisition, K.S. and A.B.; investigation, T.V.; project administration, K.S. and A.B.; software, T.V.; supervision, R.D.S., K.S., and A.B.; validation, R.D.S. and D.D.; visualization, T.V.; writing—original draft, T.V.; writing—review and editing, R.D.S., D.D., K.S., and A.B. All authors have read and agreed to the published version of the manuscript.

Funding: This work was in part supported by the Vlaio TETRA Project RustIEC (HBC.2021.0066).

Institutional Review Board Statement: Not applicable.

Informed Consent Statement: Not applicable.

Data Availability Statement: The data that support the findings of this study are available from the corresponding author, T.V., upon reasonable request.

Conflicts of Interest: The authors declare no conflicts of interest.

Abbreviations

The following abbreviations are used in this manuscript:

6LoWPAN	IPv6 over Low power Wireless Personal Area Networks
API	Application Programming Interface
CoAP	Constrained Application Protocol
GPIO	General Purpose Input/Output
HAL	Hardware Abstraction Layer
HIL	Hardware Interface Layer
IC	Integrated Circuit
ICMPv6	Internet Control Message Protocol version 6
IoT	Internet of Things
IPC	Inter-Process Communication
IPv4	Internet Protocol version 4
IPv6	Internet Protocol version 6
ISR	Interrupt Service Routine
MLFQ	Multi-Level Feedback Queue
MPU	Memory Protection Unit
MQTT	Message Queuing Telemetry Transport
OS	Operating System
PAC	Peripheral Access Crate
RAM	Random Access Memory
RTIC	Real-Time Interrupt-driven Concurrency
RTOS	Real-Time Operating System
SRP	Stack Resource Policy
SVD	System View Description
TCP	Transmission Control Protocol
UDP	User Datagram Protocol

References

1. Project Zero: About Project Zero. Available online: https://googleprojectzero.blogspot.com/p/about-project-zero.html (accessed on 6 August 2024).
2. 0day "In the Wild"—Google Spreadsheets. Available online: https://docs.google.com/spreadsheets/d/1lkNJ0uQwbeC1ZTRrxdtuPLCIl7mlUreoKfSIgajnSyY/edit#gid=0 (accessed on 23 May 2024).
3. MSRC-Security-Research/2019_01-BlueHatIL-Trends, Challenge, and Shifts in Software Vulnerability Mitigation.Pdf at Master · Microsoft/MSRC-Security-Research. Available online: https://github.com/microsoft/MSRC-Security-Research (accessed on 14 September 2022).
4. Viitanen, R. Evaluating Memory Models for Graph-like Data Structures in the Rust Programming Language: Performance and Usability. Ph.D. Thesis, Linköpings Universitet, Linköpings, Sweden, 2020.
5. Lankes, S.; Breitbart, J.; Pickartz, S. Exploring Rust for Unikernel Development. In Proceedings of the 10th Workshop on Programming Languages and Operating Systems, Huntsville, ON, Canada, 27–30 October 2019; pp. 8–15. [CrossRef]
6. Costanzo, M.; Rucci, E.; Naiouf, M.; De Giusti, A. Performance vs Programming Effort between Rust and C on Multicore Architectures: Case Study in N-Body. *arXiv* **2021**, arXiv:2107.11912.

7. Lin, Y.; Blackburn, S.M.; Hosking, A.L.; Norrish, M. Rust as a Language for High Performance GC Implementation. In Proceedings of the 2016 ACM SIGPLAN International Symposium on Memory Management, Santa Barbara, CA, USA, 14 June 2016; pp. 89–98. [CrossRef]
8. Vandervelden, T.; De Smet, R.; Steenhaut, K.; Braeken, A. SHA3 and Keccak Variants Computation Speeds on Constrained Devices. *Future Gener. Comput. Syst.* **2022**, *128*, 28–35. [CrossRef]
9. Fulton, K.R.; Chan, A.; Votipka, D.; Hicks, M.; Mazurek, M.L. Benefits and Drawbacks of Adopting a Secure Programming Language: Rust as a Case Study. In Proceedings of the Seventeenth Symposium on Usable Privacy and Security (SOUPS 2021), Berkey, CA, USA, 9–10 August 2021; pp. 597–616.
10. Pinho, A.; Couto, L.; Oliveira, J. Towards Rust for Critical Systems. In Proceedings of the 2019 IEEE International Symposium on Software Reliability Engineering Workshops (ISSREW), Berlin, Germany, 27–30 October 2019; pp. 19–24. [CrossRef]
11. Jung, R.; Jourdan, J.H.; Krebbers, R.; Dreyer, D. Safe Systems Programming in Rust. *Commun. ACM* **2021**, *64*, 144–152. [CrossRef]
12. Astrauskas, V.; Matheja, C.; Poli, F.; Müller, P.; Summers, A.J. How Do Programmers Use Unsafe Rust? *Proc. ACM Program. Lang.* **2020**, *4*, 136:1–136:27. [CrossRef]
13. Yu, Z.; Song, L.; Zhang, Y. Fearless Concurrency? Understanding Concurrent Programming Safety in Real-World Rust Software. *arXiv* **2019**, arXiv:1902.01906
14. Ayers, H.; Laufer, E.; Mure, P.; Park, J.; Rodelo, E.; Rossman, T.; Pronin, A.; Levis, P.; Van Why, J. Tighten Rust's Belt: Shrinking Embedded Rust Binaries. In Proceedings of the 23rd ACM SIGPLAN/SIGBED International Conference on Languages, Compilers, and Tools for Embedded Systems, San Diego, CA, USA, 14 June 2022; pp. 121–132. [CrossRef]
15. Uzlu, T.; Şaykol, E. On Utilizing Rust Programming Language for Internet of Things. In Proceedings of the 2017 9th International Conference on Computational Intelligence and Communication Networks (CICN), Girne, Northern Cyprus, 16–17 September 2017; pp. 93–96. [CrossRef]
16. Noseda, M.; Frei, F.; Rüst, A.; Künzli, S. Rust for Secure IoT Applications: Why C Is Getting Rusty. In Proceedings of the Embedded World Conference, Nuremberg, Germany, 21–23 June 2022; p. 10. [CrossRef]
17. Javed, F.; Afzal, M.K.; Sharif, M.; Kim, B.S. Internet of Things (IoT) Operating Systems Support, Networking Technologies, Applications, and Challenges: A Comparative Review. *IEEE Commun. Surv. Tutor.* **2018**, *20*, 2062–2100. [CrossRef]
18. Cherkaoui, A.; Merzouk, S.; Marzak, A.; Hain, M. Review on Embedded Systems and the Internet of Things: Comparative Study. In Proceedings of the 4th International Conference on Networking, Information Systems & Security, Kenitra, Morocco, 1–2 April 2021; pp. 1–7. [CrossRef]
19. Silva, M.; Cerdeira, D.; Pinto, S.; Gomes, T. Operating Systems for Internet of Things Low-End Devices: Analysis and Benchmarking. *IEEE Internet Things J.* **2019**, *6*, 10375–10383. [CrossRef]
20. Matsakis, N.D.; Klock II, F.S. The Rust Language. *ACM SIGAda Ada Lett.* **2014**, *34*, 103–104. [CrossRef]
21. Cortex-m-rt—Rust. Available online: https://docs.rs/cortex-m-rt/0.7.3/cortex_m_rt/index.html (accessed on 18 July 2023).
22. Mips-rt—Rust. Available online: https://docs.rs/mips-rt/0.3.5/mips_rt/index.html (accessed on 4 April 2024).
23. Riscv-rt—Rust. Available online: https://docs.rs/riscv-rt/0.12.2/riscv_rt/index.html (accessed on 4 April 2024).
24. Esp32c-rt—Rust. Available online: https://docs.rs/esp32c-rt/0.1.1/esp32c_rt/index.html (accessed on 4 April 2024).
25. Esp-Rs/Rust: Rust for the Xtensa Architecture. Built in Targets for the ESP32 and ESP8266. Available online: https://github.com/esp-rs/rust (accessed on 26 June 2024).
26. Rust-Embedded/Svd2rust. Available online: https://github.com/rust-embedded/svd2rust (accessed on 4 April 2024).
27. Smoltcp-rs/smoltcp. smoltcp. Available online: https://github.com/smoltcp-rs/smoltcp (accessed on 22 May 2024).
28. Levy, A.; Campbell, B.; Ghena, B.; Giffin, D.B.; Leonard, S.; Pannuto, P.; Dutta, P.; Levis, P. The Tock Embedded Operating System. In Proceedings of the 15th ACM Conference on Embedded Network Sensor Systems, New York, NY, USA, 6–8 November 2017; SenSys '17; pp. 1–2. [CrossRef]
29. Embassy. Available online: https://embassy.dev/ (accessed on 28 March 2024).
30. Tjäder, H. RTIC A Zero-Cost Abstraction for Memory Safe Concurrency. Ph.D. Thesis, Luleå University of Technology, Luleå, Sweden, 2021.
31. Hubris. Available online: https://hubris.oxide.computer/ (accessed on 28 March 2024).
32. Levy, A.; Campbell, B.; Ghena, B.; Giffin, D.B.; Pannuto, P.; Dutta, P.; Levis, P. Multiprogramming a 64kB Computer Safely and Efficiently. In Proceedings of the 26th Symposium on Operating Systems Principles, New York, NY, USA, 28 October 2017; SOSP'17; pp. 234–251. [CrossRef]
33. N7space/Aerugo: Safety-Critical Applications Oriented Real-Time Operating System Written in Rust. Available online: https://github.com/n7space/aerugo (accessed on 26 June 2024).
34. Bern RTOS · GitLab. 2024. Available online: https://gitlab.com/bern-rtos (accessed on 26 June 2024).
35. Drone OS. Available online: https://github.com/drone-os (accessed on 26 June 2024).
36. Cbiffle/Lilos: A Wee Async RTOS for Cortex-M. Available online: https://github.com/cbiffle/lilos (accessed on 26 June 2024).
37. Future-Proof-Iot/RIOT-rs: Rust & RIOT Combined for Ergonomic Embedded Development. Available online: https://github.com/future-proof-iot/RIOT-rs (accessed on 3 May 2024).
38. Google/Wasefire: Secure Firmware Framework Focusing on Developer Experience. Available online: https://github.com/google/wasefire (accessed on 26 June 2024).

39. Baker, T. A Stack-Based Resource Allocation Policy for Realtime Processes. In Proceedings of the 11th Real-Time Systems Symposium, Lake Buena Vista, FL, USA, 5–7 December 1990; pp. 191–200. [CrossRef]
40. ARMv7-M Architecture Reference Manual. Available online: https://developer.arm.com/documentation/ddi0403/d/System-Level-Architecture/System-Level-Programmers--Model/Registers/The-special-purpose-mask-registers (accessed on 3 May 2024).
41. Tracking Issue for Coroutine Memory Usage · Issue #69826 · Rust-Lang/Rust. Available online: https://github.com/rust-lang/rust/issues/69826 (accessed on 31 July 2024).

sensors

MDPI

Article

A Novel Medium Access Policy Based on Reinforcement Learning in Energy-Harvesting Underwater Sensor Networks

Çiğdem Eriş [1,*], Ömer Melih Gül [1,2] and Pınar Sarısaray Bölük [3,4]

1 Department of Computer Engineering, Bahcesehir University, Istanbul 34353, Turkey
2 Informatics Institute, Istanbul Technical University, Istanbul 34467, Turkey; omgul@itu.edu.tr
3 Department of Artificial Intelligence and Data Engineering, Istanbul University, Istanbul 34134, Turkey; pinar.boluk@istanbul.edu.tr
4 Department of Software Engineering, Bahcesehir University, Istanbul 34353, Turkey
* Correspondence: cigdem.eris@bahcesehir.edu.tr

Abstract: Underwater acoustic sensor networks (UASNs) are fundamental assets to enable discovery and utilization of sub-sea environments and have attracted both academia and industry to execute long-term underwater missions. Given the heightened significance of battery dependency in underwater wireless sensor networks, our objective is to maximize the amount of harvested energy underwater by adopting the TDMA time slot scheduling approach to prolong the operational lifetime of the sensors. In this study, we considered the spatial uncertainty of underwater ambient resources to improve the utilization of available energy and examine a stochastic model for piezoelectric energy harvesting. Considering a realistic channel and environment condition, a novel multi-agent reinforcement learning algorithm is proposed. Nodes observe and learn from their choice of transmission slots based on the available energy in the underwater medium and autonomously adapt their communication slots to their energy harvesting conditions instead of relying on the cluster head. In the numerical results, we present the impact of piezoelectric energy harvesting and harvesting awareness on three lifetime metrics. We observe that energy harvesting contributes to 4% improvement in first node dead (FND), 14% improvement in half node dead (HND), and 22% improvement in last node dead (LND). Additionally, the harvesting-aware TDMA-RL method further increases HND by 17% and LND by 38%. Our results show that the proposed method improves in-cluster communication time interval utilization and outperforms traditional time slot allocation methods in terms of throughput and energy harvesting efficiency.

Keywords: underwater acoustic sensor networks; reinforcement learning (RL); energy harvesting; lifetime

1. Introduction

Technological advances in wireless sensor networks and seamless integration with diverse technologies have led to the proliferation of underwater wireless sensor networks and their application areas. Submarine missions are increasingly utilizing underwater sensor gear [1]. Numerous vital applications, such as early warning systems, search and rescue missions, and ecosystem monitoring, can be carried out by these devices. With the collection and analysis of data in aquatic environments, sensors are crucial assets for intelligent systems that enable autonomous decision-making and data analysis. To fully realize the potential of the underwater realm, research focuses on addressing the particular limitations of the underwater medium to enable sustainable data collection in such applications. Underwater sensor nodes primarily employ acoustic communication technology to transmit data over long distances across water. However, acoustic waves have high bit-error rates; therefore, sensors need large transmission powers to avoid packet loss [2]. Considering sensor nodes are typically deployed in sub-sea zones and mostly run on batteries, energy management is crucial for building underwater sensor networks due to maintenance, and human intervention is not practical.

As energy efficiency has been the main focus of underwater communication in the past decade, there have been considerable improvements in this research field to prolong network lifetime by suggesting MAC and routing protocols to improve the utilization of limited energy resources of acoustic sensor nodes to cope with the high energy demand of underwater wireless mediums. The primary reason for energy depletion in UASNs is environmental factors such as acoustic waves. The underwater environment is particularly prone to noise from various sources, such as shipping activities, wind, and aquatic life. Consequently, this leads to a low signal-to-noise ratio (SNR), resulting in a high bit error rate (BER). Since acoustic communication is a dominant technology underwater, the high energy demand of acoustic links is usually decreased by clustering methods. On the other hand, autonomous underwater vehicles (AUVs) are common application assets to gather information collected by clusters in underwater applications.

The use of autonomous robots for data collection is another interesting viewpoint in the literature, and it has been thoroughly investigated in terrestrial wireless sensor networks. By minimizing the energy consumption of cluster heads and UAV robots, several research projects suggested mobile sinks for data gathering from clustered networks [3–6]. In the study [7], authors explore data collection in a single-hop wireless sensor network, employing a myopic policy based on a Round Robin structure. Findings reveal the suboptimality of this approach for various energy harvesting processes, emphasizing limitations while achieving optimality in specific instances. Yet, in comparison to terrestrial wireless sensors, the underwater system has higher financial costs, even though the assistance of autonomous robots lowers the energy cost of sensor equipment.

To maximize UASN lifetime, several studies in the literature focus on improving network clustering and cluster head selection methods [8–10]. Furthermore, recent studies present that harvesting ambient energy sources is a promising method to improve the life cycle of underwater sensors [11–14]. Recent studies [15,16] have demonstrated that UASN applications must optimize energy management in routing by using ambient energy to provide sustainable data collection from underwater sensor nodes. The main obstacle to optimizing energy management in submerged communication channels is the constraints of sensing apparatus and harvesting machinery.

In our previous study [17], we proposed a cluster head selection method for energy-aware routing problems in UASNs and investigated how expected available energy affects cluster head selection while accounting for the stochastic energy harvesting techniques of individual sensors. We tackle the same problem and propose a novel reinforcement learning-based algorithm for determining cluster heads (CHs), which involves sensor nodes' positions and remaining energy in addition to estimated harvested energy [18]. Numerical results validate that our introduced approach significantly increases harvested energy and, hence, extends the network's operational lifetime considerably, proving that energy harvesting awareness improves the operational lifetime of underwater sensors.

In this study, we introduce a time slot scheduling policy and improve the medium access control (MAC) protocol designed specifically for energy harvesting underwater acoustic sensor networks (EH-UASNs). The main goal of this policy is to optimize the network's lifespan while enhancing throughput. We utilize a clustered topology, leveraging its duty cycling and data aggregation nature, to enhance the efficiency of network energy utilization. We investigate the time division multiple access (TDMA) scheme for intra-cluster communication. TDMA optimizes energy usage by enabling inactive nodes to transition into sleep or idle modes until their allocated time slot for communication arrives. Our main goal is to enhance the efficiency of energy harvesting within clusters of the network by leveraging the allocation of time slots. We introduce a novel cooperative multi-agent reinforcement learning algorithm to schedule time slots of the TDMA MAC protocol for EH-UASNs to maximize harvested energy and enhance throughput through adaptive time slot allocation in intra-cluster nodes.

Our main contributions can be listed as follows:

- We propose a novel method for TDMA time slot allocation where nodes independently learn from their ambient energy resources and harvesting opportunities in order to autonomously decide their communication slots in their cluster. In our method, we model the TDMA time slot allocation task as a multi-armed bandit problem on individual nodes. We combine multi-armed bandit problem with a cooperative and independent Q-learning algorithm to maximize harvested energy in the network and mitigate the continuous scheduling duty on the cluster heads.
- To analyze the efficiency of our proposed method in realistic channel conditions, we optimized the power consumption of the sensor node to maintain connectivity in clusters via optimal carrier frequency selection according to the channel parameters and distance to the receiver.

The remainder of this paper is organized as follows: Section 2 presents the related work. Section 3 gives the system model; then Section 4 presents the problem statement. Section 5 proposes our novel approach. Section 6 evaluates the performance of the proposed algorithms numerically. Section 7 further investigates the performance of our approach. Section 8 concludes our work; Section 9 gives future work.

2. Related Work

There is growing literature about medium-access strategies to improve energy efficiency in underwater wireless sensor networks. In wireless sensor networks, the aim of MAC protocols is to decrease latency in the network and focus on the management of high traffic, which is extensively studied [19]. These efforts can be categorized as contention-based and contention-free protocols. In contention-based protocols, all nodes can transmit data packets simultaneously without any predefined scheduling algorithm. In [20], a contention-based MAC protocol, TDTSPC-MAC, is developed for three-dimensional UASNs facing challenges such as long propagation time, high bit error rate, and limited bandwidth. The protocol integrates time synchronization, power control, clustering, layering, and sleep mechanisms. TDTSPC-MAC utilizes hierarchical division of three-dimensional space and a distributed clustering algorithm, combining time synchronization and power control strategies to prevent collisions and reduce energy consumption through monitoring and sleep mode. Yet, in scenarios involving extensive data transmission or a significant number of nodes, data packets become susceptible to collisions. Large transmission delays and limited transmission rates inherent in underwater sensor networks increase collision probability and cause low energy utilization. In [21], a delayed-reward ALOHA-Q protocol is designed for UASNs. By leveraging Q-learning, DR-ALOHA-Q autonomously determines optimal time slots and offsets for data transmissions to improve channel utilization in the presence of large propagation delays. Contention-based methods require active listening and short control packet exchanges in order to mitigate long idle waiting times and improve overall energy consumption and transmission delay in UASNs. In [22], challenges in underwater sensor networks related to high latency, low bandwidth, and high bit error rate in acoustic communication are investigated. It highlights the limitations of contention-based medium access control (MAC) protocols in UASNs and proposes a novel contention-free MAC protocol called DL-MAC. The DL-MAC protocol addresses underwater MAC challenges through depth-based layering, a distributed clustering algorithm, and TDMA-based scheduling, demonstrating superior performance in terms of throughput, packet delivery ratio, energy consumption, and packet loss.

On the other hand, contention-free MAC protocols can easily address the well-known hidden node problem without extra control packet overhead and interference of neighboring nodes by utilizing scheduling nodes to distinct time slots to perform transmissions. A well-known contention-free MAC protocol, TDMA, attracted researchers, while other contention-free protocols, such as FDMA, suffer from limited available bandwidth, and CDMA faces challenges due to the near-far problem [23]. Hence, TDMA-based MAC protocols have been the main focus for long-term surveillance applications in the literature.

Numerous TDMA-based medium access methods are proposed [24–26] to leverage the benefits of simplicity, fairness, and energy efficiency by mitigating issues such as collisions, idle listening, and transmission over-hearing. However, TDMA-based MAC protocols exhibit certain drawbacks, such as suboptimal channel utilization, challenges in dynamic scalability, and the need for time synchronization. Wang et al. [27] proposed an online scheduling algorithm to calculate the optimal action, namely, the decision of transmitting the packet or holding it back in the packet queue in each time slot, with the aim of decreasing energy consumption in packet transmission. In this work, a channel state prediction algorithm is employed in order to determine the optimal action. Aiming to minimize energy consumption and considering the channel conditions in transmissions, a transmission strategy is proposed in [28]. Ref. [29] suggested channel-aware transmission scheduling, considering the duration of each slot and channel conditions and adjusting the amount of data to be transmitted.

In [30], a deep reinforcement learning (DRL) algorithm is introduced, delayed-reward deep Q-network (DR-DQN), to improve throughput degradation due to long propagation delays in underwater acoustic networks (UANs). Delayed-reward DRL multiple access (DR-DLMA) is proposed, aiming for an optimal channel access strategy that maximizes network throughput by efficiently utilizing available time slots resulting from long propagation delays. In [31], authors suggest prediction of the channel state by capturing temporal and frequency correlations in a one-dimensional convolutional neural network (CNN). In [32] a time slot allocation scheme for clustered underwater acoustic sensor networks, utilizing physical layer information to minimize energy consumption caused by unnecessary retransmissions. This enhancement aims to extend network lifetime and improve throughput. To streamline the process and reduce overhead and computational complexity. In their two-phase approach, first each member node autonomously determines the number of required time slots for the next intra-cluster cycle by solving a Markov decision process (MDP). Second, the cluster head optimizes scheduling decisions based on channel quality and an urgency factor.

Despite ongoing research efforts, existing studies mainly focus on the improvement of throughput and energy utilization, considering only the channel state and fairness. On the other hand, the impact of energy harvesting in underwater medium has proven its importance in the design of communication protocols by extending the operational lifetime of underwater sensor devices considerably [14]. A noteworthy study conducted by Ge, Y. et al. [16], focused on the improvement of throughput and energy harvesting for solar-powered and clustered WSNs. This work proposes a multi-agent reinforcement learning algorithm to maintain nodes in an energy-neutral state by balancing the consumed and harvested energy of nodes. Yet, this study focuses on the WSNs, their peculiar characteristics underwater, and the amount of available ambient energy that needs to be taken into account for UASNs. A decentralized reinforcement learning approach for random access is proposed to improve the throughput of the network, considering energy harvesting for sustainable data collection from EH-UASNs [15]. In this work, a multi-agent cooperative learning algorithm is used in the adaptive choice of contention window size to optimize throughput while maintaining fairness in the network. However, the authors focused on the throughput and the reward function, considering only the fairness and throughput of the network. Increasing energy harvesting utilization is not investigated in this study.

When considering clustered UASNs and TDMA-based protocols, it is imperative to allocate resources effectively to ensure reliable and efficient operation. Therefore, time slot allocation methods for underwater sensor networks need to be robust and accurate, as this greatly affects communication efficiency. Extensive research has been conducted on medium-access strategies aimed at enhancing energy efficiency in UASNs. Notable focus has been placed on reducing network latency, managing traffic, and minimizing energy consumption through various mechanisms such as time synchronization, power control, and sleep modes. However, these studies focus on optimizing energy efficiency rather than maximizing energy harvested from the environment. In the literature, a significant gap persists regarding MAC protocols specifically tailored to optimize and maximize energy harvesting in UASNs, accounting for the distinctive challenges posed by underwater environments. To the best of our knowledge, existing literature on MAC protocols in UASNs has mainly concentrated on enhancing network efficiency and optimizing energy usage; no prior study was specifically aimed at optimizing energy harvesting through channel access strategies. Our method combines multi-armed bandits with cooperative, independent Q-Learning and proposes a decentralized and robust solution that adapts to dynamic environments with minimal communication overhead.

3. System Model

Our system comprises 100 acoustic sensor nodes anchored to the multi-level depths across the seabed and designed to be used for long-term underwater monitoring applications. Sensor measurements such as pressure, water salinity, and temperature are relayed to a gateway (sonobuoy) on the sea surface. Nodes are able to maintain a connection to the gateway via one-hop. However, due to excessive energy depletion in data transmission over long distances, we considered a clustered network and performed a data collection task via elected cluster heads. We assume interference-free communication in inter-clusters with the use of different carriers or orthogonal spreading codes. All nodes in the network have energy harvesting equipment, and nodes perform energy harvesting only in their idle times, assuming independently and identically distributed (i.i.d.) harvesting states.

3.1. Network Model

We model the three-dimensional non-uniform distribution of 100 acoustic sensors ($N_{node} = 100$) randomly deployed in 250 m × 250 m × 250 m. There is one surface sink on the sea surface, at the top of the network. Nodes are fixed to the ocean floor, and we presume that sensor locations will not change over time. A sample 4-clustered 3D network topology consisting of 100 underwater sensor nodes is shown in Figure 1. Cluster members are connected to their cluster heads via single hop.

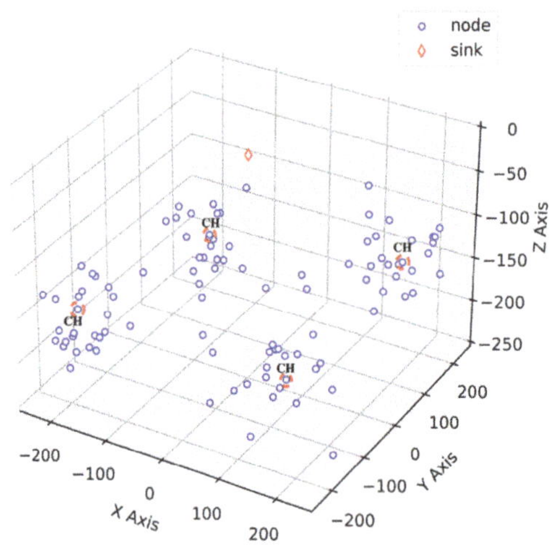

Figure 1. 3D Sample network topology showing gateway and sub-sea node placements.

Data aggregation and the transfer of aggregated data to the gateway are handled by cluster heads. There are several rounds to complete this operation. A frame consists of one packet of L bits transmitted by each node, and a round is divided into many successive frames. Keep in mind that nodes use energy for data transmission, reception, and aggregation. The length of time that a packet is transmitted and received is shown by

$\tau_{tx} = L/R$, where R is the sensor nodes' bit rate. Moreover, all nodes harvest energy only in their idle periods.

In our system, the network is divided into 4 regions by the k-means clustering method. The surface gateway divides the network into k clusters by computing the elbow method and initializing clusters [18]. Each node in the network learns their clusters from the broadcast message of the gateway station. As the next step, each node determines whether to become the cluster head for the current round. With prior knowledge of members in its cluster, cluster heads assign a unique time slot for each node in the cluster. Cluster members send their data to the cluster head in their programmed time slots to avoid collisions. After data transmission, each node becomes idle and harvests ambient energy until the next frame of data collection.

Given that underwater channels have limited capacity and high propagation delay, TDMA-based medium access protocols are widely used by cluster-based data collection [33]. These protocols have been chosen over collision avoidance-based protocols due to their poor performance in underwater acoustic networks [34]. Furthermore, time slot allocation has the potential to reduce energy usage by preventing contention and collisions among packets without extra overhead for channel reservation that requires short control packets.

3.2. Physical Layer Model

Attenuation and absorption have a significant impact on acoustic waves over long distances. To determine transmission power in acoustic modems, an underwater propagation model is presented. Depending on the location of the destination node, the source node modifies its power. Sonar equations and the propagation of underwater acoustic waves are defined in [35], and the acoustic intensity of the transmitted signal is determined as [36].

$$SL(d,f)_{ij} = A(d,f)_{ij} + N(f) + \gamma(d)_{dB} + DI \tag{1}$$

where $SL(d,f)_{ij}$ represents the sound intensity magnitude emitted by node-i at a distance d (in meters) in relation to the acoustic pressure of sound (dB ref μ Pa) and is calculated using the acoustic signal frequency f (in kHz). Path loss of acoustic waves at frequency f is represented by $A(d,f)_{ij}$, which increases with node distance d and is quantified as dB in [37]

$$A(d,f)_{ij} = 10\kappa \log_{10}(d_{ij}) + \alpha(f) \times d_{ij} \times 10^{-3} \tag{2}$$

where κ denotes the spreading factor; the absorption coefficient is expressed as $\alpha(f)$ given as dB/km in Equation (3) [38]

$$\alpha(f) = \frac{0.11f^2}{1+f^2} + \frac{44f^2}{4100} + f^2 + 2.75 \times 10^{-4} f^2 + 0.003 \tag{3}$$

The ambient noise level is computed in dB ref μ Pa accounting for the cumulative noise levels induced by water turbulence (i.e., $N_t(f)$), surface ships (i.e., $N_s(f)$), thermal activities (i.e., $N_{th}(f)$), and breaking waves (i.e., $N_w(f)$) defined in [37].

$$N(f) = N_t(f) + N_s(f) + N_{th}(f) + N_w(f) \tag{4}$$

The bit error rate (BER) is defined for 16-QAM modulation with orthogonal frequency division multiplexing (OFDM) encoding in Equation (5). The signal-to-noise ratio (SNR) can be calculated as follows in order to maintain a BER on a link (i.e., 10^{-9}) [34]

$$p_{ij}^{b} = \frac{3}{8} erfc\left(\sqrt{\frac{4}{10}\frac{B_N}{R}\gamma(d)_{ij}}\right) \tag{5}$$

where B_N is noise bandwidth (in Hz), $\gamma(d)_{ij}$ is SNR in linear form, and R is data rate in bps. The intensity level of sound (I_{ij}^{tx}) at a distance d is used to calculate the electrical power needed for transmission [34]

$$p_{ij}^{tx} = I_{ij}^{tx} \times 2\pi \times 1m \times h_i \tag{6}$$

where h_i represents the sea depth of node-i in meters. The source level ($SL(d,f)_{ij}$) is used to calculate the intensity of the acoustic signal (I_{ij}^{tx}) [34].

$$I_{ij}^{tx} = 10^{\frac{SL(d,f)_{ij}}{10}} \times I_0 \tag{7}$$

I_0 is the reference intensity at 1 m defined as 0.67×10^{-18} (Watts/m^2) [34]. To satisfy the predetermined BER and SNR threshold, the required transmission power is calculated with respect to the distance between the source and destination. Given electrical transmission power (p_{ij}^{tx}), the total energy consumption of the node transmitting a single data packet is calculated

$$E_{ij}^{t} = p_{ij}^{tx} \times \tau_{tx} \tag{8}$$

where τ_{tx} is duration of single packet transmission determined as $\tau_{tx} = L/R$.

3.3. Stochastic Model of Piezoelectric Energy Harvesting

Piezoelectric harvesters are triggered by the change of energy in flowing water. This harvester makes use of the flow's turbulence, which forms vortexes with varying rotational velocities and opposing directions. The underwater environment is characterized by high levels of variability and uncertainty. Sensor nodes are distributed across various depths, encountering a range of environmental factors that cause variations in the produced electrical energy. The pressure gap in clockwise and counter-clockwise directions is calculated using the density (ρ) and velocity of the flow as (v_f) [11]

$$\varrho_{cw} = \frac{\rho}{2} v_f^2 \tag{9}$$

$$\varrho_{ccw} = -\frac{3}{2} \rho v_f^2 \tag{10}$$

The amount of electrical power produced by a piezoelectric harvester varies depending on the pressure gap, piezo-material, and cantilever properties. The piezoelectric harvester's generated electrical energy (W_{el_cw} and W_{el_ccw}) in both clockwise and counter-clockwise directions is calculated [11]

$$W_{el} = \frac{1}{128} \varrho^2 \frac{{d_{31}^{p}}^2}{\varepsilon_0 \varepsilon_r} \frac{BL^5}{T_{pzt}^3} \tag{11}$$

where ${d_{31}^{p}}^2$, ε_0, and ε_r indicate the piezoelectric constant, absolute permittivity, and relative permittivity of the piezo-material, respectively. B, $L = 2.1D$, and T_{pzt} indicate the cantilever width, length, and thickness respectively.

As the flow velocity changes, we use the Poisson distribution to model the turbulence of the flow patterns. The mean velocity of the flow is observed in multi-level depths of the Bosphorus strait [39]. The vortex frequency at a time t, f_v, varies with respect to the velocity of the flow (v_f), bluff size (D), and Strouhal Number (S_t) is determined as [11]

$$f_v(t) = \frac{S_t \times v_f(t)}{D} \tag{12}$$

Given Poisson events, the harvested energy of a node i is calculated for $t = 0, \ldots, T$

$$E_i^h(T) = \int_{t=1}^{T} 2f_v(t)(W_{el\_cw}(t) + W_{el\_ccw}(t))dt \tag{13}$$

4. Problem Definition

As with TDMA-based and round-robin methods in clustered sensor networks, each transmission round is divided into frames, f. In each frame, cluster members send a fixed-length (L) data packet to their cluster head. We consider a data backlogging system where nodes capture measurements for long-term monitoring applications and always have data to transmit when it is their turn. In long-term monitoring applications, we consider a clustered network, assuming bi-directional communication in cluster heads to operate control signals and data aggregation. Additionally, to evaluate energy efficiency in these applications, low latency and high reliability are considered secondary concerns. This approach allows for the sustainability of the network over long periods, prioritizing energy efficiency over quality of service (QoS) and ensuring data integrity at the cluster head level. All nodes have the same data rate and are allowed to send the same number of packets in each frame. We use transmission power control (TPC) so that each transmission is held with a transmission power of nodes to satisfy a predetermined SNR for successful packet reception [34].

We consider a network of non-uniformly dispersed 100 nodes in varied depths underwater. Nodes maintain channel access in TDMA fashion, communicating with cluster heads over their scheduled time slots per frame. Cluster heads determine the time intervals and notify cluster members of their time slots for data transmission.

We denote the set of N acoustic sensor nodes by $S = \{s_1, s_2, \ldots, s_N\}$. We assume stochastic energy harvesting processes modeled by Poisson distribution at each node.

The remaining energy and the amount of harvested energy of a sensor node s_i in a time slot t denoted as $E_i(t)$ and $E_i^h(t)$, respectively. $E_i^h(TS)$ represents total harvested energy per frame. Considering frames consist of TS many transmission slots, the same as the number of nodes in clusters, the transmission slot set is represented as $TS = \{t_1, t_2, \ldots, t_N\}$, the total amount of harvested energy in cluster within time steps from 1 to TS in frame, under a policy π where t_{tx_i} is the designated time slot index of sensor i, $\mathbf{1}_{\{t_{tx_i}\}} \in \{0,1\}$ is the indicator function, and harvested energy at time slot t_m can be written as $E_i^h(t_m) = E_{i(t_{m-1})}^h \mathbf{1}_{\{t_{tx_i}\}}$. Overall harvested energy under a policy is determined as

$$V_i^\pi(TS) = \sum_{i=1}^{N} V_i^\pi(TS) = \sum_{i=1}^{N} \sum_{t=1}^{TS} E_i^h(t) \tag{14}$$

where $V_i^\pi(TS)$ is the sum of harvested energy under policy π in the cluster from starting time slot 1 through TS

$$E_i^h(TS) = \sum_{t=1}^{TS} \left[E_i^h(t) - \sum_{t=t_{tx_i}}^{t_{tx_i}+1} E_i^h(t) \mathbf{1}_{\{t_{tx_i} \in TS\}} \right] \tag{15}$$

Our objective is to maximize the total amount of harvested energy by each node over a finite time horizon,

$$\max_{\{\pi(t)\}_{t=1}^{T}} \frac{1}{T} \mathbb{E}[V_i^\pi(T)] \tag{16}$$

In clustered networks, optimal time slot scheduling algorithms employ cluster heads to schedule the transmission slots of each node. However, the cluster head may not select the optimal transmission slot without incurring communication overhead to gather knowledge on the energy harvesting states of nodes. Even when this information is provided to the cluster head, its timeliness might be compromised due to costs associated with complexity and computational delays due to slow convergence. Adopting a global optimal solution approach is not feasible. Therefore, instead of relying on centralized methods, delegating the transmission slot allocation task to cluster members not only delegates autonomy but also unveils the harnessing of ambient energy through adaptive transitions between transmission and idle energy harvesting modes. On the other hand, distributed reinforcement learning and game-theoretic algorithms offer independent learning with increased communication overhead and computational complexity. However, these methods compromise scalability at the expense of additional communication overhead and lack adaptability in dynamic environments. We model this problem as multi-armed bandits and combine the cooperative, independent Q-learning approach by leveraging shared rewards with environmental signals. In our model, slot selection with cooperation is inspired by Independent Q-Learning, aiming to balance individual optimization with cooperative behavior. Our proposed reward structure guides agents towards cooperation while maintaining independent learning at each node. Nodes can determine their slots to transmit packets, incorporating environmental conditions to determine the optimal timing for packet transmission or reverting to energy harvesting mode. In our model, we used the stochastic piezoelectric harvester, and the following assumptions were made:

- The statistical characteristic of all random quantities (flow velocity, voltage peaks, etc.) is known by observation and experiment [11,39].
- Harvested power in time slots is independent and identically distributed.
- As a well-known practice, we employ two different MAC methods on the low density (size of inter-cluster nodes) and high density (size of intra-cluster nodes) settings in clustered network topology. Namely, the TDMA MAC protocol for intra-cluster communication and the CSMA MAC protocol for determining the average power consumption of cluster heads in inter-cluster communication.

5. Transmission Slot Selection Policy with Reinforcement Learning

The underwater medium introduces uncertainties regarding water depth and environmental conditions, impacting the magnitude of underwater vibrations and movements and thereby influencing the harvested energy over time. Scheduling methods based on time slot allocation often overlook environmental factors that influence the availability of harvestable energy in the underwater environment when assigning time slots to nodes within the cluster. For this reason, nodes transmit within their scheduled time periods, regardless of available energy, resulting in a deficiency of the expected amount of harvested energy.

In our model, we adapt a multi-agent independent Q-learning algorithm with cooperation running multi-armed bandit problem on each node to autonomously select their time slot per data frame and learn from their past decision-making choices influenced by ambient conditions. In the single-agent, multi-armed bandit problem, the agent makes a choice among k different actions modeled as arms of a slot machine [40]. In this slot machine, each time after an action is performed, the agent receives a reward depending on a probability distribution in arms. The value of the actions is recorded as the mean of rewards over time steps. The agent maintains the estimated value of each action a in each time step, as $Q_t(a)$. The aim of the agent is to maximize the cumulative rewards over repeated actions in time steps.

In a single data frame, $R_t[a_i]$ denotes the reward received after action a_i is selected in time step t, and the estimated value of action a_i after $t-1$ is $Q_t[a_i]$ defined in Equation (17).

$$Q_t[a_i] = Q_{t-1}[a_i] + \frac{1}{t-1}(R_{t-1}[a_i] - Q_{t-1}[a_i]) \tag{17}$$

On the other hand, multi-agent systems (MASs) focus on developing algorithms that enable agents to learn adaptively and optimize their behavior in changing environments. Multi-agent reinforcement learning (MARL) aims to educate multiple agents simultaneously within a common environment by employing reinforcement learning (RL) techniques. In a fully cooperative setting, agents work together toward a shared goal, like assembling machines [41]. Figure 2 represents the multi-agent system, n distributed agents as underwater sensor nodes, cooperatively play the same multi-armed bandit game. Each agent has its own record of the Q table as time slot arrays. Agents choose actions independently, constructing a joint action array from received packets at the cluster head. We model k arms to represent time slots, the same as cluster size (the total number of cluster members). Note that each frame consists of k, i.e., TS many time slots. To find the best global combination of arms, agents wish to maximize a global return, or, in other words, minimize the overall regret. Associated with arms, mutually independent sequences of i.i.d.-valued rewards are modeled. Specifically, the reward is the overall energy gained in the rest of the arms except the arm selected for transmission. We run our model for a predetermined duration of a time slot. A detailed explanation of our method is given in Algorithm 1.

Algorithm 1 Distributed Multi-Agent Learning Algorithm for Transmission slot selection

Require: $0 \leqslant \gamma \leqslant 1, \alpha \in (0,1]$, small $\varepsilon > 0, n \geq 0$
  Initialize $Q_i[a] \leftarrow 0 \forall a \in A_i$ and $\forall i \in N$
  Update Q table $Q_i[a] \leftarrow E_i^h(t) \forall t \in TS$
  for each time slot **t** in frame (TS) **do**
    for each node **n** in Cluster^k **do**
      if $random(n) \geq \varepsilon$ **then**
        Choose exploitation
        Select maximizing action $a_i = \arg\max Q_i[:]$
      else
        Choose exploration
        Select a random action a_i
      end if
      node **n** selects action a_i forms the joint action $\mathbf{a} \leftarrow \langle a^1, \ldots, a^N \rangle$

      Receive local reward from environment $R_t^n(a_i)$
    end for
    Return global reward from environment $R_t^N(\mathbf{a})$
    $R_t(a_i) \leftarrow \beta R_t^N(\mathbf{a}) + (1-\beta) R_t^n(a_i)$
    Update $Q_t[a_i] \leftarrow \alpha * (R_t(a_i) + \gamma * Q_t[a_{max}] - Q_{t-1}[a_i])$
  end for

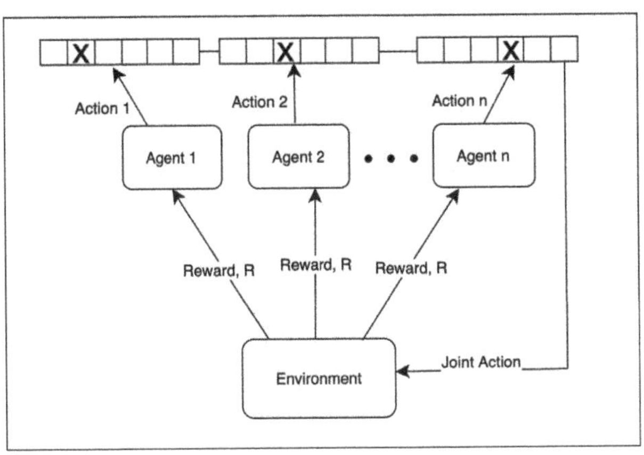

Figure 2. Training paradigm of multi-agent reinforcement learning system.

1. Agent: Every underwater sensor node in the network is an agent.

2. Action: The action is the selection of a transmission slot to maximize the harvested energy during the current frame of data transmission. A transmission slot can be selected depending on the interaction of each sensor with its environment, which affects the available energy. Transmission slots are designed as discrete time intervals. Action is the choice of the time interval for data transmission.
3. Reward: The reward calculation contains the weighted sum of two parts, namely the mutual reward and the independent local reward. The mutual reward of a cluster member after selecting a transmission slot is the total number of data packets that arrive in the cluster head R_{CH}, and it is broadcast to cluster members at the end of each frame. The weight coefficient β is fixed at 0.4. Reward function penalizes conflicted slot selection with the decreased amount of received packets. In case of conflict, nodes will wait for the next round to send their data packets. As a result, a reduction in the number of received data packets will lead to a decrease in the global reward, prompting nodes to adjust to their neighboring nodes' decisions. The total harvested energy of the cluster member serves as the agent's local reward, calculated as the overall energy gain excluding the selected time interval for transmitting a single data frame. In simpler terms, it represents the accumulated harvested energy within the cluster during the idle time of nodes in the previous frame.

$$Reward_n = \beta \sum_{t=1}^{TS} R_{CH} + (1-\beta) \sum_{t=1}^{TS} E^h_{s_n}(t) \tag{18}$$

We propose a multi-agent reinforcement learning algorithm for the optimal policy in the selection of time slots. Awareness of environmental conditions and observed energy fluctuations in ambient resources can be utilized in the determination of timing for data transmission; hence, this approach potentially alleviates the load on the cluster head. Furthermore, the selection of the best transmission slots for each node in the cluster is of mutual interest to all nodes in the system, thereby maximizing energy utilization in the cluster. With learning, each sensor can exploit the ambient resources to harvest energy to assure the maximal lifetime of the network. In our method, we consider round-based data collection. After one frame of data collection is complete, all nodes in the cluster take the same reward for the number of data packets received and a local reward for the sum of their harvested energy in the frame.

For intra-cluster communication, nodes perform data transmission in their time slots that are designated by their cluster head and switch back to an idle state until the next frame. However, instead of centralized control of medium access, nodes determine their slots by learning the environmental conditions of harvesting parameters.

In Figure 3, there is an example timeline showing our approach within a data frame in clustered networks. A round's duration is preset to guarantee that, on average, every node can function as both a cluster head and a non-cluster head several times over its lifetime [9]. CH^k represents the cluster head of kth cluster with a time slot allocation table and contains record of each packet reception from its cluster members. Here, cluster members, denoted as CM, decide their transmission slot for a packet by selecting one of Q available time slots in current frame. Nodes observe energy harvesting rates and schedule their transmission to a time slot with less available energy compared to other slots. For instance, CM_1 decides allocating time slot 2 according to its available energy. Depending on its value of Q table for time slot 2, the transmission decision is calculated based on its harvested energy in previous frame, with the lowest in time slot 2.

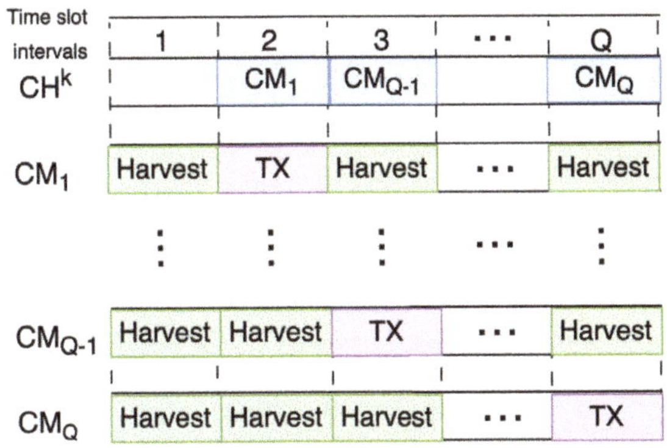

Figure 3. Example self scheduling of transmission slots representing high/low harvesting conditions.

6. Numerical Results

In this section, we compare the efficiency of our transmission slot scheduling method with the traditional TDMA approach. Additionally, the contribution of energy harvesting to the lifetime of a clustered underwater sensor network is also denoted in our Python simulations. We used the piezoelectric energy harvesting model [11] with the underwater communication channel model [34] and round-based data collection in clustered networks is adopted from [42]. We assume data is backlogged, i.e., nodes always have data to transmit to their cluster heads. Data packets are fixed in size, and transmission power is adjusted according to the channel conditions and distance of cluster members to their respective cluster heads. We present a performance comparison of 100 different network topology settings in this section. Simulation parameters are defined in Table 1.

In TDMA-based medium access methods, the transmission slot of each node in the cluster is organized by the cluster head, and cluster members are notified about their scheduled slots for communication. We investigate the performance of TDMA and the effect of piezoelectric energy harvesting on the clustered underwater sensor network. The TDMA-none curve indicates 100 nodes without energy harvesting equipment and using TDMA slot allocation for in-cluster communication. In TDMA-none, the curve cluster head schedules the transmission slots for cluster members. The TDMA-EH curve presents 100 nodes with piezoelectric harvesting equipment and the same transmission slot scheduling method as TDMA-none. We present the performance of our method in the TDMA-RL curve, the transmission slot scheduling with cooperative learning, and compare its efficiency to the traditional TDMA method.

Figure 4 depicts that our proposed method improves energy utilization as more data signals are received by the gateway station. In the TDMA-none curve, nodes perform transmissions in predetermined slots scheduled by cluster heads without energy harvesting equipment. The TDMA-EH curve incorporates energy harvesting. It is observed that nodes collect more energy as in consecutive rounds. Therefore, compared to the TDMA-none curve, the TDMA-EH curve sends 20% more data signals to the gateway. The TDMA-RL curve denotes the performance of our approach. As available energy changes during idle-tx states in frames, each node experiences varying levels of energy within its surrounding environment. As the selection of transmission slots adapts to the harvesting conditions, the potential for collecting more energy during each frame increases. It is observed that 15% more data signals can be received by gateway in the TDMA-RL curve compared to the TDMA-EH curve. However, in the traditional TDMA slot scheduling, nodes are unaware of their ambient conditions, and energy is harvested in pre-established slots during frames; compared to the TDMA-none curve, it is observed that ∼35% more data packets can be transmitted by exploiting the available energy underwater.

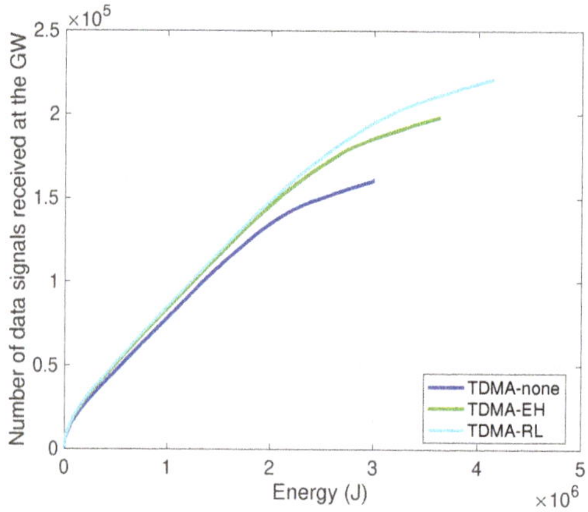

Figure 4. Number of data signals received at the gateway per energy.

Table 1. Simulation Parameters.

System & Network Parameters	Definition	Value
N_{node}	Number of nodes	100
M	Network Size (m^3)	$250 \times 250 \times 250$
h	Network Depth (m)	250
$S_{(x,y,z)}$	Sink Location	(125, 125, 0)
T_{round}	Round Duration (s)	100
Channel & Modem Parameters		
R	Data rate (kbps)	2
E_0	Initial Energy (kJ)	0.1
P_{rx}	Reception Power (W)	1.3
P_{idle}	Idle Power (mW)	2.5
f	Frequency (kHz)	25
p_{ij}^{b}	Bit error rate on link-(i,j)	10^{-10}
L	Packet size in frames (bits)	1024
κ	Spreading Factor	1.5
B_N	Noise Bandwidth (kHz)	1
E_{DA}	Data Aggregation Energy (nJ/bit/packet)	5
Stochastic Energy Harvesting Model Parameters		
L	Cantilever length (mm)	50
B	Cantilever width (mm)	3
ε_r	Relative permittivity	4000
ε_0	Absolute permittivity (F/m)	8.85×10^{-12}
T_{pzt}	Thickness (μm)	60
d_{31}^{p}	Piezoelectric constant (C/N)	300×10^{-12}
S_t	Strouhal number	0.2
v_f	Mean Flow Velocity (m/s)	0.65
ρ	Density of Ocean Water(kg/m^3)	1000
λ	Mean event rate	5

Figure 5 represents the performance of the previously mentioned methods in terms of throughput. It is observed that at the late stages of simulation in the TDMA-RL method, more data signals are received per unit of time compared to the TDMA-none and TDMA-EH methods due to better utilization of available energy. It is also observed that all curves are identical in the early stages of the simulation. In the forthcoming rounds, more energy is collected while nodes await idle and harvest energy until their communication slots in the cluster. Compared to the TDMA-none method, in TDMA-EH and TDMA-RL, as more nodes remain active in rounds, 21% and 37% more data packets can be relayed to the gateway, respectively. The TDMA-RL and TDMA-EH curves have the same characteristics, but they collect more energy in successive rounds. On the other hand, the TDMA-RL curve outperforms by selecting efficient slots to remain idle, observing the ambient available energy, selecting the most inefficient time slot in terms of available energy, and performing data transmission. Consequently, TDMA-RL captures more energy, whereas the TDMA-EH method neglects to exploit available energy by transmitting data during periods of high energy availability in time slots.

Figure 6 shows the number of available nodes over data signals received at the base station. As more energy is captured from environment, lifetime duration of nodes is improved and more data can be generated compared to TDMA-EH utilizing traditional TDMA approach. In TDMA slots, nodes communicate with their cluster heads without being aware of their ambient energy conditions. Therefore, less ambient energy can be collected. In the early phase of the simulation, it is observed that three methods have the same decrease rate in the number of alive nodes until 5% of nodes run out of energy and a few megabytes of data are received at the base station. It is observed that if energy harvesting (EH) is involved in the system, the amount of data packet reception increases by 23% regardless of the medium access method. It is clear that harvested energy significantly contributes to the battery of nodes in successive rounds; hence, nodes can perform more data transmission. The TDMA-RL curve improves the amount of data packets by 11% compared to the TDMA-EH method.

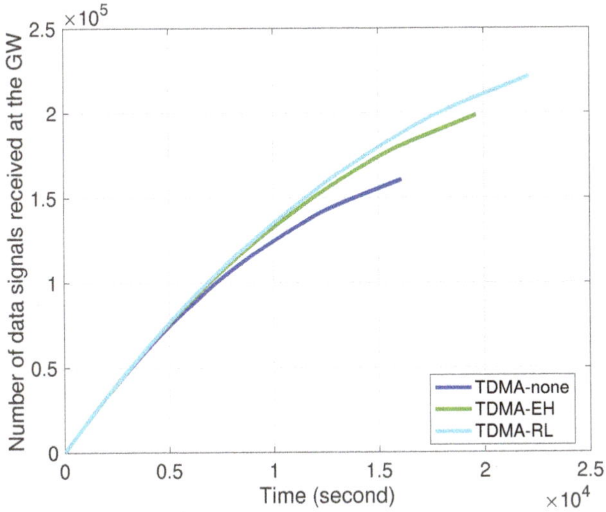

Figure 5. Number of data signals received at the gateway over time.

We present the comparison of total harvested energy in the system in Figure 7. The TDMA-Best curve represents the maximum total energy captured by all nodes in the system, assuming nodes know the least efficient transmission slots to harvest energy in advance. This curve serves as an upper bound for the total energy available in the environment. Since energy harvesting is not incorporated in the TDMA-none method, we compare the TDMA-EH and TDMA-RL methods with this upper bound of available energy. As depicted in the plot, TDMA-RL captures 96% of the available energy in the system, while the TDMA-EH curve reveals that the total amount of energy in the system can only utilize 56% of the available energy.

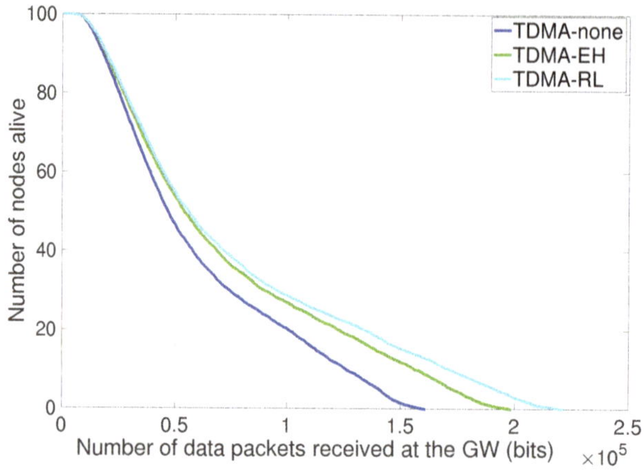

Figure 6. Number of alive nodes per data items received.

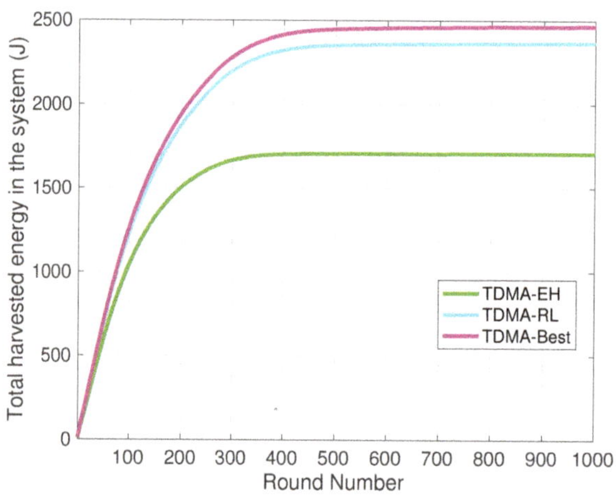

Figure 7. Total harvested energy in system in rounds.

Figures 8 and 9 depict the performance of cooperative-learning-based slot selection to the traditional TDMA protocol on a lifetime basis. Considering the rounds consist of multiple frames, the duration of each round varies depending on the number of alive nodes. Both figures acknowledge that lifetime is significantly improved in the case of cooperative selection of transmission slots in clusters. While energy harvesting improves the lifetime by adapting to the dynamic underwater environment and predicting the fluctuations in ambient energy, it is observed that transmission slots can be selected with the aim of maximizing the utilization of the available energy in the environment. Furthermore, individual transmission slot selection at each node minimizes energy waste from overhearing while also relaxing the need for strict synchronization. It is noted that in both figures, the curves for TDMA-Best and TDMA-RL exhibit marginal disparities, yet without significant alterations in the number of active nodes per unit time or across rounds. The network lifetime is defined as the duration from the initialization of the sensor network until the depletion of the last node's battery. To represent the numerical result of 100 simulation runs, the performance of each method with statistics of 100 simulation runs is depicted in Table 2. The results presented in Table 2 clearly illustrate the beneficial effect of TDMA-RL in increasing the number of active nodes over the course of rounds and enhancing the overall longevity of the network.

Note that due to the amount of harvested energy and the early steps of learning at the beginning of the rounds, the TDMA-EH, TDMA-RL, and TDMA-Best methods have a similar central tendency in FND. HND is improved 14% due to the amount of harvested energy that incorporates the traditional TDMA method. HND in TDMA-EH is improved by 2% with the TDMA-RL method. As more energy is collected towards the last stages of rounds, we observe that the efficiency of our method on LND increased by 25% and 40% in TDMA-EH and TDMA-RL, respectively.

Table 2. Network Lifetime over 100 run of simulations

FND	Min	Max	Median	Mean	Std
TDMA-none	12	46	25	25	6.5758
TDMA-EH	13	48	25	26	7.1873
TDMA-RL	13	48	25	25	7.0877
TDMA-Best	13	46	26	26	7.0437
HND					
TDMA-none	81	154	113	114	17
TDMA-EH	90	192	128	131	21.968
TDMA-RL	91	202	128	134	24.324
TDMA-Best	90	201	132	135	24.39
LND					
TDMA-none	222	1340	355	388	138.36
TDMA-EH	249	1500	442	475	168
TDMA-RL	286	1500	498	536	198.45
TDMA-Best	285	1500	510	542	205.73

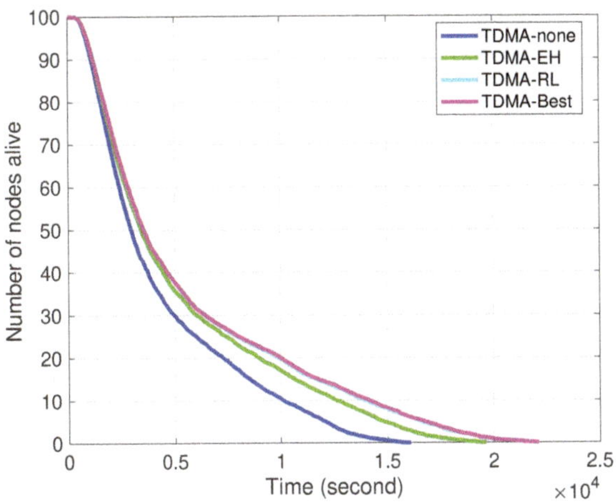

Figure 8. Number of alive nodes over simulation time.

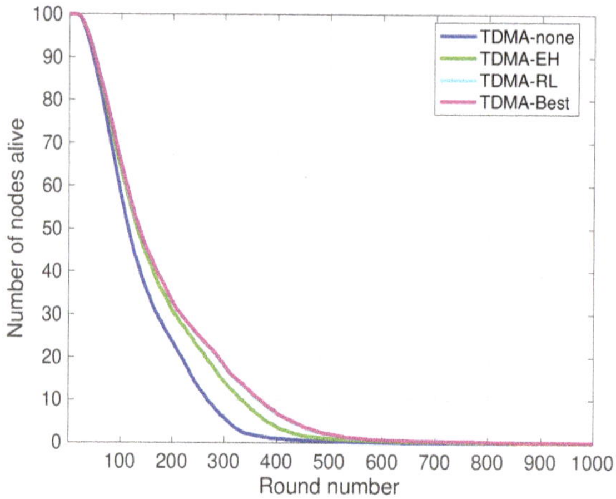

Figure 9. Number of alive nodes over simulation rounds.

7. Discussion

Underwater sensor networks encounter unique challenges, such as long propagation delays, limited bandwidth, and high attenuation, which can significantly decrease the performance of communication protocols. Therefore, traditional contention-free methods, specifically time division multiple access (TDMA), are commonly used in underwater sensor networks due to their simplicity and robustness in such demanding environments. Furthermore, clustering methods often rely on TDMA due to their efficiency in scheduling intra-cluster communication, minimizing collisions and energy consumption, which is the primary concern for the power-constrained nodes in underwater conditions. On the other hand, the dynamic nature of underwater environments causes significant variability in energy harvesting conditions. In this study, our primary objective is to augment the accumulated energy of underwater sensor nodes by dynamically selecting TDMA time slots. We specifically emphasized the integration of harvesting awareness into the transmission slot selection strategy. Our investigation revolves around assessing the impact of harvesting-adaptive slot scheduling in response to the varying levels of available energy underwater. Our results show that both TDMA-EH and TDMA-RL improve the network's initial robustness and longevity compared to the baseline TDMA method. The inclusion of energy harvesting in TDMA-EH extends the network's operational period, reflected in higher minimum and mean values for first node dead (FND). TDMA-RL further enhances performance by dynamically adapting time slots based on available energy, thus better sustaining network operations over time. However, TDMA-RL includes the added complexity of reinforcement learning, we would expect it to outperform the simpler TDMA-EH consistently. This similarity might indicate that the learning mechanism is not significant in the earliest phases of node operation compared to what is achieved by simple energy harvesting alone. One future investigation is a guided exploration strategy to quickly identify good actions.

In terms of half node dead (HND), TDMA-EH and TDMA-RL significantly outperform the baseline, indicating that they can maintain a larger portion of the network for longer periods. TDMA-RL, in particular, shows a slightly higher mean HND, demonstrating the advantages of adaptive scheduling. On the other hand, TDMA-RL shows a higher standard deviation in both HND (24.324) and LND (198.45) compared to TDMA-EH (21.968 and 168, respectively). This suggests greater variability in network performance, which might be due to the adaptive nature of the method leading to inconsistent outcomes across different simulation runs. While adaptive methods can optimize performance, it also shows that they can introduce variability. Q-learning, especially in the initial stages where the algorithm is still learning and exploring the environment. The last node dead (LND) results further confirm the superiority of these advanced methods, with TDMA-RL achieving the highest median and mean LND values, indicating its effectiveness in prolonging the overall network lifetime. The TDMA-Best method serves as an ideal benchmark, setting the highest performance targets and illustrating the maximum potential of the network with optimal time-slot assignments. This benchmark underscores the effectiveness of the TDMA-RL method, showing that adaptive learning strategies can approach optimal performance levels.

Overall, the study highlights the significant benefits of incorporating energy harvesting and adaptive scheduling into UASNs. TDMA-RL stands out for its ability to dynamically manage energy and time-slot allocation, leading to substantial improvements in network longevity and efficiency. The results suggest promising directions for future research, focusing on refining these methods and integrating advanced communication technologies to further enhance network performance and reliability.

8. Conclusions

The main issues that influence the design of underwater communication protocols are the battery life of underwater sensors and the dependability of low-rate acoustic communications. In this work, we used a stochastic model for piezoelectric energy harvesting and took into account the dynamic nature of underwater ambient resources to optimize the transmission schedule of the nodes. Our method considers spatio-temporal uncertainty in the available energy of the piezoelectric energy harvesting method. Our simulation results demonstrate that the proposed adaptive scheme, based on the decision of time slots to perform transmission, extends the network's lifespan. An approach, distributed cooperative multi-agent reinforcement learning is proposed, considering the realistic channel and environmental specifications. Nodes interact with the environment to learn energy harvesting opportunities and select their transmission times with an adaptive strategy. Our main focus is exploiting the available ambient energy while alleviating the load on the cluster head. Performance evaluations reveal that our proposed approach improves the lifetime of the network by 15%, while the incorporation of energy harvesting only contributes 10% to the lifetime. Our study aims to provide valuable insights for researchers investigating optimal time slot allocation for the sustainable operation of UASNs. Towards this aim, we show the contribution of energy harvesting to the traditional contention-free medium access methods.

9. Future Work

As part of our future work, the overhead of efficient information sharing and decentralized coordination mechanisms will be investigated while maintaining effective coordination among sensor nodes. A comparison of our harvesting-aware method in terms of throughput and energy utilization, thereby providing a comprehensive evaluation of our proposed approach, is planned for future work. Moreover, the efficiency and performance of our transmission slot selection strategy can be improved with advanced multi-agent reinforcement learning algorithms, such as proximal policy optimization (PPO) and deep Q-networks (DQN), and their complexity, will be investigated with a varied size of the network. Additionally, we intend to incorporate variations in channel state to offer a more realistic approach that accounts for the influence of energy harvesting. On the other hand, we plan to validate our proposed method in this study regarding accuracy and reliability to model real-world underwater sensor network scenarios. We plan to compare our simulation results with experimental data obtained from field deployments or test-bed environments, particularly under various environmental conditions and operational scenarios.

Underwater communication encounters significant delays, higher bit error rates, and limited bandwidth. As a result, it requires adaptive and robust reinforcement learning strategies for time slot allocation. In contrast, terrestrial wireless sensor networks benefit from higher speeds, lower BER, and greater bandwidth, enabling more aggressive and efficient slot allocation through learning algorithms. In another area of future research, we will conduct a comprehensive analysis of delay performance in the adaptive time slot allocation approach, particularly in dynamic underwater environments. This will involve detailed modeling and simulation of delays associated with different slot allocation strategies, as well as empirical validation through field experiments. Our goal is to understand the trade-offs between delay, energy harvesting efficiency, and network throughput to enhance the overall performance of underwater acoustic sensor networks.

Moreover, the rapid development of new communication techniques such as rate-splitting multiple access (RSMA) and non-orthogonal multiple access (NOMA) presents opportunities. Furthermore, hybrid approaches, combining the strengths of multiple methodologies, such as integrating TDMA with non-orthogonal multiple access (NOMA) techniques, are also promising. To date, these techniques have not been extensively investigated in underwater communication systems. As a future research direction, their potential applicability in underwater environments may be explored. By pursuing these research directions, we aim to contribute to the advancement of UASNs, enhancing their performance and efficiency through innovative communication techniques and more accurate modeling of environmental factors.

Author Contributions: Conceptualization, Ç.E. and Ö.M.G.; methodology, Ç.E. and Ö.M.G.; software, Ç.E.; validation, Ç.E., Ö.M.G. and P.S.B.; formal analysis, Ç.E. and Ö.M.G.; investigation, Ç.E. and Ö.M.G.; resources, C.E; data curation, Ç.E.; writing—original draft preparation, Ç.E. and Ö.M.G.; writing—review and editing, Ç.E. and Ö.M.G.; visualization, Ç.E. and Ö.M.G.; supervision, Ö.M.G. and P.S.B.; project administration, Ö.M.G. and P.S.B.; All authors have read and agreed to the published version of the manuscript.

Funding: This research received no external funding. The APC was funded by authors.

Institutional Review Board Statement: Not applicable.

Data Availability Statement: Data are contained within the article.

Conflicts of Interest: The authors declare no conflicts of interest.

Abbreviations

The following abbreviations are used in this manuscript:

UASN	Underwater Acoustic Sensor Networks
EH-UASN	Energy Harvesting Underwater Acoustic Sensor Networks
TDMA	Time-division Multiple Access
CDMA	Code Divison Multiple Access
FDMA	Frequency Division Multiple Access
CSMA	Carrier-sense Multiple Access
RL	Reinforcement Learning
MAB	Multi-arm Bandit
LEACH	Low-Energy Adaptive Clustering Hierarchy

References

1. Awan, K.M.; Shah, P.A.; Iqbal, K.; Gillani, S.; Ahmad, W.; Nam, Y. Underwater wireless sensor networks: A review of recent issues and challenges. *Wirel. Commun. Mob. Comput.* **2019**, *2019*, 6470359. [CrossRef]
2. Akyildiz, I.F.; Pompili, D.; Melodia, T. Underwater acoustic sensor networks: Research challenges. *Ad Hoc Netw.* **2005**, 3, 257–279. [CrossRef]
3. Gul, O.M.; Erkmen, A.M. Energy-Aware UAV-Driven Data Collection with Priority in Robotic Wireless Sensor Network. *IEEE Sens. J.* **2023**, *23*, 17667–17675. [CrossRef]
4. Gul, O.M.; Erkmen, A.M.; Kantarci, B. UAV-Driven sustainable and Quality-Aware data collection in robotic wireless sensor networks. *IEEE Internet Things J.* **2022**, *9*, 25150–25164. [CrossRef]
5. Gul, O.M.; Erkmen, A.M.; Kantarci, B. NTN-Aided Quality and Energy-Aware Data Collection in Time-Critical Robotic Wireless Sensor Networks. *IEEE Internet Things Mag.* **2024**, *7*, 114–120. [CrossRef]
6. Gul, O.M.; Erkmen, A.M. Energy-efficient cluster-based data collection by a UAV with a limited-capacity battery in robotic wireless sensor networks. *Sensors* **2020**, *20*, 5865. [CrossRef] [PubMed]
7. Gul, O.M.; Demirekler, M. Average throughput performance of myopic policy in energy harvesting wireless sensor networks. *Sensors* **2017**, *17*, 2206. [CrossRef]

8. Han, B.; Ran, F.; Li, J.; Yan, L.; Shen, H.; Li, A. A Novel Adaptive Cluster Based Routing Protocol for Energy-Harvesting Wireless Sensor Networks. *Sensors* **2022**, *22*, 1564. [CrossRef]
9. Heinzelman, W.B. Application-Specific Protocol Architectures for Wireless Networks. Ph.D. Dissertation, Massachusetts Institute of Technology, Cambridge, MA, USA, June 2000.
10. Zhu, J.; Chen, Y.; Sun, X.; Wu, J.; Liu, Z.; Xu, X. ECRKQ: Machine Learning-Based Energy-Efficient Clustering and Cooperative Routing for Mobile Underwater Acoustic Sensor Networks. *IEEE Access* **2021**, *9*, 70843–70855. [CrossRef]
11. Pobering, S.; Schwesinger, N. A Novel Hydropower Harvesting Device. In Proceedings of the 2004 International Conference on MEMS, NANO and Smart Systems (ICMENS04), Banff, AB, Canada, 25–27 August 2004; pp. 480–485.
12. McKenna, M.F.; Ross, D.; Wiggins, S.M.; Hildebrand, J.A. Underwater radiated noise from modern commercial ships. *J. Acoust. Soc. Am.* **2012**, *131*, 92–103. [CrossRef]
13. Erdem, H.E.; Gungor, V.C. Lifetime analysis of energy harvesting underwater wireless sensor nodes. In Proceedings of the 25th Signal Processing and Communications Applications Conference (SIU), Antalya, Turkey, 15–18 May 2017; pp. 1–4.
14. Erdem, H.E.; Yildiz, H.U.; Gungor, V.C. On the lifetime of compressive sensing based energy harvesting in underwater sensor networks. *IEEE Sens. J.* **2019**, *19*, 4680–4687. [CrossRef]
15. Han, M.; Duan, J.; Khairy, S.; Cai, L.X. Enabling sustainable underwater IoT networks with energy harvesting: A decentralized reinforcement learning approach. *IEEE Internet Things J.* **2020**, *7*, 9953–9964. [CrossRef]
16. Ge, Y.; Nan, Y.; Guo, X. Maximizing network throughput by cooperative reinforcement learning in clustered solar-powered wireless sensor networks. *Int. J. Distrib. Sens. Netw.* **2021**, *17*, 15501477211007411. [CrossRef]
17. Eris, C.; Gul, O.M.; Boluk, P.S. An Energy-Harvesting Aware Cluster Head Selection Policy in Underwater Acoustic Sensor Networks. In Proceedings of the 2023 International Balkan Conference on Communications and Networking (BalkanCom), Istanbul, Turkey, 5–8 June 2023; pp. 1–5.
18. Eris, C.; Gul, O.M.; Boluk, P.S. A Novel Reinforcement Learning Based Routing Algorithm for Energy Management in Networks. *J. Ind. Manag. Optim.* **2024**, *20*, 1–19. [CrossRef]
19. Gabale, V.; Raman, B.; Dutta, P.; Kalyanraman, S. A classification framework for scheduling algorithms in wireless mesh networks. *IEEE Commun. Surv. Tutor.* **2012**, *15*, 199–222. [CrossRef]
20. Chen, Y.; Jin, Z.; Xing, G.; Zeng, Q.; Chen, Y.; Zhou, Z.; Yang, Q. An Energy-Efficient MAC Protocol for Three-Dimensional Underwater Acoustic Sensor Networks with Time Synchronization and Power Control. *IEEE Access* **2023**, *11*, 20842–20860. [CrossRef]
21. Tomovic, S.; Radusinovic, I. DR-ALOHA-Q: A Q-Learning-Based Adaptive MAC Protocol for Underwater Acoustic Sensor Networks. *Sensors* **2023**, *23*, 4474. [CrossRef] [PubMed]
22. Alfouzan, F.A.; Shahrabi, A.; Ghoreyshi, S.M.; Boutaleb, T. An energy-conserving collision-free MAC protocol for underwater sensor networks. *IEEE Access* **2019**, *7*, 27155–27171. [CrossRef]
23. Pompili, D.; Melodia, T.; Akyildiz, I.F. A CDMA-based medium access control for underwater acoustic sensor networks. *IEEE Trans. Wirel. Commun.* **2009**, *8*, 1899–1909. [CrossRef]
24. Yongxin, Z.; Jianguo, H.; Jing, H. A TDMA MAC protocol for underwater acoustic sensor networks. In Proceedings of the IEEE Youth Conference on Information, Computing, and Telecommunication, Beijing, China, 20–21 September 2009; pp. 534–537.
25. Chen, Y.D.; Lien, C.Y.; Chuang, S.W.; Shih, K.P. DSSS: A TDMA-based MAC protocol with dynamic slot scheduling strategy for underwater acoustic sensor networks. In Proceedings of the OCEANS 2011 IEEE-Spain, Santander, Spain, 6–9 June 2011; pp. 1–6.
26. Han, G.; Wang, X.; Sun, N.; Liu, L. A collision-free MAC protocol based on quorum system for underwater acoustic sensor networks. In Proceedings of the 16th International Conference on Mobility, Sensing and Networking (MSN), Tokyo, Japan, 17–19 December 2020; pp. 671–676.
27. Wang, Z.; Wang, C.; Sun, W. Adaptive transmission scheduling in time-varying underwater acoustic channels. In Proceedings of the OCEANS 2015-MTS/IEEE, Washington, DC, USA, 19–22 October 2015; pp. 1–6.
28. Tomasi, B.; Preisig, J.C. Energy-efficient transmission strategies for delay-constrained traffic with limited feedback. *IEEE Trans. Wirel. Commun.* **2014**, *14*, 1369–1379. [CrossRef]
29. Lee, J.; Jindal, N. Energy-efficient scheduling of delay-constrained traffic over fading channels. *IEEE Trans. Wirel. Commun.* **2008**, *8*, 1866–1875. [CrossRef]
30. Ye, X.; Fu, L. Deep reinforcement learning based MAC protocol for underwater acoustic networks. In Proceedings of the 14th International Conference on Underwater Networks & Systems, Atlanta, GA, USA, 23–25 October 2019; pp. 1–5.
31. Liu, L.; Cai, L.; Ma, L.; Qiao, G. Channel state information prediction for adaptive underwater acoustic downlink OFDMA system: Deep neural networks based approach. *IEEE Trans. Veh. Technol.* **2021**, *70*, 9063–9076. [CrossRef]
32. Jagannath, J.; Saji, A.; Kulhandjian, H.; Sun, Y.; Demirors, E.; Melodia, T. A hybrid MAC protocol with channel-dependent optimized scheduling for clustered underwater acoustic sensor networks. In Proceedings of the 8th International Conference on Underwater Networks Systems, Kaohsiung, Taiwan, 11–13 November 2013; pp. 1–8.
33. Molins, M.; Stojanovic, M. Slotted FAMA: A MAC Protocol for Underwater Acoustic Networks. In Proceedings of the OCEANS 2006—Asia Pacific, Singapore, 16–19 May 2006.
34. Felemban, M.; Felemban, E. Energy-delay tradeoffs for underwater acoustic sensor networks. In Proceedings of the 1st International Black Sea Conference on Communications and Networking (BlackSeaCom), Batumi, Georgia, 3–5 July 2013; pp. 45–49.
35. Coates, R.F.W. *Underwater Acoustic Systems*; Halsted Pr: New York, NY, USA; Macmillan: Basingstoke, UK, 1989; pp. 92–93.

36. Urick, R.J. *Principles of Underwater Sound*, 2nd ed.; McGraw-Hill Book: New York, NY, USA, 1983.
37. Stefanov, A.; Stojanovic, M. Design and performance analysis of underwater acoustic networks. *IEEE J. Sel. Areas Commun.* **2011**, *29*, 2012–2021. [CrossRef]
38. Jornet, J.M.; Stojanovic, M.; Zorzi, M. On joint frequency and power allocation in a cross-layer protocol for underwater acoustic networks. *IEEE J. Ocean. Eng.* **2010**, *35*, 936–947. [CrossRef]
39. Jarosz, E.; Teague, W.J.; Book, J.W.; Besiktepe, S.T. On Flow Variability in the Bosphorus Strait. *J. Geophys. Res.* **2011**, *116*, 1–17. [CrossRef]
40. Sutton, R.S.; Barto, A.G. *Reinforcement Learning: An Introduction*, 2nd ed.; MIT Press: Cambridge, MA, USA, 2018.
41. Yuan, L.; Zhang, Z.; Li, L.; Guan, C.; Yu, Y. A Survey of Progress on Cooperative Multi-Agent Reinforcement Learning in Open Environment. *arXiv* **2023**, arXiv:2312.01058.
42. Heinzelman, W.B.; Chandrakasan, A.P.; Balakrishnan, H. An application-specific protocol architecture for wireless microsensor networks. *IEEE Trans. Wirel. Commun.* **2002**, *1*, 660–670. [CrossRef]

sensors

MDPI

Communication

Performance Analysis of CSMA/NP under Finite Population Environments

Ariadna I. Rodriguez-Gomez , Mario E. Rivero-Angeles , Izlian Y. Orea-Flores *, Gina Gallegos-García and Juan Carlos Chimal-Eguia

Centro de Investigación en Computación, Instituto Politécnico Nacional, Mexico City 07738, Mexico; arodriguezg2020@cic.ipn.mx (A.I.R.-G.); erivero@cic.ipn.mx (M.E.R.-A.); ggallegos@cic.ipn.mx (G.G.-G.); chimal@cic.ipn.mx (J.C.C.-E.)

* Correspondence: iorea@ipn.mx

Abstract: In this study, we analyze the CSMA Non-Persistent protocol with a finite number of nodes, providing more accurate results for applications like wireless sensor networks. The finite model addresses scenarios where the node count is moderate, capturing realistic system dynamics. Our analysis reveals a dependency on the node count, impacting system throughput. As the node count increases, throughput behavior aligns with Kleinrock's infinite model. We derive a complex closed-form throughput expression for a finite quantity of nodes in the system, solved numerically, and offer an approximate expression for specific conditions. These insights advance understanding of low-contention network performance, especially in scenarios where the infinite model becomes inadequate.

Keywords: access protocols; CSMA; finite population; throughput; WSNs

1. Introduction

In modern communication systems, we encounter many possible scenarios where the number of nodes is relatively low compared, for example, to conventional cellular systems in a macro cell where the infinite population assumption is very accurate. For example, wireless sensor networks (WSNs) are systems composed of devices distributed within a defined area based on specific application requirements. In these systems, devices must support wireless communication, computation, and sensing capabilities [1–3]. There are many possible environments where WSNs are deployed, and, in some cases, the number of nodes contending to transmit in the shared channel may be relatively low. This occurs when nodes are sufficiently separated from each other (outdoor surveillance, for instance) or when a hierarchical system is used, for example, in clustered-based WSNs. In clustered-based WSNs, although hundreds of nodes might be present, the clustering scheme effectively reduces the number of nodes contending in each cluster, thereby simplifying the management of transmissions and potentially improving network efficiency. In these systems, nodes transmit data to a central base station using media access control protocols, among them, the Carrier Sense Multiple Access (CSMA) protocol [4].

The CSMA-Non-Persistent protocol (CSMA-NP) has been extensively studied in the literature [4–8], with a primary focus on scenarios involving an infinite population. However, there may be many circumstances where this is not the case. For instance, in the previously mentioned WSNs or even in 5G cellular systems, where carrier frequencies are in the region of gigahertz, producing very narrow areas of coverage. Additionally, this can occur in Internet of Things applications where only a couple of nodes are present. Therefore, there is a pressing need to analyze the CSMA-NP protocol within the context of a finite population assumption.

The analysis of a finite population within a communication network warrants careful consideration. Therefore, several authors, such as [4–8], have delved into this subject, exploring various scenarios that consider finite populations or retransmissions. The methodologies employed to assess network performance vary. These include the utilization of Markov chains, as seen in the work of [6]. Additionally, Monte Carlo simulations are employed, as demonstrated by [7]. Another approach is the application of the Exponential Backoff Scheduling algorithm, as demonstrated by [9]. The latter approach considers a system with multiple queues and a single server.

Despite the predominant focus on throughput when analyzing the performance of finite populations in the CSMA-NP protocol, much of the existing research has primarily focused on ad hoc networks. In contrast, the analysis presented in this paper considers a central base station. However, a significant gap remains in the current literature—much of the research on CSMA protocols, even when focused on finite node scenarios, is often based on protocol variants and not specifically on the CSMA-NP protocol itself. This oversight suggests a crucial need for dedicated studies that directly address the protocol in finite populations, offering insights that could be critical for the efficient design and management of modern network systems. Building on this, the main contributions of this work are as follows:

- We provide clear insights into the dynamics of the CSMA/NP random access protocol when the number of interfering nodes is low, which the infinite population model fails to consider. Specifically, in the vulnerability period, the number of interfering nodes reduces as the number of transmissions increases, whilst in the infinite population model, the packet transmission probability remains constant.
- We develop a closed-form expression to calculate the system throughput with N nodes. The vast majority of previous works consider an infinite population, which is accurate in WiFi, and cellular systems. However, in IoT applications, where only a few nodes interact directly (even if the network comprises hundreds of nodes, just the neighbor nodes interact due to the low transmission capabilities of the nodes in a WSN or due to the use of clustering schemes to provide energy savings, among others). We prove that our model is more accurate when the number of nodes is lower than 10, while the infinite population model provides adequate results for $N > 10$.
- We propose an approximated solution to simplify the throughput calculation. Indeed, we provide an exact expression for the throughput for the finite population scenario, but it has to be numerically solved. As such, we provide an approximation that does not require the numerical solution, but it provides a direct result that is accurate in certain regions. Hence, this approximation can be used instead of the numerical solution for the appropriate system variables' range.

The remaining sections of this paper are structured as follows: In Section 2, we study the conventional CSMA-NP protocol under the infinite population model. Then, in Section 3, we introduce a novel approach to analyze the CSMA-NP protocol with a finite population assumption. In Section 4 some relevant results are presented, where we examine the system throughput using both a closed-form equation that we solve numerically and the simplified expression. We also analyze the implications of our findings when comparing them to the protocol with an infinite population. Finally, Section 5 concludes this paper and outlines potential avenues for future research.

2. CSMA-NP under the Infinite Population Assumption

The CSMA-NP protocol [10] has as its main objective to avoid collisions by rescheduling the packets when the sender node senses the channel is occupied. Conversely, if the channel is free, the node is cleared to send its packet.

This work develops an analysis that assumes an infinite population where the arrival process is considered to be a Poisson process with a packet arrival rate of g packets/s and each node sends only one packet at a time. Each of the packets is assumed to have a constant length of T seconds. When a collision occurs, the packets that collide turn into destructive interference and they cannot be decoded successfully. Also, a propagation delay of τ seconds is considered, which represents the time it takes a packet to be received by all contending nodes in the system. As such, after an idle period, when the transmitting node senses the channel, it will assume that it is free and start its transmission; if a second node attempts to transmit, it also senses the channel, but if this occurs before the first packet arrives, i.e., before τ seconds of the first transmission, this second node also senses the channel as idle and transmits its packet, generating a collision. If the second node senses the channel after τ seconds, then it senses the channel as occupied and alters its transmission, avoiding any collision. Hence, τ is usually referred to as the *vulnerability period*.

Thus, the throughput is the successful transmission rate $\bar{U}$ over the cycle of observation, which involves the expected duration of the channel in idle mode $\bar{I}$ and the expected duration of the channel in a busy period, whether a successful or packet collision occurs, $\bar{B}$ occurs. The analysis developed in [10] derives the following expression for the throughput (see (1) for further details):

$$S = \frac{\bar{U}}{\bar{I} + \bar{B}} = \frac{e^{-\tau g}}{\frac{1}{g} + T(1 + \tau + \tau - \frac{(1-e^{-g\tau})}{g})}. \tag{1}$$

However, this analysis assumes a constant arrival rate to the system (since an infinite population is considered), which is not accurate if the number of nodes is low. Indeed, as some nodes are allowed to transmit in the vulnerability period because they sensed the channel idle, the arrival rate drastically diminishes during the rest of that period, rendering a different system throughput. However, if the number of nodes is relatively high, the arrival rate remains almost constant irrespective of the number of previous transmissions. As such, the infinite population model renders accurate results for high values of g. Hence, we now study the system for a finite number of nodes in the following section.

3. CSMA-NP under the Finite Population Assumption

The finite population model (FP) assumes the same considerations as in the standardized protocol. Namely, that each node only transmits one package at a time and the packets take T seconds to be transmitted. However, the main difference falls in the arrival rate. As the number of nodes transmitting a packet increases, the remaining nodes that can transmit diminish, as opposed to the infinite population model where the arrival rate remains constant. To this end, consider that each node transmits a packet with rate α; then, the total arrival rate to the system is given by $g = \alpha N$, where α represents the rate of arrival for each node, and N represents the nodes over the network.

In Figure 1, a network scenario with three nodes is depicted. From a top-down perspective, the third node attempts its initial packet transmission, highlighted in orange. Since the channel is unoccupied, the node begins to send the packet after a propagation delay of τ seconds, with the transmission taking T seconds. Meanwhile, the first and second nodes, upon sensing the channel, detect that it is occupied and consequently do not initiate transmission. Subsequently, after the third node has completed its transmission, the first node attempts to send a packet.

However, in a third scenario depicted, all three nodes attempt to send packets simultaneously. Each node, finding the channel idle after their respective vulnerability periods, initiates the transmission. These close transmissions lead to a collision. The duration of this collision spans from the first attempt to transmit to the point where the last node sends its packet. A transmission is deemed successful if it encompasses only the period from the intent to transmit to the conclusion of the transmission.

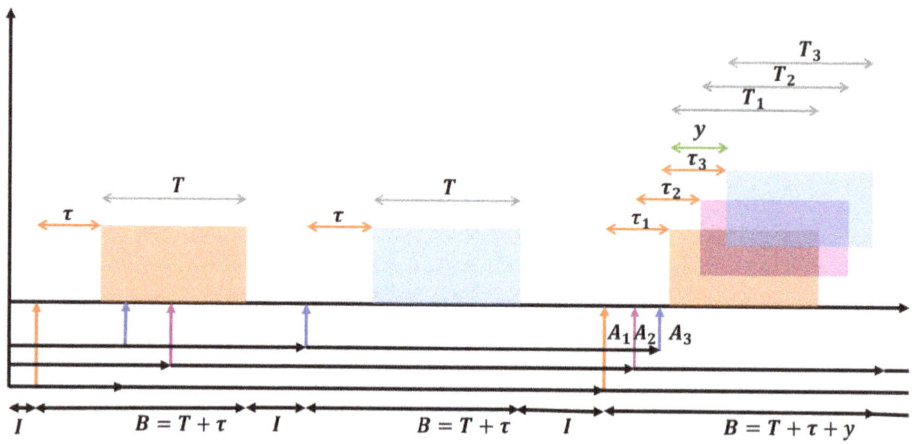

Figure 1. Non-persistent CSMA, Successful transmission and collision events.

Building on this, the average time that the shared channel is useful can be obtained by observing that in case the packet is successful, it consumes T seconds of the channel, while it is 0 otherwise, i.e., no transmissions or packet collisions. Also, once a packet has been transmitted after an idle period, the probability that such a packet is successful, P_{succ}, is given by the probability that none of the remaining nodes, $N-1$, transmit in the vulnerability period, τ. Hence,

$$\begin{aligned} P_{succ} &= Prob\{\text{None of the remaining } N-1 \text{ nodes transmit in the vulnerability period}\} \\ P_{succ} &= e^{-\alpha(N-1)\tau} \end{aligned} \tag{2}$$

From this, the average time that the system transmits useful information is given by

$$\bar{U} = T * P_{succ} = T * e^{-\alpha(N-1)\tau} \tag{3}$$

To calculate the average time that the system is idle, we first calculate its cumulative distribution function (CDF), $F_I(t) = Prob(I \leq t)$.

$$\begin{aligned} F_I(t) = \; & Prob(\textit{The first node transmits before } \tau)+ \\ & Prob(\textit{The second node transmits before } \tau)+ \\ & Prob(\textit{The N}^{th} \textit{ node transmits before } \tau)+ \\ = \; & Prob(\textit{at least one of the N nodes transmit before } \tau) \\ = \; & 1 - [e^{-\alpha t} * e^{-\alpha t} * \ldots * e^{-\alpha t}] = 1 - e^{-N\alpha t}, \end{aligned} \tag{4}$$

which is an exponential random variable with parameter $N\alpha$. Hence,

$$\bar{I} = \frac{1}{N\alpha} \tag{5}$$

Finally, to calculate the average time that the system is busy, either by a successful packet transmission or packet collision, $\bar{B}$, can be calculated as follows: Whenever a packet transmission begins after an idle period, the system will remain busy for at least T seconds, which corresponds to the duration of the packet plus the propagation time, τ, plus the time after this first transmission and the last interfering packet that is transmitted before the vulnerability period, τ, ends. Let us call this time from the first transmission to the last interfering packet, Y. Then,

$$\bar{B} = T + \tau + E[Y] \tag{6}$$

Since T and τ are constant values, we now concentrate on finding the mean value of Y. To this end, we first derive an expression for the CDF of the random variable Y, $F_Y(y)$. We can see that the probability that $Y \leq y$ is equivalent to the probability that there are no more arrivals in the vulnerability period after y seconds succeeding the first arrival, then $F_Y(y) = Prob(Y \leq y) = Prob(N(\tau - y) = 0)$.

Where the function $N(t)$ represents the number of arrivals in the period (0,t). Note that interfering nodes transmit before y; then, the non-interfering nodes have to transmit after τ, since they no longer collide with the rest of the packets. In this sense, this probability highly depends on the number of interfering nodes, N_I, because as the number of interfering nodes increases, the number of nodes that do not interfere decreases. This is the main issue in the finite population model that the finite population model cannot consider. As such, if there is only one interfering node, $N_I = 1$, and considering that the first node that transmits is not an interfering node, then

$$Prob(N(\tau - y) = 0 | n_I = 1) = e^{-(N-2)\alpha(\tau - y)} \tag{7}$$

For the case of 2 interfering nodes:

$$Prob(N(\tau - y) = 0 | n_I = 2) = e^{-(N-3)\alpha(\tau - y)} \tag{8}$$

And in general, for i interfering nodes:

$$Prob(N(\tau - y) = 0 | n_I = i) = e^{-(N-i-1)\alpha(\tau - y)} \tag{9}$$

As such, we find that:

$$Prob(Y \leq y) = \sum_{i=1}^{N-1} \binom{N-1}{i} (1 - e^{-\alpha y})^i \left(e^{-(N-1-i)\alpha(\tau - y)}\right) \tag{10}$$

From this, we find the expected value of $\hat{Y}$ as:

$$\begin{aligned} \hat{Y} &= \int_0^\tau (1 - F_Y(y))dy \\ &= \int_0^\tau \left(1 - \sum_{i=1}^{N-1} \binom{N-1}{i} (1 - e^{-\alpha y})^i \left(e^{-(N-1-i)\alpha(\tau - y)}\right)\right) dy \\ &= \int_0^\tau dy - \int_0^\tau \left((1 - e^{-\alpha y}) + \left(e^{-\alpha(\tau - y)}\right)\right)^{N-1} dy - \int_0^\tau \left(e^{-\alpha(\tau - y)}\right)^{N-1} dy \\ &= \tau - \int_0^\tau \left(1 - e^{-\alpha y} + e^{-\alpha(\tau - y)}\right)^{N-1} dy - \frac{e^{-\alpha(N-1)\tau}}{\alpha(n-1)}. \end{aligned} \tag{11}$$

Thus, by substituting (11) in the expression of $\bar{B}$, we get:

$$\bar{B} = T + 2\tau - \int_0^\tau \left(1 - e^{-\alpha y} + e^{-\alpha(\tau - y)}\right)^{N-1} dy - \frac{e^{-\alpha(N-1)\tau}}{\alpha(n-1)}. \tag{12}$$

And finally, we derived the throughput equation presented in Equation (13). This equation is solved with a closed-form solution, which renders exact results but with high computational complexity that rapidly increases as the number of nodes in the system N increases. As such, we propose an approximated solution as we now describe.

$$\bar{S}(N) = \frac{Te^{-\alpha(N-1)\tau}}{\frac{1}{N\alpha} + T + 2\tau - \int_0^\tau \left(1 - e^{-\alpha y} + e^{-\alpha(\tau - y)}\right)^{N-1} dy - \frac{1}{\alpha(N-1)} e^{-\alpha(N-1)\tau}} \tag{13}$$

Approximated Solution

As we mentioned above, we obtained the system throughput for the FP model by a closed-form solution. However, for values of N higher than 10, it requires high computational resources to solve it. Hence, we derive an approximated method to solve this integral which results in a closed expression with very low complexity for any value of N, which allows us to easily evaluate the system throughput in any condition. To this end, the integral presented in (13) can be written as (14):

$$\int_0^{\tau}\left(\left(1-e^{-\alpha y}\right)+\left(e^{-\alpha(\tau-y)}\right)\right)^{N-1}dy=\int_0^{\tau}\left(1-e^{-\alpha y}+e^{-\alpha\tau}e^{\alpha y}\right)^{N-1}dy. \tag{14}$$

Let $x=\alpha y$ and $a=e^{-\alpha\tau}$; then, $dx=\alpha dy \Rightarrow dy=\frac{1}{\alpha}dx$, substituting x and a, we get:

$$\int_0^{\alpha\tau}\left(1-e^{-x}+ae^{x}\right)^{(N-1)}\frac{1}{\alpha}dx=\frac{1}{\alpha}\int_0^{\alpha\tau}\left(1-e^{-x}+ae^{x}\right)^{N-1}dx. \tag{15}$$

By considering $e^x=1+x+\frac{x^2}{2!}+\frac{x^3}{3!}+\frac{x^4}{4!}+\ldots$, Equation (15) can be expressed as:

$$\begin{aligned}&\frac{1}{\alpha}\int_0^{\alpha\tau}\left(1-\left(1-x+\frac{x^2}{2!}-\frac{x^3}{3!}+\frac{x^4}{4!}-\theta(x^5)\right)+a\left(1+x+\frac{x^2}{2!}+\frac{x^3}{3!}+\frac{x^4}{4!}+\theta(x^5)\right)\right)^{N-1}dx\\&=\frac{1}{\alpha}\int_0^{\alpha\tau}\left(x-\frac{x^2}{2!}+\frac{x^3}{3!}-\frac{x^4}{4!}+\theta(x^5)+a+ax+a\frac{x^2}{2!}+a\frac{x^3}{3!}+a\frac{x^4}{4!}+a\theta\left(x^5\right)\right)^{N-1}dx.\end{aligned} \tag{16}$$

Reorganizing the terms, we obtain:

$$\frac{1}{\alpha}\int_0^{\alpha\tau}\left(a+x(a+1)+\frac{x^2}{2}(a-1)+\frac{x^3}{3}(a+1)+\theta(X^4)\right)^{N-1}dx. \tag{17}$$

Let us consider a function such that:

$$f(x)=(a+x(a+1)+\frac{x^2}{2}(a-1)+\frac{x^3}{3}(a+1)+\theta^4)^{N-1} \tag{18}$$

And performing an expansion of Equation (18) around 0, we obtain:

$$f(x)=\left(f(0)+f'(0)(x-a)+\frac{f''(0)(x-a)^2}{2}+\frac{f'''(0)(x-a)^3}{3!}+\ldots\right)^{N-1} \tag{19}$$

Note that:

$$f(0)=a^{N-1} \tag{20}$$

$$f'(0)=(N-1)a^{N-2}(a+1) \tag{21}$$

$$f''(0)=a^{N-3}(N-1)(a^2(N-1)+a(2N-3)+(N-2)) \tag{22}$$

And by considering Equation (19), a Taylor series can be constructed by substituting with (20), (21) and (22):

$$\begin{aligned}f(x)&=a^{N-1}+(N-1)a^{N-2}(a+1)x+\\&\quad a^{N-3}(N-1)\left(a^2(N-1)+a(2N-3)+(N-2)\right)\frac{x^2}{2}+\ldots\end{aligned} \tag{23}$$

And by substituting in (17) and organizing the terms, we obtain:

$$
\begin{aligned}
&\frac{1}{\alpha\tau}\int_0^{\tau}\Big(a^{N-1}+(N-1)a^{N-2}(a+1)x+\\
&a^{N-3}((N-1)(a^2(N-1)+a(2N-3)+(N-2))\frac{x^2}{2}+\theta(x^3)\frac{x^3}{3}...\Big)dx\\
=\ &\eta
\end{aligned}
\tag{24}
$$

$$
\begin{aligned}
\eta =&\frac{1}{\alpha}[a^{N-1}x+(N-1)a^{N-2}(a+1)\frac{x^2}{2}+\\
&\frac{1}{2}a^{N-3}(N-1)(a^2(N-1)+a(2N-3)+(N-2))\frac{x^3}{3}+\theta(x^4)]\ |_0^{\alpha\tau}
\end{aligned}
\tag{25}
$$

Then, we consider the original values of $x = \alpha y$ and $a = e^{-\alpha\tau}$, and after some algebraic manipulation, we find:

$$
\begin{aligned}
\eta =\ & e^{-\alpha\tau(N-1)}\alpha\tau+(N-1)e^{-\alpha\tau(N-2)}(e^{-\alpha\tau}+1)\frac{(\alpha\tau)^2}{2}+\\
&\frac{1}{6}e^{-\alpha\tau(N-3)}(N-1)(e^{-(\alpha\tau)^2}(N-1)+e^{-\alpha\tau}(2N-3)+\\
&(N-2))(\alpha\tau)^3+\theta(\tau^4)
\end{aligned}
\tag{26}
$$

$$
\begin{aligned}
\int_0^{\alpha\tau}\Big(1-e^{-\alpha y}+e^{-\alpha(\tau-y)}\Big)^{N-1}dy =&e^{-\alpha\tau(N-1)}\alpha\tau+(N-1)e^{-\alpha\tau(N-2)}(e^{-\alpha\tau}+1)\frac{(\alpha\tau)^2}{2}+\\
&\frac{1}{6}e^{-\alpha\tau(N-3)}(N-1)(e^{-2\alpha\tau}(N-1)+\\
&e^{-\alpha\tau}(2N-3)+(N-2))(\alpha\tau)^3+\theta(\tau^4)
\end{aligned}
\tag{27}
$$

Finally, let $e^{-\alpha\tau}$ be a, and by substituting (27) in (13), we obtain (28).

$$
\begin{aligned}
\bar{S}(N)=&\frac{\bar{U}(N)}{\bar{I}(N)+\bar{B}(N)}\\
=&\frac{Ta^{(N-1)}}{\frac{1}{N\alpha}+T+2\tau-\alpha\tau(a^{(N-1)}+(N-1)a^{(N-2)}(a+1)\frac{\alpha\tau}{2}+\frac{1}{6}a^{(N-3)}(N-1)(a^2(N-1)+a(2N-3)+(N-2))(\alpha\tau)^3-\frac{a^{(N-1)}}{\alpha(N-1)}}
\end{aligned}
\tag{28}
$$

To evaluate the performance of the proposed closed-form and the approximated solution, we develop a system simulation presented in the pseudocode Algorithm 1:

Algorithm 1: Simulation System

Input: g, τ, T, N
$\alpha = g/N$;
for *i* **in** *each node on the network* **do**
  Generate random arrivals ;
  Add arrivals as events to the list Events ;
while *arrivals* $\leq$ *iterations* **do**
  Extract the first event from the list Events ;
  Evaluate the impact of the new event on the system;
  Add time intervals of the occurrences of idle periods, collisions, and successful transmissions as appropriate;
Output: $\frac{U_{accumulated}}{I_{accumulated}+B_{accumulated}}$

The system simulation is summarized in Algorithm 1, which operates based on the discrete event paradigm. Given the input variables g, τ, T, N, and assuming that $\alpha = g/N$, the algorithm initiates by generating a first attempt to send a packet for each network node. Subsequently, these packet arrival events are sorted in chronological order. The simulation then proceeds iteratively; the first element of the sorted list is processed based on the system's current state.

The algorithm evaluates the impact of each new event on the current state of the system. Possible events include arrivals, end of transmission, and end of the vulnerability period. The variables that accumulate the time intervals for different system modes are:

- $U_{accumulated}$: The increments are $T + \tau$ for each successful transmission.
- $I_{accumulated}$: Records the time intervals from the last end of transmission until a new arrival; the increments are not standardized.
- $B_{accumulated}$: Updates with the time interval from the first arrival until the last arrival has completed its packet transmission. Note that the last arrival to send a packet occurs between the first arrival and the end of the vulnerability period of the first arrival, so the increment should be within $T + \tau$ and $T + 2\tau$.

For example, if the channel is occupied with a single transmission and a new event is an arrival, it will not be taken into account. The cycle then continues to the next event on the list without making any changes. At the end of the current transmission, the variables $U_{accumulated}$ and $B_{accumulated}$ are increased by $T + \tau$, as the channel has been busy and a successful transmission occurred.

Conversely, if an attempt to transmit information occurs before the vulnerability period has finished and the new event is an arrival, the new arrival causes a collision. In this case, $B_{accumulated}$ is updated with the time interval from the first arrival until the last arrival has sent its complete packet, representing the time during which the channel has been busy. The $I_{accumulated}$ variable records the time lapses from the last end of transmission until the first arrival, indicating that the channel has been in idle mode.

Finally, the output should be the result of $\frac{U_{accumulated}}{I_{accumulated}+B_{accumulated}}$, which corresponds to the throughput equation in Equation (1). The algorithm should ensure that the iterative process is repeated sufficiently to achieve steady-state results. In this particular case, we performed 100,000 iterations, which was a value founded based on empirical observations and testing by running the algorithm with the same variables several times.

We developed our simulator in Python due to its versatility and extensive library support. Our simulator is based on the methods mentioned above and was implemented without the use of additional simulation packages. Python's robust libraries and tools enabled us to efficiently manage the complex calculations and event-driven processes required for our simulation.

4. Numerical Results

In this section, we present the most relevant results derived from this work. In addition to the analysis developed above, we performed multiple system simulations to validate the analytical results, for both the exact and approximated throughput expressions. We first obtain the system throughput using Equation (13) and compare it to the results under the infinite population model; this infinite model considers that the packet arrival rate remains constant. Conversely, in our proposed model, the rate of packet transmissions decreases according to the number of packets previously transmitted, which renders different, more accurate results for low values of N. In Figure 2, we show the throughput for different values of N for the finite population model, varying the arrival rate (g) from 1×10^{-7} to 1×10^{-6} packets per second (pps) and the vulnerability time (τ) from 3.3×10^{-8}, taking the speed of light in a vacuum and considering a distance between the sender and receiver of 10 m, to 3.3×10^{-7} [seconds] (100 m), the T value is fixed to 0.001. We can see that the FP model differs greatly from the infinite population model when N is low and when the packet arrival rate is low, i.e., for low values of g and τ. Note that the infinite population model provides a very good approximation to the system dynamics when the traffic load remains relatively constant during the vulnerability period. This occurs for high values of g and τ, but for many IoT applications where packet transmissions are scarce, our proposed model better captures the behavior of the system.

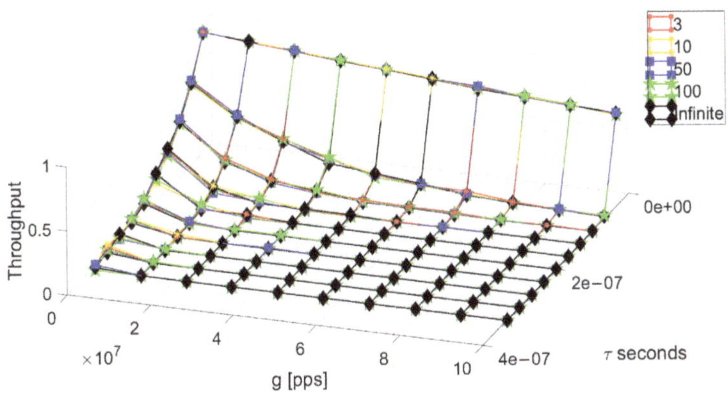

Figure 2. Throughput simulation of the system with 3, 10, 5, 100 and an infinite number of nodes.

Then, we validate our analysis by comparing the results of the closed-form (red surface) of the throughput under the finite population model to the system simulations (black surface), as depicted in Figure 3. We can see a very good match between these results and a very slight difference when a single node is in the system producing almost no packet transmissions.

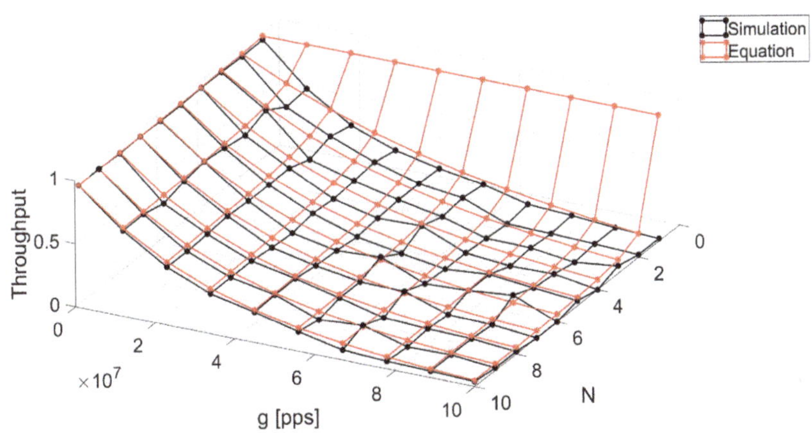

Figure 3. Comparison between the simulation of the system, and the closed-form solution for an FP with $\tau = (3.33) \times 10^{-8}$ and $T = 0.001$.

We now evaluate the accuracy of the proposed approximation (blue surface) to the closed-form expression of the system throughput under the finite population model. We can see in Figure 4 that, in general, the proposed approximation presents a very good match compared to the closed expression of the throughput (red surface) and the system simulation (black surface). Although some points present a higher discrepancy, we believe that it still accurately captures the system behavior with the great advantage that it provides results for any value of N with low computational complexity, while the closed exact expression requires numerically solving the integral, adding some inconvenient complexity. To assess the precision of the approximation, we calculate the relative error,

$RE = \sum_{\text{For all } i} \frac{(x_i - \hat{x}_i)}{x_i}$, where x_i represents the values obtained through the simulation and it acts as the reference and $\hat{x}_i$ are the values obtained through the approximation solution. It is crucial to note that the optimal application scenario for this approximation occurs when g, defined as αN, exceeds three times $1/\tau$.

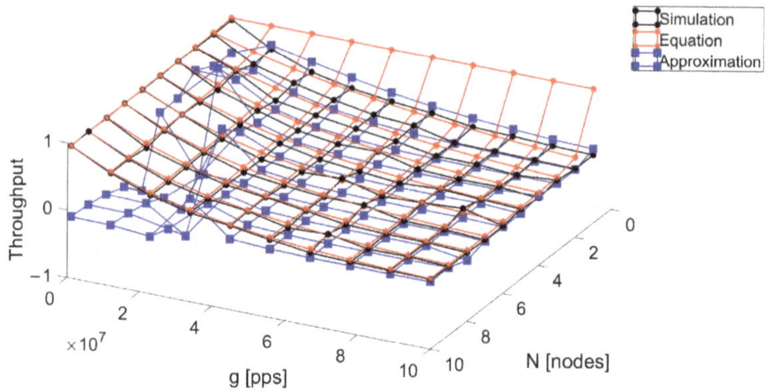

Figure 4. Comparison between the simulation of the system, the closed-form solution, and the numerical method for an FP with $\tau = 0.1$ and $T = 1$.

The relative error between the closed expression and the proposed approximation is 0.4874. It can be observed that the regions where there are the most discrepancies are when the traffic offered is below fifty percent. The rationale behind this is that the terms of the Taylor series that are ignored have an important impact on the calculation of the arrival of the interfering packets Y. We believe that including additional terms to this approximation may result in a better match but with an increased complexity. For practical effects, the proposed approximation renders a good match in most of the system parameters and we leave the study of a better approximation to future work since we believe that it lies outside the scope of this paper.

The main advantage of the proposed finite population model is that it provides more accurate results when the number of interfering nodes is reduced. Specifically, when the nodes in the transmission range are low, when some nodes have previously transmitted their packet, the remaining nodes that can transmit are reduced accordingly, which is not considered in an infinite population model. This model would render more accurate results in the context of WSN and IoT applications, where, even if the number of nodes is high, due to the low transmission capabilities of the nodes (usually 10 to 50 m compared to hundreds of meters in a cellular system), only a handful of them can interfere, or even in cases where clustering and ON/OFF schemes are used, drastically reducing the number of interfering nodes in the surroundings. We believe that our model can be used in energy consumption calculation or cyber-attack detection using more accurate results than the infinite population model. However, this analysis renders a complex equation with an integral that can only be numerically solved. As such, we provide an approximation that does not require the numerical solution of the integral, but this method is only adequate when it meets the previously mentioned relationship $g > 3/\tau$.

5. Conclusions

In this work, we studied, analyzed, and evaluated the CSMA-NP protocol for environments where the number of nodes is low or the packet arrival rate depends on the number of active transmissions. Such environments include many modern communication systems that the infinite population model cannot capture accurately. We derive a closed expression of the system throughput but it includes an integral that has to be numerically solved.

Hence, we also propose an approximation that presents a good fit in most cases and with low computational complexity. We validated our results with system simulations.

As expected, the infinite population model renders very different throughput results when there are a few nodes in the network and the packet arrival rate is low. This would generate important discrepancies in practical environments in terms of packet delay and energy consumption if the infinite population model is used in certain system conditions. Conversely, when the number of nodes is high, greater than $N = 10$, the infinite population model accurately captures the system performance since the packet arrival rate in the vulnerability period does not greatly vary anymore.

Overall, this study highlights the importance of considering finite populations in the analysis of the CSMA-NP protocol and provides valuable insights into how the system behaves as the number of nodes varies and offers a proposed equation that, while generally accurate, may require adjustments for specific scenarios. These findings contribute to a deeper understanding of network performance and open the door to future research directions for refining the proposed equation and extending the analysis to different network configurations and scenarios.

Funding: This work is partially funded by IPN SIP project 20240671, IPN SIP project 20240675, and IPN SIP project 20241113.

Institutional Review Board Statement: Not applicable.

Informed Consent Statement: Not applicable.

Data Availability Statement: Data are contained within the article.

Acknowledgments: The author wishes to express sincere gratitude to Luis Israel Ramos Perez for their invaluable assistance in rewriting the equations in LaTeX format, which enhanced the manuscript's clarity and presentation.

Conflicts of Interest: The authors declare no conflicts of interest.

References

1. Ukhurebor, K.E.; Odesanya, I.; Tyokighir, S.S.; Kerry, R.G.; Olayinka, A.S.; Bobadoye, A.O. *Wireless Sensor Networks: Applications and Challenges*; IntechOpen eBooks: Rijeka, Croatia, 2021. [CrossRef]
2. Stankovic, J.A. Wireless Sensor Networks. *Sensors* **2008**, *41*, 92–95. [CrossRef]
3. Abdirahman, M.J. Communication Protocols for Wireless Sensor Networks. ResearchGate, February 2022. Available online: https://www.researchgate.net/publication/358594142 (accessed on 17 January 2024).
4. Huang, W.; Lin, J.; Chen, C.H.; Chang, Y.-S.; Chen, Y.Y. *Accurate Analysis of IEEE 802.15.4 Slotted CSMA/CA over a Real-Time Wireless Sensor Network*; Springer eBooks: Berlin/Heidelberg, Germany, 2010; pp. 98–110. [CrossRef]
5. Coyle, E.; Liu, B. Finite Population CSMA/CD Networks. *IEEE Commun. Lett.* **1983**, *31*, 1247–1251. [CrossRef]
6. Wu, J.-L.C.; Wu, J.; Lee, T.-C. Performance Analysis of Interconnected CSMA/CD Networks with Finite Population. In Proceedings of the IEEE INFOCOM'88, Seventh Annual Joint Conference of the IEEE Computer and Communcations Societies, New Orleans, LA, USA, 27–31 March 1988. [CrossRef]
7. Wan, T.; Sheikh, A.U.H. Performance Analysis of Buffered CSMA/CD Systems. *Wirel. Pers. Commun.* **2001**, *18*, 45–65. [CrossRef]
8. Gkelias, A.; Dohler, M.; Friderikos, V.; Aghvami, A.H. Average Packet Delay of CSMA/CA with Finite User Population. *IEEE Commun. Lett.* **2005**, *9*, 273–275. [CrossRef]
9. Wong, P.K.; Yin, D.; Lee, T.T. Analysis of Non-Persistent CSMA Protocols with Exponential Backoff Scheduling. *IEEE Trans. Commun.* **2011**, *59*, 2206–2214. [CrossRef]
10. Kleinrock, L.; Tobagi, F. Packet Switching in Radio Channels: Part I-Carrier Sense Multiple-Access Modes and their Throughput-Delay Characteristics. *IEEE Trans. Commun.* **1975**, *23*, 1400–1416. [CrossRef]

sensors

MDPI

Article

A Programmable Crypto-Processor for National Institute of Standards and Technology Post-Quantum Cryptography Standardization Based on the RISC-V Architecture

Jihye Lee, Whijin Kim and Ji-Hoon Kim *

Department of Electronic and Electrical Engineering, Ewha Womans University, Seoul 04763, Republic of Korea; jihyelee317@gmail.com (J.L.); whijin98@gmail.com (W.K.)
* Correspondence: jihoonkim@ewha.ac.kr

Abstract: The advancement of quantum computing threatens the security of conventional public-key cryptosystems. Post-quantum cryptography (PQC) was introduced to ensure data confidentiality in communication channels, and various algorithms are being developed. The National Institute of Standards and Technology (NIST) has initiated PQC standardization, and the selected algorithms for standardization and round 4 candidates were announced in 2022. Due to the large memory footprint and highly repetitive operations, there have been numerous attempts to accelerate PQC on both hardware and software. This paper introduces the RISC-V instruction set extension for NIST PQC standard algorithms and round 4 candidates. The proposed programmable crypto-processor can support a wide range of PQC algorithms with the extended RISC-V instruction set and demonstrates significant reductions in code size, the number of executed instructions, and execution cycle counts of target operations in PQC algorithms of up to 79%, 92%, and 87%, respectively, compared to RV64IM with optimization level 3 (-O3) in the GNU toolchain.

Keywords: post-quantum cryptography; PQC; RISC-V; crypto-processor; programmability; domain-specific processor

1. Introduction

With the emergence of 5G communication and the development of various services, including Internet-of-Things and cloud services, a large amount of personal information, such as medical and financial records, is transmitted through communication channels. Public-key cryptography has been commonly used as a traditional method for maintaining confidentiality and integrity and preventing attackers or sniffers on the channel from disclosing this information. Diffie and Hellman introduced public-key cryptography in 1976 [1]. The cryptosystem is based on a complex mathematical problem that takes a long time to solve. Traditional public-key cryptography schemes, such as Elliptic-Curve Cryptography (ECC) [2] and the Rivest–Shamir–Adleman (RSA) algorithm [3], are based on the discrete logarithm problem and factorization problem, respectively.

In 1994, Peter Shor introduced Shor's algorithm [4], which proves that quantum computers can solve the mathematical problems for ECC and the RSA algorithm in polynomial time. This discovery makes quantum computers a potential threat to the security of traditional public-key cryptography. In recent years, Google has proposed a quantum processor called Sycamore, which takes about 200 s to solve an operation that would take a state-of-the-art supercomputer about 10,000 years to complete. In addition, IBM Q System One was introduced in 2019, and related studies are underway. As quantum computers are now widely deployed worldwide, it is necessary to develop quantum-resistant cryptosystems to ensure information security; this is known as post-quantum cryptography (PQC). As the importance of quantum-safe algorithms is well understood globally [5] and various cryptography algorithms have been developed, the National Institute of Standards and

Technology (NIST) initiated the standardization process of post-quantum cryptography in 2017.

The number of PQC publications in the past 5 years has accounted for nearly half of the articles published in this field over the past 25 years [6]. Previous works have studied the implementation of post-quantum cryptography algorithms [7]. However, due to various schemes, frequent memory access, and iterative operations, it is inefficient to implement these algorithms solely in software [8]. Various studies on hardware accelerators have recently been proposed and can be categorized into three types of implementation methods, as shown in Figure 1 [9].

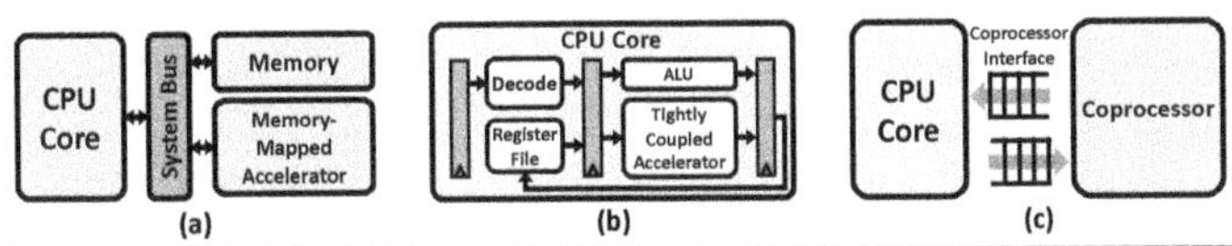

Method	(a) Memory-mapped	(b) Tightly Coupled	(c) Coprocessor
Pros	• Direct access to memory • Parallel processing to CPU	• Low area overhead • Direct access to GPR	• Flow Control of CPU • Minor modification of CPU
Cons	• Requirement for Controller	• Lower timing performance • CPU pipeline modification • Serial processing with CPU	• Requirement for interface

Figure 1. Comparison of hardware accelerator implementation methods. (**a**) Memory-mapped accelerator, (**b**) tightly coupled accelerator, and (**c**) coprocessor.

The first method attaches a memory-mapped accelerator to system buses such as AMBA AXI and AHB. The CPU core accesses this accelerator by storing values in a specific memory space allocated to the accelerator, which triggers a specific operation depending on the data written to the memory address [10,11]. This method does not require modifications to the CPU core's microarchitecture and enables parallel processing alongside the CPU. However, the memory-mapped accelerator leads to additional memory access latency due to load and store operations for workload offloading to the accelerator.

The second method implements a tightly coupled accelerator within the CPU microarchitecture as a functional unit. This method allows easy access to the general-purpose register file in the CPU core and incurs low area overhead. However, custom instructions must be decoded before execution, which requires modifications to the CPU's microarchitecture. Additionally, concurrent operation with the main thread in the CPU core is limited in a single-thread processor, resulting in lower performance compared to an external accelerator. Previous works, such as [12–14], defined custom RISC-V instruction sets for targeted post-quantum cryptography algorithms.

The third method involves a coprocessor attached to the CPU core through a dedicated interface. This method is widely adopted in modern CPU architectures such as Arm and RISC-V and allows for easy extension of the CPU core's capabilities with additional coprocessor instructions, without significant modifications to the baseline CPU's microarchitecture [9,15]. A high-performance vector coprocessor for lattice-based cryptography was designed in [16].

Our proposed programmable crypto-processor aligns with the coprocessor scheme, which reduces the design complexity caused by the use of a system bus and memory map, in comparison to studies involving memory-mapped PQC accelerators [10,11]. Also, compared to previous studies [12–14], there is no need to change the internal design of the existing CPU core because of the introduction of the coprocessor interface in this paper, which can connect the proposed crypto-processor to the main CPU core.

Several studies have been conducted on accelerating lattice-based cryptography, such as Kyber and Dilithium. Previous works, such as [11,16], mainly focused on accelerating lattice-based algorithms. However, less attention has been given to the hardware acceleration of other cryptographic schemes. Although various PQC schemes based on mathematical bases have been developed, as described in [8,17], hardware implementations of PQC algorithms commonly require a large memory footprint and highly repetitive computations, which are significant obstacles in efficient hardware implementations. To address this issue, this paper proposes a custom RISC-V Instruction Set Architecture (ISA) extension that can support all round 4 candidate algorithms in the NIST PQC standardization process, as well as algorithms yet to be standardized. This paper also introduces a programmable crypto-processor that can be attached to the main RISC-V CPU core via a widely used coprocessor interface, known as the CORE-V extension interface [15]. With the proposed RISC-V instruction set extension, the crypto-processor can flexibly support various PQC algorithms across various applications. Furthermore, this approach can reduce the code size of cryptosystems, leading to a smaller instruction memory requirement for PQC computation. Additionally, the number of executed instructions in the overall architecture and the execution clock cycle are significantly improved compared to baseline RISC-V implementations (Figure 2).

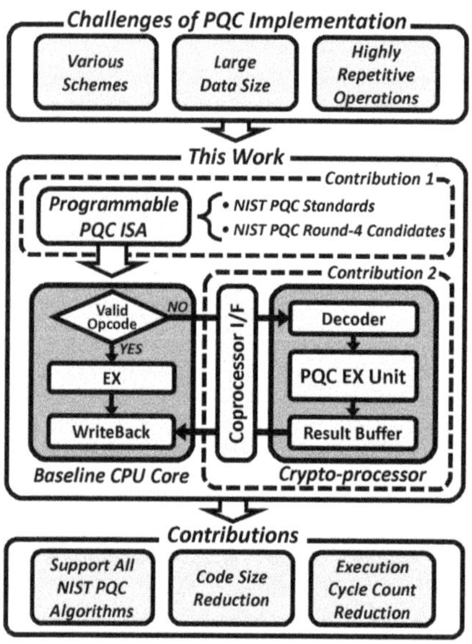

Figure 2. Proposed crypto-processor based on RISC-V architecture.

The remainder of this paper is organized as follows. Section 2 provides an overview of the targeted NIST PQC algorithms and their analysis from a performance point of view. Section 3 discusses the proposed instruction set for NIST PQC algorithms, including the algorithms to be standardized, round 4 candidates, and crypto-processor architecture that can support custom instructions. Section 4 presents the experimental results and the discussion, including a comparison with previous works. Finally, Section 5 contains the conclusions drawn in this paper.

2. Target PQC Algorithms

PQC algorithms can be categorized based on their arithmetic foundations. This section provides an overview of the NIST PQC standardization algorithms and their arithmetic background. Additionally, we describe their fundamental operations, which can result in performance bottlenecks in hardware implementations.

2.1. NIST PQC Standard and Round 4 Algorithms

The target PQC algorithms in this paper are the round 4 candidates of NIST PQC standardization and the algorithms selected to be standardized, as declared on 5 July 2022, as denoted in Table 1. The algorithms can be categorized into public-key encryption/key-establishment or digital signature algorithms.

Table 1. NIST post-quantum cryptography standard and round 4 candidates.

Class	Algorithm Type	Public-Key Encryption/ Key-Establishment	Disigtal Signature
NIST PQC Standard	Latice	CRYSTALS-Kyber	CRYSTALS-Dilithium Falcon
	Hash	-	SPHINCS+
NIST PQC Round-4 Candidate	Code	BIKE HQC Classic McEliece	-
	Isogeny	SIKE	-

The SIKE teams acknowledged that SIKE is insecure and should not be used.

Figure 3a depicts the fundamental operation flow of the key-establishment mechanism that enables key establishment. This mechanism comprises three main components: key generation, encapsulation, and decapsulation. During key generation, security parameters are input, generating a pair consisting of a public key (*pk*) and a secret key (*sk*). The public key *pk* is then transmitted to the P2 side. Encapsulation receives *pk* as input and produces a ciphertext and a shared key *K*. The ciphertext, an encapsulation of the key *K*, is sent to the P1 side. Finally, decapsulation returns a shared key based on a secret key and the ciphertext [18].

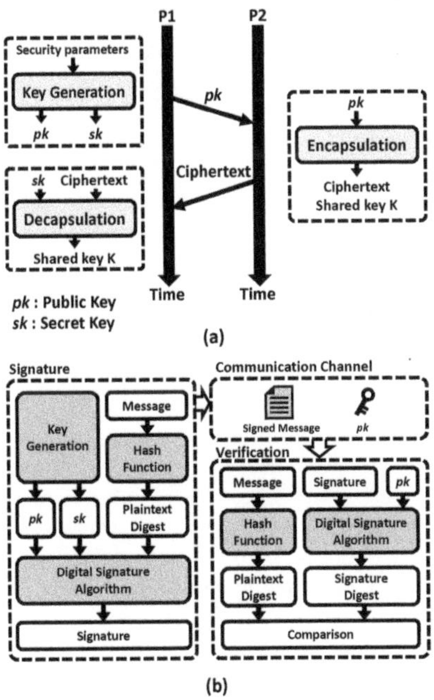

Figure 3. Fundamental flow of (**a**) key-establishment mechanism, (**b**) digital signature algorithm.

The digital signature algorithm consists of key generation, a signature, and verification steps, as shown in Figure 3b. First, the sender generates a public key, pk, and a secret key, sk, for communication. Next, the message is input to the hash function and signed by the secret key. Finally, the receiver verifies the sender's authenticity by comparing the plaintext digest and the signature digest using the sender's public key [19].

The PQC algorithms targeted in this paper can be categorized into lattice, hash, and code-based algorithms based on their arithmetic basis, as indicated in Table 1. Specifically, CRYSTALS-Kyber and CRYSTALS-Dilithium are based on the module-LWE problem, whereas SPHINCS+ relies on the security of hash functions such as SHAKE256, SHA-256, and Haraka. Code-based algorithms, including BIKE, HQC, and Classic McEliece, are based on quasi-cyclic moderate-density parity-check (QC-MDPC) codes or binary Goppa codes [20]. SIKE, based on the Supersingular Isogeny Diffie–Hellman (SIDH) protocol, is not included in the scope of this paper since the SIKE team has acknowledged potential security issues.

Lattice-based cryptography algorithms rely on the hardness of the Shortest Vector Problem (SVP), which involves finding the shortest non-zero vector in a lattice and is known to be a difficult problem [21]. A lattice is a set of points in an n-dimensional space with a periodic structure defined by n linearly independent basis vectors [22]. The most commonly used problems in lattice-based cryptography are LWE and LWR. LWE involves finding the vector s given a matrix A and a vector $b = As + e$, where e is a small additive error [23]. If there is no error on the right side, the vector s can be easily found using Gaussian elimination. However, with a small additive error, this problem becomes very hard. Ring-LWE [24] and module-LWE [25] are the main variants of the LWE problem. Ring-LWE uses polynomial rings over a finite field as a domain, where the vectors s and e are polynomials from a polynomial ring [12]. On the other hand, module-LWE replaces the single-ring elements with a matrix of polynomials.

The hash-based algorithm was introduced by Lamport in the 1970s as a one-time signature scheme, where the key pair can only be used to sign one message [26]. However, this scheme is vulnerable if the same key is used to sign two different messages. To address this issue, the extended Merkle signature scheme (XMSS) was developed as a stateful signature that can be used multiple times [27]. Nonetheless, stateful signature algorithms encounter difficulty synchronizing states between different participants in communication [28]. SPHINCS+, on the other hand, is a stateless hash-based signature scheme that is a variant of XMSS but eliminates the need to maintain state.

Code-based cryptography was introduced by McEliece in 1978 [29]. This cryptosystem is based on the property of error-correcting codes that are easy to encode but hard to decode. The Classic McEliece uses the property of the Goppa code, which is a linear error-correcting code that can encrypt and decrypt a message [30] and is defined by a sequence of distinct n elements and a Goppa polynomial $g(z)$. BIKE implements the McEliece scheme that uses QC-MDPC codes and the equivalent Niederreiter scheme. HQC employs a concatenated code of duplicated Reed–Muller and Reed–Solomon codes.

2.2. Core Operations for Post-Quantum Cryptography

The NIST PQC standards and round 4 candidates utilize the SHA-3 family [31] in their submissions, which comprises four hash functions and three extendable output functions (XOFs). A hash function takes input data of any size and generates a fixed-length digest, whereas an XOF produces variable-sized output data commonly used to randomly generate coefficients of polynomials in a lattice-based cryptosystem [13]. The hash functions in the SHA-3 family are based on the Keccak-f permutation, which is one of the most time-consuming components of PQC algorithms [12].

The Keccak-f[1600] permutation consists of iterative rounds that include five step mappings: θ, ρ, ϕ, χ, and ι, as shown in Algorithm 1. The input state for these mappings is an array of 25 elements, whose data size is determined by the permutation parameter and updated throughout the processes. The θ step mapping XORs all bits in two columns of the state array and XORs them with a bit-wise rotation. In the ρ mapping, the bits of the state array elements are rotated along the rotation offset, described as ROT in Algorithm 1, which depends on the x- and y-coordinates of the element. Then, the state array elements are rearranged in the ϕ step mapping. The bits in two state elements of different x-coordinates are XORed with a non-linear function in the χ mapping. Finally, the round constant, denoted as RC and depending on the current round index, is XORed with a state element, with both x- and y-coordinates being zero.

Algorithm 1: Keccak-f[1600] Permutation

```
Input : state[x,y] from (x,y) = (0,0) to (4,4)
        ROT[x,y] from (x,y) = (0,0) to (4,4)            ▷ Rotation offset
        RC[x] from x = 0 to NROUNDS − 1                 ▷ Round constants
Output: state[x,y] from (x,y) = (0,0) to (4,4)

RoundCount = 1
NROUNDS = 24                                            ▷ Number of rounds
while RoundCount ≤ NROUNDS do
    RoundCount++
    for x = 0; x < 5; x++ do                            ▷ θ−step
        C[x] = state[x,0] XOR state[x,1] XOR state[x,2]
               XOR state[x,3] XOR state[x,4]
        D[x] = C[x − 1] XOR RotateLeft(C[x + 1], 1)
    end for
    for x = 0; x < 5; x++ do
        for y = 0; y < 5; y++ do
            state[x,y] = state[x,y] XOR D[x]
        end for
    end for
    for x = 0; x < 5; x++ do                            ▷ ρ−step
        for y = 0; y < 5; y++ do
            state[x,y] = RotateLeft(state[x,y],ROT[x,y])
        end for
    end for
    for x = 0; x < 5; x++ do                            ▷ π−step
        for y = 0; y < 5; y++ do
            B[y, 2x + 3y] = state[x,y]
        end for
    end for
    for x = 0; x < 5; x++ do                            ▷ χ−step
        for y = 0; y < 5; y++ do
            state[x,y] = ((NOT B[x + 1, y]) AND B[x + 2, y])
                         XOR B[x,y]
        end for
    end for
    state[0,0] = state[0,0] XOR RC[RoundCount − 1]      ▷ ι−step
end while
```

Polynomial multiplication requires high computation resources and is a time-consuming operation, so it is considered a bottleneck in lattice-based cryptography [32]. The naive method for polynomial multiplication, known as the schoolbook algorithm, has a computational complexity of $O(n^2)$, where n is the degree of the polynomial. The number-theoretic transform

(NTT) [33] is an efficient method for performing polynomial multiplication, as it can reduce the time complexity to $O(nlogn)$.

$$\hat{a}_i = \sum_{j=0}^{n-1} a_j w_n^{ij} \, mod \, q, \forall i \in [0, n-1] \quad (1)$$

The NTT is a discrete Fourier transform in finite fields and is commonly used in post-quantum cryptography. It exploits polynomial multiplication over R_q, denoted by a polynomial ring $\mathbb{Z}_q[x]/(x^N+1)$, where $\mathbb{Z}_q$ represents the group of integers $0, \cdots, q-1$. ω_n is the n-th primitive root of unity in the finite ring $\mathbb{Z}_q$, also known as the twiddle factor. The twiddle factor satisfies ${\omega_n}^n = 1 \, mod \, q$ and ${\omega_n}^i \neq 1 \, mod \, q$ for all $i \in [0, \cdots, n-1]$.

$$a_i = \frac{1}{n} \sum_{j=0}^{n-1} \hat{a}_j {w_n}^{-ij} \, mod \, q, \forall i \in [0, n-1] \quad (2)$$

The NTT and inverse NTT are defined as (1) and (2), respectively. Polynomial f contains the coefficient sequence $a = \{a_0, \cdots, a_{n-1}\}$ in R_q, whose degree is n. The polynomial f is transformed into $\hat{f}$ after the NTT, whose coefficient sequence is $\hat{a} = \{\hat{a}_0, \cdots, \hat{a}_{n-1}\}$. The NTT and inverse NTT can be described as $\hat{f} = NTT(f), f = NTT^{-1}(\hat{f})$.

$$f \cdot g = NTT^{-1}(NTT(f) \circ NTT(g)) \quad (3)$$

The NTT involves several computation stages that include butterfly operations. Figure 4 illustrates an 8-point NTT based on the Cooley–Tukey butterfly algorithm [33]. For an 8-point polynomial multiplication, three stages for each NTT and inverse NTT are required. The CT butterfly multiplies an operand with a twiddle factor, which is a power of a root of unity, and then begins addition and subtraction after modular reduction. In Kyber, Dilithium, and Falcon, Montgomery reduction [34] is utilized. Modular reduction is one of the main bottlenecks during polynomial operations [35]. Algorithm 2 describes how Montgomery reduction is performed on an integer A. The Montgomery factor is $\beta = 2^{16}$ in Kyber and Falcon and $\beta = 2^{32}$ in Dilithium.

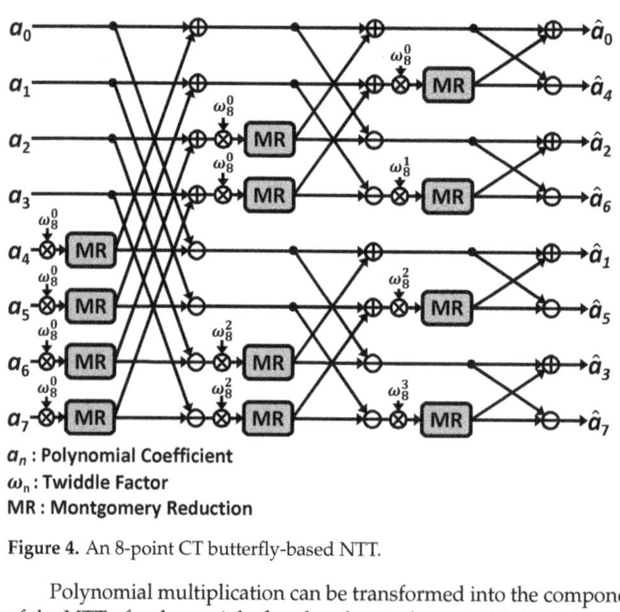

Figure 4. An 8-point CT butterfly-based NTT.

Polynomial multiplication can be transformed into the component-wise multiplication of the NTT of polynomials f and g, denoted as $\circ$ in (3). NTT-based polynomial multiplication is achieved through iterative butterfly operations, which are detailed along with our proposed instruction set in Section 3. This property makes polynomial multiplication based on the NTT a target for accelerating efficient PQC computations.

Sampling coefficients for lattice-based cryptosystems is a performance bottleneck [16]. It is more efficient to sample coefficients from a centered binomial distribution than from a discrete Gaussian distribution [13]. The centered binomial distribution, which is symmetrical around zero, is generated by computing the Hamming weight of two η-bit values and then subtracting one from the other using a modular operation. Algorithm 3 describes the centered binomial distribution of width η. The parameter η determines the range of polynomial coefficients, which is $[-\eta, \eta]$. To generate uniformly random coefficients of polynomials that do not exceed a bound, rejection sampling can be used with the modulus q as the bound to generate the polynomial coefficients in $\mathbb{Z}_q$.

The target code-based algorithms use arithmetic with bit polynomials over the finite field $GF_2[x]$, whose coefficients are either 0 or 1. Bit polynomial multiplication is a performance bottleneck in these algorithms [36,37]. In Classic McEliece and HQC, bit polynomial inversion over the finite field involves finite-field arithmetic, including repetitive multiplication and square operations. Accelerating the finite-field arithmetic can improve the execution time of the target code-based PQC algorithms.

Algorithm 2: Montgomery Reduction for PQC algorithms

Input : $2K$-bit Integer A
Montgomery Factor $\beta = 2^K$
Modulus Prime Integer q
Precomputed $q_{inv} = q^{-1} \bmod \beta$
Output: Reduced $A' = A\beta^{-1} \bmod q$

$X = Aq_{inv} \bmod \beta$
if *Unsigned Montgomery Reduction* **then** ▷ Falcon
  $Y = A + Xq$
else ▷ Kyber, Dilithium
  $Y = A - Xq$
end if
$Z = Y >> K$ ▷ Shift with Most-Significant Bit
if *Unsigned Montgomery Reduction* **then**
  if $Z > q$ **then**
    $A' = Z - q$
  else
    $A' = Z$
  end if
else
  $A' = Z$
end if

Algorithm 3: Sampling based on Centered Binomial Distribution

Input : Random Bit Vector $B = \{b_0, \cdots, b_{2N\eta-1}\}$
Output: Polynomial $f = a_0 + a_1X + \cdots + a_{N-1}X^{N-1} \in R_q$

for $i = 0; i < N; i++$ **do**
  $x = \sum_{j=0}^{\eta-1} b_{2i\eta+j}$ ▷ Hamming Weight of η bits
  $y = \sum_{j=0}^{\eta-1} b_{2i\eta+\eta+j}$
  $a_i = x - y$
end for

3. Proposed Crypto-Processor Architecture with PQC Instructions

To address the significant computational complexity and repetition involved in core operations in PQC algorithms, optimal hardware and software co-design is necessary. This section introduces the RISC-V instruction set extension that accelerates NIST PQC standards and round 4 candidates. Additionally, the hardware architecture of the proposed crypto-processor is discussed in detail.

3.1. Proposed RISC-V Instruction Set Extension

Due to its flexibility in instruction set extension, we use the RISC-V instruction set architecture as the baseline to support the NIST PQC algorithms and round 4 candidates [38]. As the primary performance bottlenecks in PQC algorithms are commonly due to the repetitive computation of similar core operations, a carefully designed instruction set extension can significantly enhance the efficiency of PQC computations.

The instruction format for the proposed RISC-V post-quantum cryptography extension is presented in Table 2. The basic formats in the RISC-V standard are Type-*R* and Type-*R4*. *R*-type instructions utilize two register values with indices *rs1* and *rs2*, whereas *R4*-type instructions require three indices for the source registers. In the proposed crypto-processor, each source register index in the *R4*-type instructions is used to access the 32 × 64-bit coprocessor register file (CR) instead of the general-purpose register in the baseline CPU core. Types *Custom*1 and *Custom*2 are newly defined PQC operations.

Table 2. Proposed crypto-processor's 32-bit instruction format.

<table>
<tr><th rowspan="2">Type</th><th colspan="32">Encoding Map</th></tr>
<tr><th>31</th><th>30</th><th>29</th><th>28</th><th>27</th><th>26</th><th>25</th><th>24</th><th>23</th><th>22</th><th>21</th><th>20</th><th>19</th><th>18</th><th>17</th><th>16</th><th>15</th><th>14</th><th>13</th><th>12</th><th>11</th><th>10</th><th>9</th><th>8</th><th>7</th><th>6</th><th>5</th><th>4</th><th>3</th><th>2</th><th>1</th><th>0</th></tr>
<tr><td>R</td><td colspan="7">Functon 7</td><td colspan="5">rs2</td><td colspan="5">rs1</td><td colspan="3">Function 3</td><td colspan="5">rd</td><td colspan="7">Opcode</td></tr>
<tr><td>R4</td><td colspan="5">rs3</td><td colspan="2">Func. 2</td><td colspan="5">rs2</td><td colspan="5">rs1</td><td colspan="3">Function 3</td><td colspan="5">rd</td><td colspan="7">Opcode</td></tr>
<tr><td>Custom1</td><td colspan="7">Immediate</td><td colspan="5">rs2</td><td colspan="5">rs1</td><td colspan="3">Function 3</td><td colspan="5">rd</td><td colspan="7">Opcode</td></tr>
<tr><td>Custom2</td><td colspan="7">Function 7</td><td colspan="5">-</td><td colspan="5">rs1</td><td colspan="3">Function 3</td><td colspan="5">rd</td><td colspan="7">Opcode</td></tr>
</table>

Table 3 provides a detailed description of the proposed instruction set, which can be classified into seven groups based on a comprehensive analysis of the target NIST PQC algorithms: Keccak-f permutation, Montgomery reduction for the NTT, binomial and rejection sampling, finite-field and conditional arithmetic, and access to coprocessor registers. Depending on the current instruction's opcode, the source operands RS1 and RS2, as well as the destination register RD in Table 3, can be selected between the GPR in the baseline core and the CR. As shown in Table 4, the proposed crypto-processor supports all NIST PQC algorithms yet to be standardized and round 4 candidates.

In post-quantum cryptosystems, the Keccak-f permutation is the basis for SHA-3, encompassing hash functions (such as SHA3-256 and SHA3-512) and XOFs (such as SHAKE128 and SHAKE256). The number of iterations and the data size of the input and output array vary according to the permutation parameter, selectable from 25, 50, 100, 200, 400, 800, and 1600. The proposed instructions in this paper can accelerate any Keccak-f permutation parameter by simply adjusting the operand data size. For instance, for the Keccak-f[1600] permutation acceleration, the user can adjust the state array element data size to 64-bit and the number of rounds to 24. However, the Keccak-f permutation is time-consuming because of the high number of iterations, and it requires a significant number of registers for storing the permutation state. With the proposed PQC instructions, the five steps in Algorithm 1 for the Keccak-f permutation can be accelerated, as explained in Section 4.

Table 3. The architecture of the proposed PQC instruction set.

Operation	Instruction	Description
Keccak-f Permutation	XOR5	RD = CR[*rs1*] ^CR[*rs1*+1] ^CR[*rs1*+2] ^CR[*rs1*+3] ^CR[*rs1*+4]
	ROLX	RD = ROL(RS1, 1) ^RS2
	ANDX	RD = CR[*rs1*] ^(~CR[*rs2*] & CR[*rs3*])
	XROL	RD = ROL(RS1 ^RS2, *Imm*)
Montgomery Reduction	MR4	RD = (RS1 - ((RS1 × q^{-1}) & 64'hFFFF) ∗ RS2) >> 16
	MR4U	RD = (RS1 + ((RS1 × q^{-1}) & 64'hFFFF) ∗ RS2) >> 16
	MR8	RD = (RS1 − ((RS1 × q^{-1}) & 64'hFFFF_FFFF) ∗ RS2) >> 32
Binomial Sampling	SND2	RD = {61'b0, ({1'b0, ({1'b0, RS1[*Imm*]} + {1'b0, RS1[*Imm*+1]})}) − ({1'b0, ({1'b0, RS1[*Imm*+2]} + {1'b0, RS1[*Imm*+3]})})}
	SND3	RD = {61'b0, ({1'b0, ({1'b0, RS1[*Imm*]} + {1'b0, RS1[*Imm*+1]} + {1'b0, RS1[*Imm*+2]})}) − ({1'b0, ({1'b0, RS1[*Imm*+3]} + {1'b0, RS1[*Imm*+4]} + {1'b0, RS1[*Imm*+5]})})}
Rejection Sampling	REJH	RD[11:0] = (RS1[11:0] < RS2) ? RS1[11:0] : 12'b0 RD[23:12] = (RS1[23:12] < RS2) ? RS1[23:12] : 12'b0 RD[35:24] = (RS1[35:24] < RS2) ? RS1[35:24] : 12'b0 RD[47:36] = (RS1[47:36] < RS2) ? RS1[47:36] : 12'b0 RD[63:48] = 16'b0
	REJ	RD[23:0] = (RS1[22:0] < RS2) ? {1'b0, RS1[22:0]} : 24'b0 RD[47:24] = (RS1[46:24] < RS2) ? {1'b0, RS1[47:24]} : 24'b0 RD[63:48] = 16'b0
Finite Field Arithmetic	SQR	RD = {1'b0, RS1[31], 1'b0, RS1[30], ... , 1'b0, RS1[1], 1'b0, RS1[0]}
	CLMUL	RD = (RS2[0] ? (RS1 << 0) : 64'b0) ^... ^(RS2[63] ? (RS1 << 63) : 64'b0)
	CLMULH	RD = (RS2[0] ? (RS1 >> 63) : 64'b0) ^... ^(RS2[63] ? (RS1 >> 0) : 64'b0)
Conditional Arithmetic	CON4	RD = RS1[15] ? RS2 : 64'b0
	CON8	RD = RS1[31] ? RS2 : 64'b0
CR Access	RDCR	GRP[*rd*] = CR[*rs1*]
	WRCR	CR[*rd*] = GPR[*rs1*]

GPR : General Purpose Register in Baseline CPU Core. CR : Coprocessor Register. ROL : Rotate Left

Table 4. Supporting algorithms for the proposed PQC ISA.

Supportin Algorithm	Proposed RISC-V Post-Quantum Cryptography ISA					
	Keccak-f Permutation	Montgomery Reduction	Sampling	Finite Field Arithmetic	Conditional Arithmetic	CR Access
PKE/KEM	Kyber	O	O		O	O
	BIKE	O		O		O
	HQC	O		O		O
	Classic McEliece	O		O		O
DS	Dilithium	O	O		O	O
	Falcon	O	O		O	O
	SPHINCS+	O				O

PKE/KEM : Public-Key Encryption / Key-Establishment DS : Digital Signature

As demonstrated in numerous prior works [14,32,39], accelerating the NTT can improve the performance of polynomial multiplication. Modular reduction is included in each operation in both the NTT and inverse NTT. Since the complexity of modular reduction is higher compared to other operations, such as addition, subtraction, and multiplication in the NTT, accelerating the reduction operation can efficiently improve the overall performance of the NTT. Montgomery reduction is the most commonly used reduction scheme in lattice-based cryptosystems that require polynomial multiplication. The proposed instruction set for Montgomery reduction supports all parameters used in PQC standards and round 4 candidates that use the NTT.

The parameter η in the binomial sampling instructions determines the number of bits used in the operation and the range of the result $[-\eta, \eta]$. For ease of use, Function 3 in the binomial sampling instruction set is equivalent to η, as shown in Table 3. The instruction set supports all possible values of η (2 and 3) used in NIST standard algorithms. In addition, the instruction set for rejection sampling includes REJH for sampling on 12-bit integers, which supports Kyber, and REJ for 23-bit integers, which supports Dilithium.

The finite-field arithmetic instructions consist of SQR for square operations and CLMUL and CLMULH for carry-less multiplication of bit polynomials. As discussed in Section 2, combining these fundamental operations can also speed up bit polynomial inversion.

CON4 and CON8 support conditional arithmetic operations. The result of the CON4 instruction depends on the value of RS1[15]. If RS1[15] is 0, the result is a 64-bit zero. If RS1[15] is 1, the result is RS2 as a 64-bit value. For CON8, the result of the instruction is determined by the value of RS1[31].

Recently, a scalar cryptography extension for RISC-V was announced, which supports the Advanced Encryption Standard (AES) and hash functions, including the SHA-2 family [40]. The proposed crypto-processor also includes a scalar cryptography extension to support NIST PQC standards, their variants, and finalists. Kyber introduced their 90s versions that use AES and SHA-2, and hardware acceleration of AES and SHA-2 can support SPHINCS+ [41]. AES is also used for random number generation in variants of PQC algorithms [42].

3.2. Proposed Crypto-Processor Microarchitecture

Figure 5 illustrates the overall architecture of the proposed crypto-processor. The coprocessor interface, a subset of the CORE-V extension interface [15], connects the crypto-processor to the baseline CPU core, CVA6 [43]. CVA6 consists of six pipeline stages and supports the RV64IMAC ISA. When an instruction is fetched from the instruction cache, it is passed to the decode stage. Since CVA6 does not support the scalar cryptography extension or any proposed PQC instructions, they are considered invalid at the decode stage and offloaded through the coprocessor interface, with source operands from the general-purpose register in the baseline core, a 32-bit instruction, and the Program Counter (PC).

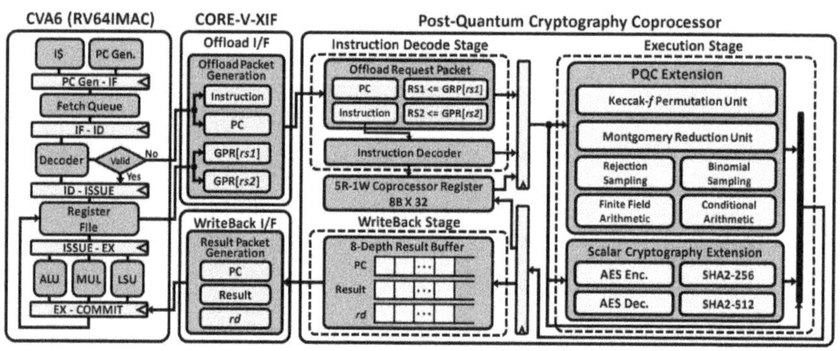

Figure 5. Overall architecture of the proposed crypto-processor.

The crypto-processor has a three-stage pipeline architecture with an instruction decode stage, an execution stage, and a writeback stage, where all instructions require only a single cycle for the execution stage. The proposed coprocessor decodes the instruction with Function 7, Function 3, and Opcode fields to generate control signals. The Opcode determines the source operands for the current instruction from either the general-purpose register in the offload request packet or the coprocessor register. Based on the PC and source operands, as well as the index of the destination register and immediate value from the instruction, the execution stage of the coprocessor initiates an operation according to the control signals from the decode stage. The result is then passed to either the coprocessor register with the *rd* index or the general-purpose register through the writeback stage, along with the PC and index *rd*. The results that need to be written back to the baseline core are stored in the result buffer and wait to pass through the coprocessor interface. In the writeback interface, they become a result packet and are passed to the general-purpose register file in the commit stage of the baseline CPU core. Data stored in CR[*rs1*] can be loaded to the CPU core through the RDCR instruction, whereas the WRCR instruction allows a source operand in the general-purpose register to be written to the CR[*rd*]. The coprocessor register reduces frequent access to memory and the register file in the baseline core.

Figure 6 shows the hardware architecture of the proposed XOR5, ROLX, ANDX, and XROL instructions used in the Keccak-f permutation in the coprocessor execution stage. By utilizing a dedicated register file in the coprocessor to store the permutation state, repetitive access to the general-purpose register file in the baseline CPU core to update the state array every round can be avoided. Instead, these instruction sets utilize data stored in the coprocessor register as operands and write back computation results. During the decode stage, the index of the coprocessor register for each instruction's source operand is determined.

The XOR5 and ROLX instructions support the θ step in the permutation. The XOR5 instruction accelerates repetitive 64-bit XOR operations with five 64-bit operands from CR[*rs1*] to CR[*rs1+4*], which would otherwise be executed for each clock cycle and repeated four times. The ROLX instruction first shifts the source operand CR[*rs1*] left by 1 bit and XORs it with CR[*rs2*]. The ANDX instruction supports the χ step in the Keccak-f permutation. In this instruction, the bit-inverted CR[*rs2*] and CR[*rs3*] are ANDed and then XORed with CR[*rs1*]. The XROL instruction accelerates the rest of the θ step and the whole part of the ρ and ϕ step mapping. The source elements CR[*rs1*] and CR[*rs2*] are XORed with each other and shifted by an amount specified in immediate[5:0]. The result is then written back to CR[*rd*].

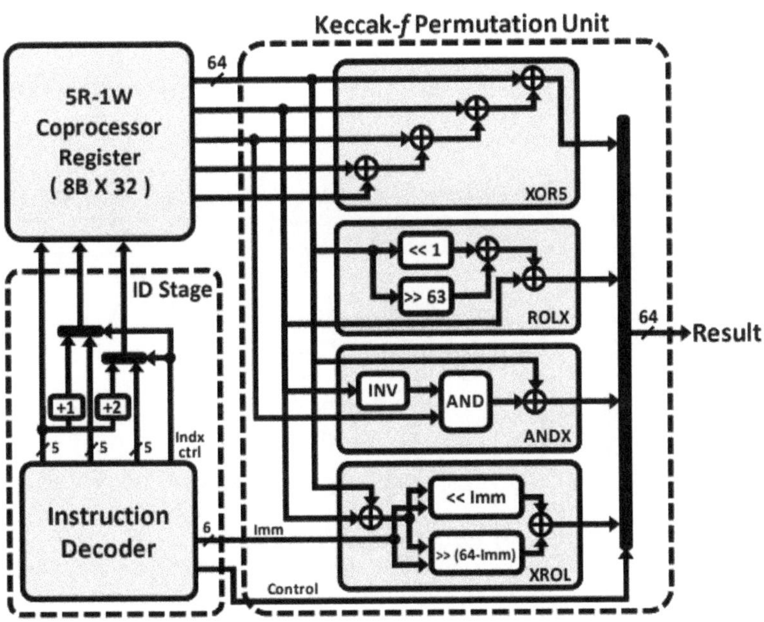

Figure 6. Hardware architecture of the Keccak-f permutation unit.

The proposed Montgomery reduction instruction set is executed, as depicted in Figure 7. The parameter q^{-1}, which is the inversion of the prime factor q, is selected based on the value of RS2. The instruction decode stage controls the number of bits to be extracted and shifted and determines whether operands should be added or subtracted. MR4 and MR8 require 32-bit addition, whereas MR4U requires 64-bit subtraction. The shift amount is 16 bits for the execution of the MR4 and MR4U instructions and 32 bits for the MR8 instruction.

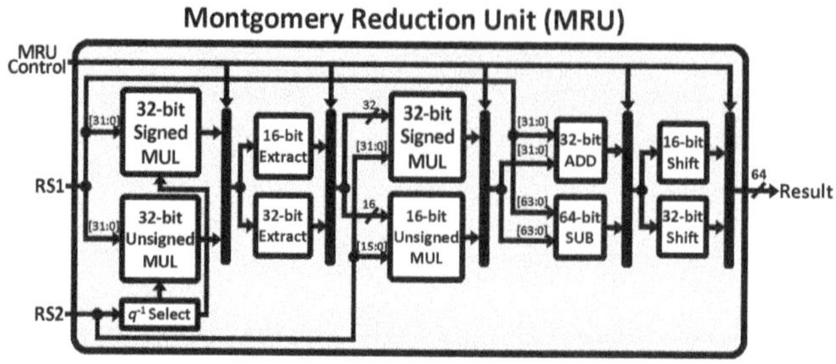

Figure 7. Hardware architecture of Montgomery reduction unit for the NTT instruction set.

Figure 8a shows the execution unit for sampling based on a centered binomial distribution. A 6-bit immediate determines the bit of the 64-bit source operand. Depending on the control signal from the instruction decode stage, η bits are extracted twice. The first set of η bits is obtained from RS1[Imm] to RS1[Imm+($\eta-$ 1)], and the second set of η bits is obtained from RS1[Imm+η] to RS1[Imm+(2$\eta-$1)]. For instance, in the SND2 instruction, where η is 2, RS1[Imm] and RS1[Imm+1] are extracted, and each bit is extended to 2 bits by zero extension. Then the two 2-bit values are added, and the result is zero-extended to 3 bits. RS1[Imm+2] and RS1[Imm+3] are computed similarly. The two 3-bit values are subtracted, extending the result to 64 bits with zero. This produces the result of binomial sampling within the range of $[-2, 2]$. The proposed instructions and crypto-processor support all η values used in the target NIST PQC algorithms.

The rejection sampling unit uses RS1 as the random bit stream generated by SHAKE or AES in PQC algorithms, and RS2 as the bound for rejection. By setting the bound as the modulus prime q, it is possible to select the polynomial coefficients within the appropriate range. The control signal from the instruction decode stage determines the bit widths of the configurable extractors, as shown in Figure 8b.

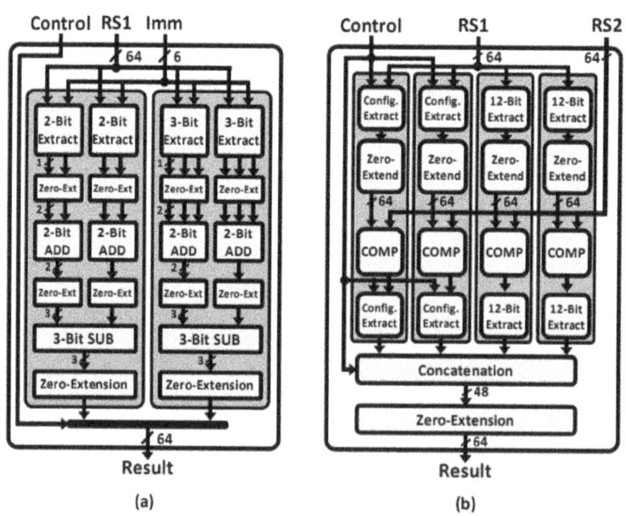

Figure 8. Hardware architecture of (**a**) binomial sampling unit; (**b**) rejection sampling unit.

The execution stage also includes units for scalar cryptography [40]. The proposed crypto-processor can support AES encryption and decryption, as well as SHA-2 hash functions, including SHA-256 and SHA-512. These algorithms' complex operations can be computed efficiently by a combination of appropriate instructions. For example, the AES unit supports instructions for key scheduling, middle encryption rounds (including

ShiftRows, SubBytes, and MixColumns steps), and final encryption rounds (including ShiftRows and SubBytes steps). The instruction extension can also support AES decryption through inverse operations. For SHA-2 hash functions, transformations such as sigma0, sigma1, sum0, and sum1, which consist of rotation operations, are mapped to the RISC-V instruction format.

4. Experimental Results

This section presents a performance analysis of the proposed crypto-processor with PQC instructions. We evaluate the code size, number of executed instructions, and execution cycle counts. Furthermore, we compare the hardware implementation results with previous works.

4.1. Performance Analysis

In addition to reducing the cycle count, which was the primary focus of most previous works, the code size and number of executed instructions are also critical in demonstrating the effectiveness of the proposed instruction set. For the experimental setup in this study, we used a 64-bit CPU core, CVA6, as the baseline, and we employed the RISC-V GNU toolchain with the golden simulator, Spike. We measured the improvement based on the RV64IM with optimization level 3 (-O3) assembly source code of the target NIST PQC algorithms. As part of standardization, the NIST releases the C-based source code of each PQC algorithm, which we used in our experiments with the RISC-V compiler. To ensure a fair comparison, we modified only the assembly instructions that can be replaced with the proposed ISA and left everything else unchanged except for the target assembly instructions. We also provided execution clock cycle count reductions for each target cryptographic operation when the proposed crypto-processor was attached to the CVA6 core through the coprocessor interface, as shown in Figure 5.

Table 5 presents the comparison results for the Keccak-f[1600] permutation. The Keccak-f[1600] permutation cycle counts of the RV64IM software implementation based on the version 2.0 ISA for 32-bit [44], hardware–software co-design [45], and this work are shown in Table 5. Our study demonstrates that compared to the RV64IM software implementation of the permutation with optimization level 3, our proposed crypto-processor reduced the execution cycle counts by up to 86%.

Table 5. Execution cycle counts (kilo cycles) for Keccak-f[1600] permutation.

RV64IM (-O3)	E31 (RV32IMAC) [44]	Cortex-M4 [44]	Accelerator [45]	This Work
11.722	13.774	12.969	1.8	1.632

Table 6 compares the NTT cycle counts according to the parameters used in NIST PQC standards. The parameter n refers to the degree of the polynomial, whereas q is a prime integer. Our work demonstrated a 46% to 50% reduction in cycle counts for the NTT compared to RV64IM with optimization level 3. Moreover, due to the well-defined instruction set, our proposed crypto-processor required fewer cycle counts for the NTT compared to previous works [14,32,39].

Table 6. Execution cycle counts (kilo cycles) for the NTT.

Parameter	Implementation				
(n, q)	RV64IM (-O3)	Accelerator [32]	Accelerator [14]	Cortex-M4F [39]	This Work
(256, 3329)	25.53	43.76	18.49	-	13.88
(253, 8380417)	29.50	43.76	18.55	-	15.16
(512, 12289)	108.20	81.06		75.90	55.20
(1024, 12289)	237.74	180.24		157.70	119.98

A comparison of execution cycle counts between the software implementation of sampling and previous works [13,46] is denoted in Table 7. The parameter n is the polynomial degree, and η determines the range of polynomial coefficients, as described in Section 2. As the rejection sampling in Kyber-512 reference implementation includes SHAKE-128, the proposed Keccak-f permutation and rejection sampling instruction set were used for the measurement. Our study shows that compared to RV64IM with optimization level 3, the proposed crypto-processor can reduce cycle counts for binomial sampling by 38% to 50% and rejection sampling by 77%.

Table 7. Execution cycle counts (kilo cycles) for sampling.

Target Algorithm	Parameter	Implementation		
		RV64IM (-O3)	Accelerator [13]	This Work
Binomial Sampling	n = 256, η = 2	2.46	-	1.24
	n = 256, η = 3	3.01	2.36	2.86
Rejection Sampling	Parameter	RV64IM (-O3)	Cortex-M4 [46]	This Work
	n = 256	206.36	60.43	47.36

Table 8 displays the execution clock cycle improvement for applications that use finite-field arithmetic, specifically the Syndrome decoder in mceliece348864 and the Reed–Solomon decoder in HQC-128. The reference implementation for NIST round 4 submissions was used for each experiment. The improvement of Karatsuba bit polynomial multiplication was measured based on the source code of the gf2x library [47], written in C. The code-based round 4 candidates, BIKE and HQC, use the gf2x library for efficient bit polynomial arithmetic, which can be supported by Karatsuba multiplication acceleration. $GF_2[x]$ polynomial multiplication significantly impacts the execution time of BIKE [36], and it is also utilized in all the primitives in the HQC implementation. The proposed crypto-processor exhibited execution cycle count improvements of 65%, 39%, and 87% for the respective algorithms.

Table 8. Execution cycle counts (kilo cycles) for applications based on finite-field arithmetic.

Target Algorithm	**Implementation**	
	RV64IM (-O3)	**This Work**
Reed-Solomon Decoder (HQC-128)	861.17	300.24
Syndrome Decoder (mceliece348864)	45,556.83	27,830.81
Karatsuba Multiplication	2311.75	305.98

The reduction ratios for the code size and executed instructions are presented in Figure 9. For the Keccak-f[1600] permutation, the proposed instruction set achieved a reduction of 79% and 81% in terms of the code size and executed instructions, respectively. Regarding the NTT with standardized parameters for NIST PQC algorithms, the proposed instruction set achieved a reduction of 13% to 20% in terms of the code size and 38% to 48% in terms of the executed instructions. Additionally, the instruction set for binomial sampling achieved reductions of 32% to 45% and 32% to 38%, respectively. For rejection sampling, reductions of 52% and 76% were achieved in the corresponding experiments. Among the applications based on finite-field arithmetic, the proposed instruction set reduced the code size from 4% to 40% and the executed instructions from 41% to 92%.

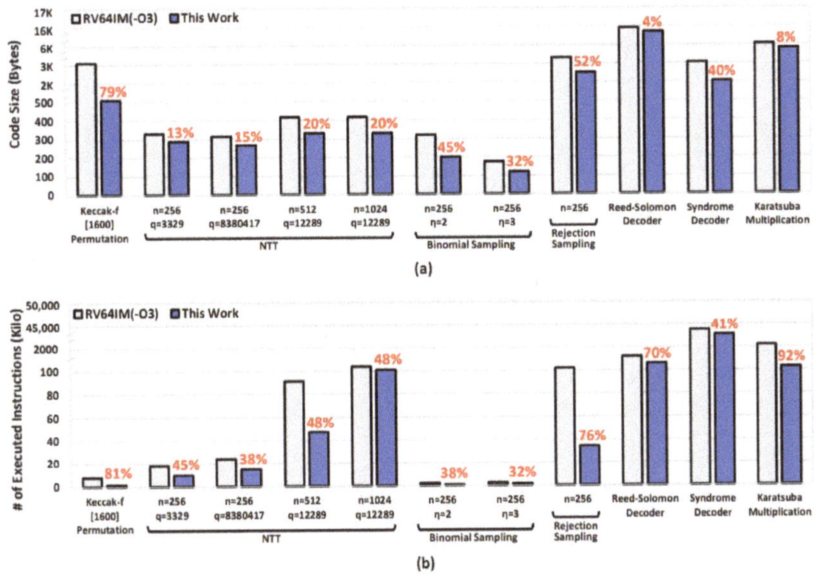

Figure 9. Comparison results of target applications. (**a**) Code size. (**b**) The number of executed instructions.

4.2. Hardware Implementation Results

The proposed crypto-processor is described in Verilog HDL and synthesized with a 28 nm CMOS process at an operating frequency of 150 MHz. The total gate count is 54 kGE (NAND2 Gate Equivalent) and the ratio of each component is depicted in Figure 10. The PQC unit and scalar cryptography unit occupy 27.8% and 17.4% of the total gate counts, respectively. The 32 × 64-bit coprocessor register and the result buffer account for 31% and 18.5% of the coprocessor, respectively.

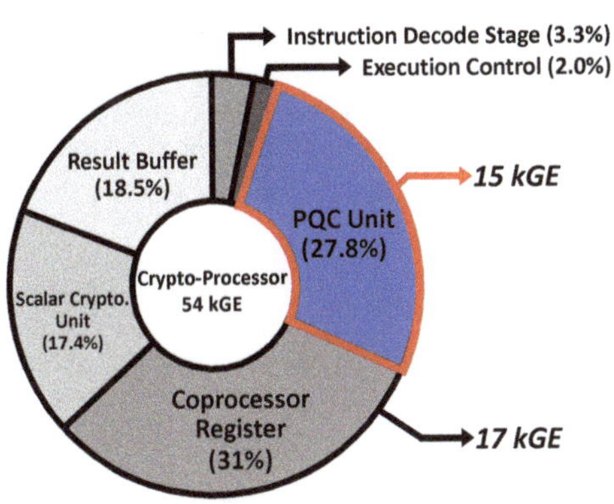

Figure 10. Gate-count ratio of proposed crypto-processor.

Although the gate count of the proposed crypto-processor is slightly higher compared to other tightly coupled PQC accelerators [13,14,32], as shown in Table 9, mainly due to the coprocessor's register file and result buffer, which occupy about 50% of the total gate count, the proposed architecture as a programmable coprocessor supports all round 4 candidate algorithms in the NIST PQC standardization process, as well as algorithms yet to be standardized.

Table 9. Comparison of hardware PQC accelerations.

Design	TCHE'20 [13]	IEEE Access'21 [14]	FPL'20 [32]	TCHE'19 [11]	TCAS-I'20 [16]	This Work
Platform	ASIC (65nm)	FPGA (ZCU106)	FPGA (VIRTEX-7)	ASIC (40nm)	ASIC (28nm)	ASIC (28nm)
Frequency (MHz)	45	100	-	72	300	150
Gate Counts (kGE)	57 [a]	-	-	106 [e]	37 + 942 [f]	477 + 54 [g]
Complexity (LUT/FF/DSP/BRAM)	-	178/0/5/0.5 [b] 377/0/10/0.5 [c]	417/462/0/0 [d]	-	-	-
Accelerator Type	Tightly Coupled	Tightly Coupled	Tightly Coupled	Memory-mapped	Coprocessor	Coprocessor
Supported NIST PQC algorithms	Kyber Saber	Kyber Dilithium	Kyber Dilithium Falcon	Kyber Dilithium	Kyber	Kyber Dilithium Falcon SPHINCS+ BIKE HQC Classic McEliece

[a] Includes Pulpino w/o FPU. [b] Only for additional ALU logic for Kyber. [c] Only for additional ALU logic for Dilithium. [d] Only for additional accelerator. [e] Includes baseline CPU core. [f] SCR1 core and the vector coprocessor, respectively. [g] CVA6 core and the coprocessor, respectively

5. Conclusions

We propose an instruction set for all NIST PQC algorithms yet to be standardized and round 4 candidates, along with a programmable crypto-processor that can be easily attached to the baseline RISC-V CPU core as a coprocessor. This proposed architecture can alleviate computational bottlenecks in PQC algorithms, such as the Keccak-f permutation, the NTT, binomial and rejection sampling, and finite-field arithmetic. Additionally, the proposed crypto-processor supports RISC-V scalar cryptography extensions, including SHA-256, SHA-512, and AES. By combining the proposed instruction set with low complexity, the proposed architecture can support various PQC algorithms and cover various applications in real life. The proposed crypto-processor can reduce the code size and number of executed instructions of target operations in PQC algorithms by up to 79% and 92%, respectively. When compared to software implementations, execution cycle counts can be reduced by up to 87%. The proposed crypto-processor operates at 150 MHz and occupies 54 kGE with the 28 nm CMOS process.

Our proposed PQC coprocessor enables more secure communication compared to existing encryption systems. It is possible to keep information secure on communication channels with PQC algorithms. However, its disadvantage is that the operation of algorithms takes a long execution time. Our proposed crypto-processor can accelerate the computation of PQC algorithms to address these shortcomings. Therefore, the crypto-processor can be used in fields where PQC algorithms must be calculated in a short time by connecting to the main CPU.

The proposed ISA in this paper targets the PQC standard and round 4 candidate algorithms. It can also be applied to other algorithms, which can be accelerated by commands supported by the ISA. However, the limitation is that PQC algorithms that mainly use operations not supported by the proposed ISA cannot be accelerated. In this case, adding new instructions to the ISA will also reduce the computational time of various newly developed PQC algorithms, which is a potential avenue for future work in this paper.

Author Contributions: Conceptualization, hardware design, test, manuscript preparation, J.L.; validation, W.K. and J.-H.K. All authors have read and agreed to the published version of the manuscript.

Funding: This work was partly supported by the MSIT (Ministry of Science and ICT), Korea, under the ITRC (Information Technology Research Center) support program (IITP-2020-0-01847) supervised by the IITP (Institute for Information & Communications Technology Planning & Evaluation) and partly supported by IITP grant funded by the Korea government (MSIT) (No.2021-0-00724, RISC-V based Secure CPU Architecture Design for Embedded System Malware Detection and Response). The EDA tool was supported by the IC Design Education Center (IDEC), Republic of Korea.

Informed Consent Statement: Not applicable.

Data Availability Statement: The data in this study are available from the corresponding author upon reasonable request.

Conflicts of Interest: The authors declare no conflicts of interest.

References

1. Diffie, W.; Hellman, M.E. New directions in cryptography. In *Secure Communications and Asymmetric Cryptosystems*; Routledge: Abingdon, UK, 2019; pp. 143–180.
2. Miller, V.S. Use of elliptic curves in cryptography. In Proceedings of the Conference on the Theory and Application of Cryptographic Techniques, Lyon, France, 23–27 April 1985; Springer: Berlin/Heidelberg, Germany, 1985; pp. 417–426.
3. Rivest, R.L.; Shamir, A.; Adleman, L. A method for obtaining digital signatures and public-key cryptosystems. *Commun. ACM* **1978**, *21*, 120–126. [CrossRef]
4. Shor, P.W. Polynomial-time algorithms for prime factorization and discrete logarithms on a quantum computer. *SIAM Rev.* **1999**, *41*, 303–332. [CrossRef]
5. Kumar, M. Post-quantum cryptography Algorithm's standardization and performance analysis. *Array* **2022**, *15*, 100242. [CrossRef]
6. Dam, D.T.; Tran, T.H.; Hoang, V.P.; Pham, C.K.; Hoang, T.T. A Survey of Post-Quantum Cryptography: Start of a New Race. *Cryptography* **2023**, *7*, 40. [CrossRef]
7. Dang, V.B.; Mohajerani, K.; Gaj, K. High-Speed Hardware Architectures and FPGA Benchmarking of CRYSTALS-Kyber, NTRU, and Saber. *IEEE Trans. Comput.* **2023**, *72*, 306–320. [CrossRef]
8. Nejatollahi, H.; Dutt, N.; Ray, S.; Regazzoni, F.; Banerjee, I.; Cammarota, R. Post-quantum lattice-based cryptography implementations: A survey. *ACM Comput. Surv. (CSUR)* **2019**, *51*, 1–41. [CrossRef]
9. Choquin, L.; Piry, F. *Arm Custom Instructions: Enabling Innovation and Greater Flexibility on Arm*; Technical Report; ARM: Cambridge, UK, 2020.
10. Fritzmann, T.; Sharif, U.; Müller-Gritschneder, D.; Reinbrecht, C.; Schlichtmann, U.; Sepulveda, J. Towards reliable and secure post-quantum co-processors based on RISC-V. In Proceedings of the 2019 Design, Automation & Test in Europe Conference & Exhibition (DATE), Florence, Italy, 25–29 March 2019; pp. 1148–1153.
11. Banerjee, U.; Ukyab, T.S.; Chandrakasan, A.P. Sapphire: A Configurable Crypto-Processor for Post-Quantum Lattice-based Protocols. *IACR Trans. Cryptogr. Hardw. Embed. Syst.* **2019**, *2019*, 1140. [CrossRef]
12. Alkim, E.; Evkan, H.; Lahr, N.; Niederhagen, R.; Petri, R. ISA extensions for finite field arithmetic: Accelerating Kyber and NewHope on RISC-V. *IACR Trans. Cryptogr. Hardw. Embed. Syst.* **2020**, *2020*, 219–242. [CrossRef]
13. Fritzmann, T.; Sigl, G.; Sepúlveda, J. RISQ-V: Tightly coupled RISC-V accelerators for post-quantum cryptography. *IACR Trans. Cryptogr. Hardw. Embed. Syst.* **2020**, *2020*, 239–280. [CrossRef]
14. Nannipieri, P.; Di Matteo, S.; Zulberti, L.; Albicocchi, F.; Saponara, S.; Fanucci, L. A RISC-V Post Quantum Cryptography Instruction Set Extension for Number Theoretic Transform to Speed-Up CRYSTALS Algorithms. *IEEE Access* **2021**, *9*, 150798–150808. [CrossRef]
15. OpenHW Group. *CORE-V Extension Interface*; Technical report; OpenHW Group: Ottawa, ON, USA, 2022.
16. Xin, G.; Han, J.; Yin, T.; Zhou, Y.; Yang, J.; Cheng, X.; Zeng, X. VPQC: A domain-specific vector processor for post-quantum cryptography based on RISC-V architecture. *IEEE Trans. Circuits Syst. Regul. Pap.* **2020**, *67*, 2672–2684. [CrossRef]
17. Fernández-Caramés, T.M. From pre-quantum to post-quantum IoT security: A survey on quantum-resistant cryptosystems for the Internet of Things. *IEEE Internet Things J.* **2019**, *7*, 6457–6480. [CrossRef]
18. Jiang, H.; Zhang, Z.; Ma, Z. Key encapsulation mechanism with explicit rejection in the quantum random oracle model. In Proceedings of the Public-Key Cryptography–PKC 2019: 22nd IACR International Conference on Practice and Theory of Public-Key Cryptography, Beijing, China, 14–17 April 2019; Springer: Berlin/Heidelberg, Germany, 2019; pp. 618–645.
19. Soni, D.; Basu, K.; Nabeel, M.; Karri, R. A hardware evaluation study of NIST post-quantum cryptographic signature schemes. In Proceedings of the Second PQC Standardization Conference, NIST, Santa Barbara, CA, USA, 22–24 August 2019.
20. Alagic, G.; Apon, D.; Cooper, D.; Dang, Q.; Dang, T.; Kelsey, J.; Lichtinger, J.; Liu, Y.; Miller, C.; Moody, D.; et al. *Status Report on the Third Round of the NIST Post-Quantum Cryptography Standardization Process*; US Department of Commerce, NIST: Gaithersburg, MD, USA, 2022.
21. Chuang, Y.L.; Fan, C.I.; Tseng, Y.F. An efficient algorithm for the shortest vector problem. *IEEE Access* **2018**, *6*, 61478–61487. [CrossRef]
22. Regev, O. Lattice-based cryptography. In Proceedings of the Annual International Cryptology Conference, Santa Barbara, CA, USA, 14–18 August 2016; Springer: Berlin/Heidelberg, Germany, 2006; pp. 131–141.
23. Khalid, A.; Oder, T.; Valencia, F.; O'Neill, M.; Güneysu, T.; Regazzoni, F. Physical protection of lattice-based cryptography: Challenges and solutions. In Proceedings of the 2018 on Great Lakes Symposium on VLSI, Chicago, IL, USA, 23–25 May 2018; pp. 365–370.
24. Lyubashevsky, V.; Peikert, C.; Regev, O. On ideal lattices and learning with errors over rings. In Proceedings of the Annual International Conference on the Theory and Applications of Cryptographic Techniques, French Riviera, France, 30 May–3 June 2010; Springer: Berlin/Heidelberg, Germany, 2010; pp. 1–23.

25. Langlois, A.; Stehlé, D. Worst-case to average-case reductions for module lattices. *Des. Codes Cryptogr.* **2015**, *75*, 565–599. [CrossRef]
26. Lamport, L. *Constructing Digital Signatures from a One Way Function*; Technical Report, Technical Report CSL-98; SRI International: Palo Alto, CA, USA, 1979.
27. Buchmann, J.; Dahmen, E.; Hülsing, A. XMSS-a practical forward secure signature scheme based on minimal security assumptions. In Proceedings of the International Workshop on Post-Quantum Cryptography, College Park, MD, USA, 28–30 September 2011; Springer: Berlin/Heidelberg, Germany, 2011; pp. 117–129.
28. Sun, S.; Zhang, R.; Ma, H. Efficient parallelism of post-quantum signature scheme SPHINCS. *IEEE Trans. Parallel Distrib. Syst.* **2020**, *31*, 2542–2555. [CrossRef]
29. McEliece, R.J. A public-key cryptosystem based on algebraic. *Coding Thv* **1978**, *4244*, 114–116.
30. Berlekamp, E. Goppa codes. *IEEE Trans. Inf. Theory* **1973**, *19*, 590–592. [CrossRef]
31. Dworkin, M.J. *SHA-3 Standard: Permutation-Based Hash and Extendable-Output Function*; Technical report; National Institute of Standards and Technology: Gaithersburg, MD, USA, 2015.
32. Karabulut, E.; Aysu, A. RANTT: A RISC-V architecture extension for the number theoretic transform. In Proceedings of the 2020 30th International Conference on Field-Programmable Logic and Applications (FPL), Gothenburg, Sweden, 31 August–4 September 2020; pp. 26–32.
33. Cooley, J.W.; Tukey, J.W. An algorithm for the machine calculation of complex Fourier series. *Math. Comput.* **1965**, *19*, 297–301. [CrossRef]
34. Montgomery, P.L. Modular multiplication without trial division. *Math. Comput.* **1985**, *44*, 519–521. [CrossRef]
35. Alkim, E.; Bilgin, Y.A.; Cenk, M.; Gérard, F. Cortex-M4 optimizations for {R, M} LWE schemes. *IACR Trans. Cryptogr. Hardw. Embed. Syst.* **2020**, *2020*, 336–357. [CrossRef]
36. Chen, M.S.; Güneysu, T.; Krausz, M.; Thoma, J.P. Carry-less to bike faster. In Proceedings of the Applied Cryptography and Network Security: 20th International Conference, ACNS 2022, Rome, Italy, 20–23 June 2022; Springer: Berlin/Heidelberg, Germany, 2022; pp. 833–852.
37. Schöffel, M.; Feldmann, J.; Wehn, N. Code-based Cryptography in IoT: A HW/SW Co-Design of HQC. *arXiv* **2023**, arXiv:2301.04888.
38. Waterman, A.; Lee, Y.; Patterson, D.A.; Asanovi, K. *The Risc-v Instruction Set Manual. Volume 1: User-Level Isa, Version 2.0*; Technical report, Department of Electrical Engineering and Computer Sciences, California University: Berkeley, CA, USA, 2014.
39. Oder, T.; Speith, J.; Höltgen, K.; Güneysu, T. Towards practical microcontroller implementation of the signature scheme Falcon. In Proceedings of the International Conference on Post-Quantum Cryptography, Chongqing, China, 8–10 May 2019; Springer: Berlin/Heidelberg, Germany, 2019; pp. 65–80.
40. Marshall, B. *RISC-V Cryptographic Extension Proposals. Volume I: Scalar & Entropy Source Instructions*; RISC-V International: Zurich, Switzerland, 2021.
41. Banerjee, U.; Das, S.; Chandrakasan, A.P. Accelerating post-quantum cryptography using an energy-efficient tls crypto-processor. In Proceedings of the 2020 IEEE International Symposium on Circuits and Systems (ISCAS), Seville, Spain, 12–14 October 2020; pp. 1–5.
42. Soni, D.; Karri, R. Efficient hardware implementation of pqc primitives and pqc algorithms using high-level synthesis. In Proceedings of the 2021 IEEE Computer Society Annual Symposium on VLSI (ISVLSI), Tampa, FL, USA, 7–9 July 2021; pp. 296–301.
43. Zaruba, F.; Benini, L. The Cost of Application-Class Processing: Energy and Performance Analysis of a Linux-Ready 1.7-GHz 64-Bit RISC-V Core in 22-nm FDSOI Technology. *IEEE Trans. Very Large Scale Integr. (VLSI) Syst.* **2019**, *27*, 2629–2640. [CrossRef]
44. Stoffelen, K. Efficient cryptography on the RISC-V architecture. In Proceedings of the International Conference on Cryptology and Information Security in Latin America, Santiago de Chile, Chile, 2–4 October 2019; Springer: Berlin/Heidelberg, Germany, 2019; pp. 323–340.
45. Li, H.; Mentens, N.; Picek, S. Maximizing the Potential of Custom RISC-V Vector Extensions for Speeding up SHA-3 Hash Functions. In Proceedings of the 2023 Design, Automation & Test in Europe Conference & Exhibition (DATE), Antwerp, Belgium, 17–19 April 2023.
46. Kannwischer, M.J.; Rijneveld, J.; Schwabe, P.; Stoffelen, K. *PQM4: Post-Quantum Crypto Library for the ARM Cortex-M4*; GitHub: San Francisco, CA, USA, 2019.
47. GF2X/GF2X · GITLAB. Available online: https://gitlab.inria.fr/gf2x/gf2x (accessed on 15 November 2023).

MDPI AG
Grosspeteranlage 5
4052 Basel
Switzerland
Tel.: +41 61 683 77 34

Sensors Editorial Office
E-mail: sensors@mdpi.com
www.mdpi.com/journal/sensors

www.ingramcontent.com/pod-product-compliance
Lightning Source LLC
Chambersburg PA
CBHW040809250926
51850CB00007BA/1123